ATTACKS on the PRESS in 2003

On the cover: Journalists record the delivery of aid by the Kuwait Red Crescent Society in the southern Iraqi city of Safwan on March 26, 2003. (Courtesy of Elizabeth Malby, *The Baltimore Sun*)

The publication of *Attacks on the Press in 2003* is underwritten by a grant from Bloomberg.

COMMITTEE TO PROTECT JOURNALISTS

330 Seventh Avenue, 12th floor, New York, N.Y. 10001
Phone: (212) 465-1004 Fax: (212) 465-9568 e-mail: info@cpj.org
Web site: *www.cpj.org*

Founded in 1981, the Committee to Protect Journalists responds to attacks on the press worldwide. CPJ documents more than 400 cases every year and takes action on behalf of journalists and their news organizations, without regard to political ideology. Join CPJ and help promote press freedom by defending the people who report the news. To maintain its independence, CPJ accepts no government funding. We depend entirely on the support of foundations, corporations, and individuals.

The Associated Press, IDT, Lexis-Nexis, and Reuters provided electronic news and Internet services that were used to conduct research for this book.

AP Associated Press · IDT · LEXIS·NEXIS A member of the Reed Elsevier plc group · REUTERS

Editor: Susan Ellingwood
Deputy Editor: Amanda Watson-Boles
Copy Editor: Jeremy Bogaisky
Design: FTK Media LLC

Printed in the United States of America.

Attacks on the Press in 2003: A Worldwide Survey by the Committee to Protect Journalists
ISSN: 1078-3334
ISBN: 0-944823-23-8

| TABLE OF CONTENTS |

PREFACE

by Ted Koppel

THIS IS NOT A GOOD DAY. As I write, pop star Michael Jackson has been arrested for allegedly engaging in sexual misconduct with a minor. His residence cum theme park, "Neverland," has been invaded by police, sheriff's deputies, and a team of forensic specialists.

I am not empathizing with Michael Jackson, although this is clearly anything but a good day for him. Instead, I'm feeling helpless; hoist, as I am, on my own petard. I once observed, before many witnesses, that simply because the entire country is obsessed with a given event is insufficient reason for "Nightline" to avoid that story. Several of my colleagues have reminded me of what I said, and so, tonight, we will do the Michael Jackson story, even though there is plenty of other news to cover from around the country and the world.

"Nightline's" ratings will go up tonight, and we are conscious of our ratings, because ratings mean advertisers, advertisers mean money, and money means survival. But not the kind of survival that preoccupies our colleagues at the Committee to Protect Journalists.

Unlike local journalists in places such as Bangladesh, Haiti, Russia, and Eritrea, we have no reason to fear execution, torture, or imprisonment. Or unlike our colleagues who remain in Iraq and face danger at every turn, an angry phone call from our publisher or corporate owner about a critical story is about as serious a consequence as any of us working in the United States is likely to experience.

Over the course of more than 40 years, I have had the opportunity to practice our trade in over 80 countries. It has been my observation that, generally speaking, there are only three broad categories or systems in or under which journalism or some facsimile thereof operates: Theocracies, like Iran; political dictatorships, like North Korea; and the democratic/market system, like the United States. Clearly, gradations exist within each of these categories; sometimes even combinations. Whatever the failings of the market system, it is without question the most benevolent and the most tolerant of the lot. It still produces the best journalism in the world—but not necessarily the best journalists.

Unfortunately, in the United States, we have been conditioned, however subtly, to apply dramatic and commercial standards to our journalism. As one who has adapted to those standards, I sometimes wonder if I could function in a more threatening environment—one in which survival and freedom are constantly at stake.

One might think that freedom from physical fear would create the most robust kind of journalism; and indeed, there are still many fine examples that flourish. On the whole, however, we American journalists are a flaccid lot—too susceptible by far to the siren calls of circulation and advertising dollars.

"One might think that freedom from physical fear would create the most robust kind of journalism. But unlike our colleagues in dangerous places, we in the United States are too susceptible by far to the siren calls of circulation and advertising dollars."

The U.S. system reduces the incentive for tough reporting on complex subjects by rewarding glittering mediocrity and bombastic banality. Our 24-7 cable news networks are, too often, in a breathless race to be first with the obvious; and we at the broadcasting networks often pant along on the same track. In the face of freedom, we have grown lazy and timid, while many of our colleagues who operate under totalitarian regimes continue to humble us by their example.

And so, if we are going to measure ourselves against those of our colleagues who operate in a police state or under the scrutiny of religious enforcers, we will have to grade on a curve because reporting in countries like Cuba or the Philippines carries a greater degree of difficulty than it does in the United States. And in turn, we must salute the local journalists in such dangerous places who have the courage and ingenuity to penetrate the restraints of their environment and endure hardship, violence, and deprivation to bring news and information to light.

Ted Koppel is anchor and managing editor of ABC News' "Nightline."

A total of 36 journalists were killed for their work in 2003, a sharp rise from 2002, when the number stood at 19. Thirteen journalists were killed covering the war in **Iraq**, by far the most dangerous beat of the year. (See pages 186 and 220.)

Of the journalists who died in **Iraq**, at least four were killed by U.S. fire, most notably in the April 8 shelling of Baghdad's Palestine Hotel and the air strike that hit the Baghdad bureau of the Qatar-based channel Al-Jazeera that same day. (See pages 188 and 223.)

In a massive crackdown on the independent media in March and April 2003, **Cuban** officials jailed 29 journalists—about one-third of the island's independent press corps—and sentenced them to prison terms ranging from 14 to 27 years. (See pages 80 and 264.)

In **Togo**, authorities accused three independent journalists of trying to send photographs of alleged election disturbances to Web sites abroad. In mid-June, the trio was arrested and eventually charged with "attempting to publish false information." All three were held for more than a month, and two were tortured while in custody. (See page 58.)

In October, the U.S. Committee for Human Rights in North Korea released an extensive report, based primarily on testimony from defectors, claiming that up to 200,000 political prisoners are currently detained in **North Korea**'s extensive gulag system. Offenses include reading a foreign newspaper and "not taking proper care of" a newspaper containing a photo of Kim Jong Il. (See page 124.)

On October 9, 2003, two unidentified assailants stabbed to death *Tolyatinskoye Obozreniye* Editor-in-Chief Aleksei Sidorov in the **Russian** city of Togliatti. He was the second editor-in-chief of the independent daily to be murdered in 18 months. (See pages 165 and 235.)

In **Chile**, the Sixth Chamber of the Santiago Appeals Court overturned in early 2003 the conviction of TV commentator Eduardo Yáñez on charges of "disrespect." Yáñez faced up to five years in jail when he was prosecuted for calling the country's judiciary "immoral, cowardly, and corrupt" for not compensating a woman who had been wrongly imprisoned. The appeals court ruled that "even though the expressions voiced by Yáñez can be qualified as excessive, vulgar, or ignorant, they do not constitute the crime of disrespect." (See page 76.)

Internet service providers and cybercafé owners are held legally responsible in **Vietnam** if their customers access banned information online. A Culture and Information Ministry official explained, "Restaurant owners must guarantee the food is free from harmful substances. Therefore it's the same with Internet cafe owners. They are not allowed to provide young people with poisonous substances." (See page 140.)

With 39 journalists in prison in 2003, **China** was the leading jailer of journalists for the fifth year in a row. As of midnight on December 31, 2003, there were 136 imprisoned journalists worldwide. (See pages 109 and 251.)

The New York Stock Exchange (NYSE) in the **United States** revoked the credentials of two reporters from the Qatar-based news channel Al-Jazeera, purportedly to reduce the number of journalists on the stock exchange floor for security reasons and to give priority to reporters from financial networks. While one NYSE spokesman denied that the move was related to Al-Jazeera's coverage in Iraq, another spokesman said the station was not a "responsible" news outlet, hinting that its war coverage may have factored into the decision to revoke the journalists' accreditation. Their credentials were restored on April 29. (See page 91.)

The government of **Sudan** suspended *Al-Sahafa*, one of the country's most popular dailies, for three days because it ran an advertisement for Ethiopian Airlines that mentioned the wine served on its flights. The government took issue with the newspaper for advertising alcohol, which is banned in Sudan. (See page 206.)

Tajikistan's press is notoriously nervous about reporting on anything that could anger the government. As a result, the media allowed President Imomali Rakhmonov to bask in two days of constant television coverage of his participation in a conference on potato farming, while a typhoid outbreak in the capital went unreported for several weeks. (See page 168.)

In **Morocco**, a group of unidentified men physically assaulted a reporter after he wrote an article alleging that a provincial governor had granted a concession for the sale of alcohol to Morocco's royal financial and economics adviser. The assailants beat the reporter and stripped him of his pants, telling him never to write about the governor again. (See page 202.)

On October 20, 2003, police in **Somalia** detained an editor for nine hours and accused him of publishing information that was "not good for the government." (See page 54.)

In **Iran**, Canadian-Iranian journalist Zahra Kazemi died in a hospital after being held in government custody for nearly two weeks. The official Iranian news agency, IRNA, reported that court officials called Kazemi's death a "quasi-intentional murder" and ordered her two interrogators, who were not identified, detained. (See page 184.)

In announcing the repressive new Mass Media Law as part of his continuing crackdown on independent journalists, President Aleksandr Lukashenko of **Belarus** noted that he was "deeply convinced" that all journalism should be state-run. (See page 150.)

INTRODUCTION

by Ann Cooper

IN REAL-TIME IMAGES, the war in Iraq splashed across television screens worldwide in March, with thousands of journalists covering the U.S.-led war against Saddam Hussein and his regime.

The conflict and its aftermath had a far-reaching impact on the press and its ability to report the news, with the reverberations felt in some surprising places and in unsettling ways.

In Iraq itself, 13 journalists died in hostile acts. Most were foreign correspondents killed in conflict situations, such as suicide bombings and air strikes, but the dead also included the Iraqi editor of a newspaper newly freed from decades of stifling censorship. Ahmed Shawkat was gunned down at his office in October in reprisal for his work. Shawkat's articles criticized Islam, Saddam Hussein, and the U.S. occupation of Iraq. The deaths in Iraq were more than a third of the global total of 36 journalists killed during 2003 because of their work.

Journalists from dozens of countries covered the war, either traveling "embedded" with U.S. or British troops or reporting "unilaterally," from Baghdad or the field. And there were great disparities in how correspondents reported. In the United States, for example, the media's dominant focus was often on the U.S. military, while Arab television was far more likely to present the story through graphic images of Iraqi civilian casualties. The choices of emphasis and images led to one of the most bizarre attacks on the press in 2003, when the New York Stock Exchange revoked the credentials of two reporters from the Qatar-based satellite TV station Al-Jazeera. The ostensible reason was that the exchange floor was overcrowded, though exchange officials also acknowledged anger at what some Americans deemed as offensive coverage on Al-Jazeera. A few days earlier, the station had aired footage of American prisoners of war and U.S. soldiers' corpses. U.S. broadcasters largely shunned those images, leading to criticism that their coverage was sanitized and overly patriotic.

And so it went around the world, with the war provoking fierce debates about the nature of truth and the role of journalism.

The war also provided cover for dictators like Cuba's Fidel Castro. Taking advantage of the world's preoccupation with Iraq during the first week of the fighting in March, Castro launched a massive crackdown on political dissidents. They included 29 journalists, all in prison at year's end, whose courageous and critical reporting, many for foreign Web sites, had provided the world with some of the only independent accounts of life under Castro's fearsome rule.

Following the 2001 terrorist attacks on the United States and the conflict in Afghanistan, the war in Iraq also reinforced a troubling new international climate in which it has grown easier for foes of press freedom to curb independent reporting in the name of fighting terrorism or defending national security.

For example, Morocco's long record of relative tolerance for critical media was marred by the arrests of several journalists, some of whom were charged under an antiterrorism law passed in 2003. And after the United States embedded several hundred journalists with military forces headed for Iraq, Indonesia embraced the idea with a disturbing twist: Those reporters allowed to accompany Indonesian soldiers into battle against rebels in the separatist state of Aceh were warned that their stories must "contain the spirit of nationalism."

If the world's new security- and terrorism-conscious atmosphere emboldened restrictive governments, it also sometimes seemed to silence more democratic states with histories of speaking up in defense of human rights. Thus, few diplomatic reprimands were heard while President Vladimir Putin presided over the continued erosion of press freedom in Russia. In fact, in September, U.S. President George W. Bush shocked even some of his conservative supporters when he called Russia "a country in which democracy and freedom and rule of law thrive." And in Africa, leaders such as South African President Thabo Mbeki kept silent while President Robert Mugabe forced almost all foreign media out of Zimbabwe and closed the country's only independent daily paper.

With diplomats and politicians less likely to defend journalists, it grew more imperative than ever for members of the media and press freedom advocates to stand up against repression. And in many cases, their advocacy made a difference, gaining the release of Internet journalists in China and Tunisia and helping secure pardons, in January 2004, for two Moroccan journalists who were imprisoned in 2003.

Journalists also played a key role in a stunning human rights victory in Hong Kong, where public protests forced the government to withdraw the controversial "subversion" legislation that, among other things, would have seriously curbed press freedoms. And in Costa Rica, a journalist's dogged fight against his conviction for criminal defamation could win an important precedent that would ease the threat of criminal sanctions against other journalists throughout the Americas.

Such a precedent would be welcome news, since imprisonment remains a common tool for silencing journalists whose work uncovers corruption, human rights abuses, or other misdeeds. At the end of 2003, 136 journalists were in prison, the same as in 2002. China was the world's leading jailer of journalists for the fifth year in a row with 39 behind bars, and Cuba leapt to number two with 29 journalists in jail. The number of imprisoned journalists remained stable in 2003 because there were significant drops in Nepal and Turkey, coupled with an enormous roundup in Cuba. In addition, a number of countries—Togo, the Democratic Republic of Congo, India, and Russia—each released one or two journalists in 2003.

The journalists who died in Iraq offered terrible reminders of the great risks faced by war correspondents. But, as in previous years, the majority of the 36 journalists killed in 2003 were murdered far from battlefields. Five were killed in the Philippines for their coverage of local corruption or criticism of public officials. Four more died in Colombia, three of them murdered for their reporting. And in Russia, the editor-in-chief of a hard-hitting provincial newspaper was stabbed to death outside his home—the paper's second editor-in-chief to be murdered for his work in 18 months.

Though 2003 began with the convictions of several men for the 2000 murder of Mozambican investigative journalist Carlos Cardoso, the Cardoso case remained an exception; most murders of journalists continue to be committed with impunity. That makes journalists very vulnerable targets in countries such as the Philippines and Colombia, where the murders of dozens of journalists remain unpunished.

War correspondents face a different kind of risk in conflict zones. They are rarely "targeted" in direct reprisal for what they have written. Yet throughout 2003, those who covered the Iraq conflict spoke often of being "targets," and in some senses they were. Their expensive computers and satellite phones made them prey to bandits, particularly on road trips into and out of the country. Some of the buildings they frequented for work or leisure—the U.N. headquarters or a popular restaurant—were prime targets of insurgency bombings. By year's end, even the most seasoned war correspondents were calling Iraq the most dangerous assignment they had ever covered.

Despite the dangers, few spoke of abandoning the story, perhaps because the conflict has implications well beyond the future of Iraq itself. In response to the danger, some media organizations, particularly television broadcasters, hired armed security professionals to escort their journalists while they traveled in Iraq to report. Others—again including many television broadcasters—angrily denounced the practice, arguing that those who use armed guards jeopardize the perception of journalists as neutral observers. The debate intensified as reports circulated about journalists (not just their guards) carrying weapons.

Shortly before the war began, CPJ published a comprehensive security handbook for journalists, called "On Assignment: A Guide to Reporting in Dangerous Situations." While noting that media organizations had hired armed guards in some particularly dangerous conflicts, including Somalia in the early 1990s, CPJ warned that journalists who carry guns or travel with armed guards endanger their status as neutral observers and could encourage combatants to view them as legitimate military targets.

A popular media Web site based in the United States carried some fierce letters on the debate, though most appeared to agree with Associated Press reporter Richard Pyle, who covered the Vietnam War, which claimed dozens of journalists' lives. Pyle argued that weapons are more likely to hurt journalists than help them. Noting how many had already died in Iraq, he wrote, "Covering that war would seem to have enough danger for the Fourth Estate without inviting more."

A WORD ABOUT THIS YEAR'S BOOK: We have not included the hundreds of individual cases of attacks on the press documented by CPJ in 2003, though many are described here in the individual country summaries. For details on all these cases, and to read about additional attacks, please visit *www.cpj.org.*

Ann Cooper is the executive director of the Committee to Protect Journalists. Before joining CPJ in 1998, she was a foreign correspondent for National Public Radio for nine years, serving as bureau chief in Moscow and Johannesburg.

AFRICA

Abuja Edition
THE DAILY NEW
Established 1999
5 -8 December 2003
TELLING IT LIKE IT IS
The voices Mug
wants to silenc

OVERVIEW: AFRICA

by Julia Crawford

ALTHOUGH THE NUMBER OF JOURNALISTS IN PRISON IN AFRICA at the end of 2003 was lower than the previous year, African journalists still faced a multitude of difficulties, including government harassment and physical assaults. Many countries in Africa retain harsh press laws. In the wake of the 2001 terrorist attacks on the United States, some countries have also moved to introduce tough antiterrorist legislation, which journalists fear could be used to stifle civil liberties, including press freedom. For example, Uganda, which faces a rebellion in the north, used its antiterrorism law in 2003 to shutter a radio station for more than a month.

Two journalists were killed in Ivory Coast, and another was shot to death while reporting in Somalia. Nineteen journalists were in prison for their work at year's end, down from 26 in 2002. Seventeen of them were imprisoned in Eritrea, which has silenced its entire independent press corps. The regime in Zimbabwe continued its efforts to do the same, closing the country's only independent daily newspaper, the *Daily News*, and banning much of the foreign press.

When Radio France Internationale's Jean Hélène was killed by a police officer in Ivory Coast on October 21, it came as a shocking reminder of the risks that journalists face. The Ivoirian government launched an inquiry, and on January 22, 2004, the officer was convicted of killing the journalist. Swift action to bring Hélène's murderer to justice was a welcome contrast to the usual pattern in Africa, where all too frequently journalists have been killed with impunity. For example, an investigation into the 1998 murder of independent journalist Norbert Zongo in Burkina Faso was still ongoing at the end of 2003, having produced few results.

In a rare case of a journalist's murderers being brought to justice, a Mozambican court sentenced six men to lengthy prison sentences for the November 2000 murder of journalist Carlos Cardoso. However, many local journalists believe that the masterminds of Cardoso's killing remain at large. During the trial, several of the defendants said that the president's eldest son, Nymphine Chissano, had ordered the journalist's murder. Chissano has denied any connection to the killing.

On May 3, World Press Freedom Day, CPJ included Eritrea and Togo on its list of the "World's Worst Places to Be a Journalist." Eritrea, which has been Africa's leading jailer of journalists since 2001, was featured on the list for the second year in a row. During the last three years, Togolese authorities have ruthlessly harassed and jailed journalists and censored publications that criticized President Gnassingbé Eyadema, who was re-elected in 2003.

Unfortunately, Togo was not the only country where the prospect of elections caused repressive regimes to tighten the screws on the independent press. It was also

Julia Crawford, CPJ's Africa program coordinator, along with **Adam Posluns**, Africa research associate, and **Alexis Arieff**, research and special projects associate, researched and wrote this section. **Kate Davenport**, former BBC correspondent in Abidjan, contributed the summary on Ivory Coast. The summary on the Democratic Republic of Congo was written by **Stephanie Wolters**, former chief news editor for Radio Okapi in Kinshasa.

Photo (previous page): A journalist from Zimbabwe's banned newspaper the *Daily News* holds up a special edition that was printed in the Nigerian paper *ThisDay* in December 2003. *AP/Ben Curtis*

ATLANTIC OCEAN
Str. of Gibraltar
MEDITERRANEAN SEA
RED SEA
Gulf of Aden
SENEGAL
THE GAMBIA
NIGER
ERITREA
SIERRA LEONE
IVORY COAST
TOGO
NIGERIA
ETHIOPIA
SOMALIA
LIBERIA
Bight of Benin
Bight of Bonny
CENTRAL AFRICAN REPUBLIC
GULF OF GUINEA
CAMEROON
KENYA
UGANDA
GABON
RWANDA
INDIAN OCEAN
DEMOCRATIC REPULBLIC OF CONGO
BURUNDI
ATLANTIC OCEAN
ANGOLA
MALAWI
Mozambique Channel
ZIMBABWE
MOZAMBIQUE
SWAZILAND
SOUTH AFRICA

an election year for Rwanda, where the editor of the only independent newspaper was jailed for a month after reporting that former Prime Minister Faustin Twagiramungu would run against the incumbent, Paul Kagame. The paper had also printed a satirical cartoon implying that Kagame would decide the election's outcome. In Cameroon, where President Paul Biya faces elections in 2004, authorities have moved against broadcast media that criticize the government. In Guinea, where incumbent President Lansana Conte was declared the overwhelming winner of polls that the opposition boycotted, officials banned foreign magazines that ran articles questioning the status quo.

Elections also occurred in Nigeria, where the press, which is relatively free, exercised self-censorship during the polling out of apparent concern for political stability. Thus, the widespread fraud, irregularities, and voter intimidation alleged by the opposition and election observers were not highlighted in the Nigerian media.

Many African countries retain legislation that allows them to bring criminal charges against journalists, and some have used this to crush dissent. For example, a journalist was jailed in Niger after reporting on government malpractice. And in Sierra Leone, the critical daily *For Di People* was closed by a series of lawsuits, while its editor faces a criminal trial that could result in a prison sentence.

Local and international press freedom groups continued to lobby for the decriminalization of press offenses. But countries such as Togo, Zimbabwe, the Gambia, and Ethiopia have moved to introduce harsh new press laws that boost, rather than reduce, authorities' powers to clamp down on the press. This is also the case in Somaliland, which claims independence from Somalia, although it is not internationally recognized. Ethiopia's government has responded to journalists' criticism of draft press legislation by consulting with them, but at year's end there was little evidence of transparency in the process, and authorities had suspended the Ethiopian Free Press Journalists Association, which was one of the most vocal local opponents of the draft law.

Even countries such as Senegal and Kenya, hailed as examples of democracy, have exhibited worrying trends. In October, Senegal's government expelled a Radio France Internationale correspondent, accusing her of "tendentious" reporting on the rebellion in the southern Casamance Region. Kenyan authorities brought criminal charges against a journalist from the country's oldest newspaper, the *East African Standard*, after it printed excerpts of leaked confessions in a sensitive police inquiry.

Some of these attacks on the press have captured the headlines, but many other stories of daily harassment and intimidation have not. Local journalists in war-torn countries such as the Democratic Republic of Congo, Liberia, Central African Republic, Burundi, and Somalia face constant danger while trying to cover the news. The governments of Rwanda and Gabon have been conducting campaigns of censorship and harassment against the independent press, as have authorities on Tanzania's semiautonomous island of Zanzibar. Although the press in mainland Tanzania is relatively free, the government of Zanzibar in November shuttered the island's only independent newspaper, which had been running articles critical of the government. Oil-rich Equatorial Guinea drew only minimal international attention when it jailed one of the few independent journalists in the country.

African governments frequently mention ethnic tensions and "irresponsibility" of the press as reasons to retain draconian laws against press offenses. They often cite the example of Rwanda, where media such as Radio-Télévision Libre des Mille Collines helped to fuel the 1994 genocide.

In December, the U.N.'s International Criminal Tribunal for Rwanda convicted three Rwandan former media executives of genocide, conspiracy and incitement to genocide, and crimes against humanity, confirming the criminal role that the media played in the 1994 genocide, which left some 800,000 Tutsis and moderate Hutus dead in just over three months. The three accused were given prison sentences ranging from 35 years to life. In 2003, there was also growing international concern about partisan and provocative reporting in Ivory Coast, where both pro-government and pro-rebel media have inflamed tensions, undermining the fragile peace process and possibly increasing the level of violence. While the motive for the murder of journalist Hélène is unknown, it occurred in an atmosphere of xenophobia and anti-French feeling that had been fueled by the local media.

Media professionalism remains a legitimate cause for concern. The first complaint of many journalists' organizations in Africa is low pay and lack of training, both of which may increase the temptation for journalists to accept bribes. But the governments that complain most about lack of professionalism in the media are often those that attack press freedoms. Governments often abuse legislation against hate speech and ethnic discrimination to suppress legitimate criticism in the press.

Radio remains the only effective way to bring information to the majority of people in most African countries, where high rates of illiteracy and the costs of print media often confine newspapers' influence to elite circles. Rwanda, Ethiopia, Eritrea, Zimbabwe, Guinea, and Equatorial Guinea have no independent radio stations.

Nevertheless, some positive developments have occurred. For example, the new transition government in Liberia has invited Star Radio to return. The popular, independent station, an initiative of the Switzerland-based Hirondelle Foundation, was closed by former President Charles Taylor in 2000. Private radio stations in Burundi faced down a government ban on interviewing rebels and exposed weaknesses in a sensitive murder inquiry. Meanwhile, globalization and the spread of mobile phones and the Internet have given journalists in Africa, as elsewhere, a new medium to exchange information and build solidarity.

ANGOLA

SINCE THE DEATH OF JONAS SAVIMBI, LEADER OF THE REBEL NATIONAL UNION for the Total Independence of Angola (UNITA), brought an end to Angola's civil war in 2002, the ruling Popular Movement for the Liberation of Angola (MPLA) has become somewhat more tolerant of the independent press. Journalists say the climate has improved, but problems remain. State media are still dominant, and the independent press is limited almost exclusively to the capital, Luanda. In 2003, the government continued to drag its heels on new media legislation and to block the spread of Catholic Church–owned Radio Ecclésia to the provinces.

President José Eduardo Dos Santos, who has been in office since 1979, promised in 2001 that he would step down at the time of the next general election. However, he was quoted in November 2003 as saying that the issue of his candidacy was "an open question within the [MPLA] party." In December, the MPLA-dominated Congress re-elected Dos Santos unopposed as the head of the party, which analysts interpreted as a sign he would run again. Dos Santos came under opposition pressure to hold elections in 2004, but he said it would take two years to prepare the country for polls. By year's end, no date for the elections had been set.

Journalists say corruption, especially in relation to Angola's oil and diamond resources, is one of the most sensitive subjects for the media. According to the International Monetary Fund, billions of dollars have disappeared from state coffers in recent years. The advocacy group Transparency International ranked Angola as one of the countries perceived as most corrupt in the world, with only Nigeria ranking higher in Africa. However, U.S. President George W. Bush brought Angola into the group of African countries that enjoy liberal trade terms under the African Growth and Opportunity Act. Thirty-seven out of 48 sub-Saharan African countries made the list for 2004, and two (Eritrea and Central African Republic) were removed. A White House spokesman said the list of countries with access to the special trade terms reflected the degree to which nations were progressing toward market-based economies and the rule of law.

Angola's constitution guarantees freedom of expression, but the government often falls short of respecting it, and the independent media continued to report threats and harassment. For example, in February, when Jorge Artur Tunda Catende, of the Luanda-based independent *Folha 8* weekly, went to interview Tourism Minister Jorge Alicerces Valentim about allegations of wrongdoing at the ministry, he was detained for 34 days before being released without charge. Instead of getting the interview he had been promised, Catende said that Valentim referred him to an "Ad-Hoc Commission," which demanded that he submit questions in writing and come back the next day. As he was leaving the ministry, Catende said that Valentim called him into his office and accused him of stealing US$400 from the minister. Catende said he was taken to the National Directorate of Criminal Investigation (DNIC), interrogated, and accused of stealing, even though he had no money on him. Upon his release, Catende lodged a criminal complaint, which was still pending at year's end.

Journalists say the most important independent news outlet in Angola is the popular Radio Ecclésia, which the Catholic Church owns and operates. The station, which broadcasts 24 hours a day on FM in the Luanda area, carries news and debates in which members of the public can participate. The Information Ministry once called Radio Ecclésia "terrorist radio" after a listener said on air that Angola's real problem was the president. In the wake of the 2002 peace agreement ending Angola's civil war, Radio Ecclésia received support from foreign donors to expand broadcasting to the provinces. Journalists said technical preparations were complete, but that at the end of 2003, the government was still refusing permission for the station to broadcast outside Luanda.

Foreign radio services such as Voice of America (VOA) and the BBC have staff in Angola. VOA has a limited FM service in Portuguese, and the BBC, which is only available on shortwave, has been negotiating with the Angolan government for five years for permission to set up an FM transmitter. According to sources at the BBC in London, the Angolan government's official reason for the lengthy negotiations is that it has to change the country's press law to make foreign ownership of a radio station legal. However, journalists suspect that the government is reluctant to open up to outside broadcasters.

Speaking at the MPLA's congress in December, Dos Santos promised that a new press law would be approved "in due time," and that it would allow for the possibility of private television stations. The government has been promising a more liberal press law for three years.

BURUNDI

BURUNDI MADE SOME PROGRESS TOWARD PEACE IN 2003, but cease-fires remained fragile and civilians continued to bear the brunt of fighting between Hutu rebels and the Tutsi-dominated army. At the end of April, under intense international pressure, Tutsi President Pierre Buyoya stepped down in favor of his Hutu vice president, Domitien Ndayizeye, in accordance with the Arusha peace accords of August 2000. A cease-fire signed in December 2002 by the largest Hutu rebel group, Forces for the Defense of Democracy (FDD), failed to end the war. However, in November 2003, the same group signed a South Africa–mediated peace deal with the government, providing for power sharing in politics and the security forces. At the start of 2004, the National Liberation Forces (FNL), the only group remaining outside the peace process, agreed to talks with the government.

The government has shown some sympathy toward press freedom issues, notably with the enactment of a new media law in late 2003 that journalists generally hailed as an improvement on previous press legislation. However, problems in the peace process have often been accompanied by attempts to censor the media and ban communication with rebel groups. This happened under both Buyoya and Ndayizeye.

In March, Buyoya banned all private radio stations from broadcasting interviews and statements from the FDD and FNL rebel groups that were continuing to fight. In September, Ndayizeye's government closed the popular private station Radio Isanganiro for seven days after it aired a debate featuring Pasteur Habimana, an FNL spokesman. A letter from Communications Minister Albert Mbonerane accused the station of "endangering national unity" by putting Habimana on the air. In solidarity with Radio Isanganiro, three other private radio stations, Bonesha FM, Radio Publique Africaine (RPA), and CCIB FM, announced that they would not broadcast any government news or statements for the duration of Radio Isanganiro's closure.

Three days later, the government ordered RPA closed for an indefinite period after it interviewed Habimana about Radio Isanganiro's closure. Journalists at RPA told CPJ that Habimana apologized for causing the ban and commented on the collapse of talks between the government and the FDD. A government letter accused RPA of "violating Article 44 of the Press Law by vilifying the government and disseminating propaganda of the country's enemy." The letter also said that authorities had warned radio stations not to broadcast "inflammatory statements against the government, which is trying to obtain a global and permanent cease-fire"—a statement also contained in the letter to Radio Isanganiro.

However, the ban on RPA was lifted three days later, and Isanganiro was allowed to resume broadcasting the same day. Bonesha FM, CCIB FM, Radio Isanganiro, and RPA then announced an end to their boycott on covering government activities. Local journalists attributed the lifting of the ban to public pressure, linked to the fact that Burundians are increasingly turning to private radio for news and information.

While print media remain weak, a number of private radio stations have been launched in recent years, providing regular and diversified news and posing a challenge to the state broadcaster, RTNB. Several private stations have been established with funds from foreign donors. Journalists say the stations are playing an increasingly influential role, especially in trying to break the culture of impunity in Burundi.

For example, RPA investigated the November 2001 murder of World Health Organization representative Dr. Kassy Manlan and began broadcasting its findings in early 2002. Although police had made several arrests, RPA charged that the real killers were still at large. Other media took up the story, and diaspora Web sites alleged that Manlan's murder was linked to the embezzlement of development funds by a senior politician. One article directly accused former President Buyoya of involvement. In May 2002, authorities tried to ban RPA from investigating the murder, saying the media were now prohibited from discussing criminal cases still under investigation. RPA nevertheless continued to air interviews with the family of the victim and lawyers involved in the case. In October 2003, five new suspects were arrested, including senior figures in the Burundian security services who had been on the original committee appointed to investigate the murder. Local journalists said RPA's reporting played a significant role in the arrests.

RPA Director Alexis Sinduhije said that he and other RPA journalists were subject to frequent harassment over the Manlan affair. He told CPJ in late 2003 that he had received death threats and did not feel safe. According to journalists, security is a continuing problem, especially when reporting on such sensitive subjects as conflict, government corruption, massacres, human rights abuses, and the 1993 assassination of Hutu President Melchior Ndadaye, which sparked the civil war.

Journalists have mostly welcomed a new media law, which they say has taken some of their concerns into consideration. For example, it provides for the protection of sources and simplifies procedures for starting a new publication. Newspapers no longer have to submit copies to authorities before going on sale, and radio license fees are also being reduced. The new law also contains a "conscience clause" whereby a journalist can invoke reasons of conscience for refusing to cover a story. An employer may fire a journalist who does this, but only upon payment of "just and equitable compensation."

Unfortunately, the new law still includes criminal penalties, including heavy fines and prison sentences, for such press offenses as insulting the head of state. The definition of this offense also remains vague. "The new law contains important advances," said Augustin Kabayabaya, president of the Burundian Journalists' Association, "but I deplore the fact that the anomalies that allow abuse of the media have not disappeared."

CAMEROON

IN APRIL, TWO DAYS AFTER CAMEROON'S ONLY PRIVATE DAILY, the French-language *Mutations*, was suspended and three of its journalists were detained, Communications Minister Jacques Fame Ndongo assured journalists that, "Cameroon's press freedom is real." The Central African country's beleaguered press corps might disagree. Amid widespread domestic and international criticism of Cameroon's dismal human rights record—and ahead of

2004 presidential elections—the ruling Cameroon People's Democratic Movement (CPDM) cracked down on the private press. Authorities censored critical media outlets and harassed local journalists, who complain of frequent threats and intimidation.

Speculation in the press about the country's political future provoked government anger, which in turn caused self-censorship, according to local journalists. Elections are expected in October 2004, although President Paul Biya has hinted he may reschedule them earlier in the year. Biya, who has been in power for 21 years, has not officially announced his candidacy.

In April, a state-owned printing press refused to print the April 14 edition of *Mutations*. Police later seized the computer disk containing the edition and detained three of the publication's journalists for questioning. The actions stemmed from a report in that issue about the president's succession speculating on the possible political and ethnic turmoil that could occur if Biya retires.

Political debates aired on television and radio—especially ones featuring members of the opposition—provoked the government's ire. In March, Communications Minister Ndongo ordered the private, Yaoundé-based radio station Magic FM to close after speakers criticized Biya's frequent trips abroad, his appointment of officials to multiple posts, and government corruption. The station was allowed to reopen 10 days later, after its directors wrote a letter of apology to the Communications Ministry.

In February, the government suspended two local television networks, RTA and Canal 2, for alleged licensing violations. However, Cameroonian journalists told CPJ they believe that was a pretext, and that the suspensions were related to the political nature of local shows, including debates featuring opposition leaders who criticized Biya's administration.

Throughout 2003, authorities used Cameroon's selective licensing system to close media outlets that threatened the status quo. While the Communications Ministry gave broadcasting licenses to three new private radio stations and four private television channels in September, local journalists say that the ministry's criteria for granting licenses remain opaque, and that many news directors wait months before being allowed to operate. Local journalists say the ministry regularly delays granting licenses to radio stations that they fear will criticize the government.

In May, officials closed and sealed the offices of the new private radio station Freedom FM, which is based in the southwestern port city of Douala. The closure came the day before the station was to begin broadcasting, according to Director Pius Njawé, who also runs the popular, private triweekly *Le Messager*. Njawé is known for his political commentary, which often targets the ruling party. The Communications Ministry said Freedom FM did not follow the proper procedures in applying for a broadcasting license and therefore would not approve the station's application. However, Njawé maintains that the station followed all necessary procedures.

In November, the Communications Ministry ordered the private, Douala-based radio station Veritas to stop broadcasting, also for allegedly failing to meet licensing requirements. The station, which had been broadcasting religious programming for two weeks, was founded by Catholic Cardinal Christian Tumi. Local journalists told CPJ that the station's closure was linked to the cardinal's frequent criticism of the Biya administration, and that the ruling CPDM fears that the cardinal might run as an opposition candidate in the 2004 presidential election. On December 12, the ministry issued a new license to the station allowing Veritas to provide religious programming for "the social and cultural education of the Catholic community of Douala."

Cameroonian journalists continue to suffer under a harsh press law, which allows authorities to imprison journalists for their work. In August, Rémy Ngono, a former journalist for the private, Yaoundé-based Radio Télévision Siantou (RTS), was imprisoned on criminal defamation charges filed by a businessman he had accused of embezzlement. Local journalists called for the decriminalization of press offenses, although many also criticized Ngono for a lack of professionalism. Ngono hosted "Kondré Chaud," a satirical program on RTS, until fall 2002, when he was fired in response to numerous listener complaints the station had received accusing him of defamation and a lack of professionalism, according to local sources.

Cameroon, which was divided between Britain and France during colonization, gained independence in 1961 as a federation of autonomous Anglophone and Francophone provinces. In May 1972, the country became a "united republic." In recent years, the separatist Southern Cameroon National Council has been pushing for the English-speaking southwestern provinces to secede.

Journalists who delve into the shaky coexistence of French and English speakers in Cameroon face government reprisals. In November, police and customs officials seized the entire print run of the English-language monthly *Insight Magazine*, which included a cover piece criticizing the country's reunification. The article, partly based on interviews with members of the minority Anglophone population, accused the government of failing to deliver on promises to integrate the English-speaking community politically and economically.

CENTRAL AFRICAN REPUBLIC

ON MARCH 15, REBELS UNDER THE COMMAND OF ousted former army commander François Bozizé captured the capital, Bangui, ending President Ange-Félix Patassé's 10-year rule over this mineral-rich but chronically unstable country. Two weeks later, Bozizé announced the formation of a transitional government with representatives from all political parties, including Patassé's Movement for the Liberation of the People of Central Africa (MLPC). He promised to organize a constitutional referendum, followed by elections in late 2004.

In a June speech commemorating the first 100 days since the coup, Bozizé also promised to protect free speech, stating, "Central Africans are free to express their opinions without fear of imprisonment. The press is free to criticize ... government actions." Among the many political prisoners released by Bozizé's troops following the coup was Mathurin Momet, publication director for the private, Bangui-based daily *Le Confident*, whom Patassé had imprisoned for "threatening state security" and "inciting tribal hatred."

The local press, weary of Patassé's often antagonistic relationship with the media, has mostly reacted positively toward the new regime, and some journalists have returned from exile in neighboring countries. Government press conferences, restricted to state-employed journalists under Patassé, are now open to all journalists.

However, Central African journalists still face stark challenges, including a harsh press law that allows journalists to be criminally prosecuted for their writing. Michel Ngokpele, publication director at the private daily *Le Quotidien de Bangui*, was arrested in May and sentenced in June to six months in prison for defamation and "inciting ethnic hatred." The verdict stemmed from an article by Ngokpele detailing corruption and embezzlement allegedly carried out by the head doctor at a local hospital. The article accused local officials of sheltering the doctor, hinting that the protection was due to ethnic allegiance. Ngokpele was released on November 26. In December, a group of journalists and editors from the private press urged the government to review laws governing the media and to decriminalize press offenses.

Additionally, several journalists faced harassment because of their work. In July, police officers summoned and interrogated Faustin Bambou, the publication director and editor-in-chief of the private biweekly paper *Les Collines du Bas-Oubangui*, after he wrote an article alleging that a local businessman was using government connections to extort money. Also in July, police arrested and detained Ferdinand Samba, publication director of the private daily *Le Démocrate*, after his article described an attack in the northern part of the country by rebels with ties to Patassé. In September, a heavily armed militia leader threatened employees at the offices of the private daily *Le Citoyen* after the paper published an article arguing that Bozizé does not control the former rebel militias who helped propel the president into power. The government sent guards to protect the office for several days after the incident, journalists at *Le Citoyen* said, but to their knowledge no disciplinary action was taken against the militia leader.

The largest problems faced by the Central African media are a lack of funding and training, and the insecurity and violence that persist despite the presence of a regional peacekeeping force. While several well-respected newspapers, such as the independent dailies *Le Confident* and *Le Citoyen*, are experiencing a renaissance in the newly relaxed political atmosphere in the capital, they are barely distributed outside Bangui. Many other private newspapers are plagued by financial problems that keep them from publishing more than a few times per month. Radio Ndeke Luka, which is managed by the Switzerland-based Hirondelle Foundation, provides an independent counterpoint to state-owned Radio Centrafricaine but does not broadcast beyond the capital. In rural areas, the only private sources of information are small religious and community radio stations.

Even state media are in financial disarray. The government plans to create a state-funded national newspaper and Web site, partly to counter the pro-Patassé news Web site *Centrafrique-Presse*, which is based in France and run by Patassé's former spokesperson Prosper N'Douba. However, given the country's desperate financial situation, journalists doubt that either initiative will be realized anytime soon. With the help of a grant from the Japanese government, the Central African Republic has embarked on a plan to repair broadcasting equipment damaged by age and warfare. In July, programming on state-run television was cut for several days because of technical problems. Local journalists say such cuts are frequent.

In the fall, the government organized a "National Dialogue," a vast undertaking aimed at reconciling the country after years of conflict. While originally planned to take place over a 10-day period in mid-September, the talks continued well into October as more than 300 delegates, representing diverse political, professional, and social organizations, discussed and made recommendations on national reconciliation; political and diplomatic issues; defense and security; the economy and finances; and educational, cultural, and social matters. During the talks, Bozizé, as well as former leader André Kolingba and the son of the late, notorious dictator Jean-Bedel Bokassa, apologized to the nation for past crimes. Among the recommendations for media development made by the commission on politics and diplomacy were the revision of the Press Law, the creation of an independent media regulatory body, and the inauguration of a communications department at the University of Bangui.

DEMOCRATIC REPUBLIC OF CONGO

PRESIDENT JOSEPH KABILA'S TRANSITION GOVERNMENT was inaugurated in June, after warring parties signed a power-sharing deal in December 2002 that ended a devastating four-year civil war. The peace accord keeps Kabila in power until 2005, with four vice presidents from both the armed and unarmed opposition. In 2005, the country will hold its first elections since independence in 1960. While foreign observers praised Kabila for the accord, local journalists remain skeptical about the new government's willingness and ability to ensure press freedom in the ravaged nation.

The Democratic Republic of Congo's (DRC) transition constitution mandates the establishment of a High Authority on Media, a body meant to act both as a media watchdog and guarantor of press freedom. The authority, which Parliament has yet to approve, had not been created by year's end. However, the government chose Modeste Mutinga, a longtime independent journalist and CPJ International Press Freedom Award recipient in 2000, to head it. Mutinga, who will have the rank of minister, is well respected, and, in addition to having been a frequent target of harassment himself, he has been an outspoken advocate of media freedom in the DRC. But his job will not be easy, in part because the new body's mandate and enforcement powers are unclear.

Congolese journalists have little protection from harassment, government-orchestrated or otherwise. They seldom have legal recourse, partly because of the high cost of legal representation, and partly because the judicial system is subject to influence from powerful local figures who are often the ones harassing journalists, according to local sources. Some local human rights organizations and press freedom groups, such as the Kinshasa-based Journaliste en Danger (JED), actively denounce abuses throughout the country. While JED has had some degree of success in raising awareness of the challenges faced by journalists, researchers at the organization say that court cases opened on behalf of local journalists are rarely resolved, and most often the perpetrators of harassment go unpunished.

Attacks against the press are often orchestrated by powerful local figures, including private citizens, members of the government, and military and former rebel officials. The most common forms of harassment are arbitrary arrests, physical aggression, and intimidation; local sources say that police officers and members of the military are often paid to arrest and detain journalists. For example, in August, National Police officers arrested Guy Kasongo Kilembwe, editor-in-chief of the Kinshasa-based satirical newspaper *Pot-Pourri*. Local sources told CPJ they believe that Kilembwe was arrested on the orders of

Parliament member Pius Mwabilu, who is also the general manager of the media company Radiotélévision Groupe L'Avenir and publisher of the pro-government daily *L'Avenir* (The Future). After arresting Kilembwe, officers took him to a police station, where Mwabilu confronted him, saying, "You humiliated me in your newspaper, and now I am going to make you suffer." On August 22, *Pot-Pourri* published a front-page article alleging that Mwabilu had used funds earmarked for collective use by parliamentarians to launch his media company. Kilembwe was released without charge after five days of detention.

The most sensitive topics journalists can cover are government corruption, shifting alliances within the new transition government, and foreign sponsorship of ex-rebel factions that continue to maintain economic networks and military links. The latter includes alleged Rwandan military support for the rebel Congolese Rally for Democracy (RCD) in the eastern region of Goma, and the financial and military support that senior Ugandan military officials have provided to local militias in the northeastern Ituri region to safeguard their economic interests in the DRC.

RCD authorities, unaccustomed to criticism, kept a tight grip on information in areas under their control. In May, RCD agents arrested and detained Joseph Nkinzo, director of the Anglican community radio station Sauti ya Rehema (Voice of Mercy), in Bukavu, a town near the Rwandan border. Local journalists said the arrest stemmed from broadcasts commenting on the RCD's decision to withdraw from negotiations establishing the national transition government. (The RCD later rejoined the talks.)

Media that criticize the Kabila administration are also subject to threats and censorship from authorities. In early June, the Congolese National Police raided and closed the Kinshasa-based Radiotélévision Message de Vie (Message of Life), a religious broadcaster owned by the prominent and outspoken evangelical minister Fernando Kutino. Kutino, who had developed a large following, had recently started a political television campaign called "Save the Congo." The campaign included thinly veiled criticisms of Kabila's government and called on citizens to take responsibility for the future of their country. Kutino fled the country soon after the raid. According to JED, the radio station began broadcasting again in December using new equipment financed by the church, but Kutino remained in exile at year's end.

Conditions for Congolese media professionals vary throughout the country. Because the transition government has not extended its authority throughout the DRC, media workers continue to be at the mercy of local officials who operate with impunity. This is particularly true in the eastern and northern areas of the country, which were previously controlled by powerful rebel movements whose leaders have been incorporated into the transition government, leaving a temporary power vacuum. In those areas, local authorities—whether they are longtime civil servants or political appointees—generally apply their own ad hoc policies on media freedom.

The ambiguity over who is in charge has led to a number of media abuses. In early August, Alimasi Mayanga, a programming director for the state-run broadcaster Radio Télévision Nationale Congolaise (RTNC) in the northern city of Kisangani, was reprimanded by local authorities for not broadcasting Congolese Rally for Democracy (RCD) political propaganda programs. An RCD official threatened Mayanga with suspension, saying that the RCD was still in charge. Though the RTNC was created by the national government, control of RTNC stations varies according to the regional authority. Weeks later, newly appointed Information Minister Vital Kamerhe clarified that the federal government in Kinshasa would make programming decisions thereafter.

With the peace accords, access to previously closed-off areas has increased. But local journalists are generally limited to taking U.N.-organized trips, while foreign journalists with the financial resources to travel can go unaccompanied. Travel to areas such as the volatile Ituri region and North and South Kivu provinces can be extremely dangerous due to the ongoing presence of heavily armed rival militias and remaining rebel forces.

In late June, local journalist Acquitté Kisembo disappeared in Bunia, the main city in the Ituri region. Kisembo, who was working as a fixer for Agence France-Presse, has not been found. Journalists suspect that he was kidnapped and killed by militiamen loyal to Thomas Lubanga, leader of the Union of Congolese Patriots (UPC), the rebel group that controlled the town of Bunia until mid-June. The motives for the kidnapping remain unclear.

Local journalists usually cannot access information from other parts of the country. Radio Okapi, created jointly by the U.N. Mission in the Congo and the Switzerland-based Hirondelle Foundation, remains the only source of news available nationally, with local affiliates and relay stations in 11 Congolese cities. Recently, several mobile phone networks were extended to most major cities, which will likely have a positive impact on journalists' ability to gather information from these areas.

However, limited financial resources hamper news gathering. Because journalists in the DRC remain severely underpaid, it is difficult for them to remain independent, and local sources say that many journalists are susceptible to bribes. According to JED, most local journalists have no contracts with their employers and often work on a project basis, so taking bribes is sometimes the only way journalists can support themselves.

A December report from JED noted there had been some improvement in press freedom conditions in the DRC during 2003, with the average duration of imprisonment for press offenses decreasing. For the first time in years, no journalists were in prison for their work in the DRC at year's end. JED attributes the improvements to the stabilizing security situation after the peace accords, as well as an increased sense of accountability on the part of officials in the new government. In December, JED launched a national campaign to decriminalize press offenses.

ERITREA

WITH 17 JOURNALISTS IN PRISON IN 2003, Eritrea was Africa's leading jailer of journalists. CPJ named the country one of the "World's Worst Places to Be a Journalist" for the second consecutive year.

Despite jubilant celebrations in the capital, Asmara, honoring the 10-year anniversary of the country's independence on May 24, Eritrea's development has been almost completely halted due to the devastating 1998-2000 border war with neighboring Ethiopia, as well as President Isaias Afewerki's increasingly dictatorial rule.

Afewerki and top government officials railed against mounting criticism from the international community over Eritrea's pitiful human rights record and failed to implement democratic reforms promised before the war. Simmering tensions with Ethiopia over border demarcation drew attention throughout 2003, but with no domestic private press and only a handful of international correspondents to cover events, the outside world remained largely oblivious to Eritrea's shattered economy and the effects of a serious drought.

The government's crackdown on the press began on September 18, 2001, when authorities banned all nonstate print media after senior politicians called for political reforms, and editorials on democracy and human rights began appearing in the local press. Authorities sealed off the newsrooms of such weekly publications as *Meqaleh*, *Setit*, and *Tsigenay*, and seized the papers' equipment.

Within days, the government began rounding up journalists, arresting at least 10 by the end of the month. Several more reporters went into hiding or fled the country. Since then, Eritrean authorities have arrested even more journalists. Almost all have been held incommunicado, without access to their families, lawyers, or international organizations such as the International Committee of the Red Cross.

The government, which admitted for the first time to a CPJ delegation in July 2002 that it was detaining journalists, has given different reasons for the arrests. Top officials have at various times accused the detained journalists of working without licenses or of evading military service, which is compulsory. In a May 20 interview with Reuters, Afewerki claimed that the media were "trying to confuse people by spreading disinformation." In an earlier interview with Radio France Internationale, he accused the journalists of being "spies" who had been bribed to create division in the country. Though almost all of the journalists were arrested long after the war with Ethiopia formally ended in June 2000, Afewerki said, "In the middle of the war we had to check them. We had to say enough is enough." Acting Information Minister Ali Abdu Ahmed has echoed that sentiment, telling the U.N. Integrated Regional Information Networks (IRIN) news agency in May that the incarcerated journalists were "mercenaries," and that their imprisonment was a matter of national security.

Despite these allegations, no formal charges have been brought against any of the journalists, and the government has given no indication that it intends to formally prosecute them.

Though CPJ research shows that a total of 17 journalists are in detention Eritrean authorities contend that some are performing their military service. All Eritrean citizens are obligated to perform military service, but the required duration of this service has been unclear since the beginning of the war with Ethiopia. Eritrean sources, however, have said the army service requirement is a pretext to arrest journalists for criticizing the government and to prevent them from working.

The July 8, 2003, arrest of Voice of America (VOA) stringer Aklilu Solomon seemed to demonstrate this point. Eritrean authorities claimed that Solomon, who was taken by police to an undisclosed location and has not been heard from since, was driven to a military camp to complete his mandatory national service. The VOA said, however, that Solomon had documents proving he had already completed part of his national service and was exempt from the remainder for medical reasons.

About 10 days earlier, officials had stripped Solomon of his press credentials for reporting on the grief of Eritrean families when the government announced the list of soldiers who died during the war with Ethiopia. Solomon's reporting contradicted the official version of events, which said that the families had celebrated with pride upon the announcement. Officials said Solomon's reporting was biased and designed to "please the enemy."

Police returned to Solomon's family home shortly after his arrest, disconnected his phone line, and confiscated his tape recorder and several cassettes. Eritrean sources questioned why police would have taken such actions if Solomon had actually been taken to perform military service. Solomon was one of only three Eritrean journalists in the country not working for the state media.

Despite the closure of the local private press, authorities maintain that Eritreans are free to express their political views and write what they want without fear of reprisal. Officials bristled when accused of human rights violations and in turn accused the international community of double standards when it threatened to make aid contingent on democratic reforms, pointing to the United States' detention of prisoners in Guantanamo Bay, Cuba, to justify their crackdown on the basis of "national security" concerns.

With the U.S. military considering building a military base in Eritrea, CPJ wrote to U.S. Secretary of Defense Donald Rumsfeld in early February urging the United States to take into account Eritrea's appalling press freedom record in its negotiations with Eritrean authorities. In December 2002, Rumsfeld had traveled to Eritrea to meet with Afewerki and discuss possible sites for a base there. When asked at a press conference about the country's press freedom record, Rumsfeld noted that Eritrea "is a sovereign nation, and they arrange themselves and deal with their problems in ways that they feel are appropriate to them."

In March, the U.S. Defense Department sent a letter to CPJ saying that Rumsfeld had discussed human rights abuses with Eritrean officials and had communicated that such abuses could hamper defense cooperation between the two countries. In the end, the United States opted for a base in Djibouti instead.

In early 2003, the U.S. State Department informed the Eritrean government that the country would be dropped from eligibility for benefits under the African Growth and Opportunity Act (AGOA) unless human rights conditions improved. At the beginning of 2004, the U.S. government followed up on its warning, canceling Eritrea's AGOA privileges.

In late July, Eritrean authorities asked the U.N. Mission to Ethiopia and Eritrea to close its two outreach centers—located in Asmara and the Western city of Barentu—calling the centers "unnecessary." The centers provided information on the peace process between Eritrea and Ethiopia, as well as general information on the United Nations, to hundreds of Eritreans. Police stationed outside the centers prevented people from entering. Negotiations with the government to keep the centers open failed, and they were permanently shuttered in September.

According to local sources, only about six international news organizations have correspondents in Eritrea, and only two of those journalists are Eritrean. The government heavily monitors foreign reporters. In March, Acting Information Minister Ahmed lambasted the BBC's reporting as "far-fetched and off the wall," according to IRIN, after a BBC reporter asked Ethiopian Prime Minister Meles Zenawi during an interview if he regretted not having pushed deeper into Eritrea during a successful offensive in the middle of the war.

In early February, CPJ launched its "Free Joshua" campaign to bring attention to the imprisonment of Fesshaye Yohannes, also known as "Joshua," one of the 17 journalists detained by Eritrean authorities and a recipient of CPJ's 2002 International Press Freedom Award. On February 5, CPJ delivered a petition signed by 607 people to the Eritrean Embassy in Washington, D.C., calling for Yohannes' release. By year's end, the number of signatories to CPJ's campaign had exceeded 800. CPJ representatives also met with members of the U.S. Congressional Human Rights Caucus to urge them to work for the release of jailed Eritrean journalists.

ETHIOPIA

DURING ITS 10 YEARS IN POWER, THE RULING ETHIOPIAN People's Revolutionary Democratic Front has come under mounting criticism for its antagonistic attitude toward the country's burgeoning private press. Authorities have used a restrictive press law to imprison journalists for critical reporting and to intimidate others into silence on sensitive issues, such as government infighting and secessionist ethnic groups. Though the government has recently attempted to improve its image by jailing fewer journalists and reforming its press law, one journalist remained in prison at year's end and a new draft press law was heavily criticized.

In January, the Information Ministry held a symposium at which it unveiled the new draft press law that Information Minister Bereket Simon had been promising. While Simon claimed that the new law would promote "constructive and responsible journalism," journalists doubted the motives behind the bill, which was drafted without the media's input. Journalists' fears were confirmed by the bill, which called for a licensing regime for all reporters, authorizing the Information Ministry to decide who could practice journalism. Journalists previously convicted of defamation would be prohibited from working.

The bill would require all foreign publications to be vetted by the Information Ministry before distribution, and it would allow the ministry to bar them from circulating for vague reasons. The bill forbids financial aid to newspapers and reporters from foreign organizations or states, a serious issue for the impoverished Ethiopian press. High printing costs and punitive fines have crippled many publications, and journalists are poorly paid.

The law would also establish a 29-member Press Council comprised of representatives from the government, the press, and civil society. According to the bill, the government would determine the council's powers and procedures to select members.

The bill also retains harsh criminal penalties, including imprisonment and fines for practicing journalism without a license and prison terms for distributing a prohibited publication or receiving contributions from foreign states or international groups. Under the draft legislation, courts would also be granted broad powers of censorship and be authorized to impose a three-year ban on media outlets for press law violations.

The Information Ministry's January symposium did not begin auspiciously, with representatives of the Ethiopian Free Press Journalists Association (EFJA) walking out to protest the government's refusal to allow private journalists or associations to formally present their views on the bill. Shortly after the symposium, the publishers of nine of the country's most prominent publications issued a joint statement on the draft law, saying it would highly restrict the activities of the private press and would infringe on citizens' constitutional right to access information.

To deal with journalists' criticism, the Information Ministry held another symposium on the bill in February. Information Minister Simon later said that the government had taken some of the journalists' comments on the bill into consideration and was making amendments. For instance, the government scrapped the law's access to government information provisions and hired a South African law firm to draft a freedom of information bill instead. Official translations of the amended draft press law and the freedom of information bill were not available at year's end.

Despite the Information Ministry's professed receptivity, the attempt to introduce another clearly repressive press law set a bitter tone to relations between journalists and the government all year long. Journalists claim that the new bill would undermine press freedom and be used to muzzle the press in the run-up to the 2005 general elections. The government countered that the new law was meant to foster professionalism in a "private press [that is] engaged in producing stories full of distortions and fabrications on a regular basis instead of offering stories based on accurate reporting."

In this heated atmosphere, the government closed EFJA's offices and suspended the organization's activities in November. EFJA, which has 155 members and has been operating for 11 years, is the country's only association open to all journalists and is a member of the International Freedom of Expression Exchange. Authorities claimed that the reason for the organization's closure was purely technical, since EFJA had failed to submit a mandatory audit of its budget to the Justice Ministry (as required of all civic organizations) and to renew its license for three consecutive years.

But EFJA representatives contended that the audit was a pretext for authorities to close an organization that has strongly criticized the government and drawn international attention to the plight of the country's beleaguered press. Around the time of the suspension, strident critiques of the organization's president, Kifle Mulat, and executive committee began appearing in state and private media accusing Mulat of corruption and the executive committee of poor leadership.

In early December, authorities banned the EFJA executive committee from conducting even the limited activities of hiring an accountant to perform the audit and holding overdue elections for a new executive committee. The government said it would call a meeting of the organization's membership to carry out these tasks. Mulat said the move was part of a plan to install a government-friendly executive committee that would allow authorities to push through the new press law with less international attention. Though authorities were criticized both locally and internationally for interfering in the internal affairs of the press association, government spokesperson Zemedkun Tekle told the U.N. Integrated Regional Information Networks news service that EFJA's suspension would be lifted as soon as the organization submitted its audit report.

Meanwhile, in June, a group of journalists established a new press association—the Ethiopian National Union of Journalists. The new union is supposed to operate independently of EFJA. Some local sources said the organization was formed by journalists who were disenchanted with EFJA's leadership. But others said the government was behind the union's creation and would use it as a counterweight to EFJA and to project a better image internationally.

During 2003, the government continued to use Press Proclamation No.34/1992 to charge and imprison journalists, particularly those working for the Amharic-language weekly *Ethiop*. Former *Ethiop* Editor-in-Chief Tewodros Kassa spent all year in prison. Kassa was sentenced to two years in prison in July 2002 on charges of defamation and incitement. Editor-in-Chief Melese Shine, who was charged with defamation, spent five months in jail in 2003, unable to pay his bail.

In an even more worrying development, in October, unidentified assailants brutally attacked *Ethiop* journalist Araya Tesfa Mariam near his home, leaving him with injuries that have impaired his mobility. Though CPJ wrote to Prime Minister Meles Zenawi calling for an inquiry into the attack, there were no reports of an investigation at year's end. Local journalists said they worried the attack may have come in reprisal for *Ethiop*'s aggressive coverage of internal struggles in Zenawi's Tigray People's Liberation Front (TPLF), one of four parties in Ethiopia's ruling coalition. In 2001, a number of hard-line TPLF members split from the party in opposition to the December 2000 peace treaty with Eritrea that ended two years of war.

The U.N. ruling on the border between the neighboring countries made headlines all year, and there was heated opposition within Ethiopia over Badme, the small but symbolic border town that was awarded to Eritrea. In a September letter to the U.N. Security Council, Zenawi called the ruling on Badme "illegal, unjust, and irresponsible" and warned that it could spark further unrest. Some of the local press, both state and private, took up the nationalistic rallying call in provocative editorials and accused the United Nations of shortchanging Ethiopia in the ruling. The feisty comments elicited the concern of the U.N. special representative to the region, Legwaila Joseph Legwaila, who appealed to journalists to "stay calm," Inter Press Service reported.

In 2002, the government opened the Ethiopian Broadcast Agency, which is charged with issuing licenses to the country's first private broadcasters, but the agency had not issued any licenses by the end of the 2003. Though Ethiopia's broadcast law—which mandates the liberalization of the airwaves—was enacted three years ago, the government has dragged its feet on putting it into action. Journalists have been left to speculate on whether any stations will be licensed before the 2005 elections, and whether the proposed press law, if it is passed, will give the government more control over private broadcasters.

In December, the Information Ministry and the British Council, a cultural and educational organization, organized a four-day training seminar in the capital, Addis Ababa, for journalists and government officials. During 2003, the U.S. government–funded broadcaster Voice of America and the U.S. Agency for International Development donated equipment to the journalism school at the private Unity University and were helping the school build its first radio studios.

GABON

IN JULY, THE GABONESE LEGISLATURE AMENDED THE CONSTITUTION to eliminate presidential term limits, opening the way for President Omar Bongo, who has been in office for 36 years, to be president for life. The state-controlled *L'Union* newspaper, the country's only daily, said the amendment would usher in "a new era for our democracy and our country." In fact, the constitutional change shows that opposition and pro-democracy movements remain weak and marginalized in this oil-rich Central African nation.

Throughout 2003, the government's National Communications Council (CNC), which is supposed to promote press freedom and ensure quality journalism, continued the crackdown on private media that it began more than four years ago ahead of presidential elections.

Continuing its pattern of shuttering any private newspapers that dare criticize authorities, the CNC in May suspended the private weekly *Le Temps* the day after the paper published an article accusing members of the government of embezzling funds meant for coordinating the national independence festival. In September, the CNC banned two other private newspapers, *La Sagaie* and *Sub-Version*, for allegedly "attacking the dignity of the institutions of the Republic," among other charges. In December, the CNC suspended the private bimonthly *L'Autre Journal*, accusing it of publishing "defamatory articles."

Meanwhile, *Misamu*, a private bimonthly known for its critical stance, remains closed. It had been banned in early 2002 for reporting on official corruption but resumed publishing in the fall of that year. In May 2003, however, the CNC suspended *Misamu* again, citing an ownership dispute between the paper's editor and a senator. In September 2003, the CNC extended the suspension, again citing the dispute. But local journalists suspect that the ownership issue is being used as an excuse to keep the paper shut.

Because the ruling Democratic Party controls all state institutions, including the judiciary and the CNC, self-censorship in the media is rife. Journalists also complain that, while a handful of private newspapers exist, many are bankrolled by members of the government and can become pawns in political power struggles. High printing costs and low salaries make it difficult for both publications and journalists to remain independent.

Financial constraints mean that most privately owned publications cannot appear regularly, and several newspapers are printed in neighboring Cameroon to reduce costs. In May, Communications Minister Mehdi Teale announced that the government would allocate 500 million CFA francs (US$937,490) to support media development. However, journalists say that in the past, the government used such funds to buy favorable coverage.

Several private radio stations broadcast in Gabon in addition to the state-run Radio Télévision Gabonaise, but local journalists say that most private stations do not focus on news. Only foreign stations provide regular independent news, including Radio France Internationale, Voice of America (VOA), and the BBC, which began broadcasting on the FM band in Gabon in 2003. Also this year, after several attempts, the BBC managed to secure a license from the CNC to operate its own antenna in the capital, Libreville. VOA programs are broadcast on FM in Libreville via cooperation with a local private radio station.

THE GAMBIA

IN 2003, PRESIDENT YAHYA JAMMEH'S RULING ALLIANCE FOR PATRIOTIC REORIENTATION and Construction (APRC) maintained a firm grip on power in this tiny West African country, despite signs of political and economic instability. In September and October, the president fired four ministers, including the communications minister, while a fifth, the justice minister, resigned.

Since the APRC swept parliamentary elections in 2002, Jammeh has used his power to silence opposition voices and the independent media. Throughout 2003, the strained relationship between the administration and the private press continued, demonstrated by the government's frequent arrest and detention of local journalists. In addition, many journalists reported receiving anonymous death threats for critical political coverage.

The government continued its crusade of harassment against *The Independent*, a private biweekly based in the capital, Banjul. In September, *The Independent*'s editor-in-chief, Abdoulie Sey, was abducted and held incommunicado at the headquarters of the National Intelligence Agency for three days after the paper ran an opinion piece titled "Jammeh Under the Microscope." The article, written by a Gambian journalist based in the United States, discussed the Gambia's endemic poverty and corruption and concluded that the president had "failed us all." In October, three unidentified men assaulted a private security guard in front of the newspaper's offices, doused the building with gasoline, and set it on fire. The fire damaged the newspaper's power supply, causing the staff to relocate temporarily. Gambian journalists said the attack, which closely resembled an arson attack in 2000 on the offices of the private Banjul-based Radio 1 FM, may have come in reprisal for *The Independent*'s critical reporting on the government.

In March, police officers arrested Pa Nderry M'bai, a reporter for the private newspaper *The Point*, after he wrote an article alleging that police frequently extorted bribes from black-market moneychangers. M'bai, who was also secretary of the Gambian Press Union, was accused of attempting to undermine the police force. He was released the same day with a warning to avoid similar topics in the future.

The government's intolerance of criticism has caused self-censorship among journalists and media outlets. For instance, after the arson attack in 2000, Radio 1 FM dropped news and moved to an all-music and entertainment-based format. The closure of Citizen FM in 2001 for alleged nonpayment of taxes left the country with no private news-based radio stations. As a result, Gambians rely on heavily controlled state radio for information. State radio rebroadcasts some Voice of America and BBC programming, although both are subject to frequent government censorship.

Tensions between the Gambia and neighboring Senegal also created problems for journalists. Senegalese politicians have accused the Gambian government of supporting a militant separatist movement in southern Casamance, a region of Senegal largely cut off from the rest of the country by the Gambian border. After Senegal won a June soccer match against the Gambia, angry crowds in Banjul attacked Senegalese nationals and Senegalese-owned businesses. The violence continued for hours before the government imposed a curfew. During the rioting, an angry mob stoned the offices of private radio station Sud FM, which is partly owned by Senegalese citizens and was broadcasting live reports on the anti-Senegalese violence. In addition, intelligence agents arrested and questioned the managing editor of *The Independent* after the newspaper ran a report on violence at the soccer match.

A media regulatory commission with jurisdiction over complaints against journalists was inaugurated in the summer of 2003 in accordance with the 2002 National Media Commission Act. The act requires journalists and media organizations to register with the commission for one-year renewable licenses. Journalists and media rights activists have heavily criticized the legislation on the grounds that its definitions of press offenses are vague and it grants the commission overly broad powers, including the rights to issue arrest warrants and force journalists to reveal their sources.

Shortly before the commission was inaugurated, the Gambian Press Union (GPU), along with private publications including *The Independent*, *The Point*, and *News and Reports*, filed a suit with the Supreme Court challenging the commission's constitutionality. When the commission sent letters to private newspapers and radio stations asking them to register, the journalists responded by filing another suit with the High Court, seeking to restrain the commission from registering publications while the Supreme Court case was pending.

The GPU also refused to nominate one of its members to fill a designated seat on the commission, protesting that it would not cooperate with the commission until its charter was amended. The government responded by pushing legislation through Parliament that allows the communications minister to appoint any journalist to the GPU's seat.

While members of the private press criticize the National Media Commission Act, most think that more training and higher professional standards for Gambian journalists are needed. The GPU hopes to start a journalism school at the University of the Gambia in 2004, in cooperation with UNESCO.

Fear of further economic troubles prompted some Gambians, who depend on revenue from the tourism industry for survival, to criticize the private press for what they perceive as inflammatory reporting that could damage the Gambia's reputation as a place of relative political stability. In an October letter to *The Independent*, one resident said the publication risked causing further economic turmoil when it ran an interview with opposition leader Lamin Waa Juwara. The article, titled "Let's Take to the Streets," quoted Juwara as calling for a mass protest against the country's economic situation. Juwara was arrested and detained for more than two weeks in response to the interview.

IVORY COAST

THE BRUTAL MURDER OF A FRENCH JOURNALIST IN IVORY COAST IN OCTOBER highlighted the lack of security in the country in 2003. The killing came after the collapse of the government of national reconciliation in September, when rebels walked out and accused President Laurent Gbagbo of refusing to fully implement the peace process. Despite a peace accord signed in France in January, the country remained divided at year's end into a mainly Muslim, rebel-held north and a mostly Christian and animist government-held south, with French and West African peacekeepers sandwiched in the middle.

On July 4, 2003, the former rebels, now known as the New Forces, and the army jointly declared the end of the war. However, good will faded as the August deadline for disarmament came and went, while the New Forces accused Gbagbo of blocking reforms. In late September, former rebels in the government withdrew to their central stronghold of Bouake, denouncing the national reconciliation government as a sham. Gbagbo in turn accused the rebels of sabotaging the peace process by refusing to disarm.

On October 21, Radio France Internationale's (RFI) West Africa correspondent Jean Hélène was shot in the head by a police officer in the capital, Abidjan, while the journalist waited outside national police headquarters for the release of 11 opposition supporters who had been detained on suspicion of plotting to kill top government officials. Hélène, 50, was an experienced journalist who had reported on many wars in Africa. On January 22, 2004, a military court in Abidjan sentenced Ivoirian police officer Sgt. Théodore Séry Dago to 17 years in prison. Séry Dago was also fined 500,000 CFA francs (US$960), stripped of his rank in the national police, and barred from voting or leaving his home for 10 years.

After Hélène's family, RFI, and the French press freedom group Reporters Without Borders applied in France to become civil parties in the case, a French public prosecutor began conducting an investigation into the murder. Under French law, French authorities have jurisdiction in the case because the victim was French. Although the French and Ivoirian inquiries are legally separate, officials have been cooperating. France and Ivory Coast have a bilateral treaty on judicial cooperation dating back to Ivoirian independence.

Although the motive for Hélène's murder is unclear, many observers linked it to the prevailing hostility against the French presence in Ivory Coast, and against the French and foreign press there. Gbagbo's ruling Ivoirian Popular Front (FPI) party has frequently accused France of backing the rebellion, which erupted into civil war in September 2002, even though many believe that the 3,800 French troops and 1,000 West African troops overseeing the cease-fire line between north and south have prevented the rebels from penetrating into government-held territory. Experts say there is no evidence to support the accusations that France has been backing the rebellion.

Days after Hélène's killing, newspaper vendors staged a national strike to protest repeated attacks by pro-Gbagbo youth in Abidjan and throughout the southwest. "They come along in plain clothes and ask for opposition papers. If we give them a copy, they rip up all our newspapers and threaten to beat us up," complained one vendor. Pro-government youth militia, known as the Young Patriots, have accused opposition newspapers, such as *Le Patriote*, *Le Nouveau Réveil*, and *Le Front*, of publishing pro-rebel propaganda.

Despite the reconciliation process, most Ivoirian media remain partisan and provocative. In fact, human rights groups, foreign journalists, and diplomats have characterized some of the commentary as "incitement to violence." One of the most blatant examples was an announcement on the state broadcaster Radio Télévision Ivoire in late 2002 calling on Ivoirians to denounce "suspicious neighbors" by reporting them to the police. This resulted in attacks on immigrants and disappearances. The communications minister, former rebel leader Guillaume Soro, attempted to introduce a number of reforms aimed at promoting a more "balanced press," including workshops to teach local journalists the importance of unbiased reporting and warn them against allowing Ivory Coast to become "another Rwanda," where some media outlets actively encouraged the 1994 genocide.

In November, *Le Patriote*, which is close to the Rally of the Republicans party of exiled opposition leader Alassane Ouattara, denounced a three-month government ban on demonstrations under the headline, "Gbagbo, the Black Hitler." Papers close to Gbagbo are also extreme and have accused France and international journalists of being close to the rebellion. While most of the dailies, including the state-run newspaper *Fraternité Matin*, carried a black page to commemorate Hélène's death, some were less sympathetic. *Notre Voie*, the newspaper of the ruling FPI, launched a campaign to defend Hélène's killer, saying that the journalist had provoked him, and that it may have been an accident. Some papers speculated that the French media provoked the murder by showing bias in favor of the rebels. There is no clear evidence of any bias in the French media, although French news coverage of the Ivoirian conflict remained a sensitive issue in France as well as Ivory Coast.

After Hélène's murder, foreign correspondents in Abidjan asked for a meeting with Gbagbo to find out what guarantees he could offer for journalists' security. The president said that although he was shocked by Hélène's death, he was equally shocked by the way the foreign press had "gone crazy" in its reporting on Ivory Coast. He insisted that he would never expel or imprison a journalist but suggested that correspondents show more self-restraint. The president was particularly outraged at a January article headlined "Gbagbo's Death Squads" in the French newspaper *Le Monde* that covered a U.N. report linking killings in Abidjan to a tribal militia close to Gbagbo's wife. Gbagbo was also angered by a cartoon in the paper that showed the United Nations fighting Saddam Hussein on one side and Gbagbo on the other.

West Africa bureaus of foreign news agencies have for many years been based in Abidjan, but most had pulled out by the end of 2003. The Associated Press moved its offices to Dakar, Senegal, in August 2002, and *The New York Times* correspondent followed suit in 2003. Reuters also relocated to Dakar in November 2003. The BBC will move its regional office to Accra, Ghana, in 2004. RFI will no longer have a permanent correspondent in Abidjan and advised its freelance reporter to leave. Agence France-Presse had not decided by year's end whether it would leave Ivory Coast.

Hélène was the second journalist killed in Ivory Coast in 2003. The body of Ivoirian journalist Kloueu Gonzreu, 51, who worked for the state-owned Ivoirian Press Agency (AIP), was found in March near the western town of Toulépleu, bordering Liberia, by a team from the Red Cross, for which he also worked. His body was found along with those of his 19-year-old son and two other local Red Cross volunteers. The victims reportedly disappeared on January 11. Local journalists told CPJ at the time that they believed Gonzreu had been kidnapped and killed by Liberian mercenaries fighting for the Ivoirian government, and that his death could have been linked to his work as a journalist. On January 30, the pro-government newspaper *Notre Pays* accused him of "voicing sympathy with the rebellion." However, the circumstances of his death remain murky, and some have also raised the possibility that he was killed in crossfire during an upsurge of fighting in early 2003 between government and rebel forces. Because Toulépleu is remote with no government authority ruling it, no inquiry has been conducted.

In January, security forces in the southwestern port city of San Pedro arrested French journalist Anne Boher of Reuters after rebels announced that they would try to take the town. Though Boher primarily reported on Ivory Coast's cocoa industry, she was accused of being a spy because she had the names and numbers of opposition members and rebels in her contact book. She was released 24 hours later in Abidjan. Boher had previously received death threats, and Reuters moved her to another country.

Attempts were under way toward the end of 2003 to salvage the peace process. In December, following a series of meetings, both sides agreed to a series of confidence-building measures, including withdrawing heavy weapons from the front lines. In early January 2004, rebel ministers returned to Abidjan, ending their boycott of the transition government, while an advance party of French peacekeeping troops began deploying in the rebel-held north.

KENYA

THE DECEMBER 2002 ELECTORAL VICTORY OF PRESIDENT MWAI KIBAKI'S National Rainbow Coalition (NARC) brought high hopes for a new era of democracy, economic recovery, and respect for human rights after the 24-year rule of former President Daniel arap Moi and his KANU party. However, the euphoric atmosphere quickly dissipated.

The new government failed to deliver on many election promises, including the introduction of a new constitution within 100 days. As the government came under attack, authorities also showed increasing signs of intolerance toward the media.

At the end of September, police arrested three senior staff members of the *East African Standard*, the country's oldest newspaper, after the *Standard* published excerpts of leaked confessions in a sensitive murder inquiry. The confessions were from a suspect in the murder of Crispin Odhiambo Mbai, who headed a key committee of Kenya's Constitutional Review Conference. Mbai was killed on September 14 in what many believe was a political assassination. The *Standard* article suggested that the police inquiry was moving too slowly.

After six hours of questioning, the police released Tom Mshindi, the managing director of Standard Group, which owns the *Standard*, and one of his editors. Another editor, David Makali, was detained for two days and charged with stealing a police videotape. He pleaded not guilty to the charge, which carries a sentence of up to three years in prison. The newspaper, whose original article on the confessions referred to a police report and not to tapes, denies that it ever had a police videotape. Makali was released on bail, but the court case remained ongoing at year's end.

In December, Attorney General Amos Wako announced a clampdown on so-called scandal sheets, publications that often carry unsigned articles with gossip about Kenya's rich and powerful. The move came after members of Parliament demanded action against the publications, saying they thrived on character assassination through unfounded and exaggerated stories. A recent edition of one sheet had listed the HIV status of some lawmakers. Wako accused six sheets of failing to comply with rules governing the publication and sale of newspapers and said vendors of these titles would be arrested and charged. Ironically, he invoked provisions of the repressive Books and Newspapers Act, introduced by the Moi government only months before the 2002 elections, which the new government had promised to overturn. The law raised the libel insurance bond that publishers must pay the government from 10,000 Kenyan shillings (US$130) to 1 million Kenyan shillings (US$13,200) and penalizes vendors who sell unlicensed publications. Anyone caught selling illegal publications faces six months in jail and a fine of 20,000 Kenyan shillings (US$265).

Scandal sheet publishers and editors deny they violated the law. They vowed to defy the crackdown and argued that civil libel laws provide adequate means for redress to individuals who feel unfairly targeted by the press. However, with vendors afraid to sell the publications, sales went underground by mid-December, according to local journalists. Although mainstream journalists question the professionalism and ethics of the scandal sheets, most agreed that the government clampdown was a threat to press freedom.

In late December, the respected daily newspaper *The Nation* reported that two government ministers and a NARC parliamentarian had been caught with prostitutes in their cars during a police raid in the capital, Nairobi. *The Nation* said police had videotaped evidence, which police denied. Labor Minister Ali Chirau Mwakwere sued Nation Media Group (NMG), which owns the paper, for civil defamation, while the other minister and the lawmaker obtained 14-day gag orders against NMG and the owners of Citizen radio and television banning them from circulating any material about the police operation. The gag orders expired at year's end, but the case remained before the courts. Kenyan law limits press coverage of matters in court.

Journalists expressed disappointment at the new government's failure to improve the legislative framework for press freedom in 2003. Despite their pre-election promises, authorities did not revoke laws that threaten press freedom, including the Official Secrets Act, which criminalizes breaches of government secrecy; sections of the Penal Code; and the Books and Newspapers Act.

Photojournalist Wallace Gichere has been fighting for government compensation since 1991, when police officers threw him from the window of his fourth-floor apartment in Nairobi, leaving him paralyzed from the waist down. The officers had gone to arrest him for writing antigovernment articles and sending information on human rights abuses to Amnesty International.

In June 2000, a government committee on human rights recommended that the government compensate him for injuries and loss of earnings, a recommendation that the previous government approved the same year, according to Gichere. In July 2002, after the journalist went on a hunger strike, Attorney General Wako admitted liability but said the journalist's compensation claim was excessive. Gichere went on a hunger strike again for two weeks in December 2003. This time, Wako offered him 9.4 million Kenyan shillings (US$124,000). The Kenya Union of Journalists (KUJ), which has taken up his case, described this as "peanuts" and said the amount would not even cover his medical bills. KUJ Secretary-General Ezekiel Mutua demanded that the government explain its offer and put it in writing. By mid-January, officials had still not done so, according to Gichere. So far, there have been no moves to prosecute the police officers responsible for crippling Gichere.

LIBERIA

WITH REBEL FORCES OVERRUNNING THE CAPITAL, MONROVIA, and the international community clamoring for his departure, Liberian President Charles Taylor resigned and accepted exile in Nigeria on August 11. Taylor's departure paved the way for a transitional national government—comprised, in part, of representatives from two rebel groups, as well as members of Taylor's government—to lead the country to elections planned for 2005.

During his six-year rule, Taylor ruthlessly cracked down on the political opposition and civil society activists to consolidate his power. As the last remaining openly critical sector of society, the Liberian private media, which Taylor regarded with a mix of suspicion and contempt, was continually subject to government repression.

The Taylor government's tactics for silencing critics were varied. Police banned independent radio stations perceived to have an "antigovernment" editorial line, and, using pretexts such as tax evasion, they closed newspapers that exposed government corruption or rights abuses. As the war between government forces and the rebel Liberians United for Reconciliation and Democracy (LURD) intensified, the Taylor regime tightened its grip on information, imposing censorship policies that required all news stories on the rebellion to receive approval from the Information Ministry before publication or broadcast.

When formal censorship policies were insufficient, journalists were co-opted with bribes, driven into exile, or cowed into self-censorship with threats of imprisonment or physical assault. The tactics of intimidation culminated in brutal attacks against two journalists in 2002. Hassan Bility, editor-in-chief of the independent *Analyst*, was held for six months incommunicado and repeatedly tortured for alleged ties to LURD. In December 2002, *Inquirer* reporter Throble Suah was viciously attacked by agents of Taylor's notorious Anti-Terrorist Unit after he covered LURD activities and the refugee crisis in the north of the country. Suah had to be flown out of Liberia for medical treatment; he did not return to Monrovia until after Taylor's departure.

In mid-January 2003, Taylor accused the Press Union of Liberia (PUL) of politicizing the attack on Suah and of blowing it out of proportion. The PUL issued a release in response saying it had no political interest and was merely concerned for the welfare of the ailing journalist. In the following weeks, PUL members reported that they had received threats and were under surveillance by suspected members of Taylor's security forces.

An indictment for "crimes against humanity" issued by the U.N.-backed tribunal in Sierra Leone followed Taylor into exile in Nigeria. His adversarial relationship with journalists followed him as well. The Nigerian Union of Journalists mounted a legal challenge to Taylor's asylum, but the suit was dropped after Taylor arrived in Nigeria. The journalists' union is still seeking redress for the death of two Nigerian journalists: Krees Imodibe of the Nigerian *Daily Champion*, and Tayo Awotusin of *The Guardian*. While fighting to depose then President Samuel Doe, Taylor's rebel forces murdered the two journalists, who were working in Liberia in the early 1990s, said Liberian sources.

As the war between Taylor's government forces and LURD rebels approached Monrovia in the spring of 2003, it became increasingly difficult for journalists to do their jobs. The fighting hit a fever pitch in July, and almost all of the Liberian media shut down. Journalists went into hiding for fear of being targeted by either side or hit in the crossfire. The only independent news source still operating in the capital in late July was the Catholic Church–owned Radio Veritas. The broadcaster was finally forced off the air on July 21, when a mortar shell hit its transmitter.

Foreign journalists flocked to the war-torn capital after U.S. President George W. Bush ordered U.S. warships to the region and Taylor's departure drew near. French photographer Patrick Robert, on assignment for the U.S.-based weekly *Time* magazine, was seriously injured in crossfire between government and rebel soldiers, and he was flown out of the country for medical treatment.

Several media companies were attacked and looted during the war, and tens of thousands of dollars in equipment was lost or damaged. Radio Veritas was unable to resume broadcasting until the end of August, and then only on the FM band, since the station did not have the funds to repair its shortwave transmitter. Talking Drum Studios, a broadcaster funded by the U.S.-based nongovernmental organization Search for Common Ground, lost an estimated $150,000 of equipment. The Liberia Institute of Journalism, a nonprofit journalism-training center, was stripped bare of its computers and broadcasting equipment.

Good news for Liberian journalists seemed to arrive with the October 14 inauguration of Gyude Bryant as chairman of the new transitional government. In his inauguration speech, the former Monrovia businessman and activist for democratic reform declared, "This government will encourage and exercise the freedom of speech and of the press which constitutes one of the basic tenets of good governance. It is only when people are free to speak, write, and print that they can help keep the government accountable and transparent."

Though Liberian journalists were used to similar-sounding empty promises from former presidents Taylor and Doe, Bryant took an early step toward reinforcing his remarks by lifting the 3-year-old ban on Star Radio in the beginning of November. Star Radio, an initiative of the Switzerland-based Hirondelle Foundation, was established in the run-up to Liberian elections in 1997 to promote democracy and provide a forum for different views. The immensely popular station was banned in March 2000 by the Taylor government for broadcasting what authorities claimed were "hate messages against the Liberian government" that threatened national security. Bryant said that the station would play a key role in the "development of communication and enhancing the integrity of our media industry."

With Liberia's literacy rate just over 50 percent, radio is the country's most important medium of mass communication. Previously, Taylor had a virtual monopoly on the airwaves beyond Monrovia. Though some "amateur" and community stations existed outside the capital, authorities banned at least five of them in the spring, according to journalists in Monrovia, because of fears that they were mobilizing the rural population against the government. Taylor allowed the state media service, the Liberian Broadcasting System (LBS), to deteriorate, preferring to disseminate propaganda through his private media empire—the Liberian Communications Network—which comprised several radio stations.

After Taylor's departure, journalists continued to fear reprisals from Taylor loyalists who remained in Monrovia. Their fears seemed warranted when, in early October, the United Nations found that Taylor was still meddling in Liberian internal affairs from exile. Meanwhile, LBS journalists protested the reappointment of J. Allison Barco as director-general of the state broadcaster, accusing Barco of corruption and partisanship toward Taylor and his National Patriotic Party (NPP). NPP members of the transitional government had been tasked with appointing the LBS director. Barco was later replaced, local sources said.

But journalists were more sanguine about the press's prospects once the transitional administration took over; U.N. peacekeepers had firm control over the capital, and disarmament of the warring factions had begun. Sources in Monrovia said the biggest obstacle to the media was no longer government repression but finding the funding to surmount the damage caused by the war and to sustain the press in a shattered economy. Nonetheless, by year's end, several new publications had appeared on Monrovia newsstands—a sign, journalists said, of the population's eagerness to engage in the country's future.

LURD forces, still armed, control the vast majority of Liberia outside the capital, and it is unsafe for journalists to work in the countryside. Journalists in Monrovia were unaware of any independent media operating in the interior at year's end.

MALAWI

PRESIDENT BAKILI MULUZI'S ELECTION IN 1994 WAS HAILED as a return to democratic rule after years of dictatorship under Hastings Kamuzu Banda. Muluzi has called himself a friend of the press, but he has proved to be a fair-weather friend. Throughout 2003, journalists in this small, Southern African country endured frequent harassment from government officials and party supporters, which took the form of threats, verbal attacks, and physical violence.

The beginning of 2003 was dominated by Muluzi's renewed bid to run for an unconstitutional third term in office. A presidential election is scheduled for May 2004. In July 2002, the National Assembly rejected proposals to amend the constitution to allow Muluzi to run. In February 2003, Justice Minister Henry Phoya reintroduced the bill, only to withdraw it when indications showed it would be defeated again. The president's actions led to protests that drew thousands of Malawians, and journalists covering the demonstrations were endangered by police attempts to control the crowds. One journalist from the privately owned *Daily Times* was hit in the knee by a rubber bullet.

The debate politicized relations between supporters of Muluzi's United Democratic Front (UDF) and independent journalists, whom Muluzi supporters accuse of attacking the president by failing to support his campaign to stay in power. In May, a senior reporter for the *Daily Times* went into hiding after receiving threats for criticizing Muluzi's bid for a third term. In February, at the peak of tension fueled by the debate, members of the UDF's youth wing, known as the Young Democrats, attacked newspaper vendors for selling allegedly pro-opposition papers. Local journalists said the attacks were provoked by a *Daily Times* article with the headline "Sayimanso," which means "he will not stand again" in Chichewa, a local language.

At a UDF party convention in July, a group of Young Democrats physically assaulted Daniel Nyirenda, a photojournalist for the independent daily *The Nation*. Nyirenda had been taking pictures of a fight that had broken out among delegates near the entrance gates of the convention hall. The youths beat him and dragged him into the mud. Nyirenda's colleagues at *The Nation* said the assailants also broke his digital camera and stole another. Following the attack, Nyirenda spent more than a week in the hospital. According to local journalists, no action had been taken against Nyirenda's assailants by year's end.

The attack on Nyirenda provoked widespread condemnation of the Young Democrats by the press and local journalists organizations. The UDF's response to Nyirenda's beating drew further criticism. While Muluzi condemned the beating and said "the media should know that I am their friend," he claimed that "enemies of the ruling party" carried out the assault. After party officials publicly admitted that Nyirenda's assailants were UDF supporters, a regional governor said at a UDF rally that Nyirenda's beating was deserved and accused the journalist of being on a spying mission for opposition leader Aleke Banda. The governor also warned *The Nation* against sending journalists to cover the party's August convention. Later, Muluzi assured journalists that they would be protected at the convention. *The Nation* editor Steven Nhlane told CPJ that the newspaper sent reporters to cover the convention despite fears for their safety, but that attendees did not target them.

In one positive development for journalists, in October the High Court awarded 48,000 kwacha (US$455) in damages to McDonald Chapalapata, a *Nation* journalist assaulted in 2002 by the financial controller of the government's National Food Reserve Agency. The suit was made possible by a legal aid fund for journalists started by the local chapter of the Media Institute of Southern Africa (MISA).

Throughout 2003, journalists and news outlets endured verbal attacks from Muluzi and party leaders. In June, after reports in the media raised questions about Muluzi's practice of distributing corn at political rallies—a powerful gesture ahead of elections in a country ridden with hunger—the president lashed out, threatening journalists that "one day I will come to your home and grab you by the collar," according to MISA.

In addition, the Malawi Communications Regulatory Authority (MACRA) threatened private radio stations that aired critical news coverage. In June, MACRA's director said that community radio stations were not allowed to broadcast news under Malawi's 1998 Communications Law. Local observers linked the director's statements to the fact that community radio stations often air live call-in programs, which allow listeners to criticize government policies. In June, MACRA warned MIJ FM, a radio station at the Malawi Institute of Journalism, which is funded by international and nongovernmental donors, that it risked losing its broadcasting license because of alleged political bias in its reporting. In September, MACRA threatened to close the popular Capital Radio, which is widely respected for its editorial independence, because the station had offered to air live political rallies. After widespread protests in the local media, the threats were quietly dropped.

Religious tensions in the country also played into media relations. In July, journalist Lameck Masina was suspended for a week from his job at Radio Islam, which is run by a an international Islamic charity, for broadcasting an interview with the wives of five alleged al-Qaeda members who Malawi had turned over to U.S. officials at the request of U.S. intelligence officers. Malawi's minority Muslim population widely criticized the suspects' transfer to U.S. custody, sparking public protests.

During the interview, the wives said that President Muluzi had apologized to them for their husbands' arrests. Muluzi, himself a Muslim, had earlier defended turning the men over to U.S. officials, saying that it was in the best interests of the nation. Some local journalists told CPJ that Masina's suspension came in response to pressure from senior

UDF officials. Hub-Eddin Abbakar, the station's manager, told The Associated Press that the suspension was "an internal issue."

Politicians continue to use litigation to stifle critical reporting. Office equipment belonging to the privately owned newspaper *The Chronicle* was confiscated in September after it lost two defamation suits, both lodged by government employees. The court ordered the confiscation after *The Chronicle* was unable to pay the legal damages awarded in the suits. The paper was able to continue publishing using borrowed equipment but faces up to six more libel cases, including one for criminal defamation, according to Managing Editor Robert Jamieson. Some journalists allege that the suits are part of a government attempt to drive the paper out of business because it is sympathetic to the opposition.

MOZAMBIQUE

THE TRIAL OF SIX MEN ACCUSED OF KILLING MOZAMBICAN JOURNALIST Carlos Cardoso in November 2000 ended on January 31. The defendants were sentenced to lengthy prison terms ranging from 23 to 28 years in jail for conspiring to kill Cardoso because of his aggressive coverage of a 1996 corruption scandal involving the state-controlled Commercial Bank of Mozambique. South African journalist Phillip van Niekerk represented CPJ at the verdict's announcement.

The rare instance of a journalist's murderers being brought to justice renewed the confidence of the Mozambican press corps. Since the end of a 16-year civil war in 1992, Mozambique's media have flourished. Today, dozens of private publications frequently criticize both the ruling Mozambique Liberation Front (FRELIMO) and the main opposition party, Mozambique National Resistance (RENAMO), which comprises members of the former rebel movement. Private and community radio stations have also proliferated. Many air daily news programs, although most recycle their information from a variety of secondary sources, including the local print media. Journalists, who say that even state media outlets enjoy editorial freedom, praise state-run Radio Mozambique—the country's only nationwide station—for its independent coverage.

However, the implications of Cardoso's murder still weigh heavily on journalists in this southern African coastal state. Many told CPJ they believe that the masterminds behind the killing remain at large. During the trial, several of the defendants said that the president's son Nymphine Chissano ordered the murder. In January, law enforcement officials announced that they were launching a separate investigation into Nymphine's role in the Cardoso case, although no developments had been announced by year's end.

Local journalists told CPJ that while reporters are not afraid to criticize government or ruling-party policies, most avoid the type of investigative reporting that Cardoso pursued and don't write about political corruption or organized crime. While the government has said publicly that protecting journalists is a priority, press freedom organizations such as the local chapter of the Media Institute for Southern Africa (MISA) say that authorities should move beyond public statements to create a truly safe environment for the press.

Reporters who do write about corruption often encounter harassment. Journalists complain of frequent calls from ruling-party officials who pressure editors to reinforce

Mozambique's international image as a place of stability and economic growth. Furthermore, journalists say that anonymous threats, while rarely carried out, are common against those who report on corruption. In March, Rui de Carvalho, a journalist with the independent weekly *Mediafax,* received threatening phone calls after he reported on illegal land deals that implicated FRELIMO leaders.

While usually supportive of media freedom, President Joaquim Chissano publicly warned the local press against "sensationalism" in March at a ceremony inaugurating new members of Mozambique's Supreme Mass Media Council, a watchdog body established under the constitution and Press Law. At the ceremony, the council's chairperson, Julieta Langa, said Mozambique's press "embraces speculation [and] does not practice constructive journalism," according to the state news agency, AIM. In April, several Supreme Court justices made similar accusations and warned journalists they would take "legal action" against reporters who defamed the court in their articles. That same month, Supreme Court Chief Justice Mario Mangaze filed a criminal defamation case against the private weekly *Zambeze* after the paper published an article accusing him of corruption. The case was pending at year's end. Mangaze also threatened to sue *Mediafax* in response to similar allegations.

While local journalists condemned the president's remarks, several also criticized *Zambeze* for poorly researched articles. *Zambeze* had earlier drawn criticism when it ran the reportedly leaked verdict and sentences in the Cardoso case the day before the verdict was announced. The real sentences varied by a few years from those in *Zambeze*'s story.

Attacks on journalists remain rare, but the local media reported several cases of harassment in the run-up to municipal elections in October and November, when tensions between FRELIMO and RENAMO made it difficult for journalists to do their jobs. In November, FRELIMO supporters harassed a *Mediafax* correspondent, tore up his notebook, and accused the publication of supporting RENAMO. In November, a stringer working for state-run Radio Mozambique in the north was kidnapped and detained for several hours by RENAMO supporters who said his coverage was biased in favor of the ruling party.

A draft freedom of information bill, written by consultants to MISA-Mozambique and designed to provide journalists with greater access to government information, was still being finalized at year's end with input from local journalists' associations. MISA hopes Parliament will introduce the bill in early 2004.

NIGER

AFTER U.S. PRESIDENT GEORGE W. BUSH CLAIMED IN HIS 2003 STATE OF THE UNION address that Iraqi leader Saddam Hussein had attempted to buy uranium from the impoverished West African country of Niger, outraged journalists and President Mamadou Tandja, who has led the nation since its return to civilian rule in 1999, rallied to the nations' defense. No evidence has been found to support Bush's accusation.

However, President Tandja and Niger's independent press agree on little else. A tense relationship exists between journalists and authorities, who accuse the private media of antagonizing the government. Journalists reject accusations of bias, maintaining that a critical stance is necessary for Niger's nascent democracy. However, many members of the media also acknowledge that financial difficulties and a lack of training make it difficult to stay independent.

In 2003, authorities used Niger's harsh press laws and the Criminal Code to crack down on journalists who criticized the government. In September, Ibrahim Souley, publication director of the private weekly *L'Enquêteur*, was imprisoned for a month pending his trial on charges of spreading propaganda and "inciting ethnic hatred." The charges stemmed from an article in the paper alleging that businessmen from eastern Niger had complained that the government was awarding too many contracts to a businessman from the west. In October, Souley was given a one-year suspended sentence and was freed the same day. Local journalists rallied to support Souley, but many also acknowledge that ethnicity is a sensitive subject that is often avoided for fear of provoking unrest.

A month after Souley's release, police imprisoned Maman Abou, director of the private weekly *Le Républicain*, a newspaper widely respected for its independence. The arrest came after an article published in July accused government ministers of using unauthorized treasury funds to pay for government contracts. The article alleged that several contracts had been awarded to government supporters without competitive bidding. The newspaper also published documents from the Public Treasury that reportedly supported the accusations.

In a closed trial in November, Abou was convicted of criminal defamation and sentenced to six months in prison. Neither Abou nor his lawyers were present at the proceedings. Despite a government order forbidding a demonstration on Abou's behalf, thousands of people protested in the capital, Niamey, in mid-November to call for the journalist's release, according to news reports. Local human rights and press freedom groups also condemned Abou's imprisonment.

On December 23, after the defamation charge against Abou was appealed, Niamey's Correctional Court amended the journalist's sentence, changing it from six months in prison to a suspended sentence of four months. However, Abou was kept in prison under preventive detention for a second charge of complicity in stealing and possessing confidential government documents. An appeals court granted him a provisional release in early January 2004.

Throughout 2003, authorities retaliated against media outlets that reported on the country's turbulent past and sensitive ethnic issues. In February, police in the town of Agadez, north of Niamey, shuttered the independent radio station Nomade FM on the orders of Interior Minister Albade Abouba. The station was accused of "inciting rebellion" by airing an interview with two former rebels who criticized the government's failure to implement the 1995 peace accords between the government and ethnic Tuareg rebel fighters. The station remained closed for three weeks before it was given permission to broadcast again.

In September and October, local government representatives, who said they were acting on orders from the president, warned private radio stations nationwide not to broadcast news that could "endanger peace and public order." Journalists said no topics were specified, and at year's end it remained unclear what had provoked the warning.

In September, Niger's High Council on Communications (known by its French acronym, CSC) revoked 15 private radio stations' authorization to broadcast. The move resulted from an internal dispute on the council, which suspended CSC President Mariama Keita because she granted the 15 stations permission to broadcast without seeking the council's collective approval. After Keita was suspended, the CSC asked the stations to resubmit their applications and revoked their authorization to broadcast pending the council's approval. Local journalists' associations criticized the move, arguing that a dispute within a regulatory body should not restrict citizens' access to information. By year's end, the council had approved several of the stations' applications.

Under pressure from human rights groups, Niger's Parliament banned the keeping or trading of slaves in May. However, local journalists said that authorities are reluctant to acknowledge that slavery still exists in the country. In December, police harassed reporters at a ceremony celebrating the liberation of several slaves in Tahoua, a town north of Niamey. According to news reports, police seized equipment from the journalists on the orders of a local government official.

NIGERIA

In Nigeria's first successful transfer between civilian administrations since independence in 1960, President Olusegun Obasanjo was re-elected in a landslide victory that also saw his ruling People's Democratic Party (PDP) make significant gains in polls across the country. Despite the relatively peaceful conduct of the election, opposition parties and election observers alleged widespread fraud, irregularities, and voter intimidation.

In its coverage of the April elections, the Nigerian media generally prized concern for stability and the success of the elections over rigorous investigation. According to local journalists, the press's acquiescent tone and wariness stemmed at least partly from the blame the media had incurred in the past for the failure of Nigerian democracy. During the previous attempt at civilian succession in the 1983 elections, media critics argue, the press's prominent coverage of alleged electoral fraud was used as part of the pretext for the military coup that interrupted democracy in the country for 15 years.

As a result, coverage of Muhamadu Buhari, the retired general who led the 1983 coup and Obasanjo's main rival in the 2003 election, was not favorable. A Muslim from northern Nigeria, Buhari was portrayed as a promoter of Shariah, or Islamic law. The press, which is concentrated in the predominantly Christian southwest, maintained that he was incapable of unifying the country. Buhari claimed that the elections were marred by fraud, but the Nigerian media barely covered his legal challenge to the results.

State-owned media outlets throughout the country tended to favor incumbents, and politicians from the smaller opposition parties complained that the press overlooked them in favor of candidates from larger and richer parties. But victorious government officials celebrated the role of the local media in the elections. At a press conference after the presidential poll, Obasanjo, who was the clear favorite in the Nigerian media, praised local journalists for their "patriotic reporting." Journalists groups, primarily concerned with postelectoral stability, commended the elections as free and fair and cautioned losing candidates against inciting the population to unrest.

Meanwhile, PDP officials lashed out at foreign media and election observers who criticized the polls and exposed alleged fraud, or who expressed concerns about the legitimacy of the results. CNN, VOA, and the BBC in particular were condemned for their "negative reportage." Information Minister Jerry Gana threatened to force CNN to replace its correspondent in the country because of the channel's coverage. Obasanjo accused European Union (EU) election observers of not understanding Nigerian democracy after the EU's monitoring team criticized the elections. The EU also criticized the Nigerian media's performance during the vote, saying the press "failed to provide unbiased coverage of the political parties and candidates contesting the elections."

Nonetheless, Nigerian journalists said the media were better equipped to cover the polls than in any previous election. With the help of the United Nations and foreign governments, the Independent National Electoral Commission opened a 24-hour media center in the capital, Abuja, that gave journalists timely access to poll results and to officials who could respond to press complaints and concerns. The National Broadcasting Commission, Nigeria's official regulatory body for broadcast media, also instituted a progressive set of guidelines ahead of the elections to try to ensure equitable access to the airwaves for all parties. Local journalists said that the most egregious breach of the guidelines occurred in southern Delta State, where, according to journalists, a gang of opposition supporters raided the private Jeremi FM radio station and forced the station's presenter at gunpoint to falsely announce that their candidate had won.

The variety and magnitude of problems facing Obasanjo have not diminished since he took office in 1999. Though he pledged to make defeating corruption his top priority, local journalists say little progress has been made on that front. The international nongovernmental organization Transparency International has consistently ranked Nigeria as one of the world's most corrupt nations. Journalists who report on corruption scandals have faced harassment and censorship from authorities. In June, State Security Service (SSS) agents attempted to purchase the entire print run of the popular *Tell* magazine after it ran an article alleging fraud in the awarding of broadcasting equipment contracts for the All Africa Games, a pan-African multisports event that Nigeria hosted in October.

State governments took the more drastic step of trying to banish reporters in reprisal for their stories. In late October, the Cross River State government attempted to expel *Daily Independent* journalist Bassey Inyang from the state after he reported on an alleged bribery scandal in the state assembly. And in August, the Akwa Ibom State Assembly attempted to expel Haruna Acheneje, a correspondent for the newspaper *The Punch*, after he reported that legislators had not been paid allowances. Both governments reversed the decisions after popular protest and pressure from journalists groups.

Nigeria is the world's seventh-largest oil exporter, but citizens complain that they have not benefited from the country's oil wealth, and authorities are sensitive to coverage of scandals relating to the industry. In early July, police attacked Associated Press photographer George Osodi and *Vanguard* newspaper journalists Funmi Komolafe and Rotimi Ajayi while they covered protests in Abuja over the federal government's decision to increase gasoline prices by more than 50 percent. In November, three journalists with *Insider Weekly* were charged with sedition and defamation after the magazine published an article alleging that presidential aides were involved in oil theft in the Niger Delta Region.

Journalists say that police harassment remains the biggest obstacle to reporting. Local police forces are often politicized, and journalists who question police allegiances or integrity often face brutality. In August, a police superintendent in Anambra State ordered a group of young men to attack Emma Nwatu of Minaj Systems Television after he helped produce a report alleging that the superintendent was extorting money from bus drivers. Worsening police antagonism toward journalists led the SSS to hold several meetings aimed at improving relations between government authorities and the media. In the run-up to the December meeting of Commonwealth heads of state in Abuja, a presidential task force explicitly warned security personnel against attacking journalists during the summit, saying the government would not tolerate any tarnishing of the country's image.

Because Nigerian journalists are poorly paid, they are susceptible to bribery by politicians and other powerful figures, local sources said. High printing costs and low sales have placed a significant financial strain on print publications. Making the situation even worse, local courts have begun awarding excessive libel damages that threaten to bankrupt media companies. In November, the president's wife sued the Independent Communication Network Limited, publishers of *The News*, for 1 billion naira (US$7.5 million) after the magazine alleged that a company she owned was awarded a large contract for the All Africa Games. The case was pending at year's end.

But the robust and vibrant Nigerian media also have considerable influence in political affairs, and journalists' organizations have effectively pushed for reforms of government policies and redress of particular offenses. In July, the federal legislature withdrew a new code of conduct for journalists covering the National Assembly following protests by the Nigerian Union of Journalists and other media rights groups. The code would have forced all reporters to confirm sensitive information with the assembly administration before publication, as well as mandating punishment for "speculative journalism" and the leaking of official secret documents.

However, journalists' groups could not persuade lawmakers to pass media-friendly legislation during Obasanjo's first term. The Freedom of Information Bill, which would allow journalists and citizens greater access to government information and provide protection for whistleblowers in the government, is still pending. Though PDP legislators promised to pass the bill during Obasanjo's first term, the bill has stagnated in the National Assembly. On a positive note, assembly members said they were considering amending broadcasting laws to allow private broadcasters to transmit nationwide. Private stations are currently prohibited from broadcasting beyond their state or allocated zones. Nigerian journalists say the restriction resulted from government fear that allowing broadcasters nationwide reach could compromise national security.

Religious tensions in the predominantly Muslim north have adversely affected the media. Nigerian journalists, who have generally tried to strike a balanced tone on issues of religious and ethnic conflict, have nonetheless been caught in the fray. According to press reports, Jama'atul Nasril Islam, an influential Islamic body based in Kaduna, reaffirmed a fatwa sanctioning the killing of two *ThisDay* journalists in its annual 2003 report. The edict was issued in 2002 by the Zamfara State government after *ThisDay* published an article that sparked religious riots in the north that killed more than 200 people. Local journalists said they believe that the action was symbolic, and that Islamic authorities do not intend to enforce the ruling. One of the two *ThisDay* journalists, Isioma Daniel, remained in exile at year's end.

RWANDA

NINE YEARS AFTER THE 1994 GENOCIDE, WHICH KILLED ABOUT 800,000 PEOPLE, Rwanda ended its transitional ruling period with a constitutional referendum, followed by the first presidential and multiparty parliamentary elections in the country since its independence in 1962. The transitional government's control of the broadcast media and its repressive tactics against the independent press helped it consolidate power in all three polls. Nevertheless, the new constitution upholds the principle of press freedom, and a new media law allows for the introduction of private radio and television stations.

President Paul Kagame—an ethnic Tutsi and former military commander who has, in effect, ruled Rwanda since 1994, when his rebel army fought its way to power and ended the genocide—was re-elected with a staggering 95 percent of the vote. His main challenger, Faustin Twagiramungu, a moderate Hutu and former prime minister, garnered only 3.6 percent. Despite "numerous irregularities" in the election, European Union (EU) observers described the poll as a "positive step" toward democracy in Rwanda.

A directive from Rwanda's Supreme Press Council mandating that all candidates receive equal treatment in broadcast and print media was well respected in slots officially allotted for election coverage, according to the EU observers. But during other news, both "the written press and the broadcast media treated the candidates unequally," reserving more positive coverage for Kagame, said EU observers.

Rwanda remains haunted by the role that some media played in the 1994 genocide, notably Radio-Télévision Libre des Mille Collines (RTLM), which helped promote the massacres. On December 3, 2003, the U.N. International Criminal Tribunal for Rwanda in Arusha, Tanzania, gave long prison sentences to three Rwandan media executives for genocide, incitement to genocide, conspiracy to commit genocide, and crimes against humanity. Ferdinand Nahimana, founder and board member of RTLM, and Hassan Ngeze, former editor of *Kangura* newspaper, both received the maximum sentence of life imprisonment. The court said that life imprisonment would also have been the appropriate punishment for Jean-Bosco Barayagwiza, an RTLM board member and former leader of a Hutu extremist political party, but it was bound by a previous ruling that his sentence should be reduced if he was convicted, because his rights had been violated while in detention. The court therefore reduced Barayagwiza's sentence to 35 years, eight of which he had already served.

Defense lawyers argued that the verdict was a serious attack on press freedom. However, most experts agree that speech intended to provoke imminent lawless violence and that is likely to do so is not protected in courts anywhere in the world. RTLM radio, for example, was used to direct gangs of killers to specific Tutsi targets. The risk remains, however, that governments—including Rwanda's—could use this verdict as a further excuse to clamp down on legitimate criticism in the press.

State TV and radio maintain a broadcast monopoly in Rwanda. The influence of the written press is limited mainly to the capital, Kigali, due to a lack of finances, poor infrastructure for distribution, and widespread illiteracy. Radio remains the most effective way to reach the population nationwide. But the government has used the example of RTLM to argue against private radio stations, claiming that they could incite ethnic division and violence. However, foreign radio services such as the BBC, Radio France Internationale, Voice of America (VOA), and Deutsche Welle broadcast in the country. The BBC and VOA carry programs in the local language, Kinyarwanda, as well as in French and English.

Private publications that have tackled sensitive subjects, such as the war in neighboring Congo, government corruption, or election irregularities, continued to face harassment in 2003. Ismail Mbonigaba, former editor of the Kinyarwanda-language newspaper *Umuseso*, which is seen as the only independent voice in the Rwandan media, was arrested and imprisoned for more than a month on charges of "inciting division and discrimination." The charges came after an article in the paper reported that Twagiramungu would run against Kagame in the August elections. Mbonigaba was released in late February and subsequently launched a new journal called *Indorerwamo* (The Mirror), whose first edition was seized in April. Police claimed that the publication had not obtained proper authorization, but local journalists believe that this was a pretext for censorship.

In November, police detained six *Umuseso* staff members, including news editor Robert Sebufirira, and confiscated copies of the newspaper, which officials accused of "inciting sectarian behavior." The action stemmed from an article that questioned why certain senior military officers were being removed from duty, and why taxpayers' money had been spent to train one of these officers abroad. The journalists were released without charge two days later but told CPJ they could not resume publishing *Umuseso* because revenue lost from the confiscation had compounded the paper's financial problems.

Internews, a U.S.-based nongovernmental media organization that conducts civic education in Rwanda on genocide-related justice issues, received authorization from Rwandan authorities to present films about the elections but was never able to distribute them. According to the organization, two films had been produced with the support of a US$250,000 grant from the U.S. Agency for International Development, but Rwandan authorities stalled on giving Internews permission to distribute the films until after the elections. The first film presented portraits of the four initial presidential candidates (one subsequently withdrew and supported Kagame), with the same questions posed to each. The second film included interviews with a range of parliamentary candidates on problems facing the country.

In March 2003, the Supreme Press Council was created in accordance with a media law passed in July 2002. The council has nine members, with three elected by the private press, one from the state media, two from civil-society groups, and three appointed by the government. Council head Privat Rutazibwa, editor of the pro-government Rwanda News Agency, told CPJ that seven authorization requests had been submitted for private radio stations, but that the requests were still being processed at press time. Some local observers expressed concerns that authorities might be deliberately stalling, adding to fears that the council may not be genuinely independent.

SENEGAL

With its relatively free and diverse press, Senegal is seen as an example of democracy in West Africa. There are more than 10 daily newspapers and a plethora of weeklies and fortnightlies, many of which frequently criticize the government. Senegal also has numerous private, community, and foreign radio stations, and the constitution guarantees press freedom. However, some signs indicate that President Abdoulaye Wade, a former opposition leader who was elected in March 2000, is becoming less tolerant of independent media.

In October, Radio France Internationale (RFI) correspondent Sophie Malibeaux was accused of threatening public security and expelled from the country following an interview with a hard-line member of a rebel group from Casamance, a region in southern Senegal. Malibeaux had been covering a congress of rebel groups in the Casamance capital, Ziguinchor, aimed at preparing peace talks with the government. Before the gathering started, RFI aired Malibeaux's interview with Alexandre Djiba, a member of the rebel movement who had boycotted the meeting.

Security agents detained Malibeaux on October 7 in Ziguinchor and flew her under military escort to Senegal's capital, Dakar, where she was served an expulsion order and told to leave the country. This drew protests from local and international media organizations. RFI protested from Paris and managed to get the order suspended pending further discussions. In a later statement, RFI said one of its top directors went to Dakar from October 20 to 22 "to convince the Senegalese authorities to reverse their decision to expel Sophie Malibeaux." The talks failed, and Malibeaux left Senegal on October 24. RFI reaffirmed its confidence in Sophie Malibeaux and condemned her expulsion.

Journalists said they viewed Malibeaux's expulsion as a "warning" to the Senegalese press. They said the separatist war in Casamance, which has been ongoing for more than 20 years, remains a highly sensitive subject.

In July, journalist Abdoulatif Coulibaly received anonymous death threats after he published a book that was highly critical of President Wade. Coulibaly told CPJ that Wade accused him of trying to damage his reputation. The president then said that while he would not respond personally to the journalist's work, others would. Coulibaly said he and his secretary began receiving threatening phone calls two days later. After Coulibaly and the Senegal Union of Information and Communication Professionals (SYNPICS) complained to authorities, a bodyguard was dispatched to protect him for a few weeks. But he told CPJ in November that he no longer had a guard and did not feel safe. He said the telephone threats had ceased, but his friends were receiving anonymous letters that cast aspersions on his character.

In March, SYNPICS and the West African Journalists' Association complained to the government about police attacks on journalists, citing three serious incidents that had occurred in the space of three months. In March, riot police assaulted two journalists from the women's community station Radio Manore FM, Fanta Badji and Cira Konate, while they were reporting on the forcible removal of residents from an illegal settlement in Dakar. Badji said that she and her colleague had identified themselves as journalists and were asking questions when the officers began to hit them.

In January, officers from the same riot squad beat Ibrahima Fall, a journalist with the daily newspaper *L'Info 7*, while he tried to cover the forcible removal of people from another settlement.

The most serious of the three cases involved Libasse Ndiaye, a cameraman for African Television News, a Senegal-based television company that acts as a local correspondent for foreign broadcasters such as France's TV5. Security forces attacked Ndiaye during a demonstration at the end of 2002, and the journalist was subsequently hospitalized. SYNPICS said it launched a legal action on behalf of Ndiaye at the beginning of 2003, but that the case was still before the courts at year's end.

Journalists told CPJ that harassment of the media in the second half of 2003 coincided with political tensions and accusations, covered in the press, that Wade's ruling Senegalese Democratic Party was not delivering on electoral promises.

In September, Public Prosecutor Abdoulaye Gaye issued a statement accusing "certain press outlets" of "providing media backup for speeches designed to attack public institutions and especially targeting the President of the Republic, the national army and the judicial system." The statement reminded journalists of legal provisions that impose criminal sanctions for reports that discredit the state, incite disorder, or disseminate "false news." These provisions remain on the books, but authorities have not been using them, said local journalists, who fear that they could now be invoked.

Political tension heightened further in October, when unknown assailants brutally attacked opposition politician Talla Sylla with a hammer, leaving him with serious injuries that required hospitalization. Several newspapers said the police inquiry pointed to the president's entourage. Investigators questioned a number of presidential bodyguards and a presidential adviser, according to local and international news reports. At the beginning of November, several thousand people marched through the streets of Dakar to protest against political violence and impunity.

While the print and radio broadcast media in Senegal are diverse and relatively free, the state controls the only national television station. According to local journalists, the state TV station tends to show "only the good things" about the president. Radio remains the most powerful channel for reaching the population, but television is also widely available.

SIERRA LEONE

SIERRA LEONE HAS CONTINUED EFFORTS TO REBUILD after a brutal 11-year civil war that officially ended in January 2002. At year's end, a large international peacekeeping force that has helped stop the fighting, disarm rebels, and retrain the Sierra Leone army remained in place. In 2003, a U.N.-backed Special Court and a Truth and Reconciliation Commission began dealing with war crimes and human rights abuses committed during the war. Peace remains fragile, but it has contributed to an improvement in press freedom and human rights.

About 26 newspapers operate in the capital, Freetown, including several private dailies, and many publications criticize the government. The opening of a number of private radio stations has ended the state-owned Sierra Leone Broadcasting Service's (SLBS) monopoly of the airwaves. This is particularly significant in a country that has a literacy rate as low as 15 percent. Freetown has about six radio stations, including private and community broadcasters and a U.N. radio network. About 10 of the 14 political districts also have their own radio stations, although many are SLBS affiliates. The Community Radio Network, an independent body created in 2002 with the support of international donors such as the Open Society Institute, aims to support the further development of community radio, notably through help with equipment.

Press freedom is constitutionally guaranteed, but repressive laws stipulating criminal sanctions for press offenses remain on the books. In particular, journalists want the government to repeal the 1965 Public Order Act, which they say is the biggest threat to press freedom. The act criminalizes libel and holds newspaper vendors, printers, and publishers as liable alongside editors and reporters in a libel suit. *For Di People* editor Paul Kamara and employees at the printer of the popular daily were prosecuted in 2003 under the act after the paper ran a front-page article criticizing President Ahmad Tejan Kabbah.

In October, Kamara and three workers at the John Love Printing Press were detained and charged with seditious libel over the article, which alleged that Kabbah was a "true convict" and constitutionally unfit to hold office. The article reported that a 1967 Commission of Inquiry had found Kabbah guilty of fraud. *For Di People* had also been serializing verbatim the report of the commission, which examined fraud allegations at the Sierra Leone Produce Marketing Board at a time when Kabbah helped oversee the board as a permanent secretary at the Trade Ministry. Bail was set at Le50 million (US$20,400), which the detainees were initially unable to pay, forcing them to spend several weeks in jail.

At the end of November, while Kamara was appearing in court, armed police raided the offices of *For Di People* and confiscated the newspaper's equipment to pay off a hefty damages award in a civil libel case brought by a local judge. Kamara served a six-month prison sentence after a criminal conviction in November 2002 for defaming the judge in *For Di People*. Kamara said the police took computers, printers, desks, telephones, and his car. At year's end, the two cases against *For Di People* remained unresolved, and the paper had ceased publishing.

According to local journalists, the legal persecution of *For Di People* has underlined the necessity of eliminating the criminal libel law. However, some say that Kamara has a history of provoking authorities, and the tense relations between *For Di People* and the government are not typical of the press as a whole.

The Sierra Leone Association of Journalists (SLAJ) has undertaken a media law reform project with support from the Ghana-based Media Foundation for West Africa. One of its key demands is the repeal of the 1965 Public Order Act. SLAJ President Tayyib Bah said his association planned a lobbying campaign and would, if necessary, file suit with the Supreme Court on the grounds that the 1965 Act was unconstitutional.

Local journalists say lack of training and few financial resources are among the biggest obstacles they face. Newspaper journalists also complained about vendors' stranglehold on distribution. Vendors determine on a daily basis which newspapers they will buy and how many copies. They also charge high commissions. Newspapers fear further economic hardship as a result of government efforts to enforce tax collection and introduce a tax on newspaper vendors starting in April 2004.

SOMALIA

SOMALIA HAS HAD NO EFFECTIVE CENTRAL AUTHORITY since the fall of dictator Siad Barre in 1991. A peace agreement in 2000, which led to the installation of the weak Transitional National Government (TNG) in the capital, Mogadishu, fueled the revival of independent media, including local radio stations, newspapers, and Internet sites. Somalia's high rate of illiteracy means that radio continues to be the most effective form of communication.

Local journalists said the biggest problem they face is violence. It makes objective coverage of all Somali territories almost impossible, they say, and puts reporters at constant risk. For example, on January 24, journalist Abdullahi Madkeer, of Democratic Media Concern (DMC) Radio, was accidentally shot in the stomach by a faction of the Rahanweyn Resistance Army (RRA) while covering the reopening of Baidoa Airport in the southwest. The airport had been closed for months because of fighting between rival RRA factions. According to Somali journalists' organizations, militia members fired on the crowd at the airport to protect a cargo of khat, a narcotic plant. Madkeer was taken to the hospital, but doctors refused to operate on him because he was HIV-positive. He died later that day.

Hornafrik, a well-respected Mogadishu-based radio station founded in 1999, said it was forced off the air on January 10 when militiamen stormed its offices. Journalists said the takeover stemmed from a Hornafrik news item that quoted a book alleging that businessman Mohamed Daylaf had financial ties with the militant Islamic group Al-Ittihad al-Islamia. The siege ended later that night, after local elders intervened to mediate between the gunmen and the station's staff.

Somalia is still fragmented into rival fiefdoms, with some areas enjoying relative stability and security, while others remain subject to lawlessness and outbreaks of fighting. Peace talks involving the TNG and faction leaders that began in Kenya in October 2002 raised hopes of reunification, but the negotiations have made little progress and were ongoing after more than a year. The self-declared Republic of Somaliland has refused invitations to join the talks.

There is at least some authority in Mogadishu, in Somaliland in the northwest, and in the self-declared autonomous region of Puntland. Unfortunately, authorities in these regions have shown a tendency to repress the media and, in some cases, have directly threatened and harassed journalists.

For example, in April, TNG militia came looking for Internet journalist Omar Faruk Osman, according to witnesses, after the Web site he worked for in Mogadishu, *Ruunkinet.com*, posted a controversial photograph. The photo showed the heads of TNG President Abdiqasim Salad Hassan and several faction leaders pasted on the bodies of soccer players, with a caption presenting them as the "team" responsible for the failure of peace in Somalia. Faruk told CPJ he had received warnings before from the TNG's presidential staff. He went into hiding for several days, and on April 20, he fled to Kenya.

In Puntland, journalists' organizations said that the mayor of the city of Galkayo ordered the detention of Adan Nur Mohamed, editor of *Yameyska Weekly Press*, and Dahir Abdulkadir Ahmed, of the weekly *Bulsho*, after they published an article about the allegedly corrupt sale of state property by a local politician. On August 23, authorities detained the journalists for about 30 hours and then released them.

In Somaliland, authorities maintain a tight grip on the broadcast media, with state-owned Radio Hargeisa still the only station allowed to carry news. Private radio remains banned, pending the continually delayed adoption of licensing regulations.

Somaliland declared independence from the rest of Somalia in 1991 but has not obtained international recognition. Somaliland has managed to maintain relative peace and stability in recent years and in 2003 held its first multiparty presidential elections. The election results were contested, with incumbent President Dahir Riyale Kahin declared the winner by only 80 votes. The authorities' control of the broadcast media helped the ruling party during the elections by ensuring that the majority of the population received pro-government news.

Somaliland authorities have also moved against critical print content. On October 20, police detained Hassan Said Yusuf, editor of the daily newspaper *Jamhuuriya*, for nine hours in the Somaliland capital, Hargeisa, and accused him of publishing information that was "not good for the government."

In early July, the Somaliland government tabled a new press law that would, according to the independent research and analysis organization International Crisis Group, proscribe media "interference" in politics, religion, or culture; impose an annual tax on journalists; assign responsibility for the admission of foreign journalists to an interministerial committee; and permit the courts to order the temporary suspension of media licenses. The Somaliland Journalists Association has strongly protested the bill.

SOUTH AFRICA

SOUTH AFRICA HAS THE MOST DIVERSE AND SOPHISTICATED MEDIA on the continent. Although freedom of the press is enshrined in the constitution, a number of old laws that restrict freedom of expression remain on the books. For example, the publication of information on police and security forces is restricted, and the Criminal Procedure Act can be used to require a person to reveal sources of information to a judicial officer or face imprisonment.

Journalists and media lobby groups have expressed fears that the Anti-Terrorism Bill, now under consideration by Parliament, could be used to bring journalists before investigative hearings and force them to tell what they know about any "terrorist organization." Journalists also said that the proposed law's definition of terrorism is too broad and could be open to abuse.

South African journalists criticized President Thabo Mbeki's "quiet diplomacy" approach to human rights abuses in Zimbabwe. They lambasted his failure to take a more active stance against the Zimbabwean government's repression of the press. Journalists were dismayed that the South African government offered no criticism when Zimbabwean authorities closed the *Daily News*, Zimbabwe's only private daily newspaper, in September.

In October, a government-appointed commission of inquiry headed by a retired former judge of the Supreme Court of Appeal, Joos Hefer, issued a subpoena to four journalists, including Ranjeni Munusamy, a former writer for the weekly newspaper *Sunday Times*. The commission wanted the journalists to reveal their sources for reports that the African

National Congress (ANC) had investigated National Director of Public Prosecutions Bulelani Ngcuka as an apartheid spy.

Munusamy, backed by media organizations, challenged the subpoena on the grounds that it violated press freedom and the constitution. But the High Court ruled that since Munusamy had written the article that led to the establishment of the Hefer Commission, she was a primary source and the commission had a right to know how she conducted her investigations. Munusamy vowed to take her case to the Constitutional Court.

In December, however, Hefer withdrew subpoenas for journalists to testify, saying he believed that Munusamy's testimony was of "peripheral value," and that her appeal to the Constitutional Court could unduly delay the work of the commission. Media organizations welcomed the decision.

Munusamy still plans to take her case to the Constitutional Court. According to her and the media groups that support her appeal, a favorable ruling recognizing a constitutional right for journalists to refuse to testify on professional grounds would be extremely important for South Africa and the entire continent.

Allegations of internal censorship at the South African Broadcasting Corporation (SABC) drew protest from civil society and the media. An internal SABC memo leaked to the press in August told station managers not to discuss politics outside the designated current affairs programs, especially in relation to allegations that Deputy President Jacob Zuma tried to bribe a French company in connection with a large arms deal. SABC denied that it was trying to gag its presenters and said it would investigate the memo. According to press freedom monitors, SABC did not introduce a news blackout of the Zuma investigation.

Although the ANC has done much since taking power in 1994 to reverse the policies of white rule and instill a culture of democracy, much of the black population still lives in poverty. The role of media in black empowerment remains a focus for debate as the country prepares to celebrate 10 years of freedom from apartheid. White-owned companies dominate the country's printed press, with only a small percentage of newspapers under black management. The press has also been seeking to consolidate through mergers and acquisitions to stay commercially viable. The picture is different in the broadcast sector, where the government has been able to foster black ownership through licensing policies. Deregulation has led to a mushrooming of radio stations, including many small community stations. Many of these, however, are struggling financially.

In 2003, the Media Diversity and Development Agency (MDDA) was launched, aimed at redressing some of the imbalances in the media sector through financial and technical support. The MDDA is a joint initiative between the government and the private sector funded by the government and the media industry. The bulk of the MDDA's support is expected to go to community radio stations, but it will also fund small commercial media projects. Media organizations have generally welcomed the creation of the MDDA but stressed that at year's end, the organization had not yet started operating. "It remains to be seen how fair the MDDA decision makers will be in allocating grant funding," said Tusi Fokane of the Media Institute of Southern Africa.

SWAZILAND

KING MSWATI III, RULER OF AFRICA'S ONLY ABSOLUTE MONARCHY, retained tight control over the media in this tiny southern African nation in 2003. In April, newly appointed Information Minister Abednego Ntshangase announced a censorship policy for state media, saying that "the national television and radio stations are not going to cover anything that has a negative bearing on government." Ntshangase specifically indicated that state broadcasters would not be allowed to cover the controversy surrounding the government's plans to purchase a luxury jet for King Mswati.

The ban on negative content was directed toward the Swaziland Broadcasting and Information Services, which operates the only news-carrying radio channels in the country, and Swazi TV. Both are state-run. While local journalists concede that state media had little editorial freedom to begin with, many feared that the minister's statements could lead to a crackdown on the tiny private press.

In late July, an official from the Justice Ministry announced that the government would pass legislation allowing it to force journalists to reveal their sources. Heavy fines and/or jail time would be imposed on journalists who refused. However, the attorney general later denied the existence of such an initiative.

The repressive Media Council Bill, which was proposed in the late 1990s and calls for the creation of a regulatory council with punitive powers, remained shelved in 2003. However, journalists fear that it could be revived. In an effort to stave off the reintroduction of the bill in Parliament, public and private media took steps toward self-regulation. With help from the United Nations Development Program and the British government, state and private journalists drafted a charter for a Media Complaints Commission. In April, the charter was presented to representatives from Swaziland's Editors' Forum, the Media Institute of Southern Africa, and the Swaziland National Association of Journalists. The journalists agreed to select a board to serve on the commission, and to adopt their first journalistic code of ethics. Both the code and the commission remain works in progress.

Lack of financial resources and credibility issues continue to pose problems for the Swazi media. In the spring, Phesheya Dube, a journalist for state-owned radio, pretended to broadcast reports from Baghdad, while in fact he never left Swaziland. Making it sound as if he was calling from the war zone, Dube culled all of his information from foreign press and wire service reports. Once the ruse was discovered, Information Minister Ntshangase criticized Dube for making Swaziland "an object of scorn." However, no disciplinary action was taken against the journalist, and he was not fired.

Recently, community radio initiatives have challenged the government's monopoly on broadcast media. One pilot station, based in the central Lubombo Region, obtained several temporary permits to broadcast. Local journalists fault unclear licensing procedures for the Lubombo station's sporadic activity but agree that licenses for community stations—even if they are not news-based—could open the way for more private ownership.

In the fall, King Mswati received a draft constitution written by the Constitutional Drafting Committee—a project many years in the making. On November 14, he postponed its approval until the document could be translated into Siswati. The constitution had not been adopted by year's end. The draft, designed to balance the royal establishment's desire to retain power against growing domestic and international demands for democratic reform, guarantees some civil liberties, including press freedom, while preserving the king's ability to overrule laws. The constitution also preserves the country's long-standing ban on political parties. Local independent journalists view the document with mixed feelings and hope that it will be subject to further reform, with input from civil society and pro-democracy advocates.

Swazi journalists were also cautious in evaluating the outcome of parliamentary elections, which were held in October. While the poll ushered in several progressive new ministers, Parliament remains mainly an advisory body to the king, who can dissolve it at his whim.

A Commonwealth election monitoring team criticized Swaziland's lack of press freedom and expressed disappointment at government-owned Radio Swaziland's reporting on the elections, saying that restricted campaign coverage reduced voters' knowledge of the candidates and harmed their ability to hold candidates accountable.

TOGO

WITH A PRESS CODE THAT IMPOSES SENTENCES of up to five years in prison and a hefty fine for "insulting the Head of State," and as much as three years in jail for defaming the courts or the armed forces, Togo earned a spot on CPJ's list of the "World's Worst Places to Be a Journalist" in 2003.

During the last three years, several journalists have been imprisoned for press offenses, while others have gone into hiding to avoid arrest. On the orders of the Interior Ministry, police have confiscated thousands of copies of private publications from printing facilities. Authorities have closed down media outlets, blocked news Web sites, and jammed the frequencies of broadcasters deemed critical of President Gnassingbé Eyadéma or his ruling Rassemblement du Peuple Togolais (RPT). In response to this deterioration in press freedom conditions, in late August 2003, CPJ conducted a research mission in Lomé, Togo's capital.

The most controversial story of 2003 was the June 1 presidential election. In 1999, Eyadéma announced that he would abide by the constitutional limit of two terms in office and not run again. In December 2002, however, the RPT-dominated legislature amended the constitution to allow for an indefinite number of terms in office. To no one's surprise, Eyadéma, Africa's longest-serving head of state, won the presidential election with 57 percent of the vote amid allegations of fraud.

In the run-up to the poll, Togolese authorities clamped down on news organizations that questioned the government's commitment to democracy. In late December 2002, *Le Courrier du Citoyen* Publication Director Sylvestre Nicoué was charged with "inciting rebellion" after his paper ran an editorial suggesting that the Togolese people would rebel if democratic reforms were not instituted after the 2003 election. Nicoué spent more than four months in prison without trial before being released on May 7.

In late February, the High Authority for Audiovisual Communications (HAAC), Togo's official media regulatory body, ordered the independent Tropik FM closed after the radio station aired a political debate during which callers questioned Eyadéma's apparent intention to run for a third term. The station was allowed to reopen days later after negotiations with HAAC. Authorities also briefly closed Nana FM, an independent radio station located in the heart of Lomé's Grand Marché, after it aired a debate between youth groups on RPT governance and the possibility of Eyadéma running for re-election. HAAC officials claimed the closure was prompted by a property dispute, and Nana FM later moved its offices out of the market area.

In late March, the Communications Ministry banned correspondents from the BBC, Radio France Internationale (RFI), Reuters, and Agence France-Presse (AFP) from working in the country after the international press failed to cover a government-sponsored seminar on African elections. The ban was lifted after a few days.

Though the government touted media access to the election campaigns, Togolese journalists complained of discrimination in the campaign accreditation process. Communications Minister Pitang Tchalla claimed that nearly 80 journalists working for media from various countries were allowed to cover the elections, but few journalists working for the Togolese private media were given accreditation, and those who were hailed from pro-RPT media outlets, local sources said.

HAAC officials claimed that all journalists could get accreditation, and that the paucity of coverage in the private media was because most journalists could not afford to cover the campaigns outside Lomé. Tchalla, however, later said that HAAC refused to accredit journalists who applied late or who had a reputation for biased coverage of Togolese politics. The latter was used as a basis for rejecting the accreditation of RFI correspondent Karine Frenk, whom Tchalla accused of unbalanced reporting and of harboring opposition sympathies. RFI declined to send a correspondent in Frenk's place. Tchalla likewise accused the French daily *Le Monde* and AFP of lacking objectivity in their coverage of the election and of glorifying veteran opposition leader Gilchrist Olympio, a son of Togo's first president whose presidential aspirations have been thwarted.

Though all political candidates were allotted space in the state media—the only media to have a countrywide reach—journalists said state media coverage heavily favored Eyadéma by giving time to other RPT politicians as "official personalities" who were campaigning on the president's behalf. Opposition candidates also complained that their broadcast messages were being censored. The HAAC required all political messages to receive its approval before they aired on the state broadcasters or appeared in *Togo Presse*, the state newspaper and Togo's only daily.

The media were not given access to ballot-counting centers and were not allowed to broadcast election results before they were announced by the official electoral commission. Togolese journalists said that this prevented them from exposing possible ballot tampering and ensuring a transparent election.

By far the most alarming attack on press freedom occurred in mid-June, when *L'Evénement* Editor-in-Chief Dimas Dzikodo and Publication Director Philip Evégno and *Nouvel Echo* reporter Jean de Dieu Kpakpabia were arrested and eventually charged with "attempting to publish false information." Authorities accused the three of trying to send photographs of alleged election disturbances to Web sites abroad. The charge itself was unprecedented and is not in the country's press code. All three were held for more than a month, and several sources said that Dzikodo and Kpakpabia were tortured while in custody. Only Dzikodo was convicted and fined 500,000 CFA francs (US$865). The government Web site *republicoftogo.com* hailed the "lenient" sentence, saying it demonstrated the judiciary's independence.

Local journalists say the biggest obstacle to press freedom in Togo is economic. The media are polarized between pro-RPT and pro-opposition publications. Because businesses are reluctant to advertise in private media that are critical of the ruling regime, newspapers rely on sales to survive and journalists often go unpaid. This leaves reporters open to bribes and has fostered what is known locally as the "combat press"—publications that are financed with the exclusive aim of attacking political enemies.

Authorities often criticize private journalists' lack of professionalism, but journalists complain of government intolerance, refusal to grant access to ministers and official information, and the government's reluctance to subsidize media development. While the independent journalists' resource center Maison du Journalisme, in Lomé, frequently holds seminars sponsored by foreign embassies, the country's journalism school has been closed for years.

On July 23, journalists created a new association named the Togolese Council of Private Press Publishers (CTEP). While previously established unions comprise publishers from either the pro-RPT or pro-opposition newspapers exclusively, CTEP includes publishers from both sides. Independent Togolese sources doubt the motives behind the creation of CTEP, saying they believe that the government is subsidizing the union in return for more favorable coverage from its members. Shortly after CTEP's inauguration, four journalists from pro-RPT publications who were excluded from CTEP membership were arrested for vandalizing the offices of the CTEP vice president. They were released the next day without charge.

Since the introduction of the press code amendment in September 2002, the number of journalists prosecuted and newspapers seized has actually dropped. Authorities attribute this fact to government generosity with press subsidies and counseling on professionalism. Journalists, however, say it is due to increased self-censorship and the government's growing preference to pay off journalists rather than arrest them. Local sources also said it is due to the government's desire to project a better image internationally to persuade the European Union to lift economic sanctions that have been in place for a decade.

UGANDA

IN MARCH 2003, PRESIDENT YOWERI MUSEVENI PROPOSED extending presidential term limits, allowing him to run for a third five-year term in office. Museveni, who came to power in a 1986 coup, retained power in the country's first presidential election in 1996 and was re-elected in 2001. His proposal for a third term drew criticism from many sectors of Ugandan society, including some of Museveni's own ministers. The president also suggested that a 17-year ban on multiparty politics could be lifted, subject to a referendum. Press reports and political commentators speculated that the president could be trying to secure a compromise by allowing multiparty politics in return for a third term.

The debate over the presidential term affected government relations with the media. When *The Monitor*, Uganda's largest independent newspaper, reported in November that a Constitutional Review Commission (CRC) had rejected a Cabinet proposal to lift the two-term limit on the presidency, the government sought a court injunction banning the paper from publishing details of the leaked report. Granting this injunction on December 8, the judge ruled that *The Monitor* should wait for the CRC to submit its final report to the government before publishing its details.

Since coming to power in 1986, Museveni has introduced political and economic reforms that have done much to set the country on the road to stability and development. His reforms include liberalization of the media, and Uganda now has a competitive broadcast sector with more than 100 licensed radio stations. In the written press, even the state-owned *New Vision* newspaper runs articles critical of the government.

However, Museveni has failed to end the war in the north of the country, where the Ugandan army has been fighting the rebel Lord's Resistance Army (LRA) since 1988. The conflict has left hundreds of thousands of people dead, maimed, and displaced, including children, whom the rebels frequently abduct and use as soldiers and sex slaves. In 2003, U.S. President George W. Bush included Uganda in his five-nation Africa tour, which was hailed as a sign of close relations between the two countries, particularly in the context of the "war on terror." The United States classifies the LRA as a terror group.

Although Uganda enjoys a relatively liberal media climate, journalists say authorities have shown an increased tendency to harass the media when they become too critical or tackle sensitive subjects, such as Uganda's involvement in the civil war in the Democratic Republic of Congo (DRC), possible reform of Uganda's "no party" political system, government corruption, and, especially, the war in the north.

For example, in June 2003, authorities closed the Catholic church–owned Radio Kyoga Veritas in Soroti, northeastern Uganda, for more than two months after the station broadcast interviews with people fleeing LRA attacks. Station manager Father Athanasius Mubiru told CPJ that authorities were particularly angered by interviews with people who had been abducted and subsequently released by the LRA. Mubiru said his station was accused of subversion and of promoting the rebel cause because the interviewees said they had not been mistreated. Mubiru said he believed that the station had been allowed to reopen because of domestic and international pressure on the government.

In May, three journalists from *The Monitor* went on trial for allegedly publishing false news and information prejudicial to national security. The charges stem from articles the paper ran in 2002 alleging that the LRA had shot down an army helicopter. In response, police raided *The Monitor*'s offices, seized equipment, and closed the paper for one week in October 2002. When the paper reappeared, it carried an apology to the government. At year's end, the trial was ongoing. The journalists could face jail sentences of two to five years, according to sources at *The Monitor*.

Journalists complain that the government uses outdated, colonial-era laws to silence the press on sensitive subjects. They argue that legal provisions on sedition, criminal defamation, and publishing false news violate the 1995 constitution. An antiterrorism law enacted in 2002 imposes the death sentence for journalists who air or publish information deemed to promote terrorism. Local press freedom activists say the definition of terrorism is too vague, and that the law is designed to stop journalists from reporting on the war in the north. The law makes it a criminal offense for journalists to interview people the government considers to be terrorists. On a positive note, the government is working on a freedom of information law that would allow the media access to official government information.

Nabusayi Linda Wamboka, president of the National Institute of Journalists in Uganda, told CPJ that the main problem facing the press was "working under insecure conditions," including threats of persecution and beatings, especially when dealing with politically sensitive issues. For example, in October, police beat and briefly detained three journalists from *New Vision* newspaper who were trying to photograph riot police at a peaceful strike by female textile workers in the capital, Kampala. The journalists were released after a police spokesman intervened on their behalf.

At the end of 2003, no charges had yet been brought in connection with the killing of journalism student Jimmy Higenyi, who was shot by police in January 2002 while covering a banned opposition rally. According to local journalists, a police officer was arrested at the time but then released.

Radio remains the most effective medium for reaching Ugandans. Of the more than 100 licensed radio stations, about half were operating at the end of 2003. Most local radio stations are commercial, community, or religious based. The BBC and Radio France Internationale both have FM relays in Kampala.

FM broadcasters initially vowed to ignore a 2002 ban on talk shows, or *ekimeeza* (table talk), but local observers said they have stopped airing them. *Ekimeeza* involved broadcasting from a public place, such as a bar or restaurant, where ordinary people could gather and participate in discussions. In introducing the ban, authorities said that broadcast licenses did not extend to bars. Local observers said FM stations have replaced *ekimeeza* with phone-in shows. Some journalists said they believed that the government wanted to stop *ekimeeza* because the shows had become popular forums for expressing political views and criticizing authorities. However, one journalist claimed that the authorities only wanted to prevent drunkenness on air, and another said he believed *ekimeeza* sometimes "went overboard."

ZIMBABWE

DESPITE WIDESPREAD INTERNATIONAL CRITICISM of Zimbabwe's appalling human rights record, President Robert Mugabe and his ruling Zimbabwe African National Union–Patriotic Front (ZANU-PF) continued to silence voices of dissent in 2003. During the last four years, the government has pursued a relentless crackdown on the private press through harassment, censorship, and restrictive legislation. 2003 saw the most significant blow to press freedom yet, with authorities shuttering the *Daily News*,

Zimbabwe's only independent daily and one of the most persistent critics of the Mugabe regime.

On September 11, Zimbabwe's Supreme Court declared that the *Daily News* was violating provisions of the repressive Access to Information and Protection of Privacy Act (AIPPA). Under AIPPA, all media companies are required to register with the Media and Information Commission (MIC). Individual journalists must also be accredited by the commission, whose members are appointed by the information and publicity minister in consultation with the president. When the registration law took effect, Associated Newspapers of Zimbabwe (ANZ), the company that owns the *Daily News*, decided not to register the newspaper and challenged the legislation in court as unconstitutional. In a peculiar turn of legal reasoning, the court said that because ANZ had not registered with the commission, it was "operating outside the law," and that the court would only hear the company's constitutional challenge once it had registered.

On September 12, police raided the newspaper's offices and ordered all journalists to leave the building, using the Supreme Court's declaration as a pretext. On September 15, the *Daily News* filed an application to register with the MIC. The following day, security agents raided the newspaper's offices again, confiscating computers and equipment. The agents did not have a warrant, and the *Daily News* legal adviser said the police were acting illegally since the newspaper had not been convicted of any offense. The High Court ruled on September 18 that the newspaper could resume publishing, and staff began work on a new edition. Nevertheless, police closed the paper's offices the same day.

The following months saw frenetic legal maneuvering by both the government and the ANZ, but authorities demonstrated a singular determination to keep the paper off the market. Though Administrative Court judges twice ordered the MIC to register the *Daily News* and allow the paper to reopen, as soon as journalists went back to work, police closed the offices. Meanwhile, authorities arrested ANZ's directors in September and October and charged them with publishing a newspaper without a license. Police also began charging *Daily News* journalists for practicing journalism without accreditation. The journalists had applied for accreditation earlier in the year but were denied on the basis that they were working for an unregistered publication. Throughout 2003, *Daily News* reporters were denied access to Parliament and State House press briefings. At year's end, 16 journalists had been charged, and their cases were pending.

ZANU-PF officials claimed that the government was not meddling in the judicial proceedings. But with the government frequently accusing the independent press of serving "Western" interests, the authorities were clearly satisfied with the *Daily News*' closure, said several sources. In early October, Information Minister Jonathan Moyo turned his customary invective against two other publications, *The Standard* and *The Independent*, calling them "running dogs of imperialism." Local reports said the head of the MIC later warned the two papers they were being investigated, though they are both registered.

The closure of the *Daily News*, which has been unremittingly harassed since its inception in 1999, left an information vacuum in Zimbabwe. The paper was distributed throughout the country—Zimbabwean journalists estimate that its readership was close to 1 million—and it was most citizens' only consistent independent source for news. Aside from shortwave broadcasts from abroad and independent weeklies, whose circulation is mainly confined to urban areas, most Zimbabweans are left to get their information from government media such as *The Herald* (the country's only remaining daily) and pro-ZANU-PF publications.

In December, while the Zimbabwean government was suspended from the Commonwealth meeting of the heads of former British colonies in Nigeria, an edition of the *Daily News* was distributed on Nigerian streets during the summit. The special edition, which featured photos of state oppression of the Zimbabwean opposition and media and was headlined, "The Voices Mugabe Wants to Silence," (See page 13.) was tucked inside the popular Nigerian daily *ThisDay*. After the paper's closure, *Daily News* staffers also launched an Internet version of the paper from South Africa and managed to publish short editions that appeared in South Africa's *Mail and Guardian* and the South African edition of *ThisDay*, which was distributed in Zimbabwe's capital, Harare.

International rights groups have repeatedly pressured South Africa to take a more active role in resolving the political and human rights crisis in Zimbabwe, and South African President Thabo Mbeki has come under fire in both the Zimbabwean and South African media for his seemingly ineffective policy of "quiet diplomacy" toward his neighbor. In May, Agence France-Presse (AFP) reported that the South African government had rejected a formal request from Zimbabwean Information Minister Moyo to curb the "relentless demonization" of Mugabe in the South African media. A spokesperson for Mbeki told AFP, "South Africa has laws that govern the freedom of the press and we have no intention of interfering with that." However, South African authorities greeted the closing of the *Daily News* with silence.

In February 2003, Mbeki told the South African Broadcasting Corporation that he had recently discussed with Zimbabwean officials "complaints raised about ... legislation passed that has an impact on the press." Mbeki said that the Zimbabwean government had agreed to amend the legislation, and the following month, Moyo confirmed this. "We are amending [AIPPA] because we realize at the time we enacted it the temperatures were very high, but when the storm has gone you sit back and rationalize," Moyo claimed. AIPPA was passed soon after Mugabe's March 2002 election victory, which was marred by allegations of fraud and violent voter intimidation. Within a year of AIPPA's enactment, Zimbabwean authorities had charged more than a dozen journalists under its provisions and those of the Public Order and Security Act.

In May, Zimbabwe's Supreme Court ruled that Section 80 of AIPPA, which stipulated that it was an "abuse of journalistic privilege" to publish false information whether intentionally or not, violated the constitutional guarantee of freedom of expression. The ruling came on a challenge filed by former *Daily News* Editor-in-Chief Geoff Nyarota and former reporter Lloyd Mudiwa. Both were charged under Section 80 in 2002 after the *Daily News* ran a story alleging that pro-government militia members had beheaded an opposition supporter. The story turned out to be false, and the newspaper published an apology. While press freedom advocates celebrated the ruling, the government feigned indifference, reminding journalists that the legislation was being amended anyway.

When Parliament finally passed the amended version of AIPPA in June 2003, journalists said the changes only strengthened the government's power over the press. On the upside, Section 80 was changed to stipulate that it is an offense to "intentionally" or "recklessly" publish false information, putting the burden on the government to prove the falsification was intentional. But the amended law still carried harsh criminal penalties for other vaguely defined offenses, such as publishing information that threatens the "economic interests of the state" and "public morality." The revised law also included under its definition of mass media products "the total data, or part of the data of any electronically transmitted material." Journalists said that this addition could include e-mails or Web-based content, indicating the government's desire to restrict online dissent.

Legalities have not prevented Zimbabwean authorities from finding more direct ways of harassing the press. The most serious attack in 2003 was on Andrew Meldrum, the Zimbabwe correspondent for the U.K-based *Guardian*, who had lived and worked in Zimbabwe for 23 years. Meldrum had written about Zimbabwe's deteriorating political and economic climate and police brutality. In early May, Meldrum was forced into hiding when security agents began visiting his house at night. Soon after, he was called to the Immigration Department, where his passport and residence permit were confiscated. Meldrum was later served with a deportation order and told to leave the country. The deportation order, signed by Home Affairs Minister Kembo Mahadi, called Meldrum "an undesirable inhabitant" of Zimbabwe but said it was not in the public interest to disclose why.

Although Meldrum's lawyer obtained a High Court stay against the deportation, which she presented to officials at the airport, authorities ignored the ruling and forced Meldrum onto a plane bound for London. Meldrum, a U.S. citizen, was the last foreign reporter based in Zimbabwe.

Authorities were particularly sensitive to coverage of political unrest and the country's severe economic problems. Police arrested and beat *Daily News* photographer Philimon Bulawayo in March for covering mass demonstrations organized by the opposition Movement for Democratic Change (MDC). Police had also beaten Bulawayo in February, when he attempted to photograph long food lines in Harare, a common sight countrywide that partly stems from the government's land-reform policies and economic mismanagement. While police arrested journalists who reported on pro-democracy rallies, ZANU-PF supporters attacked vendors who sold critical newspapers and destroyed all their copies.

Though private broadcasters have been legally allowed to operate in Zimbabwe since 2000, authorities have used strict legislation to prevent any from obtaining a license. In September, the Supreme Court struck down the part of the Broadcasting Services Act that made the information and publicity minister the ultimate authority in granting broadcasting licenses. The court said this provision was unconstitutional because it undermined the independence of the authority created to issue broadcast licenses. Zimbabwean journalists, however, said they believe that the ruling will have little immediate impact, and there was no movement on any private license applications at year's end.

Critical content from independent radio stations based abroad, which use shortwave transmitters to broadcast into Zimbabwe, has infuriated the government. These stations include the London-based SW Radio Africa, the U.S.-based Voice of America's "Studio 7," and the Voice of the People (VOP), which broadcasts into Zimbabwe from Madagascar using a Radio Netherlands transmitter. Zimbabwean authorities have tried to jam the signal of SW Radio Africa and have banned six staff members—all Zimbabwean expatriates living in London—from returning to Zimbabwe. In August 2002, unidentified men bombed the offices of the VOP in Harare. Journalists who report for these stations in Zimbabwe are frequently arrested and harassed.

In December, the government announced ambitious plans to counter foreign broadcasters by setting up a new 24-hour shortwave station. Also in December, the pro-government *Daily Mirror* reported that the government planned to purchase US$5 million worth of equipment to monitor cyberspace, apparently confirming earlier suspicions about the amendment to AIPPA regarding electronic text as a mass media product. Most journalists doubted that the government could follow through on these plans, given Zimbabwe's shattered economy and poorly valued currency.

Toward the end of 2003, Moyo announced plans to establish a network of community radio stations that would mainly relay agricultural information in local languages to farmers. Though authorities have opposed all previous attempts to set up community broadcasters, state media immediately began touting the benefits of the proposed network. Media rights advocates welcomed the initiative but were skeptical that the stations would have any independence from the government. ■

POLICIA
AZA

OVERVIEW: THE AMERICAS

by Carlos Lauría

WHILE VIOLENCE AND REPRESSION AGAINST the press continued unabated and even increased in some countries, public trust in journalists and the press suffered in much of the Americas, jeopardizing support for reforms of archaic press laws and opening the door for governments to take a more confrontational approach with the media.

In 2003, seven journalists were killed in the region for their work, according to CPJ research, compared with five in 2002. Colombia, where violence amid a four-decade civil war is a major problem, remained Latin America's most dangerous country for the press. While journalists in the capital, Bogotá, are sometimes targeted, those working in rural areas face the greatest risks; the four Colombian journalists killed for their work in 2003 all came from the provinces.

Taking advantage of the fact that international attention was focused on the U.S.-led war with Iraq, the Cuban government launched a massive attack against the independent media and political dissidents. Twenty-nine journalists were arrested, convicted, and given prison sentences ranging from 14 to 27 years. The crackdown—which made Cuba one of the world's leading jailers of journalists, second only to China—was the culmination of years of repression and intimidation.

Although the press is still one of Latin America's most trusted institutions, popular credibility has dropped significantly. According to an October report by the Chile-based polling firm Latinobarómetro, popular confidence in Latin American television—the region's main source of information—has dropped 14 percentage points, from 50 percent in 1996 to 36 percent this year. Years of economic stagnation, ethical lapses, and politicization of the media in some countries have increased the public's skepticism of democratic institutions in general, and the press in particular.

Nowhere is this more evident than in Venezuela, the clearest example in the region of how intolerance in a polarized society can multiply risks for journalists. The charged rhetoric of Venezuelan President Hugo Chávez Frías against the press, combined with the active political role that the media have taken in opposing his government, have made local journalists extremely vulnerable to physical attacks from all sides.

In both Guatemala and Haiti, the private media became powerful sources of government opposition in 2003. Many Haitian radio stations are openly partisan and broadcast either pro-government or pro-opposition reports. According to CPJ research, the murders of two Haitian journalists in recent years, the flight of dozens of others into exile, as well as ongoing attacks against those still working in the country, have made

Carlos Lauría is CPJ's program coordinator for the Americas. CPJ's Americas research associate, **Sauro González Rodríguez**, did extensive research and writing for this section. CPJ's deputy director, **Joel Simon**, also contributed to this section. **The Robert R. McCormick Tribune Foundation** provided substantial support toward CPJ's work in the Americas in 2003. **The Tinker Foundation** is supporting CPJ's campaign to eliminate criminal defamation laws in the Americas.

Photo (previous page): Cuban police take journalist Oscar Espinosa Chepe (in the middle of the back seat) to court on April 3, 2003. *AP/Jose Goitia*

UNITED STATES
ATLANTIC OCEAN
GULF OF CALIFORNIA
MEXICO
GULF OF MEXICO
CUBA
HAITI
DOMINICAN REPUBLIC
CARIBBEAN SEA
ACIFIC OCEAN
GUATEMALA
COSTA RICA
PANAMA
VENEZUELA
COLOMBIA
ATLANTIC OCEAN
BRAZIL
BOLIVIA
PACIFIC OCEAN
CHILE
ARGENTINA
ATLANTIC OCEAN
SCOTIA SEA

Haiti one of the most violent places to practice journalism in the Western Hemisphere, second only to Colombia.

In Guatemala, the government has accused the media of serving the interests of local businessmen. In the months preceding Guatemala's November 9 presidential elections, CPJ documented an increased number of press freedom abuses, ranging from anonymous threats to physical attacks. CPJ fact-finding missions to Haiti and Guatemala confirmed the dangerous climate of threats and intimidation against the local press in both countries and demanded that both governments send a clear message to their societies that attacks and threats against journalists will not be tolerated.

The growing concentration of media ownership also poses problems across the region. Media conglomerates in many countries have limited choices for consumers, while owners—who often see their media holdings as tools to obtain political power—have relationships with either politicians or corporations, which can distort coverage.

In the United States, the Federal Communications Commission (FCC) approved new media ownership rules in June, allowing television broadcasters to expand their reach and lifting a ban that prevents a company from owning both a newspaper and a television or radio station in the same market. Critics argue that the decision will stifle different voices, pointing as an example to the consolidation in radio ownership after rules in that sector were modified in 1996. In September, the U.S. Senate passed a resolution to overturn the FCC decision, but the House had yet to pass a similar measure by year's end, and President George W. Bush has promised to veto any such legislation.

In Mexico and Brazil, media conglomerates such as Televisa and Globo, respectively, have consolidated their control, particularly in broadcasting, though they also own companies in print, music, and radio. Grupo Clarín in Argentina, Organización Carlos Ardila Lule and Grupo Empresarial Bavaria in Colombia, and Grupo Cisneros in Venezuela have become powerful forces, clearly dominating the media markets in their countries. Elsewhere in Latin America, media outlets are typically controlled by a handful of family-owned companies that are frequently tied to political parties or corporations.

Global corporations have also entered many markets in Latin America, partnering with local conglomerates. Two Spanish corporations, Telefónica and Grupo Prisa, have become a presence in the region by acquiring media outlets in several countries. Grupo Prisa has purchased most of the shares of Caracol Radio in Colombia, and Telefónica owns television and radio stations throughout the region.

In the United States, concerns about potential terrorist attacks increased government secrecy, with profound implications for the press. A report by the Washington, D.C.–based Reporters Committee for the Freedom of the Press describes how the federal government is limiting public access to terrorism and immigration proceedings and subverting the intent of the 1974 Freedom of Information Act by routinely denying information requests.

While no journalists in the Americas outside Cuba are currently incarcerated, a number of short detentions in 2003 highlighted the pressure that journalists in the region continue to face from criminal defamation laws. Legislatures remain reluctant to repeal these archaic laws, and public figures who benefit from them have successfully blocked reform. In Panama—despite stated commitments from President Mireya Moscoso to repeal the country's remaining "gag laws"—almost half of the journalists there face criminal libel charges, the majority of them filed by public officials angered by the media's exposure of corruption.

In a development that could have profound implications for press freedom and the campaign to eliminate criminal defamation from the Americas, the Costa Rica–based Inter-American Court of Human Rights agreed in February 2003 to hear a criminal defamation case involving a Costa Rican journalist convicted of libeling a diplomat. Journalist Mauricio Herrera Ulloa, of the daily *La Nación*, was convicted of defamation by a Costa Rican court in 1999. Herrera Ulloa originally took his case to the Washington, D.C.–based Inter-American Commission on Human Rights, arguing that his right to freedom of expression, guaranteed under the American Convention on Human Rights, had been violated. The commission sought a friendly settlement with the Costa Rican government but was unable to resolve the dispute. The commission then referred the case to the Inter-American Court. A decision is expected in early 2004, and any ruling will be binding on the Costa Rican government.

If the court determines that criminal defamation laws violate the freedom of expression guarantees contained in the American Convention, such a ruling could set a broad precedent for the entire region.

Even though 2003 has been a difficult year for the region's press, many countries have adopted freedom of information laws, important steps toward guaranteeing citizens' access to information. In Mexico, for example, the government finally began to enforce the Federal Law on Transparency and Access to Public Information on June 12. In practice, however, access often remains restricted by the laws' ambiguous language, overly bureaucratic procedures, and the influence of politicians responsible for releasing information.

In some countries, the media were able to report on corruption and official malfeasance without reprisal. In Argentina, where the press continues to struggle with economic difficulties, an interview published in December in *TXT* magazine shed light on a notorious corruption scandal after a former congressional official described how he personally delivered a US$5 million bribe to a number of senators at the request of then President Fernando De la Rúa in April 2000. In another encouraging development, the Chilean press reported freely about the abuses of Gen. Augusto Pinochet's dictatorship on the 30th anniversary of the 1973 military coup that brought him to power.

ARGENTINA

WHILE THE ECONOMY BEGAN TO RECOVER IN 2003 after the worst socioeconomic crisis in the country's history and the political situation regained stability under a new president, the Argentine press continued to struggle with significant budgetary difficulties.

Argentina's economic collapse not only caused about a dozen media outlets to fold, it has also meant that a society that once prided itself on its consumption of newspapers and magazines was forced to cut back. However, despite a shrinking media market, at least three newsmagazines were launched in 2003.

Although the economic recovery halted a free fall in circulation and advertising revenue, media owners complained about tax regulations that imposed "a discriminatory burden" on Argentina's smaller newspapers and magazines, according to publishers with the Asociación de Entidades Periodísticas Argentinas (Association of Argentine Journalistic Entities). While other small and medium-size businesses in Argentina pay a 10.5 percent tax, small and medium-size newspapers and magazines must pay double that amount. However, on December 17, the Senate passed a law reducing the tax for small and medium-size publications with yearly advertising revenue of less than 43 million pesos (US$14.3 million).

Attacks on journalists covering demonstrations increased in the run-up to Argentina's presidential elections but dwindled when Peronist candidate Néstor Kirchner was elected president in May after Carlos Menem withdrew from a runoff election. Kirchner, former governor of Santa Cruz, an oil-rich province in Patagonia, took office on May 25. He promptly gained popularity by challenging the military for past human rights violations, attacking police corruption, and pressuring an unpopular Supreme Court chief to resign.

In the fall, the government lambasted a cover story in the October 18 issue of the newsweekly magazine *Noticias*. The article argued that Kirchner's administration used the distribution of official advertising to reward supportive media and punish critical publications. A number of journalists said they agreed with *Noticias*, but others said the article exaggerated the facts.

The media supported the president's embrace of progressive policies. The daily *Página12*, which uncovered many corruption scandals during Menem's two presidential terms in the 1990s, became an active supporter of the administration's human rights and anticorruption policies. Although some journalists complained that *Página12* was rewarded with state advertising for its supportive coverage, an editor of the paper said the allegation was false. "The paper has the right to back the government if we agree on certain issues," Sergio Kiernan, *Página12*'s weekend editor, told CPJ.

On May 8, the Chamber of Deputies, the lower house of Congress, passed a bill on freedom of access to public information, which was drafted by the government's Anti-Corruption Office, along with a large group of nongovernmental organizations and civil society advocates. The bill was under consideration by the Senate Constitutional Affairs Commission at year's end. Meanwhile, the Senate Defense Commission was debating a bill to regulate state secrets that would determine what information could be classified by government agencies and for how long. On December 3, President Kirchner signed a decree guaranteeing, among other things, public access to both government information and meetings between officials and lobbyists.

On November 13, an Appeals Court in Buenos Aires Province reduced the sentences of six individuals convicted for the 1997 murder of José Luis Cabezas, a photographer with *Noticias* magazine. The sentences for Gustavo González and Horacio Braga were reduced to 20 years; José Luis Auge to 18 years; Sergio Camaratta and Aníbal Luna to 25 and 24 years, respectively; and Gregorio Ríos to 27 years. Due to provisions in Argentina's legal system, however, some of them could be released in late 2004.

Cabezas was killed in January 1997 in Pinamar, one of Argentina's most exclusive beach resorts. Armed men kidnapped the journalist while he was leaving a celebrity party where he had photographed reclusive business tycoon and reputed mafia kingpin Alfredo Yabrán. The men shot Cabezas twice in the head, placed his body in his car, and ignited it. Yabrán committed suicide in 1998, after being subpoenaed to testify in the murder trial.

BOLIVIA

THE POLITICAL CRISIS THAT HAS GRIPPED BOLIVIA since June 2002 elections peaked in October 2003, when President Gonzalo Sánchez de Lozada resigned amid violent protests. During the unrest, journalists were attacked and threatened by both the Bolivian military and civilian protesters.

The year began inauspiciously for Sánchez de Lozada, a close ally of the United States who was elected with just over 22 percent of the vote. In January, coca growers erected roadblocks on some of the country's main highways to protest the U.S.-backed eradication of coca crops in the tropical region of Chapare. Soon after, indigenous leaders from mining regions joined coca growers to organize roadblocks and vowed to fight for Sánchez de Lozada's resignation.

In early February, the government announced new austerity measures to reduce the budget deficit. On February 12 and 13, after the government attempted to introduce a new income tax, crowds of civilians in the capital, La Paz, joined thousands of striking police officers in a massive antigovernment protest. Military forces clashed with demonstrators near the presidential palace, leading to riots that killed more than 25 people and injured over 100. A dozen government buildings were also looted and burned during the riots. One journalist was shot, two others were wounded after being hit by tear gas canisters, and two more were beaten by civilians who apparently had joined in the looting.

With rioting in the streets around their offices, the state-owned television station Canal 7 and the private Canal 5–Bolivisión decided on February 12 to go off the air to guarantee the safety of their personnel and facilities. The two stations resumed broadcasting the next day.

In the fall, violence erupted again with the "Gas War," a series of antigovernment protests that began in mid-September in La Paz and the neighboring city of El Alto and then spread to the rest of the nation. The protests rallied union workers, members of neighborhood associations, miners, students, and coca growers against government plans to export natural gas to the United States and Mexico. Many Bolivians rejected the project, which involved the construction of a pipeline from landlocked Bolivia through Chile, because they consider the export of the country's natural gas reserves a theft. Many also view Chile, to which Bolivia lost its coastal area in an 1879 war, as a historical enemy.

After clashes between soldiers and demonstrators killed more than 50 people and injured hundreds, protesters began clamoring for the ouster of Sánchez de Lozada, who was forced to resign on October 17. He was replaced by Vice President Carlos Mesa, a well-known former TV journalist who had earlier withdrawn his support for the president to distance himself from the government's violent repression of the protests.

On October 12, just days before Sánchez de Lozada left office, five journalists from the state-owned Canal 7 resigned, denouncing government attempts to manipulate news coverage during the Gas War. The journalists, who claimed that they had been told by station management and the government press department not to show images of violence, also cited threats from protesters who were angry at the station's coverage.

Several journalists and media outlets were attacked or threatened during the Gas War. Oruro-based TV station Canal 13 and Catholic radio station Radio Pío XII, which extensively covered the mass protests, had their transmission equipment blown up by unidentified attackers. One journalist was assaulted and threatened by the military, while several journalists were harassed or beaten by protesters. While insisting that they had respected freedom of the press, government officials declared that some media outlets had incited the population to commit illegal acts, including "sedition." However, the government took no legal action against any journalists or their employers.

The La Paz weekly *Pulso* reported that some copies of its special October 15 issue, which contained an editorial calling on Sánchez de Lozada to resign, were confiscated. According to *Pulso* Editor-in-Chief Gustavo Guzmán, several individuals in a green van pretending to be *Pulso* staff members took copies of the weekly in a southern area of La Paz. Newspaper vendors later confirmed those reports. *Pulso*, which otherwise circulated normally in the rest of the city, also discovered that someone had been buying copies in large numbers in a northern area of La Paz. Guzmán said they suspected that government officials might have attempted to take copies of the weekly out of circulation, but the government denied any responsibility.

BRAZIL

ALTHOUGH BRAZILIAN MEDIA OUTLETS GENERALLY OPERATE in a free environment, they have increasingly been targeted with defamation lawsuits that seek to silence them. Judicial interference and censorship, under the guise of protecting privacy and honor, continues unabated.

Defamation lawsuits—mostly civil complaints—against the media are on the rise, according to the trade magazine *Consultor Jurídico*. Businessmen, politicians, and public officials file multiple lawsuits against news outlets and journalists as a way to pressure them, strain their resources, and force them to halt their criticisms. Frequently, plaintiffs seek disproportionately high amounts of money as reparation for "moral and material damages," which has given rise to an "industry of compensation" where people sue the media as a way of becoming rich. Judges increasingly admit such lawsuits in court and rule against the press. Some journalists argue that the media have become an easy target for defamation lawsuits because of flawed reporting and blurred boundaries between entertainment and news.

Throughout 2003, judges granted injunctions against the press that amounted to prior censorship. For example, in February, local media reported that a judge had ruled that the monthly *Você S/A*, owned by the Editora Abril publishing house, could publish a critical cover story about a job placement firm only on the condition that it included, with the same space and prominence, the firm's reply to each individual claim in the article. If *Você S/A* failed to comply, it would have been held in contempt of court and subjected to civil and criminal penalties. The magazine chose to pull the story and, as a result, had to change the issue's cover. Editora Abril appealed, and in late February, a three-judge panel from the São Paulo Justice Tribunal revoked the injunction, freeing *Você S/A* to publish the story without restrictions.

Having predicted a tough first year for President Luiz Inácio da Silva, known as Lula, and his Workers Party, the Brazilian media generally praised Lula's commitment to austere economic policies. In October, several associations of media owners requested public financing from the government to bail out some of Brazil's indebted media companies. Some critics of this proposal argued that the media were compromising their independence, while others argued that the government should not be rescuing cash-strapped companies. At the end of the year, the government was still considering the request.

Brazil continues to be a dangerous place for journalists. In July, Luiz Antônio Da Costa, a photographer with the weekly *Época*, was shot dead by robbers while working on an assignment in São Bernardo do Campo, São Paulo State. In June, unidentified men murdered Nicanor Linhares Batista, owner of a radio station and an on-air host in Limoeiro do Norte, in the northeastern state of Ceará. A controversial journalist, Linhares' hard-hitting commentaries angered many local politicians and public officials. In October, the Ceará Public Prosecutor's Office identified two public officials—a judge from the neighboring state of Pernambuco and his wife, Limoeiro do Norte's mayor—as the individuals who ordered Linhares' murder. Because of their status as public officials, the case was transferred to federal and state prosecutors, who had not brought formal charges against them by year's end.

CPJ continued to follow developments in the case of murdered journalist Domingos Sávio Brandão Lima Júnior, the owner and publisher of the Cuiabá-based daily *Folha do Estado* in the state of Mato Grosso. Hired gunmen killed Brandão in September 2002. João Arcanjo Ribeiro, a police officer turned businessman who has been identified by federal and state prosecutors as the head of the Mato Grosso mafia, is suspected of ordering Brandão's murder in retaliation for his newspaper's criticism of organized crime and illegal gambling. Ribeiro is currently imprisoned in Uruguay while awaiting extradition.

In some cases, the Brazilian media engage in unethical conduct. In September, Brazil's leading daily, *Folha de S. Paulo*, reported that the former government of the state of Paraná had "purchased" articles for 6.4 million reals (US$2 million) in the Paraná media in 2002. The articles, which did not disclose to readers that they were paid for and thus equivalent to advertisements, were glowing reports about the opening of public works commissioned by the former state governor and highlighted his achievements. The Paraná Public Prosecutor's Office has since opened an investigation into the purchase of these articles. According to the *Folha de S. Paulo* report, the practice of publishing paid articles without proper disclosure to readers is widespread in the Brazilian media, particularly in small and medium-size publications.

The Brazilian media industry is highly concentrated, particularly the broadcasting sector, which is dominated by the huge Organizações Globo media group. In some of the largest markets, the same media group controls newspapers, network and cable television channels, several radio stations, and Internet portals. Insufficient, outdated, and lax regulations governing media concentration mean that the news and opinions that many Brazilians have access to lack diversity.

Throughout 2003, the government telecommunications agency, ANATEL, closed several community radio stations that had been operating without broadcasting licenses and confiscated their equipment. According to some estimates, more than 4,000 community radio stations currently on the air have formally requested licenses, but ANATEL has not responded to their requests. In March, the Communications Ministry, which controls ANATEL, decided to create a working group charged with finding ways to expedite, and add transparency to, the processing of license requests.

Meanwhile, the suspects accused of murdering TV Globo reporter Tim Lopes have yet to be tried. Lopes was beaten by members of an organized crime gang and brutally murdered by the group's leader on June 3, 2002, while working on an investigative story about drug traffickers allegedly involved in the sexual exploitation of minors in one of Rio de Janeiro's favelas, or shantytowns.

CHILE

In 2003, the Chilean press reported extensively on human rights abuses during Gen. Augusto Pinochet's dictatorship and played a positive role in uncovering local corruption. Still, legal restrictions continued to hamper the press.

As 2003 came to a close, President Ricardo Lagos' bill to amend several articles of the Penal Code and the Code of Military Justice, which make it a criminal offense to insult the "honor or dignity" of public officials, was approved by the lower house of Congress. The deputies, however, made their approval conditional on the discussion of a privacy bill that would allow civil and criminal charges to be brought against journalists who invade the privacy of a public or private figure and his or her family. The Chilean press called the privacy legislation, which the Senate was considering at year's end, a serious setback for freedom of expression in Chile.

The threat to press freedom posed by many of Chile's archaic laws was illustrated on April 2, when the Appeals Court in the capital, Santiago, overturned TV commentator Eduardo Yáñez's January 31 conviction on "disrespect" charges. The conviction stemmed from a November 2001 program on Chilevisión's debate show "El Termómetro," during which Yáñez described the Chilean judiciary as "immoral, cowardly, and corrupt" for not providing compensation to a woman who had been imprisoned for a crime she did not commit. The Chilean Supreme Court then filed a criminal complaint against Yáñez.

On September 3, Supreme Court Judge Domingo Kokisch summoned reporter Ximena Marré and Editor Mario Ovalle, both of the Santiago-based daily *El Mercurio*, to clarify information published in the paper about the theft of classified financial data. According to the journalists, Kokisch repeatedly hit his desk while talking to them and demanded that Marré reveal her sources. After Marré refused, the magistrate threw both of them out of his office. As they were leaving, Kokisch pushed and attempted to punch Ovalle. Soon after, the magistrate expressed regret and apologized to the daily's director. Later that week, the local press reported that in January, Kokisch had also allegedly attacked journalist Luis Narváez, of the daily *La Nación*.

In a decision that sparked debate in the local media, the entire editorial staff of the Sunday edition of *La Nación* resigned on May 24 to protest the paper's refusal to run a story by investigative journalist Alejandra Matus about alleged corruption involving the government's Institute of Agricultural and Livestock Development (INDAP). The news staff claimed that the state-run paper's management succumbed to political pressure and censored the article.

La Nación published the article a few days later. The paper's director, Alberto Luengo, justified the delay by saying the paper needed to give INDAP an opportunity to respond. (INDAP never responded.) On August 14, the staff members who had resigned, including Matus, launched the independent biweekly tabloid *Plan B*, which started with a circulation of 3,000 and was selling 20,000 copies per issue at year's end.

The 30th anniversary of the military coup that led to the suicide of President Salvador Allende was widely covered in the Chilean press, and journalists reported freely about the abuses of the 17-year Pinochet regime. The September arrest of Santiago businessman Claudio Spiniak on pedophilia charges spawned reports that high-level politicians have had sexual encounters with minors. Members of the rightist Independent Democratic Union (UDI) party chastised the press for excessive reporting on the pedophilia charges, which they said were rumors and part of a press conspiracy intended to spoil UDI candidate Santiago Mayor Joaquín Lavín's bid for the presidency in 2005.

On December 10, retired security officer Rafael González was indicted in the slaying of U.S. journalist Charles Horman, whose execution in the early days of the Pinochet regime became the basis of the film "Missing." González is the first person formally charged in Horman's murder. González's defense attorneys appealed the indictment, which a Chilean Appeals Court upheld on December 15. According to Sergio Corvalán, the attorney for Horman's widow, other indictments are expected to follow.

COLOMBIA

COLOMBIAN JOURNALISTS CONTINUED PAYING AN EXTREMELY HEAVY PRICE for practicing their profession amid a 40-year-old civil war pitting two major leftist guerrilla groups against the Colombian army and right-wing paramilitary forces. At least four journalists were killed in reprisal for their work in 2003, and CPJ continues to investigate the deaths of three others.

Sixteen months into a four-year term, President Álvaro Uribe—a close U.S. ally—experienced a major political setback when voters rejected a referendum that the notoriously thin-skinned president claimed would have expanded his powers to fight terrorism and corruption and bolster a faltering economy. Even though Uribe attempted to strengthen the army and took steps to weaken the rebels and disarm death squads, the absence of state control in certain regions of the country left the media open to attacks. In 2003, Colombia was again featured on CPJ's list of the "World's Worst Places to Be a Journalist."

The northeastern department of Arauca, which has been a hotbed of civil unrest, is the clearest example of how the government's lack of control over vast areas of the country has affected the media. Following the March 18 murder of Luis Eduardo Alfonso Parada, an on-air host with Radio Meridiano 70, fourteen other Arauca journalists fled to the capital, Bogotá, after receiving death threats from both rebels and paramilitaries. The journalists returned three months later, but the intimidating environment has encouraged self-censorship.

During campaigning for state and municipal elections, which were held on October 26, paramilitary groups and guerrillas murdered dozens of political candidates. This wave of violence posed an additional threat for journalists covering political corruption. Guillermo Bravo Vega, an investigative journalist with the regional Alpevisión Radio who had frequently accused municipal and departmental government officials of mishandling public funds, was shot dead on April 28 in the southern town of Neiva in Huila Department. The next day, unidentified gunmen murdered Jaime Rengifo Revero, host of a weekly program on Radio Olímpica, in the northern town of Maicao in La Guajira Department. Rengifo frequently criticized state security forces and accused local politicians of corruption.

The government's failure to prosecute these crimes led many journalists to leave the country. More than 40 journalists received death threats in 2003. Six of them fled the country, including Fabio Castillo, head of the investigative unit for the weekly *El Espectador*. Castillo, a well-respected Colombian journalist, left in July after being fired on June 6. Though the paper claimed that it fired him for budgetary reasons, Castillo, as well as other Colombian and international journalists, said it was an effort to silence him following his report on alleged illegal business dealings involving Interior and Justice Minister Fernando Londoño Hoyos.

Many journalists who remain in Colombia feel that the pressure of working in a hostile environment, as well as the concentration of media ownership among businessmen with ties to the government, has kept them from reporting openly on the grave problems facing Colombia and has forced them to restrain criticism of the government and Uribe's policy initiatives.

According to some Colombian journalists, the consolidation of media ownership by a handful of large groups is eroding media diversity and limiting political debate. Three powerful corporations with close ties to the political establishment own broadcasters that claim more than 80 percent of the country's radio and television audience. Organización Carlos Ardila Lulle controls RCN, while the Spanish company Prisa has purchased most of the shares of Caracol Radio from Grupo Empresarial Bavaria. Grupo Empresarial Bavaria, which is controlled by the Santodomingo family, still holds a portion of Caracol Radio and owns Caracol Televisión.

The country's most influential daily and the only paper with national circulation, *El Tiempo*, and the company that controls it, Casa Editorial El Tiempo, have become a powerful business entity. Casa Editorial El Tiempo owns the daily business paper *Portafolio*, the tabloid *Hoy*, regional outlets in five regions of the country, a large magazine publishing company, and the television station CityTv.

Foreign correspondents have generally not been subjected to the kind of violence that regularly imperils Colombian journalists, but that changed in January, when rebel fighters kidnapped two *Los Angeles Times* journalists. They were freed within days. Even though the abductions have not prevented correspondents from traveling to the country's most dangerous areas, some said they are taking greater precautions and talking to authorities before entering those regions.

On November 6, Colombia's House of Representatives passed an antiterrorism bill that would allow the army to conduct searches, tap telephones, and intercept private correspondence without a warrant in cases involving individuals suspected of terrorist links. A controversial clause that would have banned the media from revealing the names of detainees during the first 72 hours of arrest was eliminated during the debate in the lower house of Congress. On December 11, the Senate passed the bill, which at year's end was awaiting approval by the nation's Constitutional Court.

The difficulties journalists face while covering the civil war encouraged the local press freedom organization Fundación para la Libertad de Prensa (FLIP) to publish a security manual aimed at keeping journalists safe from attacks by the armed factions involved in the conflict. The manual includes a map showing areas where each armed group holds sway and details of the different subgroups of the armed organizations: the leftist Revolutionary Armed Forces of Colombia (FARC) and the National Liberation Army (ELN), and the right-wing paramilitary United Self-Defense Forces of Colombia (AUC).

To promote the release of the manual, FLIP and its umbrella group, the press freedom organization Proyecto Antonio Nariño, which is funded by Nobel Prize–winning author Gabriel García Márquez, organized a three-day workshop on security issues for Colombian journalists. During the seminar, sponsored by International Media Support and the International News Safety Institute with support from CPJ, journalists received training from experts from Centurion Risk Assessment Services, a U.K.-based hostile-environment training firm. Frank Smyth, CPJ's Washington, D.C., representative and security expert, also led a panel on journalism and trauma.

COSTA RICA

WHILE OUTDATED MEDIA LAWS THAT ENCOURAGE SELF-CENSORSHIP among journalists remain on the books in Costa Rica, the decision by the Organization of American States' (OAS) Inter-American Court of Human Rights to hear a criminal defamation case involving a Costa Rican journalist may have a profound impact on the region's press. A ruling could set a precedent to determine whether criminal sanctions for defamation in the Americas are permissible under international law.

In 2003, the Costa Rica–based Inter-American Court of Human Rights agreed to hear the case of journalist Mauricio Herrera Ulloa, who was convicted of criminal defamation in 1999 by the Penal Court of the First Judicial Circuit in Costa Rica's capital, San José. The charges stemmed from a series of 1995 articles Herrera Ulloa wrote for the San José–based daily *La Nación* citing European press reports alleging corruption by former Costa Rican diplomat Félix Przedborski. The court ordered the journalist to pay a fine equivalent to 120 days' wages, the plaintiff's legal fees, and

60 million colones (US$190,000) in damages to Przedborski. It ordered the journalist's name added to an official list of convicted criminals, and it also instructed *La Nación* to remove all links to the offending articles from its Web site and to publish parts of the ruling.

The Inter-American Commission on Human Rights (IACHR), an entity of the Washington, D.C.–based OAS, submitted the case to the Inter-American Court of Human Rights on February 3, asking for the dismissal of the sentence against Herrera Ulloa. According to the IACHR, the conviction violates the journalist's right to freedom of expression as established by the American Convention on Human Rights.

Decisions of the Inter-American Court are legally binding on 21 countries in South and Central America and the Caribbean that have accepted the court's jurisdiction, including Costa Rica. On CPJ's behalf, the law firm of Debevoise and Plimpton agreed to submit an amicus curiae brief to the court supporting Herrera Ulloa's complaint. The court has no deadline to hear the case, but a ruling is expected in early 2004.

Meanwhile, more than two years after the assassination of popular radio journalist Parmenio Medina, investigators arrested the two suspected masterminds behind the murder: Businessman Omar Luis Chaves Mora was detained on December 26, and priest Mínor de Jesús Calvo Aguilar was arrested a day later. Calvo was the founder of Radio María, a local Catholic station that Medina denounced for financial irregularities, and Chaves was one of Radio María's main financial backers. Both suspects have denied involvement in the murder. Medina, host of the satirical weekly radio program "La Patada" (The Kick), was killed outside his home on July 7, 2001, by three gunshots fired at close range.

Prior to these arrests, the Costa Rican media had reported that two suspects—Nicaraguan-born Luis Alberto Aguirre (known as "El Indio") and Andrés Chaves Matarrita—have been incarcerated in connection with Medina's murder. A third suspect, Colombian-born John Gilberto Gutiérrez, was arrested on December 23, 2002. He was accused of acting as an intermediary between the killers and the planners of the murder, but he was released on March 26, 2003, due to insufficient evidence. On September 26, Gutiérrez was arrested again, but this time on charges stemming from two unrelated kidnappings that occurred in 2002. In November, Gutiérrez told investigators he had acted as an intermediary in the killing, a confession that led to the arrests of the alleged masterminds, Chaves and Calvo.

Several Costa Rican editors and the country's Colegio de Periodistas (Association of Journalists) have criticized the lack of progress by the legislative commission tasked with revising press laws in the wake of Medina's murder. After Medina's assassination, Costa Rican journalists were timid in reporting on the official investigation into the murder because they feared they could be prosecuted on defamation charges. Under Costa Rica's Penal Code, anyone who libels, slanders, defames, or reproduces offensive statements against someone, even public officials, can be fined or placed on an official list of convicted criminals.

CUBA

UNLIKE PREVIOUS YEARS, WHEN CUBAN AUTHORITIES were mostly content to merely harass and threaten independent journalists and their families, in 2003, authorities launched an all-out assault against the opposition and the independent press. Officials jailed 29 journalists—about one-third of the island's independent press—and sentenced them to lengthy prison terms. Those who continue to work face systematic police harassment and threats.

The detention of political dissidents and journalists—who are often accused of being "counterrevolutionaries" at the service of the United States—began on March 18, during the first week of the Iraq war, and continued for three days. Police raided and searched the journalists' homes, confiscating books, typewriters, research materials, cameras, computers, printers, and fax machines.

The journalists were taken to the headquarters of the State Security Department (DSE)—the political police—across the island. Their summary trials were held on April 3 and 4 behind closed doors, after which the courts declared that the cases were ready for sentencing. Many journalists did not have access to their lawyers before the trials. In several cases, the lawyers representing the journalists only had a few hours to prepare their defenses.

Some journalists were tried under Article 91 of the Penal Code, which imposes lengthy prison sentences or death for those who act against "the independence or the territorial integrity of the State." Other journalists were prosecuted for violating Law 88 for the Protection of Cuba's National Independence and Economy, which mandates up to 20 years in prison for anyone who commits acts "aimed at subverting the internal order of the Nation and destroying its political, economic, and social system."

On April 7, courts across the island announced prison sentences for the journalists ranging from 14 to 27 years. They remained imprisoned in jails administered by the DSE until April 24, when most were sent to prisons located hundreds of miles from their homes. In June, the People's Supreme Tribunal, Cuba's highest court, dismissed the appeals for annulment (*recursos de casación*), which the journalists filed in April, thus upholding their convictions.

The imprisoned journalists, who are being held in maximum-security facilities and are handcuffed any time they leave their cells, have denounced their unsanitary prison conditions, inadequate medical care, solitary confinement, and lack of access to the press and television. They have also complained of receiving foul-smelling and rotten food.

To demand better conditions, some imprisoned journalists went on hunger strikes several times during 2003. After learning about the hunger strikes, other jailed journalists joined them in solidarity. Because prison authorities refused to allow outside contact with the strikers or to disclose information about them, their families were unable to check on their health. As punishment for their involvement in the strikes, the journalists have been dispersed and transferred to other prisons.

Throughout 2003, several of the imprisoned journalists smuggled out reports and letters denouncing their situation. Independent journalist and CPJ 2003 International Press Freedom Award recipient Manuel Vázquez Portal wrote a prison diary, which was later smuggled out, describing the harsh conditions in Boniato Prison, in eastern Cuba, where he was being held. In retaliation, prison authorities transferred Vázquez Portal to another prison.

In early July, renowned Peruvian journalist Gustavo Gorriti traveled to Cuba on behalf of CPJ and confirmed the dire situation for independent journalists and their families there. During his stay in the capital, Havana, Gorriti visited the families of several imprisoned journalists to convey CPJ's concern.

In September 2003, the independent journalists' association Sociedad de Periodistas Manuel Márquez Sterling, which lost many of its members in the March crackdown, published the third issue of the association's magazine, the bimonthly *De Cuba*. In October, Claudia Márquez Linares, the vice president of the association, was taken to a DSE office in Havana and was warned not to publish another issue of *De Cuba*.

Facing worldwide condemnation for the crackdown—even from some leftist intellectuals who had previously supported the Cuban government—Cuban officials began using their well-funded, well-oiled propaganda machine, which now relies heavily on government-sponsored Web sites, to counter international pressure. In August 2003, the government launched a new Web site called Cubadebate, which seeks to "destroy the calumnies against Cuba." The site has been used to promote books and articles that denounce dissidents and independent journalists as "mercenaries."

To complement the government's Internet campaign—which mostly targets the international community because the government tightly controls Cubans' access to the Web—the official press unleashed an intense campaign inside the island to discredit independent journalists and dissidents. Books and radio and television programs portrayed them as "agents" on the U.S. government's payroll.

The government also stepped up its attacks on the popular quarterly magazine *Encuentro de la cultura cubana*, which is published by an association of Cuban exiles based in Madrid, Spain. Official media aired charges linking the magazine to the U.S. Central Intelligence Agency. The magazine and the online daily *Encuentro en la red*, published by the same group, provide a forum for cultural and political debate between Cubans from the island and abroad. Although banned in Cuba, the magazine is passed from reader to reader throughout the island.

DOMINICAN REPUBLIC

GOVERNMENT EFFORTS AIMED AT PUNISHING CRITICS led to a deterioration of press freedom in the Dominican Republic in 2003. Moreover, news coverage of scandals involving private financial institutions that own many Dominican media outlets seriously damaged citizens' confidence in the press.

During 2003, the government of President Hipólito Mejía hardened its stance against critical journalists. In June, officials from the National Department of Investigations (DNI) interrogated journalist Marino Zapete Corniel and accused him of insulting President Mejía in a series of critical articles about the president's alleged attempts to build two countryside mansions for himself using public funds. DNI officials also tried to pressure Zapete to reveal his sources. In July, police detained Radio Montecristi hosts Horacio Emilio Lemoine and Carlos Martínez after they conducted an on-air poll about Mejía. Lemoine and Martínez were held for more than two days, and their program was suspended for three days.

Coverage of the collapse of Banco Intercontinental (BANINTER), one of the country's largest banks and owner of the nation's largest media group, badly damaged the credibility of a large sector of the Dominican media and called into question their independence. In 2002, the nation's Central Bank had pumped billions of pesos into BANINTER to keep it afloat, to no avail. As a result, in April 2003, the Central Bank took over the failing bank's operations. A month later, the Central Bank took administrative control over BANINTER's assets—including media outlets—and asked the Public Prosecutor's Office to seize or freeze them. In addition, Central Bank officials sued the bank's owners and several executives on a host of charges, such as fraud and embezzlement. Dominican authorities are expected to auction off all of BANINTER's assets.

On May 13, when Central Bank Governor José Lois Malkun announced that the government had taken over the administration of BANINTER's assets, he said the Central Bank had asked the executive branch "to consider as an attack on national security any declaration or statement by anyone aimed at creating uneasiness and uncertainty over the Dominican banking system." Dominican journalists angrily rejected Malkun's statements, saying they could lead to censorship.

Media outlets owned by BANINTER immediately published a flurry of editorials and letters claiming that the government's seizure of news organizations was aimed at using them to advance political interests—including Mejía's re-election bid in 2004. A May 14 editorial in *Listín Diario*, the country's leading daily and a property of BANINTER, argued that, "More than the ownership of a company, what is at stake in these moments is freedom of the press itself, threatened not only through the use of an illegal, dictatorial, and blatant control, but also through attempts to silence those media outlets that dare mention the country's banking crisis." The next day, the directors of all the newspapers owned by BANINTER resigned to protest the government's action.

In the aftermath of BANINTER's collapse, some Dominican journalists warned that local banks had been buying media outlets during the last few years to shield themselves from negative publicity and to pressure the government and competitors. In addition to *Listín Diario*, BANINTER had acquired the dailies *Última Hora*, *El Financiero*, and *El Expreso*; several network and cable TV channels; and more than 60 radio stations, some of which were heavily in debt or allegedly involved in financial irregularities, such as getting secret loans from BANINTER, at the time of the Central Bank's intervention. A month after BANINTER's assets were seized, *Última Hora* and *El Financiero* closed, claiming they weren't profitable. Some journalists argue that since large banking groups began acquiring media outlets in the 1990s, newsrooms have become increasingly subject to pressure and censorship by management and owners.

In early July, several journalists resigned from the TV channel Telecentro, which was owned by BANINTER and is now run by a government-appointed administrator. The journalists charged that they had been pressured to portray the Mejía administration in a more favorable light.

The legal case surrounding the 1975 murder of journalist Orlando Martínez Howley continued in 2003. In August 2000, a retired air force general and three accomplices were convicted for the killing and sentenced to 30 years in prison each. But in November 2002, the Santo Domingo Appeals Court annulled the sentences because of procedural errors and ordered the defendants retried. The men were retried in July

2003 in the same court, convicted, and sentenced to prison terms ranging from 10 to 15 years. Both the journalist's family and the Public Prosecutor's Office appealed the verdict to the Supreme Court of Justice, contending that the new sentences were too short compared with the original 30-year sentences. The Supreme Court had not heard the case by year's end. Martínez's family and friends have pursued the case for years, arguing that Martínez was killed because his reporting had angered then President Joaquín Balaguer.

GUATEMALA

SEVEN YEARS AFTER THE GOVERNMENT AND FORMER GUERRILLAS SIGNED the last of a series of peace accords ending Guatemala's 36-year civil conflict, the nation continued its struggle with a legacy of massive human rights violations and impunity.

As relations between the government and the local press became more hostile, the number of attacks and threats against journalists increased significantly in 2003, making Guatemala one of the most dangerous places in the Americas to work as a journalist. That, along with a general increase in crime and violence during an election year, added to the tense political environment.

Although Guatemalan journalists express their views freely, many suffer retaliation for what they publish. Journalists who report on such sensitive topics as human rights, government corruption, and crime faced death threats and harassment by politicians, drug traffickers, and organized crime groups. The situation is even more difficult for provincial journalists, who are often pressured by local politicians.

During the run-up to the November 9 general elections, attacks and threats against journalists intensified. In one of the most serious incidents, José Rubén Zamora, publisher of the Guatemala City daily *elPeriódico* and a former CPJ International Press Freedom Award recipient, was attacked at his home on June 24 by a group of men who held him and his family for two hours. The men put a gun to Zamora's head and told him they were going to execute him. They also told Zamora they knew his family's routine and would kill them if he reported the attack. According to Zamora, an underground group with government connections may have been responsible for the incident.

On July 24 and 25, followers of former dictator Efraín Ríos Montt, founder of the ruling Guatemalan Republican Front (FRG) party, held violent protests in several areas of the capital, Guatemala City. The protesters, who were armed with sticks and machetes—and, according to some reports, firearms—burned tires, threw stones at buildings, and erected barricades to demand that Ríos Montt be allowed to run for president. The Constitutional Court twice rejected Ríos Montt's candidacy in the 1990s because Article 186 of the Guatemalan Constitution bars coup leaders and former dictators from running for president.

Some protesters turned their wrath against journalists who were covering the protests, threatening, harassing, and attacking them. Reporter Héctor Ramírez died from a heart attack after being assaulted and chased by protesters. Despite the violence, the police did not act to disperse the protesters. Subsequently, Ramírez's family filed a criminal complaint against President Alfonso Portillo Cabrera, Ríos Montt, and several government ministers and high-ranking FRG officials, accusing them of being responsible for the journalist's death.

Prompted by these numerous press freedom abuses, CPJ sent a delegation to Guatemala in October. In meetings with journalists from several media outlets, CPJ Americas Program Coordinator Carlos Lauría and Research Associate Sauro González Rodríguez confirmed the existence of a threatening climate for the press there. In addition, the delegation found that the lack of concrete results in investigations of attacks against journalists has reinforced the climate of impunity that prevails in the country.

The CPJ delegation also met with human rights activists, staff from the U.N. Verification Mission in Guatemala, and government officials. During one of the meetings, Marco Antonio Cortez, the Attorney General's Office's special prosecutor for crimes against journalists and trade unionists, told CPJ that because of the July violence and the Ramírez family's criminal complaint, he had asked the Supreme Court to initiate preliminary proceedings (*antejuicios*) against President Portillo, Ríos Montt, and senior officials to determine if their immunity can be lifted so they can be tried as private citizens. The proceedings had not yet begun at year's end.

In a press conference held at the conclusion of its mission, CPJ urged the government to speak publicly in support of press freedom, to end the impunity surrounding the threats and attacks against journalists, to investigate intimidation by armed underground groups, and to dismantle those groups. CPJ also called on presidential candidates to refrain from making statements that could be interpreted as license to attack journalists covering the elections.

Meanwhile, President Portillo maintained that the media have diversified and grown during his four years in office. But he continued to accuse the local press of ignoring his achievements and of serving the interests of local oligarchs. "There are some powerful people who feel they own the country, who have companies, who have banks, who have farms, who have television programs, who have newspapers.... They disrespect the people, they disrespect politicians, they disrespect peasants," Portillo stated in an October 17 speech.

The ownership of Guatemalan media is highly concentrated. Media tycoon Remigio Ángel González, a Mexican national, controls the broadcasting media. Through front companies, González owns all four of Guatemala's network television stations, which violates constitutional provisions against both monopolies and foreign ownership of the media. González, who also owns a leading radio network, wields enormous influence over Guatemalan politics. According to local press reports, González is so powerful that political candidates often try to secure his endorsement before the elections because they know he controls all the TV stations and can determine how much airtime they receive.

A few economically powerful business groups own the country's leading dailies: the more serious papers *Prensa Libre*, *Siglo Veintiuno*, and *elPeriódico*, as well as the tabloids *Nuestro Diario* and *Al Día*. Human rights groups and some journalists criticize the print media for being too focused on events in the capital, Guatemala City, at the expense of developments in the interior of the country. Some sectors of the population, particularly peasants and indigenous peoples, are routinely excluded from the news agenda.

Two years after the murder of radio journalist Jorge Mynor Alegría Armendáriz, no one has been tried for the crime. Alegría, who was murdered in September 2001 outside his home in the Caribbean port city of Puerto Barrios, hosted an afternoon call-in show that often discussed corruption and official misconduct. The three men allegedly hired to kill Alegría remain in jail awaiting trial. In September 2003, a judge ordered the detention of FRG parliamentary deputy David Pineda, who is accused of masterminding the murder, after the Supreme Court of Justice lifted his immunity from prosecution.

HAITI

NEARLY A DECADE AFTER THE UNITED STATES RESTORED Haitian President Jean-Bertrand Aristide to power in an attempt to encourage democracy there, Haitian journalists continued to face routine threats, harassment, and physical violence, while perpetrators of these attacks were rarely punished.

The murders of two prominent Haitian journalists in recent years, the flight of dozens of others into exile, and ongoing attacks against those still working in the country have made Haiti one of the most violent places to practice journalism in the Western Hemisphere, second only to Colombia, according to CPJ research.

On March 21, Judge Bernard Saint-Vil charged six men with the murder of outspoken radio broadcaster Jean Léopold Dominique, owner and director of Radio Haïti-Inter, who was gunned down in April 2000. The men had already been in jail for more than two years on suspicion of involvement in the killing.

On April 3, Dominque's widow, Michèle Montas, who has run Radio Haïti-Inter since his death, appealed the indictments, saying the investigation into her husband's killing was "incomplete," and that the indictments "failed to charge the masterminds behind the murder." On August 3, Haiti's Court of Appeals ordered a new investigation and released three of the six men accused of the killing. A new examining magistrate, who had not yet been selected by year's end, will conduct another investigation.

On February 22, Radio Haïti-Inter stopped broadcasting indefinitely because of constant threats and harassment of its staff. The closure came not long after a December 25, 2002, assassination attempt against Montas at her home, during which one of her bodyguards was killed. After Montas closed the station, she and journalists Jean Roland Chery, Immacula Placide, Guerlande Eloi, Pierre Emmanuel, and Gigi Dominique left Haiti to live in exile. Meanwhile, the December 2002 attack remains unsolved.

The investigation into the murder of journalist Brignol Lindor, who was hacked to death by a pro-government, machete-wielding mob on December 3, 2001, showed no progress in 2003. All but one of the 10 men indicted for Lindor's killing had been released by year's end.

Six of seven threatened radio journalists in Gonaïves, a town northwest of the capital, Port-au-Prince, fled Haiti in February, fearing for their lives. Radio Etincelle owner Esdras

Mondélus remains in the country, but he went into hiding in December 2002 after receiving death threats from a pro-government militia, or popular organization, known as the "Cannibal Army."

After the mutilated body of the gang's leader, Amiot "Cuban" Métayer, was discovered on September 22, violent protests erupted in Gonaïves, his hometown, and other cities, including Port-au-Prince. The slain leader's supporters in the militia group accused the government of murdering him and demanded that President Aristide resign.

The popular organizations, which have close ties to both the Aristide administration and the ruling Fanmi Lavalas party, continued to target journalists who criticized the government, accusing them of working for the opposition. Using methods ranging from death threats to physical attacks, these groups enjoy virtual immunity and are heavily involved in arms trafficking and the drug trade, according to CPJ sources. In one chilling incident in April, one of these organizations sent a 12 mm bullet cartridge in a letter to prominent radio reporter Lilianne Pierre-Paul, the journalist told CPJ.

Given Haiti's 55 percent illiteracy rate, radio is the country's most popular communications medium. Between 150 and 200 stations operate nationwide, but 10 Port-au-Prince–based stations garner much of the nation's audience. Radio coverage reflects the extremely polarized political situation in the country. Many stations are partisan, and they broadcast reports that are either blatantly pro-government or pro-opposition. The government denounces independent stations, calling their coverage reckless. Authorities also argue that the stations air insults against the president and other officials.

Despite all the difficulties journalists face, they continue to work, covering potentially dangerous street protests and political meetings. Nonetheless, reporters avoid delving deeply into sensitive issues. "There is so much corruption in Haiti, and there are so many shadowy interests that reporters who dare investigate such cases would be killed," said Max Chauvet, owner of Haiti's major daily, *Le Nouvelliste*.

Television news in Haiti is equally partisan. According to Guyler Delva, a reporter with *Le Nouvelliste* and the secretary-general of the Association of Haitian Journalists, the country's four TV stations, with the exception of the cable network Télé Haïti, are government-controlled. When an Aristide loyalist purchased the last independent channel, Télémax, in May, most Haitians were left with no independent TV stations. Journalists complain that the government exploits its control over television stations for propaganda and to attack the independent press.

In August, a CPJ delegation that included Executive Director Ann Cooper, Americas Program Coordinator Carlos Lauría, and board members Franz Allina, Clarence Page, and Paul C. Tash visited Haiti and met with journalists and top government officials, including President Aristide, to discuss press freedom concerns. During the five-day visit, CPJ confirmed the risks that Haitian journalists face while working in an intimidating environment. Prime Minister Yvon Néptune agreed to report on the status of judicial investigations into press freedom abuses documented by CPJ and respond within 30 days after CPJ sent him a letter on September 18. By year's end, CPJ had received no response.

MEXICO

WHILE THE MEXICAN PRESS WAS ABLE TO REPORT MORE FREELY about government corruption, an increase in criminal defamation charges and government pressure on journalists to reveal their sources cast a pall over the media in 2003.

As President Vicente Fox hit the halfway point of his six-year presidency, his chances of transforming the country were slipping away, and with it, the nation's optimism. On June 12, however, Mexico took a step toward curbing official corruption when the Federal Law on Transparency and Access to Public Information came into effect, opening the government's closely guarded secrets to public scrutiny.

The law allows any citizen to request information about public officials' salaries, government contracts, internal reports, and the use of public money. Government organizations must comply within 30 days, and officials who refuse to provide information can lose their jobs or face fines and criminal charges. If officials deny an information request, the legislation grants the public the right to appeal to the Federal Institute of Access to Public Information, an agency responsible for dealing with problems surrounding such requests. If that appeal is lost, citizens can take the case to court.

But according to the law, each federal branch can withhold requested information for up to 12 years for reasons of national, trade, industrial, or financial security. The law also restricts public access to records pertaining to ongoing judicial proceedings and criminal investigations.

Though the law is perceived as an important step in Mexico's path to a more open democracy, local journalists warned that the process of shedding light on government activities will be a long one. In August, during a visit to Mexico, Eduardo Bertoni, the Inter-American Commission on Human Rights' special rapporteur for freedom of expression, noted that laws on access to public information had not been enacted in various states, even though the bills had been introduced in the local legislatures.

A few short detentions in 2003 highlighted the pressure that Mexican journalists continue to face from the application of criminal defamation laws. Isabel Arvide, a Mexico City–based journalist and author who has written many exposés about drug traffickers, corruption, and violence, as well as the book *Muerte en Juárez* (Death in Juarez), was detained on March 4 in Chihuahua City. Chihuahua State Attorney General Jesús Solís Silva charged her with criminal defamation, and Arvide spent about 24 hours in jail at Chihuahua's Social Rehabilitation Center before being released March 5 on bail. Arvide, whose trial was ongoing at press time, is required to appear every two weeks in Chihuahua City before Judge Octavio Rodríguez Gaytán, of the Second Penal Court, in connection with another criminal defamation complaint filed against her in 2002. (That case was also ongoing at year's end.)

Attorney General Solís' charges stemmed from a June 2, 2001, article by Arvide that appeared on the journalist's Web site and in the Mexico City daily *Milenio*. The piece alleged that a number of state government officials, including Solís and newspaper publisher Osvaldo Rodríguez Borunda, had organized a new drug cartel in Chihuahua.

On August 26, Francisco Barradas, director of the biweekly magazine *Bi*, was detained for five hours at Cieneguillas Prison in Zacatecas State. He was charged with libeling local city council trustee Rafael Medina Briones before being released on bail. The charges stemmed from an article that Barradas published in July 2002 when he was editor of the daily *Imagen*. In the article, the journalist alleged that Medina Briones had been seen on the roof of a house stealing water from a neighbor's tank. Medina Briones said the information was false. Barradas was required to register every eight days in Zacatecas City before Judge Miguel Luis Ruiz Roble of the Fourth Criminal Court. On November 25, a superior court dismissed the charges against the journalist.

Government officials pressured several journalists to reveal their sources in 2003. In one prominent case, on September 4, federal police agents went to the offices of the Mexico City daily *La Jornada* to speak with reporter Gustavo Carrillo García about his sources for a June 19 article about drug trafficking. On September 5, the Attorney General's Office ordered an investigation to determine if the agents were attempting to harass the journalist. As a result of this incident and others, on November 28, Attorney General Rafael Macedo de la Concha issued an order to his employees to respect the anonymity of journalists' sources in court proceedings.

Almost five years after the murder of U.S. journalist Philip True, two people who defended a pair of Huichol Indians accused in the case said they now believe that the men are guilty. In late November, both the private investigator who worked to win their release and the U.S. citizen who funded portions of their defense said the two men, Juan Chivarra de la Cruz and his brother-in-law Miguel Hernández de la Cruz, privately confessed to killing True and should be brought to justice. At year's end, the legal impact of these new developments remained unclear.

True, the *San Antonio Express-News* Mexico City bureau chief, was killed in December 1998 while working on a story about the Huichol Indians, an indigenous population that lives in a mountainous area stretching across Jalisco, Nayarit, and Durango states. Police arrested Chivarra and Hernández shortly after the murder, but a municipal judge released them in August 2001. In February 2003, a federal court overturned a later appellate court sentence of 13 years. Chivarra and Hernández are now free pending a ruling by the Jalisco State Supreme Court.

PANAMA

PANAMA IS KNOWN FOR ITS INSTITUTIONALIZED SYSTEM of legal harassment against the press. Journalists there confront antiquated media laws that impose prison terms for defamation, criminalize criticism of public officials, and permit prior censorship.

In July, Eduardo Bertoni, the Inter-American Commission on Human Rights' special rapporteur for freedom of expression, visited Panama and recommended that the government eliminate all *desacato* (disrespect) provisions and repeal criminal defamation statutes. President Mireya Moscoso responded by assuring that her administration would lift such laws before the end of her term in August 2004. But by the end of 2003, authorities had taken no steps in that direction, and public officials continued to use the country's infamous "gag laws" to stifle critical voices and intimidate independent journalists with the threat of jail time.

On August 1, three weeks after President Moscoso promised to repeal criminal provisions for press offenses, Jean Marcel Chéry and Gustavo Aparicio, reporters with the Panama City–based daily newspapers *La Prensa* and *El Panamá América*, respectively, were each sentenced to one year in prison. Their sentences were later commuted to fines of US$600 each. They were prosecuted for a 2001 report that allegedly "insulted" then Minister of Government and Justice Winston Spadafora. The article claimed that public money was used to finance the construction of a road leading to private property owned by Spadafora, who is now a Supreme Court judge, and Comptroller Alvin Weeden.

On April 14, Chéry and three colleagues from *La Prensa*—reporters Alcibíades Cortés and Julio Aizprúa and photographer Bernardino Freire—were detained for allegedly breaching the security perimeter around President Moscoso's beach house in Punta Mala. The journalists were reporting on the president's house there, which has raised public concern because of high remodeling and maintenance costs. The men were released after being held for 26 hours, and a municipal judge later dismissed all charges.

Media ownership concentration, particularly in television, limits the range of opinions that Panamanians can access, according to some journalists. For example, supporters of one of the two leading presidential candidates in elections scheduled for May 2004, former President Guillermo Endara, are regularly excluded from one nationwide morning talk show.

The Medcom Corporation operates the country's two most popular networks (RPC Canal 4 and Telemetro Canal 13), it has 75 percent of the viewing audience, and it also owns the cable station Cableonda and several radio stations. There is only one state-owned network, Televisón Educativa Canal 11, which is run by the Education Ministry.

Limited access to government information is also a problem for local journalists. In January 2002, President Moscoso approved a transparency law expanding access, but in June that year, the government issued a decree that essentially neutralized the law by attaching regulations that, among other things, exempt officials' salaries, benefits, bonuses, and travel expenses. The regulations also require that those seeking information have some direct or personal relationship to it—in effect barring the press and the public from taking advantage of the law. The People's Ombudsman Office challenged the decree in the Supreme Court, which had not ruled on the matter by the end of 2003.

On October 27, a Panamanian court barred renowned Peruvian journalist Gustavo Gorriti—in the country to attend a conference about corruption—from leaving Panama and ordered him to stand trial on criminal defamation charges. The case stemmed from a July 1996 article by Gorriti in *La Prensa* reporting that current Panamanian Attorney General José Antonio Sossa, who was then running for re-election to the legislature, had received campaign funds from a company that was allegedly a front for drug traffickers. Sossa filed a suit against Gorriti, who at the time was associate director of *La Prensa*. On October 29, the court order holding Gorriti in the country for trial was overturned, and the journalist was allowed to leave Panama.

UNITED STATES

THE U.S. MEDIA WENT TO WAR IN 2003, with both embedded and independent reporters pouring into Iraq to cover the U.S.-led invasion and its aftermath. U.S. officials called the invasion the best-covered conflict in history, but it was also one of the most deadly for journalists. All told, 19 reporters died while working in Iraq, 13 of them killed by hostile acts.

CPJ took a wide variety of actions to safeguard the welfare of journalists covering the Iraq war. On March 6, for example, CPJ sent a letter to U.S. Secretary of Defense Donald Rumsfeld outlining a series of concerns, ranging from possible military strikes against Iraqi media to restrictions on embedded and independent reporters. Once the invasion began, CPJ worked to provide journalists covering the war with up-to-date safety information while documenting and denouncing press abuses and violations. For example, CPJ protested the April 8 strike by U.S. forces on Al-Jazeera offices in Baghdad, which killed one reporter, as well as the shelling of the Palestine Hotel later that morning, which left two more journalists dead. A detailed report on the Palestine Hotel incident released in May by CPJ found that the shelling, while not a deliberate attack on journalists, was avoidable. More detailed information about the attacks on Al-Jazeera and the Palestine Hotel and on press freedom conditions in Iraq is on page 186.

Foreign journalists in the United States faced additional scrutiny and pressure in 2003. On February 13, the U.S. government ordered the expulsion of Iraqi News Agency U.N. correspondent Mohammad Alawi because his presence was deemed harmful to the "interests of the United States." *The Washington Post* reported that U.S. officials suspected Alawi of espionage. The Iraqi government responded by expelling a Fox News reporter.

On March 24, the New York Stock Exchange (NYSE) revoked the credentials of two Al-Jazeera reporters, citing a desire to reduce the number of reporters on the exchange floor. However, the revocation came just after the channel aired controversial footage from Iraqi state television of U.S. prisoners of war (POWs). On April 9, CPJ board member James C. Goodale wrote to NYSE Chairman Richard Grasso, calling the move a "huge mistake for the NYSE to appear to have gotten in the business of censorship." The journalists' credentials were restored on April 29.

On May 10 and 11, six French and two British journalists who arrived in Los Angeles to cover a video game convention were barred from entering the country, searched, questioned, detained, and deported. There were several other similar incidents involving foreign journalists throughout 2003. U.S. immigration officials say they are now scrupulously enforcing a law requiring that journalists obtain a visa to enter the country. While citizens from 27 "friendly" countries may enter the U.S. for business or pleasure for up to 90 days without a visa, journalists are required to secure a visa. Press groups in both Europe and the United States have called for changes in the regulations.

U.S. law enforcement officials cited terrorism concerns in justifying several investigations involving journalists. In March, the Federal Bureau of Investigation (FBI) acknowledged it had seized a package, which U.S. Customs had intercepted in

September 2002, sent via Federal Express from The Associated Press (AP) bureau in Manila, Philippines, to AP's bureau in Washington, D.C. The package contained an unclassified but sensitive internal FBI lab report. A customs agent in Indianapolis opened the package and turned it over to the FBI; the AP was not notified. The FBI finally returned the document in May to the AP and later conducted an internal investigation into the incident.

In July, a Secret Service agent visited the *Los Angeles Times* and asked to speak with cartoonist Michael Ramirez regarding a political cartoon the newspaper had published showing a gun pointed at President George W. Bush's head. (The cartoon was intended to suggest that Bush is the victim of political assassination.) An attorney for the *Times* met with the agent but declined to allow him to see Ramirez.

In two cases, one directly involving a journalist, government officials leaked damaging information to the press in order to discredit critics. In July, after ABC News correspondent Jeffrey Kofman did a story on poor morale among U.S. military forces in Iraq, a White House aide planted a story with Internet columnist Matt Drudge that Kofman is gay and Canadian. That same month, Bush administration officials alerted several journalists that the wife of a U.S. diplomat was an undercover agent with the Central Intelligence Agency. Her husband had publicly cast doubt on the validity of President Bush's assertion in the 2003 State of the Union Address that Iraq had tried to purchase uranium from Niger, forcing the White House to admit the statement was inaccurate. In October, the Justice Department opened an investigation into the leak and threatened to subpoena conservative columnist Robert Novak, who broke the story.

Concern about possible terrorist attacks also led to increased government secrecy, with broad implications for the press. In September, the Washington, D.C.–based Reporters Committee for the Freedom of the Press released a revised and updated edition of its report on government secrecy, *Homefront Confidential*. The report describes how the U.S. government is limiting public access to terrorism and immigration proceedings and subverting the intent of the Freedom of Information Act by routinely denying requests for information. The report also documents how state legislatures are curtailing access to basic public information at the state level.

Several important court decisions in 2003 shielding judicial proceedings from press scrutiny or compelling journalists to testify were not directly related to national security concerns. In October, a federal judge ordered reporters from the *The New York Times*, *Los Angeles Times*, AP, and CNN to provide information about former nuclear scientist Wen Ho Lee, who was indicted on espionage charges by the U.S. government, which later dropped the charges. Lee is suing the government for damage to his reputation caused by the release of derogatory information to the media. Meanwhile, the Houston judge hearing the criminal cases against two former Enron executives accused of fraud refused to make available to the press transcripts from closed-door hearings because of possible "embarrassment" to the defendants and the court. "Embarrassment is not an exception to the First Amendment," noted *Houston Chronicle* Editor Jeff Cohen. The transcripts were released in October.

In June, a decision by the Federal Communications Commission (FCC) to relax media ownership rules to allow newspapers to own broadcasters in the same market and permit national broadcast networks to acquire additional stations sparked widespread controversy. Advocacy groups lobbied fiercely against the new regulations, arguing that further concentration of media ownership would allow a few giant corporations to control the information available to the public. The FCC countered that the current rules were antiquated, and that because of the explosion of news outlets on cable and the Internet, fears about corporations controlling information are unfounded. While a Senate resolution to override the FCC regulations was passed in September and a similar vote was pending in the House at year's end, President Bush has said he will veto the resolution. Opponents of the FCC ruling have also challenged the decision in court.

While the expansion of government secrecy in the United States remains troubling, fears have not been justified that, in the aftermath of the September 11 attacks, the U.S. government would seek to limit the ability of journalists to protect their sources. The kind of charged government rhetoric that followed the attacks—when Attorney General John Ashcroft claimed that criticism of the administration "only aids terrorists"—has also largely abated.

Nevertheless, 2003 was a very difficult year for the U.S media, not only because of the loss of so many colleagues in Iraq. (Four American journalists died.) Journalism reviews and editorial pages were full of warnings that overly credulous reporting from Iraq—as well as a major scandal involving *New York Times* reporter Jayson Blair, who was fired for both fabricating and plagiarizing stories—could damage public trust in the media. Critics noted that reliance on government sources led to misleading or erroneous reporting on the Jessica Lynch POW saga and the hunt for weapons of mass destruction in the immediate aftermath of the conflict.

The perception that the U.S. government was able to control and manipulate reporting during the Iraq war was damaging not only to the U.S. media but also to journalists worldwide who faced pressure from repressive governments to produce "patriotic" reporting of their own. Indonesia, for example, introduced a highly restrictive embedding program for journalists covering the government military offensive against separatist rebels in Aceh Province. Maj. Gen. Endang Suwarya, the military commander in Aceh, told journalists, "I want all news published to contain the spirit of nationalism. Put the interests of the unitary state of Indonesia first."

VENEZUELA

THE CONFLICT BETWEEN PRESIDENT HUGO CHÁVEZ FRÍAS AND THE PRIVATE MEDIA showed no signs of subsiding in 2003. In his weekly radio and TV call-in program "Aló, Presidente" (Hello, President) and in frequent speeches, Chávez continued to lambaste the private press and accuse media owners of being "coup-plotters" and "fascists." Chávez continued to use *cadenas*—nationwide simultaneous radio and television broadcasts that pre-empt all regular programming—and state-owned media to counter private news coverage, which remained heavily biased toward the opposition.

The political situation in Venezuela is defined by a polarization between supporters of Chávez, a populist president who has maintained considerable support among the poor, and his political opponents, who feel threatened by Chávez's agenda of radical reform. This crisis sparked an upheaval in the country several years ago that has more recently evolved into a political stalemate.

The private media continued to plunge into the political arena in 2003, unabashedly promoting the agenda of opposition parties while ignoring professionalism and balance. According to local sources, because opposition parties in Venezuela are either discredited or divided, the media have stepped in to fill the vacuum, becoming an extremely powerful source of government opposition.

In early 2003, while the country was engulfed in a nationwide, two-month general strike called by opposition forces and supported by private media, Chávez repeatedly threatened to cancel broadcasting concessions held by private television channels. In January and February, the National Telecommunications Commission (Conatel) launched administrative proceedings against the private channels Globovisión, RCTV, Televén, and Venevisión to determine whether they had violated media broadcast regulations. The channels could be fined or have their licenses suspended temporarily or permanently. Based on CPJ research, the proceedings, which remained pending at year's end, are based on telecommunications regulations inconsistent with international standards on freedom of expression and could foster a climate of self-censorship.

In October, Conatel confiscated Globovisión's microwave broadcasting equipment and opened new administrative proceedings into the 24-hour news channel's alleged use of unauthorized broadcasting frequencies. Globovisión rejected Conatel's allegations and said that, as a result of the confiscation, it could not broadcast live from outside its headquarters.

On October 3, the Washington, D.C.–based Inter-American Commission on Human Rights (IACHR), an entity of the Organization of American States (OAS), issued precautionary measures in favor of Globovisión asking the Venezuelan government to suspend the proceedings and return the confiscated equipment. On October 24, the IACHR further requested that the Venezuelan government urgently guarantee Globovisión access to a simple and swift appeal process before impartial judges. However, in December, Conatel fined Globovisión 582 million bolívares (US$360,000) and kept the confiscated equipment. Globovisión announced it would appeal the decision to the Supreme Tribunal of Justice (TSJ), Venezuela's highest court.

In a worrying development, on July 15 the TSJ upheld several "contempt" and criminal defamation provisions in the Penal Code. The TSJ's Constitutional Chamber dismissed a March 2001 appeal filed by Rafael Chavero Gazdik, a lawyer who has written numerous articles on constitutional issues. Chavero's appeal claimed that Penal Code Articles 141, 148-152, 223-227, 444-447, and 450 violate the Venezuelan Constitution, as well as Venezuela's international obligations, particularly under Article 13 of the American Convention on Human Rights, which guarantees the rights to freedom of expression and information.

Articles 148-152 and Articles 223-227 include *desacato* (contempt) provisions, which criminalize expressions that are offensive to public officials and state institutions; Articles 444-447 and Article 450 address criminal defamation and slander; and Article 141 establishes criminal penalties for destroying the Venezuelan flag and other national symbols.

Chavero filed the appeal as a private citizen, a procedure that is legally available to all Venezuelans. He cited the IACHR's 1994 "Report on the compatibility of *desacato* laws with the American Convention on Human Rights," which argued that *desacato* laws contravene Article 13 of the convention because they restrict freedom of expression. He maintained that as an OAS member, Venezuela should repeal *desacato* provisions or amend them in accordance with international standards, as recommended by the IACHR report.

Chavero also asked the TSJ to repeal criminal defamation provisions or update them by introducing the "actual malice" standard in cases where the person offended is a public official or a public person. (The "actual malice" standard, first articulated by the U.S. Supreme Court in the 1964 case *New York Times Co.* v. *Sullivan*, requires a plaintiff to prove not only that the offensive expression or published information is false, but also that the defendant knew or should have known it was false at the time the expression or information was disseminated.)

The TSJ ruling, written by Justice Jesús Eduardo Cabrera Romero, rejected Chavero's arguments and instead ordered that the wording of Articles 223, 224, 225, and 226 be amended slightly. Explaining his opposition to the repeal of *desacato* laws, Justice Cabrera maintained that state institutions could not stand defenseless against abuses of the right to freedom of expression, and that, at least in the context of Venezuela, *desacato* laws served as a barrier against such abuses.

In addition, the TSJ ruling found that Venezuelan laws are compatible with the American Convention on Human Rights. The tribunal stated that Articles 57 and 58 of the Venezuelan Constitution, which establish the right to freedom of expression and the right to information, offered broader protection to society as a whole than that provided under Article 13 of the American Convention, and, therefore, should be applied with preference. Furthermore, the TSJ's decision specified that the recommendations issued by the IACHR in its 1994 report were not legally binding.

After the ruling was delivered, Eduardo Bertoni, the IACHR's special rapporteur for freedom of expression, issued a communiqué decrying the tribunal's decision. Although the IACHR's recommendations are not legally binding, they represent the commission's interpretation of existing international law regarding freedom of expression.

The Law of Social Responsibility in Radio and Television, a controversial bill drafted by Conatel and introduced in January before the National Assembly by Chávez's ruling Movimiento Quinta República (MVR), was approved in committee. At the end of 2003, the law was awaiting a second debate by the full National Assembly, which is controlled by the MVR and its allies. While the government says the bill is needed to "establish the social responsibility" of television and radio broadcasters, the private broadcasting media view the bill as an attempt to muzzle them and as a way to impose censorship on the press. Although the bill was stripped of some of its most onerous provisions by the National Assembly's Science, Technology, and Media Committee, the legislation still contains broad restrictions that could affect the right to freedom of expression. The bill is also excessively punitive, local sources said. For instance, television and radio broadcasters that disseminate messages that "promote, defend, or incite a breach of the legal order in force" may be suspended for up to 72 hours. If a media outlet repeats the infraction within the next five years, its broadcasting concession may be suspended for up to five years.

In November, government and opposition representatives met with directors of private and state-owned media organizations to seek guarantees that their political advertising campaigns would have equal access. At the end of 2003, government and opposition representatives were collecting signatures for possible recall referendums on several legislative and presidential terms. The lawmakers were concerned about balanced coverage in the media. ■

Kabul Weekly
Failed Afghan asylum seekers arrive home after being flown out from UK
Afghanistan
Floods hit Afghanistan

OVERVIEW: ASIA

by Abi Wright

ACROSS ASIA, PRESS FREEDOM CONDITIONS VARIED RADICALLY in 2003, from authoritarian regimes with strictly regulated state-controlled media in North Korea and Laos, to democratic nations with outspoken and diverse journalism in India and Taiwan. Members of the media throughout the region struggled against excessive government interference, outdated press laws, violent attacks, and imprisonment for their work on the Internet. Five journalists were killed in the Philippines, Asia's most dangerous country for the press. Meanwhile, 39 journalists remained behind bars in China.

While journalists in places such as China, Vietnam, and Afghanistan are experiencing greater freedom than they have in years past, these opportunities have come at a price. In Afghanistan, where, until two years ago, the press was barred under the Taliban regime, as many as 150 newspapers and magazines are now available in the capital, Kabul. But many topics remained risky and even taboo in 2003, including criticizing the powerful regional warlords. Afghan journalists who dared to write about abuses of power risked threats and attacks.

Although journalists in Vietnam remained tightly regulated by government censors, state-run media were allowed to cover crime and corruption, a change from previous years. However, online journalists and writers were increasingly targeted and silenced by the Vietnamese government. The Chinese media have become significantly more diverse during the last decade, but attacks on journalists also appeared to be on the rise, and China remained the world's leading jailer of journalists. Meanwhile, in a positive regional development, journalists in Hong Kong successfully challenged restrictive press legislation sanctioned by Beijing in July.

Asian leaders in Taiwan, Pakistan, Burma, and Indonesia seized on national security as an excuse to stifle critical voices. Taiwanese authorities used vaguely worded national security laws to prosecute Hung Che-cheng, a reporter for the now defunct daily *Jin Pao* (Power News). Pakistan's president, Gen. Pervez Musharraf, accused the English-language monthly *The Herald* of being "anti-army" and "damaging our national interest" at a meeting with editors in November. And in Burma, Zaw Thet Htway, editor of the sports magazine *First Eleven*, was convicted of high treason and sentenced to death for allegedly plotting to overthrow the ruling military junta. Although death sentences are rarely carried out in Burma, according to exiled Burmese journalists, the harsh sentence was an unmistakable warning to the press.

Continuing this trend of citing national security issues to harass journalists, Indonesian authorities restricted reporters' access to the military's offensive in the restive Aceh Province and encouraged editors to rally patriotic support for the operation. Following the lead of the U.S. government, the Indonesian military embedded local journalists with military units, discouraged independent reporters from covering the war, and banned journalists from contacting the separatist rebels of the Free Aceh Movement, known by its Indonesian acronym, GAM.

Abi Wright is CPJ's Asia program coordinator. **Sophie Beach**, senior research associate for Asia, and **A. Lin Neumann**, Asia program consultant, contributed to the research and writing of this section.

Photo (previous page): A man reads a newspaper at a stand on the streets of Afghanistan's capital, Kabul, in May 2003. *AP/Silvia Izquierdo*

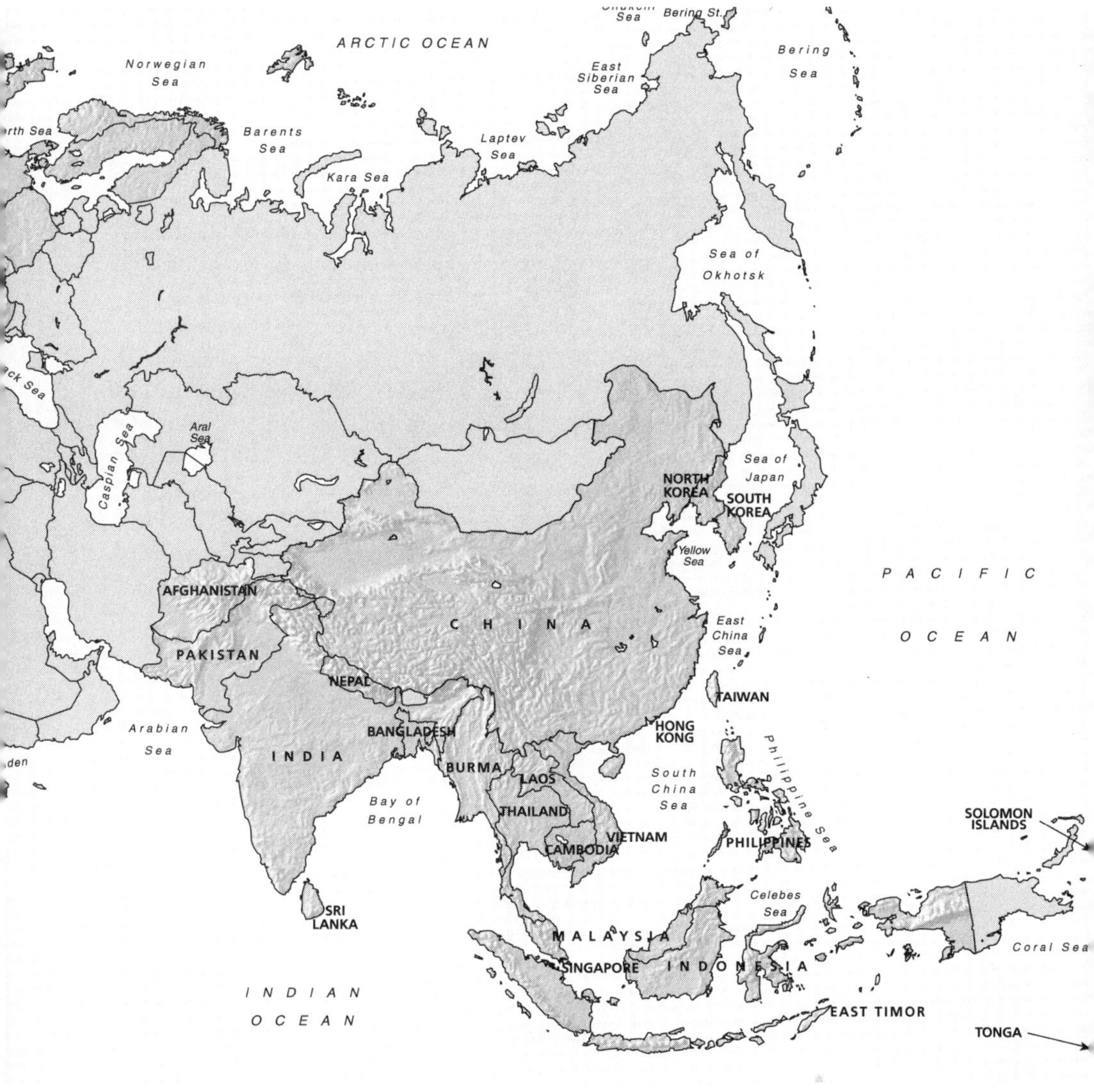

ARCTIC OCEAN
Norwegian Sea
Barents Sea
Kara Sea
Laptev Sea
East Siberian Sea
Bering St.
Bering Sea
Sea of Okhotsk
Aral Sea
Caspian Sea
Sea of Japan
NORTH KOREA
SOUTH KOREA
Yellow Sea
PACIFIC OCEAN
AFGHANISTAN
CHINA
East China Sea
PAKISTAN
NEPAL
TAIWAN
Arabian Sea
BANGLADESH
HONG KONG
INDIA
BURMA
LAOS
South China Sea
Philippine Sea
Bay of Bengal
THAILAND
VIETNAM
CAMBODIA
PHILIPPINES
SOLOMON ISLANDS
Celebes Sea
SRI LANKA
MALAYSIA
SINGAPORE
INDONESIA
Coral Sea
INDIAN OCEAN
EAST TIMOR
TONGA

Antiquated and punitive press laws were often used against journalists in 2003 in reprisal for negative coverage of government officials and other powerful individuals. Indonesian President Megawati Sukarnoputri utilized colonial-era "insult" laws to sentence the editor of the popular tabloid *Rakyat Merdeka* to a six-month suspended prison sentence for criticizing her in print. With presidential elections on the horizon for 2004, this case could have a chilling effect on Indonesia's media.

One of India's oldest newspapers, the English-language daily *The Hindu*, was slapped with 20 separate criminal defamation cases by the chief minister of the southern state of Tamil Nadu in retaliation for critical editorials and articles. Each case carries a maximum penalty of two years in prison, but even without prison time, the cases could grind on for several years, requiring hefty legal fees and multiple court appearances by editors and reporters.

In Afghanistan and Pakistan, blasphemy laws were used against journalists who published stories on sensitive subjects. Two journalists from the Kabul-based weekly *Aftab* in Afghanistan were arrested and charged with blasphemy in 2003 for publishing a series of controversial articles condemning crimes committed by senior Afghan leaders in the name of Islam. Sayeed Mirhussein Mahdawi, *Aftab*'s editor, and Ali Payam Sistany, the newspaper's assistant editor, were released from jail on June 25, but their case raised questions about the future application of Shariah, or Islamic law, in Afghanistan. In January 2004, a *loya jirga*, or grand council, ratified Afghanistan's constitution, but it was not clear whether moderate or conservative interpretations of the press law will prevail.

In Pakistan's Northwest Frontier Province, Munawar Mohsin, a former subeditor at the Peshawar-based newspaper *Frontier Post*, was convicted of blasphemy and sentenced to life in prison on July 8. The court ruled that Mohsin had "intentionally and willfully committed an offense" by publishing a letter to the editor in 2001 that made derogatory references to the Prophet Muhammad. Mohsin said he ran the letter by accident and admitted in an interview that at the time of the incident, he had recently completed a drug rehabilitation program. Four other journalists from the *Frontier Post* were also arrested, but only Mohsin remains in jail.

Journalists throughout Asia faced violence in 2003, particularly in Bangladesh, Vietnam, and the Philippines. The vast majority of attacks went unpunished. In Bangladesh, reports surfaced almost daily of brutal assaults on local journalists in reprisal for reporting on official corruption and crime.

In December, members of the youth wing of the ruling Bangladesh Nationalist Party, the Jatiyatabadi Jubo Dal, went on a rampage against the press in the southern Jhalakhati District. The Jubo Dal group beat and stabbed Humayun Kabir, local correspondent for the regional daily *Dakkhinanchal*, on December 4 in the town of Jhalakhati in retaliation for an article he wrote alleging a connection between the group's leader and an attack on a local engineer, according to press reports. After Kabir was rescued and hospitalized, local journalists tried to organize a protest against the violence at the local press club. In response, Jubo Dal targeted them for additional harassment and attacks. At least 10 journalists in the region were forced to go into hiding after Jubo Dal members threatened them and their families. At year's end, no charges had been filed against any of the journalists' assailants.

The Vietnamese government allowed journalists more leeway to cover crime and corruption in 2003, but they were also increasingly subject to attacks in retribution for investigative reporting. CPJ documented four attacks on journalists in 2003, a marked increase over previous years. In one of the most egregious examples, two reporters from government publications were beaten by the chairman of a village cooperative while investigating villagers' complaints about embezzlement by local officials. Police later filed a report accusing the journalists of "disorderly conduct." Police are often slow to respond to such incidents.

In Afghanistan, where the press has enjoyed a dramatic increase in freedom since the fall of the Taliban in 2001, journalists also risked attack for their work. In April, prominent journalist Dr. Samay Hamed, a recipient of CPJ's 2003 International Press Freedom Award, was attacked in Kabul by a knife-wielding man who cut him in the chest, arms, and hands after Hamed denounced the power of local warlords in an interview with the BBC. Other journalists also reported death threats and harassment for their work, including Zahur Afghan, editor of the Kabul-based daily *Erada*.

In Asia, the Internet is providing new challenges to journalists, with governments trying to restrict online speech in China, Vietnam, Singapore, and Malaysia. The Internet poses a significant threat to the government's control over information in China, where an estimated 78 million people are online.

Using sophisticated technology, officials monitor what people post on the Internet and threaten imprisonment as a way to control critical commentary. Six Internet essayists were jailed in China in 2003, bringing the total number of people imprisoned there for writing or distributing information online to 19. Du Daobin, a prolific and prominent writer, was arrested after posting a number of essays calling for the release of Liu Di, a college student in Beijing known by her pen name, "Stainless Steel Mouse," who was imprisoned in 2002 after writing pro-reform essays. Liu was freed on November 28, but Du, charged with subversion, remained in jail at year's end.

The threat of jail time is also used to silence critics in Vietnam, where five of the eight journalists in prison were targeted after writing or distributing information online. After handing down a 13-year sentence to Internet essayist Pham Hong Son in June, the Hanoi Supreme Court bowed to international pressure and reduced his sentence to five years on appeal. Prior to his arrest in March 2002, Son had translated and posted an essay titled "What is Democracy?" that first appeared on the U.S. State Department Web site.

Ten journalists died for their work in Asia in 2003, five of them killed in the Philippines, the biggest annual tally there since 1997, when 13 journalists were killed in the region. As in the past, Philippine police made few arrests; suspects in only two of the murders were detained, and authorities had not filed charges in any of the five cases by year's end. Most victims were low-paid, little-known journalists working in rural areas. Since the restoration of democracy in 1986, more than 40 journalists have been murdered in the Philippines for their work, according to CPJ research. There has not been a single conviction in any of these cases.

Hong Kong celebrated a rare press freedom victory for Asia in July, when popular street demonstrations led to the repeal of drafted government legislation that would have imposed stiff sentences for sedition, subversion, and the theft of "state secrets." A broad spectrum of journalists, lawyers, and others rallied against the bill's passage, and on July 1, the sixth anniversary of Britain's handover of Hong Kong to China, an estimated 500,000 citizens took to the streets in protest. Despite the embarrassment to Beijing, Chief Executive Tung Chee-hwa managed to survive the politically tumultuous summer and announced in September that he had shelved the proposed legislation indefinitely.

AFGHANISTAN

PRESS FREEDOM CONDITIONS HAVE IMPROVED DRAMATICALLY since the fall of the hard-line Taliban regime in December 2001. However, Afghanistan's rocky transition to democracy has not removed all obstacles for the media, and local journalists remain under threat.

In 2003, supporters of powerful government officials and military leaders intimidated, harassed, and attacked independent journalists in retaliation for critical articles, resulting in widespread self-censorship. In April, Zahur Afghan, editor of the Kabul-based daily *Erada*, received eight death threats in a 24-hour period after publishing an article that criticized the Education Ministry. That same month, a knife-wielding man attacked Dr. Samay Hamed, a prominent journalist and a recipient of CPJ's 2003 International Press Freedom Award, after he denounced the power of local warlords in an interview with the BBC. Hamed sustained injuries to his chest, arms, and hands.

In the western province of Herat, local governor and warlord Ismail Khan, who has been widely accused of human rights violations, continued to clamp down on the local media. At the opening of the Afghan Independent Human Rights Commission office in March, Radio Liberty reporter Ahmed Behzad was beaten, thrown in jail, and expelled from the region on Ismail Khan's orders after he overheard the reporter asking the interior minister about the human rights situation in Herat. A group of Herat-based journalists went on strike in protest and traveled to Kabul to meet with President Hamid Karzai about the incident, but their actions had little impact. Two days after the attack on Behzad, Ismail Khan condemned journalists who work for foreign radio broadcasters, warning that they would "meet a bad end."

In Kabul, police told Sayeed Mirhussein Mahdawi, editor of the independent weekly *Aftab*, that they could not guarantee his safety after he published a series of controversial articles in March and April calling for a secular government and condemning crimes committed by senior Afghan leaders in the name of Islam. In April and May, Mahdawi and his assistant editor Ali Payam Sistany received numerous threatening phone calls and visits from individuals pressuring them to stop writing.

The journalists continued publishing *Aftab* until June, when Mahdawi penned a controversial article accusing senior leaders of the Northern Alliance, other mujahedeen leaders, and the Taliban of wrecking Afghanistan in the name of Islam. On June 17, Mahdawi and Sistany were arrested and charged with blasphemy, and *Aftab* was closed. They were released from jail on June 25, but their arrest and prosecution raised new questions about the future application of Shariah, or strict Islamic law, in Afghanistan, as well as the influence of the country's conservative Supreme Court.

Almost mirroring the views of the former Taliban regime, Afghanistan's Chief Justice Mawlavi Fazl Hadi Shinwari closed cable television channels across the country in

January because their programming was "offensive" and "un-Islamic." Shinwari told Reuters that the channels were airing "half-naked singers and obscene scenes from movies." The ban was lifted in April and then re-imposed in Jalalabad in September because of reported complaints about "shocking" Western and Indian programming showing men and women dancing together.

Journalists remained vulnerable in 2003 amid a basic lack of security, renewed fighting between armed factions, guerrilla warfare, and terrorist activities. In April, officers from the criminal division of the local police beat and threatened television and radio broadcasters in the eastern province of Nangarhar for not broadcasting stories about the officers' work, according to local journalists. That same month, a local Reuters journalist was robbed by armed gunmen in Mazar-e-Sharif.

There were far fewer reports of interference in the press by U.S. troops in Afghanistan in 2003, in contrast with the year before, when U.S. soldiers threatened a *Washington Post* reporter and barred him from working near the site of a U.S. missile strike, and when a Pakistani journalist was detained at the Afghan-Pakistani border on suspicion of being a Taliban member.

In 2003, a growing number of journalists in Afghanistan received professional training in news and reporting from such organizations as Radio Free Europe/Radio Liberty and the Institute for War and Peace Reporting. New radio stations and publications opened throughout the country, including several dedicated to women's issues, such as the Voice of Women radio station. Unfortunately, political and ethnic rivalries in the journalism community thwarted attempts to form an independent journalists' union in May.

No journalists were killed for their work in the country in 2003. Far fewer foreign journalists were operating in Afghanistan since the world's attention shifted to the conflict in Iraq. In April, Afghan security forces arrested several people suspected of involvement in the killing of four foreign journalists in late 2001 while the Taliban were collapsing across the country, but the two main suspects were reportedly freed a few months later. On November 7, the U.S. State Department issued a warning to U.S. journalists in Afghanistan and foreigners working for U.S. media outlets that they could be targeted for kidnapping in exchange for Taliban members in U.S. custody.

In the run-up to the presidential elections scheduled for June 2004, Afghan journalists find themselves increasingly caught in the growing tensions between moderate and conservative government factions. President Karzai and other officials have promised to uphold press freedom in the country's newly revised constitution, which was ratified in January 2004. Debates about the extent of presidential powers and the role of women in the country's future have dominated discussions about the constitution. However, with parts of the government advocating the application of Shariah to the press, it remains to be seen whether hard-line Islamists or moderates will shape Afghanistan's new media.

BANGLADESH

IN 2003, BANGLADESH WAS ONE OF THE MOST VIOLENT COUNTRIES in the world for journalists, with almost daily cases of physical assaults and intimidation—particularly in rural areas. Local journalists say they are increasingly under threat for reporting on political violence, graft, and organized crime, but that the main cause of brutality against the press in Bangladesh is pervasive corruption.

For the third consecutive year, Transparency International, a nonprofit group dedicated to combating corruption, named Bangladesh the most corrupt country in the world. In response to criticism that her government has not done enough to stop corruption and criminal gangs, which are often linked to political parties, Prime Minister Khaleda Zia launched a massive crackdown on crime in October 2002, dubbed "Operation Clean Heart." Military units were deployed nationwide, but after police and human rights groups reported that more than 40 suspects had been killed in custody, the soldiers were withdrawn in January 2003. In February, however, a paramilitary task force was redeployed. Police were granted authority to shoot criminals on sight, and President Iajuddin Ahmed signed a controversial bill granting troops immunity from prosecution for killings and other alleged human rights violations committed during the crackdown.

One victim was journalist Hiramon Mondol, a correspondent for the daily *Dainik Prabarttan*, who was brutally assaulted by members of the government's joint task force in the southwestern town of Khulna on August 8. Soldiers beat him with rifles and hockey sticks after he wrote an article alleging that joint task force members had stolen fish from locals. Mondol was treated for his wounds then taken into custody by the joint task force, which charged him with extortion. Although he was eventually tried, acquitted, and freed six weeks after his arrest, Mondol says he still feels threatened.

CPJ documented several other cases in 2003 where journalists who reported on crimes committed by government officials were falsely charged with crimes in reprisal. Editor and publisher Mahmudul Haq was imprisoned for several weeks in May on extortion charges in Sitakunda, an industrial town in the southeastern Chittagong District, after exposing local political corruption. Akkas Sikder, a reporter for the local newspaper *Ajker Barta*, was charged with murder in July and detained for a month after he wrote about police corruption in the southern Jhalakati District. The charges were eventually dropped.

Partisans and gangs associated with Prime Minister Zia's ruling Bangladesh Nationalist Party (BNP)—including the party's student wing, Jatiyatabadi Chhatra Dal (JCD)—were responsible for many other brutal assaults against journalists. (Before the Awami League Party [ALP] lost power to the BNP in the 2001 elections, ALP members were also known for their brutal assaults on the media.) On July 31, a group of 20 JCD members viciously attacked Hasan Jahid Tusher, a reporter for *The Daily Star*, in his dorm room at Dhaka University in retaliation for articles he wrote about their violent activities. The gang beat Tusher with iron rods, severely injuring his back and shoulders, and then dragged him downstairs from his third-floor room.

In the Shariatpur District of southern Bangladesh, JCD members kidnapped the local correspondent for the national newspaper *Janakantha*, Abul Bashar, from his office on June 19. They took the journalist to district BNP headquarters, where armed party members shot him and beat him, injuring his spine, skull, and eyes. Prior to the kidnapping, *Janakantha*, which is known for its critical coverage of the BNP, ran an article detailing attacks on Shariatpur residents carried out by the JCD. By year's end, no arrests had been made in the attacks on Tusher and Bashar.

In addition to the government officials, police, and party leaders who threatened and attacked journalists, criminal gangs also endangered the Bangladeshi press in 2003. In July, Shafiq Shaheen, a reporter for the newspaper *Manabzamin*, was severely beaten with hockey sticks by suspected gang members for writing about their illegal activities in the capital, Dhaka.

While no journalists were killed for their work in 2003 in Bangladesh, six have been murdered in the last seven years. No one has been convicted for any of the killings. The investigation into the 2000 murder of Shamsur Rahman, a *Janakantha* correspondent known for his articles exposing local criminal gangs, led to the arrest and charging of 17 men beginning in May 2003, including five journalists. One of the journalists, Farazi Azmal Hossain, a reporter with the Dhaka-based daily *Ittefaq*, was a close friend of Rahman's. Hossain was formally charged in September but remained free on bail at year's end. According to The Associated Press, the government suspects that "professional jealousy" may have led Hossain to murder Rahman. But Hossain's lawyer claims that the charges are a "conspiracy" and a form of harassment because Hossain has protested Rahman's killing. Rahman's widow, meanwhile, has asked that the charges against Hossain be dropped.

Sensitivity to foreign media coverage remained high in 2003 after investigative articles in the U.S. newsweeklies *Time* and *Far Eastern Economic Review* in 2002 raised the possibility of an al-Qaeda presence in Bangladesh. In November 2002, two U.K.-based filmmakers with Britain's Channel 4 were accused of sedition and held for 16 days before being deported. Two Bangladeshi journalists working with them were also detained and charged with "anti-state activities." In February 2003, Prime Minister Zia accused the foreign media of slander at a conference for the Commonwealth Journalists Association. Visas for foreign reporters became difficult to obtain, and in July officials banned an issue of *Newsweek* containing an article examining different interpretations of the Quran.

While the number of independent publications in the country continues to grow, television is still severely restricted. The state-run Bangladesh Television and its radio counterpart, Bangladesh Betar, dominate the market. The country's only private channel that is not broadcast via cable or satellite, Ekushey Television (ETV), was closed in August 2002 after the Supreme Court ruled that the station's license had been obtained improperly. Local sources believe that the ruling was a pretext because the BNP has accused the channel of being biased in favor of the opposition Awami League Party. According to local journalists, the station plans to relaunch in early 2004.

Bangladesh has three other private channels, NTV, Channel I, and ATN, but they can only be viewed by satellite or cable. The government allows private cable companies to broadcast foreign programming such as CNN and the BBC. But channels risk losing their licenses if they are overly critical of the government, leading to self-censorship by local journalists.

In a country where impunity is the norm for those who attack journalists, a significant development occurred in 2003 in the case of 2002 CPJ International Press Freedom Award recipient Tipu Sultan. Two-and-a-half years after he was savagely attacked in the southwestern district of Feni, arrest warrants were finally issued in April for former member of Parliament Joynal Hazari and 12 of his aides on charges of violent assault and the attempted murder of Sultan. In January 2001, Sultan was abducted and savagely beaten with iron rods and hockey sticks by a gang of Hazari's thugs. During the assault, they crushed the bones in Sultan's hands, arms, and legs. Hazari, a local political leader who belonged to the then ruling Awami League Party, reportedly ordered the beating in retaliation for articles by Sultan accusing him of corruption.

Sultan's case shocked journalists in Bangladesh and worldwide, and Hazari was forced to flee the country, reportedly to India. On April 16, after a 28-month investigation, Hazari and 12 of his associates were charged in absentia. Hazari was formally indicted in October. The trial began in November and was ongoing at press time. Sultan testified against Hazari on December 17 and was scheduled to be cross-examined by defense lawyers in early 2004.

Despite progress toward justice in the case, Hazari made threatening phone calls in August to Sultan's home saying he would kill the journalist and his family unless the journalist withdrew the case, said Sultan. That same month, in an unrelated case, Hazari was convicted in absentia on two counts of illegal arms possession and sentenced to life in prison. Although Hazari's conviction in Sultan's case would send a message that those who try to silence journalists will be held accountable, he must be apprehended first.

BURMA

BURMA'S RULING MILITARY JUNTA LAUNCHED A MAJOR CRACKDOWN on pro-democracy activist Aung San Suu Kyi and her National League for Democracy (NLD) party on May 30, when a mob of government-backed thugs ambushed her convoy while she was driving through the remote northern town of Ye-u. Since her release from house arrest in May 2002, Suu Kyi had been visiting thousands of her supporters, angering authorities.

On "Black Friday," as her supporters refer to May 30, Suu Kyi was physically attacked, detained, and placed in "protective custody" along with as many as 17 of her supporters. Radio Free Asia reported that about 100 people were killed during the ambush. The next day, universities were closed, and NLD offices were sealed. International news agencies reported the incident as a premeditated attack on Suu Kyi, but inside Burma, the heavily censored press gave readers a very different story.

Both the state media and private weekly newspapers carried extensive coverage of the military government's version of events, reflecting the junta's total control of the Burmese press. Articles accused Suu Kyi and the NLD of plotting an armed uprising and committing "acts counter to democracy" and claimed that the military government was detaining Suu Kyi for her own safety.

Radio Free Asia reported that at the time of the incident, villagers were threatened with harsh penalties for listening to foreign radio news services, but they were still the major source of information for many Burmese in 2003. In addition to four state-controlled daily newspapers, which are published by the Information Ministry, as many as 50 private weekly newspapers and monthly magazines are in circulation. Private publications have to operate within strict boundaries set by the government. They must apply annually for printing licenses and carry pro-government stories, according to exiled Burmese journalists.

On July 17, military intelligence agents raided the offices of the well-regarded sports magazine *First Eleven* and arrested five staff members, including editor and former dissident Zaw Thet Htway. Exiled Burmese groups claim that Htway was beaten during his arrest. The four other *First Eleven* journalists were soon released, but Htway remained in jail, with the government claiming to have uncovered another plot to overthrow it.

In June, *First Eleven* had received a government warning after it published an article that month questioning how grant money from the international community for the development of soccer in the country had been spent, according to *The Irrawaddy*, a Bangkok-based news magazine run by exiled Burmese journalists. Exiled journalists also told CPJ that unauthorized office equipment was confiscated during the raid, including fax machines, a computer with Internet access, and a satellite dish.

In a statement released soon after the arrests, the government denied that Htway was arrested because of his work as a journalist and said he was detained "on a totally different subject." The government provided no further details, according to The Associated Press.

At a special court session in Burma's notorious Insein Prison on November 28, Htway was convicted of high treason and sentenced to death along with eight other individuals. Htway was accused of plotting to assassinate government officials and of attempting to create instability. Though it is unlikely that his sentence will be carried out, it was interpreted as a warning to Burmese journalists not to test the boundaries of press freedom.

According to CPJ research, at least nine other journalists remain behind bars in Burma, including U Win Tin, one of the country's most well-respected journalists and a close associate of Suu Kyi's. Now 73 years old, U Win Tin was arrested in 1989, and his health continues to deteriorate under harsh prison conditions, according to a recently released political prisoner. The veteran reporter was allowed medical treatment for a hernia problem in 2003, according to the BBC. Another imprisoned journalist, Tha Ban, was also permitted to have an eye operation in November. The United Nations estimates that as many as 1,300 political prisoners are jailed in Burma.

Fax machines must be licensed in Burma, and Internet use is strictly regulated. Although two public Internet cafés opened in July in the capital, Rangoon, users are required to register their names, and only 10,000 of the Internet's millions of Web sites are accessible, according to *The Irrawaddy*.

In September, Suu Kyi was finally allowed to return home, under house arrest again, after undergoing major gynecological surgery at a Rangoon hospital. In his inaugural speech to the nation on August 30, newly appointed Prime Minister Gen. Khin Nyut announced Burma's "road map to democracy" and pledged to hold elections at an unspecified future date. The speech was broadcast on Burmese state television and radio, but no reporters were allowed to cover the event. According to the BBC, the ruling junta was holding secret talks with Suu Kyi at year's end in the hopes of moving the political dialogue forward and legitimizing the government's plans.

CAMBODIA

NOMINALLY DEMOCRATIC, CAMBODIA CONTINUES TO STRUGGLE with its official commitment to press freedom while the government frequently uses its power to influence, control, and bully the press.

The Cambodian print media are famously free and infamously full of gossip. Some 200 newspapers are licensed for publication, but virtually all Khmer-language publications are subsidized, directly or indirectly, by political interests, and the quality of the press remains wildly erratic. A high degree of illiteracy nationwide and poor distribution outside the capital, Phnom Penh, further mutes the impact of these publications.

Prime Minister Hun Sen's government firmly controls the electronic media. Strict licensing and opaque business relationships conspire to keep the six private television stations close to the ruling Cambodia People's Party (CPP); the seventh station is owned directly by the government. On the radio dial things are only marginally more open, with all but three stations controlled by the government. The exceptions are the largely noncontroversial FM102, operated by the Women's Media Centre, a nongovernmental organization, and Beehive FM105, the country's only independent news station. The opposition National United Front for a Neutral, Peaceful, Cooperative, and Independent Cambodia (FUNCINPEC), was finally granted a license for its own station, Ta Prum, in late 2002. The other major opposition party, the Sam Rainsy Party, has been waiting years for the government to approve its application for a broadcast outlet.

In recent years, with Cambodia emerging from decades of repression and civil war, once common physical attacks on journalists have decreased considerably. But in October, Chou Chetharith, the deputy editor of Ta Prum radio station, was assassinated in the capital, Phnom Penh, by a gunman riding on the back of a motorcycle. The killing heightened political tension in the city and came when the government and the opposition were locked in bitter negotiations to form a coalition government. The day before the shooting, Hun Sen had criticized Ta Prum's reporting, saying the station was insulting his leadership.

Cambodians with an interest in unbiased reporting rely on foreign sources. Three expatriate-owned local newspapers, two in English and one in French, are far and away the most reliable local sources of news. Voice of America (VOA), Radio Free Asia (RFA), the BBC, and Radio France Internationale all beam Khmer-language news into the country on shortwave. VOA and RFA purchase time on Beehive radio to rebroadcast news on the FM dial, a source of continuing conflict between Beehive and the government, which has periodically banned the rebroadcast of foreign-sourced news. In 2002, Beehive was ordered to stop rebroadcasting the reports, but the ban was lifted in 2003.

During campaigning in July for the general elections, most observers reported that the CPP maintained an overwhelming advantage in access to the electronic news media. In the aftermath of the elections, which resulted in a sweeping victory for the CPP, opposition parties were again given scant coverage during a lengthy period of negotiations to form a coalition government.

The tendency of the media to report rumors and foment conflict had disastrous consequences for the country in January. The local media wrongly quoted a popular Thai actress as saying that the Angkor Wat temple complex, the national symbol of Cambodia, should properly belong to neighboring Thailand. The false accusation fueled historic tensions between the two countries when local politicians repeated the rumor. On January 29, despite the actress's denials, mobs in Phnom Penh burned the Thai Embassy and destroyed numerous Thai-owned businesses, forcing the evacuation of Thai citizens. Diplomatic relations were suspended briefly between the two governments.

Eventually, Cambodian officials apologized to Thailand and agreed to pay tens of millions of dollars in damages.

Two journalists were arrested and blamed for the rioting. In Chan Sivutha, editor of *Rasmei Angkor* (Light of Angkor) newspaper, admitted to publishing the rumor two weeks before the riots without checking its veracity. Court papers cited the second journalist, Mam Sonando, owner and manager of Beehive radio station, for allowing a caller to his station to repeat a false rumor on air that anti-Cambodian rioting was under way in Bangkok. The two were charged with disseminating false information. Both news outlets were threatened with closure, and the journalists, if convicted, could be imprisoned for 10 years. Beehive was off the air for several days under government orders before reopening.

CPJ expressed concern that the issue was being used to single out the journalists for harassment. Pro-government media also reported on and amplified the rumors immediately before the rioting, with government officials, including Hun Sen, denouncing the actress on the air without checking the accuracy of the rumors first. No legal action was taken against other media or officials.

The government action against Beehive was particularly disturbing because Mam Sonando has long been a vocal critic of Hun Sen, and opposition parties and political activists have frequent access to the station. Diplomats and international aid organizations pressured the government to allow Beehive to remain on the air. Because of the slowness of the Cambodian court system and widespread international condemnation of the prosecution, at year's end, it seemed unlikely that the charges against either Mam Sonando or In Chan Sivutha would lead to convictions.

CHINA (INCLUDING HONG KONG)

WITH THE COMMERCIALIZATION OF THE PRESS, the rapid spread of the Internet, and international condemnation of a government cover-up of the SARS virus, the new administration of President Hu Jintao and Premier Wen Jiabao faced a series of tests over government censorship policies in 2003. Although Hu initially called for the press to take on a more active watchdog role in society when he took power in March, by year's end, he had confirmed that stringent government control over the media would remain the status quo.

As 2003 began, the Severe Acute Respiratory Syndrome (SARS) virus was spreading across southern China, generating what would soon become an international health crisis. The local propaganda bureau in Guangdong Province, where the virus first appeared, initially banned journalists from reporting on the illness. According to press reports, by early February, Guangdong authorities had notified central officials of the epidemic. Yet as it spread to Hong Kong and throughout the world, Beijing continued to deny its severity.

In the run-up to the annual March meeting of the National People's Congress, which formally transferred power to Hu and Wen, propaganda officials banned all negative reporting, including news about SARS. In mid-March, the World Health Organization (WHO) issued travel warnings for Hong Kong and southern China. The government ordered the media not to report the warning, and three days later, Chinese Health Minister Zhang Wenkang announced at a press conference that, "SARS has been placed under effective control."

In early April, whistle-blower Jiang Yanyong, a doctor at a Beijing military hospital, exposed the prevalence of SARS cases in Beijing to the international media, escalating pressure on the government to acknowledge the crisis. On April 17, President Hu admitted the SARS cover-up to the powerful Politburo and called for immediate and forceful action to fight the disease. Three days later, Health Minister Zhang and Beijing Mayor Meng Xuenong were fired for their role in the cover-up. By the time the epidemic abated in July, 774 people had died in 11 countries, including 349 in mainland China and 299 in Hong Kong, according to the WHO.

Following the government's delayed but candid response to SARS, many observers believed that China's leaders had learned an important lesson about the dangers of information control. But this optimism was tempered when authorities continued to censor stories about a number of sensitive issues, including AIDS, labor unrest, the retirement of outgoing Premier Zhu Rongji, a wave of violent crime, North Korean refugees, and popular protests in Hong Kong against proposed anti-subversion legislation.

In March, *Ershiyi Shiji Huanqiu Baodao* (21st Century World Herald), a newspaper owned by the Nanfang Daily Group, was suspended after it ran an interview with Mao Zedong's former secretary Li Rui, who criticized the current political system and called for reforms. The paper, which had run stories about SARS and other sensitive topics, gained instant popularity when it was launched in May 2002. Authorities also continued the ongoing assault on *Nanfang Zhoumo* (Southern Weekend), another Nanfang Daily Group newspaper, which was China's most progressive and daring paper before a crackdown in 2001 in which top editors were dismissed. One month after the *21st Century World Herald* was suspended, Zhang Dongming, an official from the Guangdong Propaganda Bureau, was installed as editor-in-chief of *Southern Weekend* as part of an officially mandated restructuring of the Nanfang Daily Group.

The government initiated far-reaching media reforms in 2003 by instituting regulations requiring all publications to earn at least 50 percent of their revenue from voluntary subscriptions. These reforms dealt a huge blow to the hundreds of government publications that had subsisted on mandatory subscriptions that government offices required of civil servants and party cadres. In November, authorities closed 673 unprofitable official newspapers and made 87 more free of charge, according to official press reports. Journalists will thus find themselves increasingly caught between readers' demands for aggressive reporting and propaganda officials' demands for whitewashed news.

The new commercial pressures on the media have already yielded positive results for journalists, seen in the unprecedented coverage of the United States' military action in Iraq in the spring. Television stations fed live broadcasts from Baghdad and launched a new 24-hour news program on China Central Television. Newspaper reporters were embedded with U.S. troops; in total, about 100 Chinese journalists were sent to Iraq to cover the war. That was a stark contrast to the 1991 Gulf War, which was mentioned briefly at the end of the nightly news broadcast. Only one Chinese journalist, from the official Xinhua News Agency, reported from Iraq during the Gulf War.

During the September 11, 2001, attacks on New York and Washington, Chinese TV stations had to wait to broadcast the breaking news until they had received official sanction, so viewers turned to the Internet or overseas publications for information. In 2003, media owners didn't want to lose out again to online or foreign competitors, and the government, which officially owns all media, did not object. Chinese journalists attributed the change in official attitude to increased tolerance for more open reporting about issues in which China is not directly involved. One Chinese reporter told Agence France-Presse, "The guidelines are that if it doesn't concern China directly you can go with it, but if it concerns the Chinese government you still have to toe the official line."

The humanitarian plight of North Korean refugees in China proved to be an example of the latter. The Chinese government treats the refugees—who cross the border by the thousands to escape food shortages and political repression at home—as economic migrants and regularly repatriates them to North Korea. The issue has become thornier for Beijing in recent years, with refugees and their supporters staging well-publicized raids of foreign embassies in efforts to claim asylum. Journalists who try to document these asylum attempts face harassment or arrest. Jae Hyun Seok, a South Korean freelance photographer who worked regularly for *The New York Times*, was arrested in January while filming a group of North Korean refugees attempting to flee China by boat for South Korea and Japan. In May, he was sentenced to two years in prison on charges of "human trafficking." In August, South Korean journalists Kim Seung Jin and Geum Myeong Seok were also arrested while documenting refugees' attempts to enter a school run by the Japanese government in Shanghai. They were released and deported three weeks later.

Jae Hyun Seok was one of 39 journalists imprisoned in China at year's end, and the only foreigner on that list. Six journalists—Jiang Qisheng, Wang Daqi, Qi Yanchen, Liu Di, Kang Yuchun, and An Jun—were released in 2003. Seven more were arrested: Seok and six Internet essayists—Luo Yongzhong, Du Daobin, Luo Changfu, Yan Jun, Cai Lujun, and Kong Youping. Prolonged international and domestic pressure to release imprisoned journalists helped in some cases. Internet essayist Liu Di was freed before being formally charged, and, in a rare move, the Liaoning Provincial Higher Court reduced the eight-year sentence of journalist Jiang Weiping to six years on appeal. Jiang was arrested in 2000 for his reporting on high-profile corruption cases in northeast China and received CPJ's International Press Freedom Award in 2001. He is now eligible for parole.

Local officials and private citizens implicated in investigative media reports increasingly use physical force to threaten and intimidate journalists. In November, the official press reported that journalism had become the third most dangerous career in China, following coal mining and police work. In December, *Fazhi Ribao* (Legal Daily) published a report titled "Journalists' right to report challenged," which documented 11 attacks on reporters throughout 2003. In one of these incidents, in August, security guards at the Jiangsu Provincial Education Bureau beat eight journalists who tried to attend a private meeting there. One of the journalists told *Southern Weekend* that it was the third time in a year he had been violently attacked for his reporting. While journalists' demands for laws to protect their "right to report" have gone unheeded, beleaguered reporters scored a victory in June, when two assailants who had attacked *Jinghua Shibao* (Beijing Times) reporter Yang Wei in 2002 were sentenced to one year in prison. According to a report on the *Renmin Ribao* (People's Daily) Web site, the arrest marked the first time an assailant was convicted for attacking a journalist in Beijing.

The Internet played an increasingly important role for independent writers, academics, and others whose opinions the traditional media did not welcome. In several cases, online exposure of stories about crime, corruption, and industrial accidents pressured the mainstream media into reporting on previously taboo topics. With 78 million people online in China by year's end, the government faced an uphill battle in controlling Internet speech, with Web users becoming more adept and forceful in defending their right to free expression. Nevertheless, officials continued to use sophisticated technology, require Internet Service Providers and cybercafé owners to censor clients, and threaten imprisonment to control online activities. Several especially outspoken Internet writers were targeted for arrest in 2003. Liu Di, a college student in Beijing who was arrested in November 2002, spent more than a year in incommunicado detention after writing a series of sarcastic essays advocating political and social reforms in China. Her case became a cause célèbre among Chinese Internet users around the world, and on November 28, 2003, authorities released her on bail.

In October authorities arrested Du Daobin, one of China's most prominent and well-respected Internet essayists, who led an online movement demanding Liu's release. He was charged with "subversion" but had not been tried by year's end. More than 1,000 of his supporters—including mainstream journalists, lawyers, academics, and others—signed open letters to Premier Wen demanding his release and the right to free expression, which the Chinese Constitution guarantees.

HONG KONG

JOURNALISTS AND CITIZENS IN HONG KONG SCORED an unprecedented victory in 2003 by overturning government plans to implement legislation that would have outlawed subversion.

Throughout 2003, Hong Kong journalists reported aggressively on the raging debates over the proposed legislation, as well as on the SARS epidemic, which killed 299 people in the territory. Both issues helped embolden the territory's media, which have occasionally been criticized in the past for practicing self-censorship and tailoring reporting to cater to corporate or political interests.

In February, the Beijing-backed government in Hong Kong introduced draft legislation outlawing sedition, subversion, secession, and the theft of state secrets, as required under Article 23 of the Basic Law, Hong Kong's mini-constitution. The draft, which was submitted after a three-month "public consultation" period, ignored many concerns raised by critics that the proposed legislation seriously threatened press freedom. The government also ignored calls for a "White Bill" that the public could review and amend before submission to the Legislative Council.

A broad spectrum of Hong Kong society—including the U.S. Chamber of Commerce, the Hong Kong Bar Association, journalists, librarians, lawyers, legislators, banking officials, and religious figures—rallied against the law and staged public protests opposing its passage by the Legislative Council, of which only 24 of 60 members are directly elected by the public.

Anger over Article 23 fueled widespread discontent over the administration of Chief Executive Tung Chee-hwa and his handling of the economy and the SARS crisis. The public's dissatisfaction peaked in a protest march on the sixth anniversary of the July 1, 1997, handover of the territory to China from the United Kingdom. The demonstration, which was expected to attract 100,000 people, drew a crowd of 500,000—

the largest march in Hong Kong since 1989, when hundreds of thousands of people gathered to protest the military crackdown on pro-democracy demonstrations in Beijing.

In late July, Security Minister Regina Ip resigned, citing personal reasons, after becoming a target of anti-Article 23 protesters for her uncompromising support of the legislation. In a matter of days, Tung announced that he had withdrawn the proposed legislation "to allow sufficient time for the community to study the enactment question." The government is expected to reintroduce the bill in the future, but Tung has not yet announced a timetable or specific plans to involve the public in the process.

Hong Kong citizens have been galvanized by this issue, and in District Council elections in November, a record number of voters turned out to support the opposition Democratic Party, which had led the protests against Article 23. The movement's momentum carried through to the year's end, with citizens escalating calls for a more representative government and greater democracy.

EAST TIMOR

Despite widespread poverty in this tiny half-island nation, a fledgling press has developed out of the destruction that followed the territory's vote for independence from Indonesia in 1999. Since May 2002, East Timor has been sovereign, with only a small U.N. presence remaining until 2004 to provide defense and security assistance.

Given East Timor's tiny, impoverished media market, the handful of newspapers and radio stations there remain largely dependent on international aid donors. Government radio is people's largest news source. With the ruling Revolutionary Front for the Independence of East Timor (FRETILIN) party of Prime Minister Mari Alkatiri holding a large parliamentary majority and controlling most important government posts, journalists complain that the government uses its power to control the press through intimidation and subtle pressure. The government-run radio and television service is particularly susceptible, according to local journalists.

Government influence could become a more serious problem in the future if FRETILIN continues to resist efforts to create a truly independent public broadcaster. The president of the Public Broadcasting Service, Virgilio Guterres, has criticized the state secretary for the Council of Ministers for sending a reprimand to the Public Broadcasting Service regarding a number of stories about internal government conflicts that aired on the service in July, though the service was never officially sanctioned.

The courts have also begun to side with those in power. Two of the country's newspapers face large civil defamation judgments that, if imposed after appeals, could threaten their financial operations. For several years, some political leaders and media figures have called for the creation of a press council to mediate disputes and avoid costly legal battles.

In October, during a state visit to East Timor, outgoing Malaysian Prime Minister Mahathir Mohamad had some unwelcome advice for the Timorese media. "An independent media, able to criticize the government, is good, but that independence can be abused," he told the Timorese Parliament. His remarks were widely discussed in Timorese newspapers. Mahathir, who resigned in 2003 after 22 years in power, designed a system in Malaysia that tightly controls the press and political opposition. He was also a staunch defender of Indonesia's occupation of East Timor.

In a reminder of the heavy price journalists paid for covering East Timor, the families of five television journalists killed by Indonesian soldiers during the 1975 invasion gathered in October in the tiny hamlet of Balibo, about 70 miles (112 kilometers) southwest of the capital, Dili, to dedicate a memorial. The slain journalists, from the United Kingdom and Australia, were documenting incursions by Indonesia in advance of the full-scale seizure of the territory when Portuguese colonial rule ended. While investigators have identified some of those allegedly responsible for the Balibo killings, Indonesia has refused to turn the suspects over for prosecution in East Timor.

Indonesian authorities have also refused to extradite two Indonesian soldiers indicted for the 1999 murder of *Financial Times* reporter Sander Thoenes, who was killed in the aftermath of East Timor's vote for independence from Indonesia. The two soldiers were both members of Battalion 745, which has been implicated in numerous rights abuses in East Timor. Efforts to prosecute Thoenes' murder in Indonesia have stalled.

Between 1975 and 1999, a total of nine foreign journalists were killed, all allegedly by Indonesian forces. It is a measure of progress that physical attacks on journalists in East Timor are now rare.

INDIA

ALTHOUGH INDIA IS THE WORLD'S LARGEST DEMOCRACY, with a diverse and expanding media, government authorities remained sensitive to criticism in the press in 2003. Officials harassed journalists through lawsuits, using restrictive laws governing criminal defamation, contempt of court, and national security to silence reporters' accounts of corruption. Meanwhile, violence in the disputed state of Kashmir continued to endanger journalists.

In the southern state of Tamil Nadu, the respected English-language daily *The Hindu* faced a slew of lawsuits from the state's chief minister, a former actress known by her first name, Jayalalitha. In April, the minister expelled 43 opposition members from the state legislature and briefly jailed them. When *The Hindu* ran two articles and an editorial lambasting her actions, Jayalalitha responded by filing as many as 17 separate criminal defamation cases against *The Hindu*, according to the paper's editor, Narasimhan Ram, known as N. Ram. Another editor and the publisher are named in all the cases, along with eight staff members who are cited in different individual cases against the paper. If they are convicted, the journalists face up to 17 two-year sentences each, which could be served either concurrently or consecutively.

Further pressuring the paper, on November 7, the Tamil Nadu legislature ordered *The Hindu*'s five senior editors, as well as an editor from the Tamil-language newspaper *Murasoli*, jailed for 15 days each. The lawmakers passed a resolution formally charging the journalists with breach of privilege and "gross contempt" of the legislature because their articles "cast a slur on the chief minister's actions." India's Supreme Court halted the order on November 10, but the defamation cases against *The Hindu* continued. On December 15, *The Hindu* mounted a legal challenge against the criminal defamation law in the Supreme Court, arguing that the law violates the free speech provisions in the Indian Constitution. By year's end, Jayalalitha had filed three additional criminal defamation cases against *The Hindu*.

In the southeastern state of Karnataka, 30 journalists from 11 newspapers were charged on March 17 with contempt of court for reporting on an alleged sex scandal that occurred in November 2002 involving three judges from the state's High Court. Although the Karnataka High Court ruled on October 23 that each journalist would be tried separately, the Supreme Court temporarily suspended proceedings against the journalists on November 18.

The Prevention of Terrorism Act (POTA), which is designed to protect India's national security, was enacted in April 2002. The law allows police to demand any information they believe could help to curb terrorism, and local journalists remain concerned that it could infringe on their rights. Although the act was meant specifically to fight Islamic militants in areas like Kashmir, it has mainly been used in other states, including Tamil Nadu. R.R. Gopal, editor of the Tamil-language magazine *Nakkheeran*, became the first journalist to be arrested under POTA on April 11, 2003, when he was accused of aiding a banned Tamil militant group because he allegedly possessed some of the group's leaflets at the time of his arrest. Gopal denies the charges and accuses Tamil Nadu Chief Minister Jayalalitha of trying to punish him for his articles exposing corruption in her administration. The Madras High Court ordered Gopal released on bail on December 20. A Judicial Committee is scheduled to meet in January 2004 to review the legality of the Tamil Nadu government's use of POTA against Gopal.

On July 27, 2003, a group of journalists from the now defunct online news agency *Tehelka.com* were charged under the Official Secrets Act, a draconian, colonial-era law, for possessing "secret documents" deemed harmful to the state. The charges stemmed from a story titled "Are Dutch Innocent?" that ran on the Web site on October 9, 2000. India's Home Ministry claimed that the story contained information from secret government file number 11011/40/99, titled "Dutch Interest in India's Fringe Politics," which included the minutes of a confidential government meeting with the Dutch ambassador. The government alleged that *Tehelka.com* reprinted the minutes almost verbatim from the secret file. At year's end, the case against the Web site had not been heard in court. That was not the first time Indian officials had targeted *Tehelka.com*. In 2001, the site made headlines when it obtained a video of senior politicians from the ruling Bharatiya Janata Party (BJP) accepting bribes. Revenge from officials came in 2002, when two journalists from the site were arrested and later released on bail.

Iftikhar Gilani, the New Delhi bureau chief for the Jammu-based newspaper *Kashmir Times*, was also charged under the Official Secrets Act. He was arrested in June 2002 and jailed for seven months for allegedly possessing classified documents. The documents in Gilani's possession, which were about military operations, were actually readily available to the public on the Internet. The charges against him were eventually dropped, and he was released on January 13, 2003.

Despite peace efforts in Kashmir, which both India and Pakistan claim, violence increased in the disputed territory. Journalists have long been vulnerable to attack, and

2003 was no exception. In April, when the prime ministers of India and Pakistan made a conditional agreement to hold peace talks, a surge of violence killed at least 30 people in 10 days. On April 26, separatist militants detonated a car bomb in front of the offices of the state broadcasters Doordarshan Television and Radio Kashmir, which the militants view as mouthpieces for the Indian government. Five people, including three separatist gunmen and two security guards, were killed in an ensuing gunfight. Four days later, on April 29, a local news service reported a threat from the militant group Tehrik-ul-Mujahideen, which accuses local journalists of being on the payroll of Indian intelligence agencies. The militants wrote, "We inform such journalists that they will be killed if they fail to mend their ways."

Two journalists were killed in India in 2003, one of them in Kashmir. On January 31, Parvaz Mohammed Sultan, editor of the independent wire service News and Feature Alliance (NAFA), based in Srinagar, the summer capital of Jammu and Kashmir State, was shot and killed at his office by unidentified gunmen. Sultan's colleagues believe that he was targeted because of his work, although he had received no known threats before his killing and no one has claimed responsibility for the murder. Wire services like NAFA are frequently under pressure from both sides of the conflict. Since the fighting in Kashmir erupted into a civil war in 1989, ten journalists have been killed there, according to CPJ research. No one has been brought to justice in any of these cases.

The other journalist killed in India in 2003, Parmanand Goyal, was shot dead in his home north of the capital, Delhi. *The Tribune* newspaper reported that Goyal's son claims to have overheard men threatening his father to stop writing about a local political figure and the police, but the motive behind the murder has not yet been determined.

The deep-rooted tensions between India's Hindu majority and Muslim minority populations are exploited by local leaders for political gain. In February 2002, sectarian riots swept through the western state of Gujarat and killed hundreds, but the attacks remained a controversial subject for the Indian media in 2003. Journalists, diplomats, and human rights groups have reported that much of the violence was actually organized and encouraged by political leaders and groups associated with the ruling BJP. Journalists who covered the violence were vulnerable to attack by the unruly mobs, as well as to harassment and assault by police who did not want evidence of their complicity in the attacks publicized.

In 2003, officials continued their efforts to silence stories about the riots. In March, India's Central Board of Film Certification, which has the authority to alter or ban movies it deems controversial, censored a Hindu-language documentary called "Aakrosh" (Cry of Anguish), which featured interviews with survivors of the communal violence. In the letter denying certification to the film's producers, the board wrote that "the film depicts violence and reminds the people about the Gujarat riots last year. It shows the Government and Police in a bad light. The overall impact of the film is negative as it leads to communal hatred."

With its population of 1 billion people and low literacy rate, India increasingly gets its news from a wide variety of satellite and cable television channels. According to the ratings service TAM Media Research, India's television news audience has grown 80 percent in the last two years. As many as six new 24-hour cable news channels were scheduled to be on the air by the end of 2003, in addition to the existing news channels TV Today, NDTV, BBC, and CNN. The Indian government still controls most nonsatellite television and radio stations through the public broadcaster Prasar Bharati.

International media companies, including Rupert Murdoch's News Corporation, covet access to India's expanding news audience. The Hong Kong–based Star Group, a subsidiary of News Corporation and Asia's largest broadcaster, was planning to launch its own satellite news channel, Star News, in India in April. But on March 18, the Cabinet voted to tighten restrictions on foreign access to news channels, capping ownership at 26 percent. By year's end, Indian officials had worked out a deal to facilitate the channel's launch after Star News partnered with an Indian company, but the Information and Broadcasting Ministry continued to delay final approval for the project.

INDONESIA

INDONESIA'S PRESS FREEDOM CLIMATE REMAINS FRAGILE, without the constitutional and legal safeguards necessary to guarantee journalists' safety and access to information. In 2003, military restrictions on reporters' access to conflict areas and harsh lawsuits presented the greatest threat to the media since former dictator Suharto was ousted in 1998.

Despite operating under a reform-minded press law passed in 1999, the Indonesian media still must run a gauntlet of other restrictive, colonial-era laws. Powerful business and political leaders routinely bring criminal libel charges against journalists, forcing them to face the possibility of jail time for their reporting. In addition, military authorities have demonstrated their eagerness to restrict press access in the name of national security. Legislators have resisted repealing a host of colonial-era laws that affect the press, and efforts to push through a constitutional amendment guaranteeing press freedom have gone nowhere.

One of Indonesia's most respected publications, *Tempo* magazine, and several of its staff members are battling libel charges brought by powerful businessman Tomy Winata, one of the country's wealthiest entrepreneurs. The charges stemmed from a March 3 story citing allegations that Tomy, who goes by his first name, stood to profit from a fire in Jakarta's sprawling Tanah Abang textile market in February and raising questions about his possible involvement in the blaze. The piece included a statement from Tomy denying the allegation. The article also reported on an alleged proposal the tycoon had made to Jakarta officials to renovate the huge market at government expense, which Tomy denies as well.

Shortly after the *Tempo* piece appeared, and one day after the magazine received a written complaint from Tomy's lawyers, some 200 people from a pro-government youth group supporting the tycoon attempted to force their way into *Tempo*'s offices, saying they intended to burn down the building. Police initially stood by and watched before turning away the mob.

Tempo Chief Editor Bambang Harymurti, Editor Iskandar Ali, and reporter Ahmad Taufik were charged with criminal defamation, punishable by up to four years in prison, and with "publishing an article that could cause unrest," punishable by up to eight years.

In a bizarre twist, Tomy also brought charges against one of the magazine's co-founders, Goenawan Mohamad, after he made a statement about the suit urging that the country not be allowed to fall into the hands of criminals. After a September hearing in the case against Goenawan, a Jakarta court ordered his private house confiscated as collateral against possible damages, although he has been allowed to continue living in it. The highly unusual move was widely denounced as harassment, especially since Goenawan, one of Indonesia's most prominent media figures, is no longer involved in *Tempo*'s operations.

With Goenawan's trial under way, the complex case is certain to drag on well into 2004, but the message has been clear to most observers from the start: The government may no longer directly attack the press, but business interests angered by the independent media's investigations into their operations can rely on punitive laws and weak courts to harass journalists.

The choice of *Tempo* as a target is particularly ironic. The magazine, founded in 1971, was twice closed by the Suharto regime, most recently in 1994. Its 1998 reopening was taken as a sure sign that press freedom had been restored. Two of those embroiled in the current case are longtime heroes of Indonesia's press freedom struggle. Taufik was arrested in 1994 and imprisoned for three years for publishing an underground magazine protesting Suharto's clampdown on the press. Goenawan, in addition to founding the magazine, is the key figure behind an entire generation of journalists who have changed the face of the profession in Indonesia. Both men received CPJ's International Press Freedom award—Taufik from prison in 1994, and Goenawan in 1998.

In October, editor Supratman (like many Indonesians, he uses only one name) faced the wrath of Indonesia's legal system when police charged him with insulting President Megawati Sukarnoputri in the extremely popular tabloid *Rakya Merdeka*. In banner headlines and raunchy cartoons, the paper compared the president to a cannibal and accused her of corruption during a series of protests against fuel-price hikes in early 2003. Under outdated "insult" laws inherited from Indonesia's Dutch colonial rulers, Supratman received a six-month suspended prison sentence.

Following his sentencing, Supratman said the verdict would force him to use self-censorship to survive. "We can no longer use these types of headlines to lambaste the country's leaders," he said. "It's a step backward for the country's press freedom."

Only a month earlier, the same court had sentenced *Rakyat Merdeka*'s former editor, Karim Paputungan, to a five-month suspended sentence for publishing an allegedly defamatory cartoon of Parliament Speaker Akbar Tandjung, who was convicted of corruption in 2002 but refused to leave office.

The press's troubles were hardly confined to the courtroom, however. Military authorities launched an offensive against separatist rebels in restive Aceh Province in May and have since pursued a strict policy of controlling access to the conflict. Borrowing directly from the U.S. script in Iraq, the military embedded local reporters with units and tried to prevent others from covering the war.

As soon as the offensive began, military authorities ordered the local press not to print statements from the rebel Free Aceh Movement, known by its Indonesian acronym, GAM. Armed forces chief Gen. Endriartono Sutarto met with editors of major newspapers and broadcast outlets to rally patriotic support for the offensive. "In solving the Aceh case, public support plays a major role. If Indonesian media report news coming from GAM, we should question the depth of their nationalism," Endriartono told reporters after the meeting. The military threatened lawsuits against newspapers that published early reports of military atrocities in the campaign, according to *The Jakarta Post.*

Shortly after the offensive began and negative publicity began to appear in the foreign press, foreign reporters found themselves virtually shut out of the conflict. They had to apply for special permission from a number of government agencies to venture into Aceh, and many were banned from the province. Those who did make it to Aceh were told to stay in major cities or risk arrest. Reporters were officially banned from contacting rebels or visiting rebel areas

"These regulations were sent to us by the U.S. Pacific Command. It is what they used in Iraq," Maj. Gen. Sjafrie Sjamsuddin, chief of information for the Indonesian armed forces, told foreign reporters at a press briefing in Jakarta on June 20 to formally unveil the tight restrictions. "Of course, we have adapted them to our local environment."

U.S. freelance reporter William Nessen violated the restrictions by covering the war from the rebel side. He was with the rebels when the offensive started and remained with the insurgents for several weeks. Nessen, who writes for the *San Francisco Chronicle* and other publications, surrendered to Indonesian military authorities in June after facing death threats from local army commanders. He was arrested, jailed, convicted of visa violations, and sentenced to time served, one month and 10 days, before being deported on August 4.

LAOS

LAOS LIKES TO KEEP TO ITSELF, AND THE COMMUNIST GOVERNMENT does everything in its power to see that it stays that way. The country is one of the most isolated and information-starved in Asia, with no independent media of any kind. In 2001, the government announced that limited ownership of private media would be allowed, but for the second year in a row, no progress was made toward implementing the promise. The secretive regime controls the country's few newspapers and broadcast outlets, closely regulates the activities of the local journalists' association, and does not tolerate dissent at any level.

Foreign journalists frequently have to wait months for visas, and government "escorts" are mandatory inside the country. If the government suspects that a critical news report is in the works, the visa will be denied. As a result, journalists wanting to cover sensitive issues frequently travel on tourist visas but are subject to arrest and prosecution if caught.

In May, two journalists from the U.S.-based weekly magazine *Time* reported on the plight of the beleaguered Hmong rebels, bringing their story to light for the first time in years and drawing the anger of the Laotian government, which denounced the article. One of the *Time* journalists, Andrew Perrin, told CPJ that government soldiers had fired on him after he emerged from a remote rebel camp, and that he narrowly escaped being captured by Laotian forces.

The Laotian government has long denied that the Hmong rebellion still exists. The guerrillas are remnants of a secret army formed by the CIA in the 1960s to battle the communist guerrillas who eventually came to power in the capital, Vientiane, in 1975. The tiny band of Hmong rebels have been in the hills ever since but have never posed a threat to the regime. Human rights groups have consistently criticized the government's treatment of the ethnic minority, and the issue is extremely sensitive.

In June, two freelance foreign journalists based in Thailand and their translator, an American of Laotian origin, were arrested after traveling with a band of Hmong guerrilla fighters in rural Laos. On June 30, a Laotian court, following a two-and-a-half-hour trial, sentenced Thierry Falise, a Belgian photojournalist, and Vincent Reynaud, a French cameraman, to 15 years in prison for their alleged involvement in the death of a village security guard in a clash with rebels. They were formally charged with "obstructing police and possessing illegal explosives." The journalists denied the charges. According to Falise, the trial was rigged.

The journalists had entered Laos on valid tourist visas, but they had technically violated the regulations requiring that they obtain journalist visas. However, they were not charged with visa violations. Shortly after the verdict, intense diplomatic and international pressure led the government to deport the two journalists and their translator. Somewhat paradoxically, Laos is welcoming to foreign tourists as a source of badly needed foreign exchange.

There is a loophole for foreign news to reach the country. For instance, use of the Internet is allowed, but monitored, and officials have attempted to block sites that carry antigovernment reports from exile groups. Foreign newspapers circulate openly in the cities, although they are prohibitively expensive by local standards. Thai broadcast television and other media are heard throughout much of the country, and Radio Free Asia and other international Lao-language services aggressively cover Laotian politics for their shortwave broadcasts.

MALAYSIA

AFTER 22 YEARS OF AUTOCRATIC LEADERSHIP, ASIA'S LONGEST SERVING RULER, Malaysian Prime Minister Mahathir Mohamad, stepped down from his post in October, leaving behind a legacy of rapid economic growth. He also left strict controls on the press enforced through virtual one-party rule, crony ownership of most media outlets, and a pervasive climate of self-censorship.

His hand-picked successor, Abdullah Badawi, appeared to lack either the stature inside the dominant United Malays National Organization (UMNO) or the inclination to relax the tough controls on the media imposed by Mahathir. Badawi served as home minister for many years under Mahathir and was the official in charge of enforcing the country's press laws. Within his first few weeks in office, he began to show his stripes when the editor of a major state-controlled newspaper was sacked in what was likely a politically motivated dispute.

Abdullah Ahmad, editor of the UMNO-owned New Straits Times newspaper group, had written an article criticizing the harsh form of Islam practiced in Saudi Arabia and calling for reform of the Saudi monarchy. After Saudi Arabia formally protested the article, the management committee of the newspaper group, which is chaired by the prime minister, used the article as a pretext for firing the editor. However, most observers believe that the editor, a Mahathir appointee, was let go because he had criticized Badawi publicly and had questioned his staying power as prime minister.

The incident underscored the tight relationship between the government and the media. Under Malaysia's complex and sometimes tense racial balancing act—power is essentially divided among the majority Malay population, an economically powerful Chinese minority, and a smaller ethnic Indian minority—all daily newspapers are owned by UMNO; its partner, the Malaysian Chinese Association; or businessmen allied with the government. The editors of major media outlets are political appointees and serve at the pleasure of the nation's rulers. Changes in editorial management are often signs of internal political conflict.

Journalists are kept in line through a combination of management pressure and threats of prosecution under the tough Internal Security Act. Few mainstream journalists ever step out of line.

In January, what is arguably Malaysia's only independent news organization, the Internet newspaper *Malaysiakini.com*, had it offices raided, computers confiscated, and staff interrogated by police acting on a complaint from the youth wing of UMNO, which was angered by a letter published in *Malaysiakini.com* complaining about the official pro-Malay racial preferences in the country. Soon, businesses fearful of government reprisals pulled their advertising and the landlord threatened to evict the company from its offices. An international outcry accompanied the raid, which was widely seen as an act of harassment. By year's end, the Attorney General's Office had yet to file formal charges against *Malaysiakini.com* or the publication's editor, Steven Gan, a 1991 CPJ International Press Freedom Award recipient.

"We hope they are going to let it go," said Premesh Chandran, the chief executive officer of *Malaysiakini.com*, "But we have no guarantees." Fortunately, Chandran said, advertising revenue has rebounded, the landlord lost his eviction case in court, and news-hungry Malaysians still subscribe to the rapidly growing site in record numbers.

The Internet has been the one bright spot in the otherwise dreary landscape of curtailed expression in Malaysia. Mahathir long pursued the goal of making Malaysia an information technology research and development center and, as a result, allowed the Internet to flourish uncensored. So far that remains the case, although conservative elements in the ruling party have called for greater restrictions on the Internet.

The openness exists only in cyberspace, however. *Malaysiakini.com* applied for permission to publish a daily newspaper in late 2002 but had received no answer to its application by year's end. Similarly, a long-standing campaign by some loosely affiliated mainstream journalists to repeal the highly restrictive 1984 Printing Presses and Publications Act, which gives the government the power to license and close newspapers, has gone nowhere.

The Malaysian government's relationship with the foreign press has been contentious for years, and 2003 was no different. Despite his many accomplishments in the economic sphere, during his long tenure Mahathir has frequently acted as if criticism of his government in the foreign press is an affront to the entire nation. The government routinely attacks foreign publications verbally, hauls them into court, or bans their distribution.

In April, the government threatened to ban the U.K.-based *Economist* magazine over an article that praised the economic accomplishments of Mahathir but urged him to step aside gracefully for the good of the country. Pro-government organizations staged public burnings of the magazine, and Foreign Minister Syed Hamid Albar said, "I think we have to take serious action [on the matter]." In the end, the magazine was not banned.

NEPAL

THERE WAS HOPE FOR A PEACEFUL RESOLUTION TO THE POLITICAL VIOLENCE IN NEPAL on January 29, 2003, when the government and Maoist rebels signed a cease-fire agreement to halt their seven-year civil conflict. However, the deepening political crisis within the country's constitutional monarchy and the eventual collapse of the cease-fire in August sparked a sharp increase in violence, with grave consequences for the press.

Nepal's King Gyanendra initiated the cease-fire with Maoist rebel forces through back channels, according to international news reports, and both sides of the conflict participated in three rounds of peace talks before the rebels declared an end to the cease-fire on August 27. The government refused to accept the Maoists' main demand: the formation of an assembly to draft a new constitution that could redefine or even abolish the king's role.

King Gyanendra, who took the throne in 2001 after his brother and eight other members of the royal family were gunned down by the crown prince in a palace massacre, is reportedly unsupportive of a reduction in the monarchy's power. After mass protests in 1990, a new constitution was written that ended absolute monarchy in Nepal and created a multiparty democracy. Twelve governments have been formed in 13 years.

The king dismissed the government in October 2002 because of "incompetence," which led to a standoff with Nepal's five political parties, and he appointed as prime minister Lokendra Bahadar Chand, a member of the conservative, royalist Rastriya Prajatantra Party (RPP). Amid protests by opposition parties and charges that the king was acting unconstitutionally, Chand resigned in May and another RPP member, Surya Bahadur Thapa, was appointed prime minister. The ensuing stalemate between the king and the political parties hampered peace efforts in 2003.

While the cease-fire lasted, it brought a degree of stability for the press in Nepal for the first time since November 2001, when the previous cease-fire was broken and attacks against journalists escalated. At that time, King Gyanendra declared a state of emergency, mobilizing the Royal Nepal Army to fight with the police under a unified command against the Maoists. Previously, only the police had been engaged in the conflict. As a result, the fighting intensified. Of the estimated 8,000 people killed during Nepal's civil conflict, half of them have died since the army joined the fighting in 2001.

The king also suspended all civil liberties, including press freedom, through August 2002. During that time, the government detained more than 100 journalists, and Maoist rebels were responsible for kidnapping and torturing one journalist and murdering at least one other.

After the cease-fire was declared, reports of harassment of journalists decreased, even as skirmishes between security forces and the Maoists continued. However, rebel forces continued to threaten journalists whose reporting criticized the "people's war," particularly in rural districts. In February, CPJ documented two such cases. Local Maoist leaders confined Deepak Bahadur Thapa, a reporter for the national newspaper *Nepal*

Samacharpatra, to his village in the western district of Accham. Thapa's editor, Kapil Kafle, said the rebels had accused Thapa of reporting against them. On February 24, Rabin Prasad Thapalia, a journalist who contributed to the weekly newspaper *Ruprekha*, reported receiving death threats from the Maoists after he wrote an article profiling government security officers' widows.

Journalists found themselves targeted by both sides after the cease-fire collapsed in August, much like the last time peace talks failed in November 2001. Government security forces detained as many as eight journalists without charge in the fall. Nepalese security forces in Kathmandu abducted one of them, Sitaram Baral, the assistant editor of the weekly *Janaastha*, on September 13 while he was on his way to conduct an interview. When he was released five days later, Baral alleged that he had been blindfolded and subjected to "mental and physical torture." Local journalists told CPJ that another journalist, Subhashankar Kandel, editor of the weekly *Janadharana*, was reportedly taken from his home in the capital, Kathmandu, on September 9 by plainclothes security forces. He was held in army custody before being released on October 3. Kandel said that soldiers severely beat him while he was in custody.

Maoist rebel forces also terrorized journalists in the fall of 2003. On September 7, a group of suspected Maoist rebels in Nepal's eastern Sindhupalchowk District brutally murdered Gyanendra Khadka, a journalist with the government news agency Rastriya Samachar Samiti (RSS). According to RSS, the group took Khadka from a school where he taught part-time and led him to a nearby field, where they tied his hands to a pole and slit his throat. Gyanendra's murder alarmed and outraged Nepalese journalists, and more than 100 defied a government ban on public gatherings to protest the killing. According to news reports, at least 40 journalists were arrested for breaking the ban, which had been imposed in the wake of the cease-fire breakdown, but they were released after a few hours.

Local journalists told CPJ that Gyanendra's murder, detentions of journalists in Kathmandu and around the country, and torture allegations have had a chilling effect on the media in Nepal, spreading fear and self-censorship. While some publications have been more daring in their coverage in 2003, criticizing the army for human rights violations and reporting on atrocities committed by Maoist rebels, other newspapers have been cowed by threats in retaliation for their articles. Rajendra Dahl, editor of the Nepali-language bimonthly *Himal Khabarpatrika*, told CPJ that he started receiving threatening phone calls after he ran an issue in October reviewing the king's performance on the throne in 2003. Dahl said his investors have also received threats and pressure to stop critical reporting about the king.

NORTH KOREA

NORTH KOREA'S ROLE IN A GLOBAL NUCLEAR CRISIS put the country on the front page of international papers throughout 2003. But the regime's absolute control over news and information ensured that the world continued to know little about what happened inside the country's tightly fortified borders.

Six-nation talks—between the United States, North Korea, South Korea, China, Japan, and Russia—made little progress toward negotiating an end to the nuclear standoff between the U.S. administration and the regime of Kim Jong Il. After the first round of talks in August, both sides made demands that the other was unwilling to accept: North Korea wanted the United States to lift "its political, economic, military sanctions and blockade" before freezing its nuclear program; the Bush administration demanded that North Korea first fully dismantle its nuclear facilities. In December, a diplomatic impasse forced the postponement of a second round of talks until 2004.

The official Korean Central News Agency (KCNA) and other arms of the North Korean propaganda machine are often the only means through which international observers can learn the reclusive Kim Jong Il's position on the nuclear issue, as well as his regime's view of the world. After various members of the Bush administration criticized Kim's government, KCNA called Defense Secretary Donald Rumsfeld a "psychopath" and a "typical stupid man"; U.S. Undersecretary of State John Bolton was termed "human scum" after he called Kim a "tyrannical dictator"; and President Bush was referred to as "maniac," "lunatic," or just, "that man." KCNA, which employs 2,000 people, broadcasts worldwide in Korean, English, Russian, and Spanish.

Foreign journalists are rarely permitted inside North Korea, and those allowed in are assigned government minders. In 2003, British journalist Jonathan Watts had a rare opportunity to accompany a World Food Programme monitoring mission in Songrim, North Korea. Despite restrictions on his reporting, he was able to describe the desolate and impoverished conditions of a children's hospital in Songrim, where a third of the population relies on international food aid. In March, Pyongyang admitted that 200,000 people died of starvation between 1995 and 1998, but human rights activists believe that the death toll may be as high as 2 million.

Often, the only insight into life in North Korea comes from defectors, who flee the country by the thousands, most often across the border into China, where they seek asylum through a third country. In October, the private, bipartisan U.S. Committee for Human Rights in North Korea released an extensive report, based primarily on testimony from defectors, claiming that up to 200,000 political prisoners are currently detained in North Korea's extensive gulag system, where slave labor and torture are rife. Some of those imprisoned in the camps had committed the offense of reading a foreign newspaper, or "not taking proper care of" a newspaper containing a photo of Kim Jong Il.

All televisions and radios in North Korea must be registered, and those sold or imported into the country are programmed to receive only official government broadcasts. Those who surreptitiously listen to shortwave broadcasts from South Korea, the Voice of America, or other international services risk imprisonment. In August, South Korean police foiled an attempt by human rights activists to use helium balloons to smuggle radios into North Korea that were programmed to the frequencies of international broadcasters.

North Korean journalists were allowed two rare opportunities to glimpse the world outside their borders in 2003. In August, reporters from state media outlets were allowed to attend the World University Games in Daegu, South Korea, which was organized to promote reconciliation between the two neighbors, which have technically been at war since the 1950-1953 Korean War ended without a peace treaty. The reporters themselves made news when they berated and punched protesters carrying placards denouncing Kim Jong Il, launching a 10-minute brawl that had to be broken up by armed riot police.

In October, the Reuters Foundation was allowed to hold an unusual weeklong workshop in Pyongyang on business news reporting for researchers and editors from the Korea Trade and Economy Institute. The participants are responsible for distributing financial news from Reuters and other sources to the business community in North Korea—an elite and privileged group that is allowed access to information forbidden to the general population. The workshop, led by two Reuters journalists, focused on reporting on free markets and introduced the participants to the concept of a press conference.

PAKISTAN

ALTHOUGH THE PRESS IN PAKISTAN HAS ENJOYED GREATER FREEDOM under its president, Gen. Pervez Musharraf, who took power in a military coup in 1999, journalists there still operate under pressure from the military, religious hard-liners, intelligence agencies, and the country's antiquated blasphemy laws.

Since parliamentary elections in October 2002, which were held with the stated goal of restoring democracy and civilian rule in Pakistan, the government has been locked in a power struggle between Musharraf's attempts to strengthen the presidency and Parliament's demand that he relinquish his title as head of the army and rule the country as a civilian president. On December 24, Musharraf finally agreed to step down as military head in 2004 as part of a deal to extend his five-year term with the approval of Parliament's major parties, including the Islamist coalition Muttahida Majlis-e-Amal and the Pakistan People's Party.

The role of the military within the government will continue to be a critical issue for Pakistan's future, especially after Musharraf narrowly escaped two assassination attempts in an 11-day period in December in Rawalpindi, the town outside the capital, Islamabad, where the military is headquartered.

In this climate, the country's nuclear policy, religious issues, and any criticism of the army remained taboo for the Pakistani press. Pakistan's blasphemy laws (sections 295 A, B, C, and 505 of the Penal Code) state that anyone who "directly or indirectly defiles the sacred name of the Holy Prophet Mohammed shall be punished with death, or life imprisonment, and shall also be liable to a fine." According to local journalists, the laws were used to persecute journalists and led to self-censorship among the press in 2003.

On July 8, Munawar Mohsin, a former subeditor at the Peshawar-based national daily *Frontier Post*, was sentenced to life in prison by a court in Northwest Frontier Province on charges of blasphemy for publishing a letter to the editor in January 2001 titled "Why Muslims Hate Jews," which included derogatory references to the Prophet Muhammad. Hundreds of demonstrators gathered outside the *Post* the day after the letter appeared and set fire to the building housing the paper's printing press. District officials charged Mohsin and six other staff members with blasphemy; two went into hiding, and the other four were arrested but later released. Mohsin is the only *Post* staff member still in jail. Although a judicial inquiry into the case found that the offending letter was published by mistake, and the *Post* placed prominent advertisements in all of Pakistan's major newspapers apologizing for the incident, the court ruled that Mohsin "intentionally and willfully committed an offense."

The severity of Mohsin's sentence was seen as a warning to local journalists not to print anything that could offend Pakistan's religious groups. The July 28 edition of the U.S.-based weekly *Newsweek* magazine was banned and all copies were seized because of an article about the original language of the Quran, which Information Minister Sheikh Rashid Ahmed said could "incite religious sentiments." In an interview with Agence France-Presse, Ahmed said the government "expected the media to be careful about the religious sensitivities of the Muslim people."

The media also had to be careful about the sensitivities of the Pakistani army in 2003. Amir Mir, former editor of the *Weekly Independent*, a Lahore-based English-language newspaper, was forced to resign in June under pressure from local government officials who accused the paper of running articles that were "against the national interest," and of having an "anti-army policy." A former head of Pakistan's powerful Inter-Services Intelligence (ISI) also threatened the paper, and the local Punjab government withheld advertisements in retaliation for the *Weekly Independent*'s critical articles about the military.

Undaunted, Mir moved on to the monthly magazine the *Herald*, a publication known for highlighting Musharraf's suppression of civil liberties, and continued writing articles that questioned the actions of the military. According to a report in the daily *Jang*, the largest circulation national Urdu-language newspaper, Musharraf criticized the *Herald* and accused the paper of "damaging our national interest" during a meeting with newspaper editors on November 20. On November 22, Mir's car was set on fire in front of his house in Lahore, and he said shortly after that, he received a phone call from a member of the ISI telling him that this was "just the beginning."

On December 4, Information Minister Ahmed denied that Musharraf had made the reported comments about Mir and reaffirmed Pakistan's commitment to press freedom, saying that the government would "safeguard and protect freedom of the press as it believes that a free and vibrant media are essential for the consolidation of democracy."

The March arrest of senior al-Qaeda operative Khalid Shaikh Mohammed in Rawalpindi marked a potential breakthrough in the investigation of the January 2002 kidnapping and murder of *Wall Street Journal* South Asia Bureau Chief Daniel Pearl. Mohammed is reportedly a top aide to Osama bin Laden and allegedly organized the September 11, 2001, attacks on New York City and Washington, D.C. According to an October report in *The Wall Street Journal*, U.S. authorities have strong evidence that Mohammed himself killed Pearl, who was kidnapped in Karachi on January 23, 2002, while researching a story about Islamic extremists. He was held by a group that issued statements in the name of the previously unknown National Movement for the Restoration of Pakistani Sovereignty, and it was not known whether Pearl was alive or dead until a videotape of his murder was delivered to the U.S. Embassy in Islamabad on February 21, 2002. At year's end, Mohammed was in U.S. custody at an undisclosed location.

In 2002, four men were convicted of Pearl's murder. Ahmed Omar Saeed Sheikh was sentenced to death, and Fahad Naseem, Salman Saqib, and Sheikh Mohammed Adeel received 25-year sentences. Naseem, Saqib, and Adeel denied any involvement in Pearl's killing and appealed their convictions. Their hearings were delayed six times in 2003. At year's end, Pakistani police were still looking for seven other suspects in the case.

In 2003, two Islamic extremist groups linked to Pearl's murder, Jaish-e-Mohammed and Lashkar-i-Jhangvi, were banned in Pakistan for preaching militancy and hatred. According to local journalists, the ban includes monitoring publications associated with these groups. After a suicide attack on a Shiite mosque in the southwestern city of Quetta in July killed as many as 54 people, Musharraf launched another crackdown on outlawed militant groups under the country's antiterrorism law. In 2002, more than 1,000 alleged militants were rounded up and then released. This time, Pakistan's Central Bank asked members of militant organizations to submit security deposits that would be forfeited if they rejoined the outlawed groups, and the Interior Ministry closed their offices.

In October, two journalists in the Khyber Agency Region of Pakistan's tribal areas on the western border with Afghanistan were threatened and briefly detained by an outlawed extremist group after reporting on the group's activities. Other local journalists said that Taliban and al-Qaeda members have harassed them for reporting on their activities in the region.

Due to outcries from the press, a series of restrictive defamation laws proposed in 2002 were not formally approved by Parliament in 2003. The government retained its control of the electronic news media in Pakistan, but authorities took their first steps toward liberalizing media policy in January, when the government issued licenses to 22 companies to open private FM radio stations and allowed private companies to apply for TV station licenses. For now, the radio stations are only allowed to broadcast music and entertainment, but a senior official told the BBC in January that they may be allowed to broadcast news in the future. Pakistani satellite news channels, which are not permitted to broadcast from inside the country, are operated out of Dubai and the United Kingdom.

PHILIPPINES

THE OVERWHELMING ISSUE FACING THE PHILIPPINE PRESS IN 2003 was the increasing number of journalists murdered with impunity. In the last year alone, at least five journalists were slain in the course of their work—a toll surpassed only by war-related killings of journalists in Iraq. But in the Philippines, this violence is not a temporary aberration; it has become the normal state of affairs, year after year. While the Philippine media have been among the freest in the developing world since democracy was restored in 1986, more than 40 journalists there have been slain. No one has been convicted in any of the killings.

Most of those murdered have been provincial radio journalists, frequently on the strife-torn island of Mindanao. Often, the slayings came in revenge for outspoken criticism of powerful local political leaders. Nationally known radio commentator Juan "Jun" Pala, who was gunned down near his home in September, had already survived two attempts on his life. Pala, a hard-line anticommunist conservative and critic of the mayor of his hometown of Davao City, was, like many Philippine radio journalists, opinionated, enmeshed in local politics, and vocal in his diatribes against his enemies. Before his murder, Pala accused the mayor on the air of plotting to kill him.

Despite his background, Pala's death brought condemnation even from mainstream press groups. "He may have used his radio program for his own interests," said the National Union of Journalists in a statement, "but his murder and its particular brutality reinforces the idea that, in this country, people who dare to speak out—for whatever reason—are fair game, that violence is the only response to the power of the word."

Unlike Pala, it is rare that those killed are known beyond their communities, so they are easy targets. On May 17, unidentified men ambushed Apolinario "Polly" Pobeda, a commentator on radio station DWTI in Lucena City, in southern Luzon, while he was riding his motorcycle to the studio. The suspects, who have been arrested, are reportedly bodyguards for the son of the town's mayor, whom Pobeda frequently targeted in his broadcasts, according to press reports. The mayor has denied any involvement in the killing.

Other journalists killed for their work in the Philippines in 2003 were: Bonifacio Gregorio, of *Dyaryo Banat* newspaper in La Paz, Tarlac (July 8); Noel Villarante, of DZJV Radio and the *Laguna Score* newspaper in Santa Cruz, Laguna (August 19); and Rico Ramirez, of DXSF Radio, San Francisco, Agusan del Sur (August 20). The only link between these victims is that they were all working as low-paid journalists in provincial areas, and that no one has been charged with their murders.

Taking account of this carnage, several Philippine press organizations joined forces in early 2003 to form the Freedom Fund for Filipino Journalists, a coalition devoted to providing assistance to victims' families and pressuring the government to respond forcefully to the murders. In November, President Gloria Macapagal Arroyo offered a 1 million peso (US$18,000) reward for information leading to the arrest of anyone responsible for killing a journalist in the last five years.

The reward may be more of a public relations stunt than a serious attempt to pursue justice, since deep problems in the criminal justice system often keep suspects from being brought to trial. The high-profile murder of broadcaster Edgar Damalerio in Mindanao in April 2002 is a case in point. Two witnesses identified a local police officer by name as the assailant. Police and prosecutors failed to act for months until local and international pressure finally forced a judge to issue an arrest warrant for the suspect in February 2003. But it was too late. The officer, who had been under house arrest in police headquarters, disappeared shortly after the warrant was issued and has not been seen since. Damalerio's widow, who has been in hiding since the killing, told CPJ that she and her family still face death threats because of their desire to push for justice in the case.

Philippine journalists suffer from poor working conditions and low pay. Corruption within the press is also common. Frequently, politicians and other powerful figures will pay radio commentators and newspaper columnists to attack their enemies or promote their agendas in the media. Companies and government agencies routinely offer stipends to favored journalists, and some reporters extort money from politicians by threatening to write negative stories unless they are paid.

In terms of safety, a huge gap exists between conditions for journalists working for national outlets in Manila and their colleagues in the provinces. In rural areas, members of the press must face criminal justice systems that are often at the mercy of local political bosses, as well as guerrilla warfare in such places as Mindanao—all of which becomes especially dangerous when journalists speak out against abuses and corruption.

Journalists in Manila tend to be hit by lawsuits rather than bullets or fists. In August, officials arrested well-known *Daily Tribune* Publisher and Editor Ninez Cacho-Olivares after she wrote an article accusing a powerful local lawyer with ties to the president of trying to extort money from a company involved in the construction of a new terminal at the Manila international airport. The lawyer filed a criminal libel suit against her, and she was taken to a police station, where Olivares appeared on TV and radio to denounce the charges. By year's end, the case had not yet gone to trial.

The murders and other pressures have done little, however, to silence the outspoken press in the Philippines. Paradoxically, violence committed with impunity in the provinces coexists with some very high-caliber journalism produced in Manila. The national press, both print and broadcast, is very outspoken, with politicians generally courting journalists, not attacking them. Philippine journalists can—and have—brought down presidents and fought long battles to preserve and expand their freedoms. The Philippines has the oldest independent press in Asia and was the first country in the region to have private broadcasting stations. Much of the Philippine media are seen as good examples of professionalism throughout the region, making the record of killings and violence in the country all the more troubling.

SINGAPORE

SINGAPORE CONTINUED TO PROMOTE ITS BID TO BECOME A "GLOBAL MEDIA CITY" in 2003 but failed to take any concrete steps toward loosening stringent controls over free speech and the press.

As part of a campaign to liven up its stuffy international image, the government liberalized a number of its draconian social controls: Bungee jumping is now permitted, for example, and citizens will soon be allowed to buy chewing gum, but only for therapeutic purposes from a pharmacy. "If we want our people to make more decisions for themselves, and if we are to encourage a derring-do society, we must allow some risk-taking and a little excitement," Prime Minister Goh Chok Tong said in announcing the bungee-jumping initiative. However, risk-taking by the nation's journalists was still frowned upon. Strict censorship guidelines were upheld in 2003, and the ruling People's Action Party (PAP) continued to exert significant legal, financial, and political control over all major media outlets.

Relations with the United States warmed considerably in 2003, with Singapore showing enthusiastic support for the Bush administration's military action in Iraq, and the two nations signed a historic free trade agreement. In October, Bush visited Singapore, making him only the second U.S. president to do so. International standards of freedom of expression were not high on the bilateral agenda, and Bush overlooked Singapore's repressive practices in favor of securing the city-state's cooperation on antiterrorism efforts.

The Censorship Review Committee (CRC), launched in 2002 to restructure the national censorship policies that regulate licensing and media content, presented its findings to the public in July. The CRC report, which focused predominately on arts and entertainment media, claimed that 70 percent of the public expressed satisfaction with the existing censorship guidelines and, therefore, recommended very few substantive changes. The report recommended that the government uphold existing bans on "content that undermines public order and the nation's security, denigrates race and religion or erodes moral values." The government adopted almost all of the committee's recommendations.

Singapore Press Holdings (SPH), which has close ties to the PAP, owns most of the print press in Singapore, while the government-owned Media Corp. dominates the broadcast media. In this tightly circumscribed press environment, the Internet has provided Singaporeans with a rare alternative voice, although tough government controls have limited online content.

Singapore has one of the highest Internet penetration rates in the world, with almost 60 percent of citizens online. Yet regulations mandate that all sites with political content register with the Singapore Broadcasting Authority, and Internet service providers are required to filter content from pornography sites or unsanctioned newsgroups.

New regulations passed in November give security agencies the power to monitor the Internet and pre-emptively crack down on hackers suspected of "cyberterrorism." Free speech advocates raised concerns that the new laws violate Internet users' right to privacy and could be abused by the government to further stifle online speech.

A few savvy Internet users have skirted the content controls by anonymously creating newsgroups from undisclosed locations, which are difficult for censors to trace. Primarily through e-mail, these groups—including Singapore Review, New Sintercom, and The Void Deck—distribute a wide variety of content focusing on local social and political issues that are banned from the traditional media. Although most have been able to escape direct political interference, hackers have hit some newsgroups. In October, after the Singapore Review newsgroup was mentioned in a *Straits Times* article, a hacker accessed the site and bombarded subscribers with mass e-mails. Editors do not know who is responsible, though the Singapore Review editor told CPJ that such computer attacks "are not isolated, sporadic, random incidents. The attacks all focus on 'alternative media groups' like ours who struggle to maintain existence outside of the stable of SPH-owned print journals."

Officials continued to use the threat of hefty fines and libel lawsuits to silence their critics. WKRZ radio was fined 15,000 Singapore dollars (US$8,670) after the government deemed the station's morning show "obscene and in bad taste." When asked about the government's penchant for using libel suits against its opponents, Prime Minister Goh replied, "It is a pattern because there is a pattern among the opposition leaders to be accusing us of wrongdoing."

SOLOMON ISLANDS

AFTER FOUR YEARS OF FIERCE CIVIL CONFLICT IN THE SOLOMON ISLANDS, an Australian-led international peacekeeping force managed to pacify the country in 2003. The media, which had been a frequent target of armed militias and corrupt local officials, enjoyed a respite under the international presence and operated with relative freedom.

Since 1998, the Solomon Islands have been ravaged by persistent war between the indigenous residents of the main island, Guadalcanal, and immigrants from neighboring Malaita Island. Despite a peace deal signed in 2002, groups from both sides have remained armed and violent. The government, led by Prime Minister Allan Kemakeza, has been accused of maintaining links with militia leaders and has failed to bring stability to the country.

In July, Parliament unanimously agreed to invite the Regional Assistance Mission to Solomon Islands (RAMSI) to the country. Led by Australia, RAMSI includes more than 2,000 heavily armed troops from Australia, New Zealand, Fiji, Tonga, and Papua New Guinea. The forces confiscated thousands of illegal weapons, arrested several powerful militia leaders, and initiated corruption investigations within the government.

The country's journalists especially welcomed the mission, since it offered them a degree of protection they had not enjoyed since before the conflict. "With RAMSI in town, the media has been operating more freely than within the past four years," said Johnson Honimae, general manager of the Solomon Islands Broadcasting Corporation. Journalists used their newfound freedom to aggressively investigate and report on allegations of official corruption and abuses committed by both the government and militias during the conflict.

Despite the dramatic improvement in the situation after RAMSI's arrival, militia members continued to threaten the media, even across national boundaries. Harold Keke, a notorious warlord from Weathercoast Region of Guadalcanal Island, was perhaps the year's worst offender. In August, a group of armed men claiming to be Keke's supporters forced their way into the offices of the *Papua New Guinea Post-Courier* in Buka, Bougainville Island, part of neighboring Papua New Guinea. The men threatened to burn the newspaper's offices if journalists continued reporting on Keke's ties in Bougainville. The *Post-Courier* had reported that Keke planned to escape RAMSI by fleeing the Solomon Islands to Bougainville. The newspaper remained defiant and issued a statement condemning the attack, though management closed the Buka office and flew its chief correspondent to a secret location to ensure her safety.

Keke surrendered to RAMSI in August and is being held on several charges, including the murder of seven missionaries his militia had taken hostage in early 2003. During the negotiations with Australian diplomats that led to Keke's surrender, he warned the media against reporting from his stronghold of Weathercoast.

Solomon Islander government officials also threatened the media in 2003. In August, the mayor of the capital, Honiara, visited the offices of the daily *Solomon Star* and warned staff against writing about the city council. "As of today, I will ban any news items regarding the council from your paper. Don't you know I am the mayor?" he asked. While the mayor has not acted on his threat, local reporters expressed fear that the media may once again face routine threats and harassment when RAMSI leaves. By year's end, some RAMSI forces had begun to withdraw from the country, though Australian officials said they expect to keep troops there for at least a decade to maintain order.

SOUTH KOREA

After coming to power in February pledging to combat widespread corruption, President Roh Moo Hyun ended 2003 in disgrace, with several of his top aides under investigation for illegal campaign finance activities. Throughout 2003, the liberal president fought a heated battle with the largely conservative mainstream press, while the development of Internet news sites presented a significant challenge to traditional media outlets.

An already contentious relationship between Roh and the mainstream media that developed during the campaign season deteriorated as soon as he was sworn in as president. Much of the press had backed his opponent in the election, Lee Hoi Chang of the conservative Grand National Party (GNP), and opposed Roh's liberal policies, which include support for economic and diplomatic engagement with North Korea. Roh returned the favor by verbally lashing out at his critics in the media.

Roh took several steps aimed at revamping the media that were met with mixed reactions from local journalists. A former human rights lawyer, Roh put a high priority on reforming the newspaper industry, which he has called "a dangerous power in need of public scrutiny and verification." One of his first actions upon assuming office was to close the country's press clubs, which had granted only the major mainstream media outlets access to government ministries, and to initiate daily government briefings for all media. The reforms also mandated that government officials get permission from their supervisors before granting interviews to the press. Foreign media are now required to buy press passes before covering government briefings at Blue House, the presidential office.

While smaller media outlets that had been excluded under the previous system welcomed the changes, some mainstream journalists protested that the new "permission" requirement limited their access to officials. Nevertheless, some observers pointed out that, in practice, little had changed in the relationships between journalists and government officials, some of whom were known to offer lavish gifts or cash in return for positive press coverage.

While South Korea participated in negotiations aimed at diffusing mounting tensions between North Korea and the United States over Pyongyang's nuclear capabilities, the government allowed South Korean journalists to cover some special cross-border events from North Korea and to file pool reports. Foreign journalists, however, were not granted the same access.

Roh took his fight against the media one step further in August, when he filed civil defamation charges against the country's top four newspapers—*Chosun Ilbo*, *Dong-A Ilbo*, *JoongAng Ilbo*, and *Hankook Ilbo*—after they reported that Roh had made questionable real estate investments, accusations that he denies. In the lawsuit, Roh accused the papers of "comprehensive, persistent, and massive defamation of my character that, not as president but as a human being, caused me psychological agony hard to express in words," according to press reports. In doing so, Roh became the first South Korean president ever to file a lawsuit against the press.

Also in August, a senior aide of Roh's resigned after footage of him accepting food and drinks from a businessman at a nightclub was broadcast on SBS-TV. The footage allegedly proved that the aide had violated government ethics rules. Roh's supporters said the footage, which had been filmed secretly, appeared to be premeditated and claimed that the incident was a setup. SBS-TV producers said the tape had been delivered anonymously, and that they did not know who filmed it.

The entrenched media faced another challenge in 2003 with the rise of Internet news sites, especially *OhMyNews.com*, a free online news service. The site was founded by

Oh Yeon Ho, a veteran reporter for the underground press during the military dictatorship in the 1980s. He launched *OhMyNews.com* as an alternative to the conservative press, which he felt monopolized the country's media. South Korea has one of the highest Internet penetration rates in the world, and 70 percent of households have broadband access. *OhMyNews.com* targeted this market with a unique format that enlists citizens to contribute news stories, which are then fact-checked and edited by a small staff of journalists. In 2003, about 26,000 people were registered contributors to the site.

Launched in 2000, the Web site gained popularity during Roh's election in 2002, when it registered 20 million hits a day. Some observers, including Oh, partially attributed Roh's election victory to the success of *OhMyNews.com* and other online news sites, which are popular among the young, pro-reform citizens who overwhelmingly voted for Roh. "In the past, the conservative papers in Korea could—and did—lead public opinion.... In our battle between the conservative media and the netizens of Korea, the netizens won," Oh told the BBC in March 2003.

Roh himself has helped boost *OhMyNews.com* and other Internet news sites. The press club reforms allowed online news services access to the Blue House for the first time, and soon after his inauguration, Roh chose *OhMyNews.com* as the forum for his first presidential interview.

Despite the shifting dynamics of the Korean press in Roh's favor, he was unable to avoid widespread public discontent with his handling of a number of issues, including the economy, negotiations with North Korea, labor protests, and relations with the United States. In October, Roh planned a public referendum on his presidency, saying, "I reached a situation in which I cannot conduct the presidency. I have no confidence in doing my job under this situation."

At year's end, the referendum was delayed amid an escalating scandal in which several of Roh's former aides were under investigation for accepting illegal campaign donations during the 2002 election. As the scandal broke and three of his former aides were charged, Roh promised that he would resign if it was proven that his party had taken an amount greater than 10 percent of the illegal campaign donations allegedly received by the opposition GNP. GNP candidate Lee has admitted to accepting US$43 million in illegal contributions during the 2002 campaign.

SRI LANKA

The Sri Lankan government's fragile cease-fire with the separatist Liberation Tigers of Tamil Eelam (LTTE), reached in February 2002 after 20 years of fighting, held throughout 2003 and brought a measure of stability to the media. But political tensions reached a crisis point on November 4, when President Chandrika Kumaratunga suspended Parliament and deployed troops in the capital, Colombo, while her political rival, Prime Minister Ranil Wickremesinghe, was out of the country on an official visit to the United States.

Citing security concerns, Kumaratunga fired key ministers and replaced them with her own appointees, including the minister of information, who is in charge of Sri Lanka's far-reaching state-controlled media. The president also replaced the editors of state-run print and broadcast outlets with journalists aligned with her People's Alliance party. The surprise move came one week after the Tamil rebels proposed a peace plan that formally renounced their goal of a separate state for Tamil nationals in Sri Lanka's northern and eastern territories.

On November 5, Kumaratunga declared a state of emergency and introduced temporary emergency provisions, including media censorship and a ban on demonstrations. However, none of these provisions was enacted since the state of emergency was lifted two days later, on November 7, and replaced with less severe regulations giving extended power to the military. In an address to the country that day, Kumaratunga blamed the prime minister's government for lapses in security and criticized his handling of the peace process. Talks with the Tamil rebels were suspended while the president and the prime minister faced off in a political showdown over the right to represent the country at the negotiating table. Unable to reach a compromise, Kumaratunga and Wickremesinghe remained deadlocked at year's end.

Amid the political crisis, local journalists groups called for the reform of Sri Lanka's state-controlled media. In a November 6 press release, the Sri Lankan press freedom group Free Media Movement called the state-run media a "one-party propaganda machine," criticized the government for appointing political allies to high-ranking positions at media outlets, and urged the government to take "steps to transform state media into genuine public service media institutions."

The cease-fire brought journalists greater access to northern and eastern Sri Lanka in 2003. The military removed roadblocks and checkpoints, and there were fewer reported attacks on members of the media, according to local journalists. However, journalists say that self-censorship remains a major obstacle. Many media outlets are state-run and toe the government's party line, while other private publications and broadcasters reflect specific political or ethnic viewpoints.

Journalists who wrote critical stories about government officials and Tamil rebel groups still risked threats and harassment in 2003. On May 7, Ponniah Manikavasagam, a regular contributor to the BBC and a correspondent for the Tamil-language daily *Virakesari*, received a phone call at his home in Vavuniya accusing him of supporting the LTTE and warning him that he would be "killed very soon." The call was traced to an office run by the Eelam People's Revolutionary Liberation Front, a Tamil group strongly opposed to the Tigers.

On August 7, a group of LTTE activists ambushed a truck delivering the Tamil-language weekly *Thinamurasu* in Sunkankeni and burned about 5,000 copies. *Thinamurasu* is known for its reporting on LTTE human rights abuses and supports the Eelam People's Democratic Party, a Tamil opposition party. According to the newspaper, two of its local correspondents also received death threats in June from an LTTE leader in the northern district of Mannar.

In July, Fisheries Minister Mahinda Wijesekera threatened to have Lasantha Wickramatunga, the editor of *The Sunday Leader*, stabbed or shot to death in retaliation for a series of investigative articles exposing corruption in his ministry. The minister made the threat in the lobby of Parliament in front of other government officials and also alluded to plans to kill two other newspaper editors, *Ravaya* editor Victor Ivan and *Satana* editor Rohana Kumara, according to a report in *The Sunday Leader*. Although the minister issued a statement denying those allegations, he reportedly made similar threats against the journalists in a closed government meeting on August 4. Sri Lankan press freedom groups condemned Wijesekera, but police never investigated the threats, showing that a climate of impunity continues to exist in Sri Lanka.

TAIWAN

TAIWAN'S MEDIA CONTINUED TO OPERATE WITH LITTLE INTERFERENCE IN 2003, though the conviction of a reporter on charges of revealing state secrets renewed an ongoing debate about the importance of national security concerns versus press freedom.

Tensions remained high between Taiwan and mainland China, which considers Taiwan a renegade province and has threatened to take the territory by force. As a result, President Chen Shui-bian's government is very sensitive about media coverage of the military and national security affairs. In recent years, the government has utilized vaguely worded national security laws to prosecute journalists who report on sensitive political issues. In July, the High Court concluded a 3-year-old case by sentencing Hung Che-cheng, a reporter for the now defunct *Jin Pao* (Power News), to 18 months in prison, suspended for three years, on sedition charges. The government alleged that Hung revealed military secrets by reporting that a Chinese warship entered the Taiwan Straits during President Chen's 2000 inauguration. Liu Chih-chung, a Taiwanese army officer, is already serving a two-year sentence for providing the journalist with the so-called secrets.

In response to recent prosecutions of reporters on national security charges, Taiwanese journalists have pointed out that existing laws are too vague and do not spell out clear definitions of "state secrets." In January, Taiwan's legislature, the Legislative Yuan, passed the National Secrets Protection Law, which may help clarify the issue by setting clearer legal boundaries. The new law, which went into effect on October 1, classifies three categories of confidential material and sets a penalty of up to seven years in prison for revealing state secrets. It is not yet clear what, if any, impact the new legislation will have on press freedom.

Tensions with the People's Republic of China also played out in the cross-straits media exchanges that have been set up in recent years. In February, the Taiwanese government suspended broadcasts of China's state-owned China Central Television in response to the mainland's refusal to broadcast Taiwanese television stations. The ban was still in effect at year's end.

The contentious issue of Taiwanese independence will likely be a focus of the presidential election scheduled for March 2004, in which Chen, who supports formal independence from the mainland, will run against Kuomintang (KMT, or nationalist) party candidate Lien Chan. At year's end, cross-straits relations had deteriorated to the lowest point in years after Beijing protested Chen's plan to hold a public referendum asking China to remove missiles aimed at Taiwan.

Chen's Democratic Progressive Party (DPP) took concrete steps in 2003 toward eradicating political ownership of media outlets, which has long been an issue of contention between government officials and press freedom advocates. The DPP proposed revisions to existing broadcasting legislation that would ban civil servants, officials, and political parties from owning, funding, or holding key positions in radio and television companies. All of Taiwan's four major commercial noncable broadcasting outlets—China Television Company, Chinese Television System, Taiwan Television Enterprise, and Formosa Television—are at least partially owned by either the ruling DPP or the KMT, which ruled Taiwan from 1949 until 2000. Some of the stations are widely considered to have a political slant, yet the recent proliferation of independent cable broadcasters has diluted their political influence by giving Taiwanese audiences a broader range of programming.

In June, Chen, who is also chairman of the DPP, called on his party colleagues to show support for the proposal by quitting their media jobs. In response, 12 DPP officials announced at a party meeting in September that they would do so, including legislator Trong Chai, the founder and chairman of Formosa Television. In December, the Legislative Yuan passed the revisions. Under the new laws, all political parties are required to sell their stake in broadcasting stations within two years.

Taiwan's free media often serves as its own best defense, as was evidenced in April, when the government proposed a government-backed system for evaluating news coverage. The Government Information Office announced that it had hired a private foundation to rate the content of the six major Chinese-language newspapers according to standards of justice, objectivity, appropriateness, and accuracy. The evaluation results were to be published every two months. Journalists immediately responded with outrage and accused the government of interfering with the free press. Within a few days, Premier Yu Shyi-kun announced that the plan had been scrapped, but he encouraged the media to practice self-discipline to rein in sensationalistic and inaccurate reporting.

THAILAND

FOR THE LAST TWO YEARS, THAILAND'S POWERFUL AND FREEWHEELING MEDIA have been reeling from the effects of a popular and savvy prime minister who seems intent on using his absolute majority in Parliament to control the press. The process has been as subtle as it has been painful, with journalists saying that most pressure is felt behind closed doors.

Prime Minister Thaksin Shinawatra's powerful political machine and conservative, populist message have enabled the government to stifle criticism since he came to power in 2001. Journalists and editors say privately that they are routinely pressured by the government to alter news coverage and rein in overly critical reporters. On the business side, government advertising has been used to reward some media outlets and punish others.

Occasionally, however, the tensions come to the surface. In November, several newspapers revealed that a family closely allied with Thaksin's ruling Thai Rak Thai party had acquired the largest stake in the Nation Multimedia Group, which is traditionally the most independent media company in the country. Relatives of Thaksin's transport minister purchased about 20 percent of the company, more than twice as much as the next two leading shareholders, causing some critics to fear that *The Nation* newspaper, which is owned by the Nation Multimedia Group, might soon be tamed. "This purchase is linked with political clout and that's what makes us really worried," said prominent academic analyst and government critic Supinya Klangnarong of the nonpartisan Campaign for Media Reform.

Supinya herself is being sued for civil libel by Shin Corporation, the telecommunications empire founded by Thaksin and now formally controlled by members of his family, for comments she made in the *Thai Post* newspaper in July claiming that government policies had benefited the company. Shin Corp., Thailand's largest telecommunications and mobile phone company, is also suing three editors of the *Thai Post* over the article, which charged that the Thai Rak Thai party, founded by Thaksin in 2000 as a platform for his bid for the premiership, had pursued policies aimed at boosting the value of Shin Corporation's core businesses.

The case, which was scheduled to go to trial in 2004, seems destined to become a battle between reform advocates, such as Supinya, and Shin Corporation. At a preliminary hearing in December, some 50 representatives of activist organizations expressed support for Supinya, while lawyers for the company denied any links between the Thaksin government or Thai Rak Thai and Shin Corp. Thaksin, who is believed to be Thailand's richest man, has also denied having any current involvement in his family's businesses.

Thailand has some of the strongest legal and constitutional protections for the media of any country in Asia, and the print media remain largely free despite pressures from the regime. The constitution calls for the privatization of the country's radio and television frequencies, almost all of which are held by the military or government agencies. But procedural delays and wrangling over the shape of broadcast regulations stalled liberalization in 2003, according to critics. Meanwhile, the government, through the military and the office of the prime minister, has the ability to greatly influence radio and television news. The country's sole private television channel, iTV, is controlled by Shin Corp., a purchase that was made in 2000 just in advance of Thaksin's rise to power.

In February, 20 Thai Rak Thai parliamentarians proposed a bill to create a broadcast media council that would have the power to issue ethical guidelines and punish offending outlets with sanctions, including jail and closure. The Thai Journalists Association, Southeast Asian Press Alliance (a regional press freedom group), and other organizations denounced the move as inimical to press freedom. According to many observers, the bill, which had yet to be passed at year's end, was part of a conservative attempt to shape the direction of a planned National Broadcast Commission, which will be in charge of frequency allocation and privatization under a constitutional mandate. Critics contended that academics, journalists, and others were being frozen out of the process in favor of a secretive pro-business agenda pushed by the government. The legislation creating the commission should be finalized in 2004.

Nongovernmental organizations, press groups, and opposition legislators have failed to make progress on other elements of their broad reform agenda. Harsh criminal defamation laws remain on the books, and lawmakers have refused to repeal the 1941 Printing Act, an outdated law that gives authorities the power to close media outlets in times of emergency despite constitutional provisions that contradict the legislation.

Thaksin is famously prickly in his attitudes toward the press, which often engages in self-censorship to avoid his wrath. For example, the government launched a particularly bloody campaign in 2003 to "eliminate" the methamphetamine drug trade. As the death toll soared past 2,000, television news anchors took the government line and repeatedly announced without skepticism that the deaths were the result of gang feuds. Protests by scholars, human rights groups, and senior public figures, who claimed that the police were engaged in extrajudicial executions, went unreported or were relegated to the inside pages of the Thai-language press. Not surprising, there was little or no investigative coverage in the Thai press of the death toll, despite international alarm over the campaign.

Thaksin's attitude toward the media seemed to be summed up in remarks he made to the press corps in May, following a visit to Europe to promote Thai trade relations. "You media people have to believe me," he said. "Today, serving the country is more important than sending your news dispatches daily to your editors. Think before you do anything that damages the country."

TONGA

TONGA'S SMALL MEDIA SECTOR SUFFERED A MAJOR ASSAULT in 2003 from the monarchy of King Taufa'ahau Tupou IV. One of the country's few independent news outlets, *Taimi 'o Tonga* (Times of Tonga), was banned for much of the year, and in October the government passed an amendment that weakens constitutional guarantees of free speech.

Unlike most of its Pacific neighbors, the archipelago nation of Tonga was never colonized by a foreign nation. The current king has ruled since 1965. With the power to appoint heads of state and the Cabinet, the king has installed his son, Crown Prince Tupoutoa, as prime minister. Dissenting views are not easily tolerated, and journalists who expose official wrongdoing are routinely persecuted.

Tonga has only a handful of media outlets, most of which are government owned. The country's few independent publications are routinely harassed for reporting on official scandals or abuses of power.

In 2003, ongoing persecution of the popular, independent, Tongan-language *Taimi 'o Tonga* escalated when authorities banned the paper and declared it an illegal publication that had "ruthlessly campaigned for the overthrow" of the government. The paper's editors told CPJ they believe that the crackdown stemmed from several recent articles that exposed corruption among government officials and the royal family. After the paper challenged the ban in court, Tonga's chief justice declared the government's action illegal.

In July, Parliament passed the Media Operator's Bill, which limits foreign ownership of media organizations. This move was widely viewed as an effort to further silence *Taimi 'o Tonga*, which is published from New Zealand by Kalafi Moala, a native Tongan who has U.S. citizenship.

In October, Parliament passed an amendment to Clause 7 of the Tongan Constitution, which guarantees freedom of expression. The amendment empowers the government to issue laws controlling speech and the media and limits the courts' right to review royal ordinances. Some government officials have claimed that the proposals are aimed at curbing obscenity and nudity, which are not tolerated in the conservative

Christian country. While local reporters have expressed concerns about rumor-mongering and sensationalism in the Tongan media, many agree that increasing government control is not the solution.

The proposals spurred a rare public protest, and about 10,000 people marched to government headquarters on October 6 to deliver a petition opposing the amendment. However, the government ignored the public's anger. According to a report in *Matangi Tonga* magazine, when one citizen told officials that he thought the amendment was unnecessary and was intended to protect those in power, the solicitor general replied, "Well, the media are always targeting the people at the top!"

VIETNAM

THE ALREADY DIRE SITUATION FOR VIETNAMESE JOURNALISTS deteriorated in 2003, with attacks increasing against reporters covering crime and corruption. Those who used the Internet to distribute independent news and opinion faced harsh prison sentences and increasing surveillance. The traditional media remained under the tight regulation of government censors.

In response to escalating repression of independent journalists and political dissidents in 2003, CPJ named Vietnam one of the "World's Worst Places to Be a Journalist." In doing so, CPJ noted that "the government typically accuses independent journalists of endangering national security and treats even moderate criticism of the government or support for democratic reform as treasonous offenses." The arrest of Nguyen Dan Que brought the total number of journalists in prison at year's end to nine. Most of the imprisoned journalists were charged with national security crimes. Three of the journalists in prison had not yet been put on trial by year's end, although two of them—Tran Khue and Pham Que Duong—had been detained for at least a year.

Foreign governments and international human rights and press freedom organizations, including CPJ, expressed outrage at a 13-year prison sentence handed down to Internet essayist Pham Hong Son in June. Three months later, in unusual deference to international pressure, the Hanoi Supreme Court reduced Son's sentence to five years on appeal. In November, after spending more than nine months in incommunicado detention, elderly writer Tran Dung Tien was given a 10-month sentence on charges of "abusing democratic rights to harm the interests of the state." He was released a week after his trial.

Authorities routinely use the threat of jail time to silence those who use the Internet to distribute information or viewpoints banned from the official press. Five of the eight journalists in prison, including Son, were targeted after writing or distributing information online.

Vietnam currently has 2.7 million Internet users, double the number of a year ago, according to official figures, and the technological infrastructure has not been able to keep up with this rapid increase. In 2003, the government announced initiatives to improve Internet connections by allowing new Internet service providers (ISPs) to operate and by installing two new gateways linking Vietnam to Hong Kong and Shanghai, China. The government determines what information Internet users can access by directly controlling the gateways that link Vietnamese ISPs with the rest of the world, and by a series of regulations limiting online content. An April editorial in the *Hanoi Quan Doi Nhan Dan*, the official publication of the Vietnamese army, acknowledged that the firewall has "caused serious bottlenecks to Internet connection and traffic." The editorial advocated a more efficient censorship system and called for the consolidation of technical Internet controls, a comprehensive list of banned Web sites, and severer punishments for individuals who access forbidden sites.

ISPs and cybercafé owners are held legally responsible if their customers access banned information online. As a way of justifying such regulations, a Culture and Information Ministry official explained, "Restaurant owners must guarantee the food is free from harmful substances. Therefore it's the same with Internet café owners. They are not allowed to provide young people with poisonous substances."

The Culture and Information Ministry oversees all traditional media content, and harsh penalties threaten journalists who overstep the official boundaries in their reporting. In July, the ministry suspended *Sinh Vien Vietnam* magazine, which was very popular among students and youth, for "serious wrongdoings in the content of its news and articles, photo selection and layout." Among the offending issues was one that included a picture of a banknote imprinted with a photo of revolutionary leader Ho Chi Minh floating in a toilet, and another that ran a cover photo of a nude statue.

Top government officials have acknowledged that crime and corruption are among the most severe challenges facing Vietnamese society and politics, and in response, the state-run media have reported more vigorously on these issues. Journalists faced an additional threat in 2003, with corrupt officials and criminals implicated by press reports seeking violent retribution. CPJ documented four attacks on journalists in 2003, a marked increase over previous years. In one of the most egregious examples, two reporters from official publications were beaten by the chairman of a village cooperative while investigating villagers' complaints about embezzlement by commune officials. Police later filed a report accusing the journalists of "disorderly conduct." While the official press does occasionally report on incidents of violence against journalists, police are often slow to respond to such attacks. ■

КУЧМА, ДЕ
ГОНГАДЗ

OVERVIEW: EUROPE AND CENTRAL ASIA

by Alex Lupis

WHILE INTEGRATION INTO NATO AND THE EUROPEAN UNION has had a positive effect on press freedom conditions in most of Central Europe and the Baltic states, the situation for journalists in Russia and the former Soviet republics has worsened steadily, with governments relying on authoritarian tactics to silence the media. Even reformist governments in the Balkans failed to make significant improvements in press freedom conditions because most leaders in the region avoided addressing the lawlessness, government corruption, and organized crime that plague their societies.

Despite advocating democratic reforms, many progressive politicians in the Balkans continue to believe that independent media should not criticize government policies. The assassination of Serbian Prime Minister Zoran Djindjic in March, for example, led to the imposition of a state of emergency for 42 days, during which journalists were prohibited from reporting or commenting on "the reasons for the declaration of the state of emergency." The Culture Ministry used the vaguely defined restrictions to fine and shutter media outlets in an arbitrary and heavy-handed manner. Throughout the rest of 2003, journalists in the Balkans endured threats, politically motivated lawsuits, and violent attacks, mostly from politicians and government officials.

Although the number of journalists in Europe and Central Asia killed or imprisoned for their work decreased in 2003—from three to one killed and from eight to six imprisoned—these smaller numbers did not reflect an improvement in safety or growing tolerance for independent news reporting. Rather, they highlighted the success of silencing journalists through more subtle forms of intimidation, such as politicized court rulings and financial pressure on media owners. Government repression of online reporting increased. And in Russia, the government continued its ferocious restrictions on coverage of the conflict in the southern republic of Chechnya while the rest of world stood by, ignoring the information void about a war that has claimed tens of thousands of lives during the last decade.

In 2003, one journalist was killed in Russia for his work. Aleksei Sidorov, editor-in-chief of the independent newspaper *Tolyatinskoye Obozreniye* in the Volga River city of Togliatti, was stabbed to death outside his home in October because of the paper's reporting on organized crime and local government corruption. He was the newspaper's second editor-in-chief to be murdered in 18 months.

Two other murdered journalists in Europe and Central Asia may have been targeted in retaliation for their reporting. Dmitry Shvets, deputy director of the independent TV-21 station in the northern Russian city of Murmansk, was shot dead outside the station's offices in April, possibly because of the station's coverage of a politician's links to organized crime. Ernis Nazalov, a Kyrgyz journalist for the Bishkek daily *Kyrgyz Ruhu*, died in the southern Kara-Suu District in September while investigating government corruption in the Osh regional administration. His body was found on the bank

Alex Lupis is CPJ's program coordinator for Europe and Central Asia. Freelance writer **Genine Babakian** and CPJ Research Associate **Nina Ognianova** contributed to the research and writing of this section.

Photo (previous page): A man in Ukraine's capital, Kyiv, marks the third anniversary of the September 16, 2000, murder of journalist Georgy Gongadze with a candle and a photo of the journalist. *AP/Efrem Lukatsky*

RUSSIA
BELARUS
UKRAINE
MOLDOVA
CROATIA
ROMANIA
BOSNIA AND
HERZEGOVINA
SERBIA AND
MONTENEGRO
ALBANIA
GEORGIA
ARMENIA
AZERBAIJAN
KAZAKHSTAN
UZBEKISTAN
TURKMENISTAN
KYRGYZSTAN
TAJIKISTAN

of a canal, and an incomplete police investigation has raised suspicions that he may have been murdered.

Almost all of the murders of journalists in the region during the last decade remain unsolved. Ukrainian authorities, for example, continued to actively obstruct the investigation into the September 2000 disappearance and murder of Georgy Gongadze, editor of *Ukrayinska Pravda*, an online publication that often reported on government corruption. In neighboring Belarus, authorities obstructed an investigation into allegations that senior government officials were involved in the July 2000 disappearance and murder of Russian cameraman Dmitry Zavadsky. One of the few cases that has actually gone to trial, the October 1994 assassination of Dmitry Kholodov, a reporter for the independent Russian newspaper *Moskovsky Komsomolets* who had investigated corruption in the Defense Ministry, took six years to go before the courts and had not produced a conviction by year's end.

The legacy of unsolved murders has fostered a culture of fear and self-censorship in countries such as Tajikistan, where dozens of journalists were killed during the 1992-1997 civil war between the People's Front, a paramilitary organization led by the current president, Imomali Rakhmonov, and opposition parties. CPJ sent a delegation to Tajikistan in July that pressed senior officials from the Interior Ministry and Prosecutor General's Office to investigate and prosecute those responsible for the murders. Little or no progress has been made in most cases, and local journalists expressed skepticism that the government has any interest in solving them. In August, CPJ sent a list of journalists killed during the civil war to the Prosecutor General's Office. The prosecutor general replied in December that an investigative group would initiate inquiries into a number of murder cases that officials had not been aware of.

Not surprisingly, self-censorship is on the rise throughout the region, encouraged by politicized media regulators, bribery, and judges who are holdovers from the Soviet era and habitually rule in favor of the state. Growing self-censorship is also reflected in the steady decline of investigative reporting on some of the region's most serious problems, such as rampant government corruption, organized crime, and human rights violations. Alexei Simonov, president of the Glasnost Defense Fund, a Moscow-based nongovernmental organization that monitors press freedom, believes that, "Investigative journalism is becoming an extraordinarily dangerous profession," and this is depriving Russian society of its "eyes and ears."

While some Russian newspapers like the Moscow-based twice-weekly *Novaya Gazeta* have developed a strong tradition of exposing government abuses and continue to do so, others have been dissuaded after seeing colleagues murdered, beaten, prosecuted, and fined. Journalists who have opted for publishing on the Internet—like Andrei Soldatov, who runs the Web site *Agentura.ru* and specializes in writing about Russia's powerful security services—have been detained and questioned by security forces angered by articles about their activities.

The number of imprisoned journalists in the region dropped slightly, from eight at the end of 2002 to six at the end of 2003. In Belarus, three journalists were released, while Russian authorities freed one, military journalist Grigory Pasko. However, two others were put behind bars in Uzbekistan.

Uzbekistan remained the region's leading jailer of journalists, with five imprisoned at year's end. Mukhammad Bekdzhanov, editor of *Erk*, a newspaper published by the banned opposition Erk party, and Yusuf Ruzimuradov, an *Erk* employee, were sentenced to 14 years and 15 years in prison, respectively, in August 1999 for distributing *Erk* and criticizing the government. Madzhid Abduraimov, a correspondent with the national weekly *Yangi Asr*, was sentenced to 13 years in August 2001 for writing about corruption.

The two new journalists jailed in 2003 in Uzbekistan reflected the regime's efforts to silence the country's younger and more independent-minded journalists who criticize government polices. In February, Gayrat Mehliboyev, a 23-year-old freelancer, was charged with anticonstitutional activity and sentenced to seven years in prison after an April 2001 article in the state-run Tashkent newspaper *Hurriyet* questioned the compatibility of Islam and democracy. In August, Ruslan Sharipov, a 25-year-old press freedom activist and reporter for the Russian news agency Prima, was sentenced to five-and-a-half years in prison on charges of homosexuality. For years, police and National Security Service agents have harassed Sharipov—who is openly gay—because he has criticized police abuses and press freedom violations.

Sharipov was also jailed in part because his articles were posted on the Internet in English, making his criticisms of the Uzbek government accessible to a wider international audience. Previously, governments in the region were content to block controversial news and opposition Web sites. But in 2003, officials became more sensitive to online criticism and blatantly disregarded efforts by international and nongovernmental organizations to promote greater tolerance for dissent.

In early 2003, a court in Kazakhstan's financial capital, Almaty, sentenced Sergei Duvanov, a prominent independent journalist who wrote for opposition-financed Web sites and edited a human rights bulletin, to three-and-a-half years in prison for allegedly raping a minor. The trial was closed to the public and marred by numerous procedural violations. Duvanov, who denied the rape charges and claimed that they were politically motivated, is known for his criticism of high-level Kazakh officials, and authorities have frequently harassed him in reprisal for his work. In December, a court ruled that Duvanov could serve the rest of his term in a low-security facility.

Russian authorities also conducted a campaign to suppress news on the Internet by pressing neighboring Estonia and Lithuania to close the pro-independence Chechen news Web site *kavkazcenter.com*. Sergei Yastrezhembsky, an adviser to Russian President Vladimir Putin, warned Estonian authorities in April that, "Countries which aspire to partnership and mutually advantageous relations with the Russian Federation should bear in mind Russia's categorical objection to the hosting of information resources on behalf of Chechen separatists," the ITAR-TASS news agency reported.

The Kremlin's aggressive efforts to close Web sites reporting on the conflict in Chechnya were part of a broader campaign to silence all independent coverage of the conflict. Despite a public relations campaign by the Kremlin claiming that life in Chechnya is returning to normal, few journalists dared to travel to the region, and those who did remained at serious risk. In July, unknown armed assailants in Ingushetia, a southern republic neighboring Chechnya, abducted Agence France-Presse correspondent Ali Astamirov. In the months prior to his abduction, police officers and FSB agents had repeatedly harassed Astamirov and obstructed his efforts to report on developments in Chechnya. At year's end, no progress was reported in the investigation into his kidnapping.

Various branches of Russia's government continued to intimidate journalists reporting on the conflict. In February, the Media Ministry issued an official warning to the Moscow-based, ultranationalist weekly *Zavtra* for publishing an interview with an exiled Chechen separatist leader. That same month, an Interior Ministry unit in Chechnya's capital, Grozny, detained and assaulted Zamid Ayubov, a journalist for the local pro-Russian administration's thrice-weekly *Vozrozhdeniye Chechni*, while he was researching the activities of police units conducting evening patrols. In March, the Prosecutor's Office in the Siberian city of Nizhnevartovsk cleared a military officer accused of issuing death threats against Anna Politkovskaya, a war correspondent covering Chechnya for *Novaya Gazeta*.

In Azerbaijan, a repressive regime underwent a dynastic change in 2003, and analysts speculate that other despots in the region will soon follow suit. The country's ailing leader, President Heydar Aliyev, appointed his son Ilham Aliyev as prime minister in August, clearing the way for a transfer of power during presidential elections scheduled for October. Authorities aggressively cracked down on the independent and opposition media to suppress reporting on the president's deteriorating health and his son's ascent to power in what international observers characterized as a fraudulent vote. Heydar Aliyev passed away in December, and his son continued to rely on the police, courts, and security services to suppress independent news reporting. Regional analysts pointed out that the presidents of Kazakhstan and Uzbekistan appeared to be grooming their daughters to succeed them, a development likely to perpetuate the region's restrictive policies toward the media.

Perhaps the most hopeful development in the former Soviet republics was Georgia's so-called velvet revolution: the forced resignation of the country's corrupt and highly unpopular president, Eduard Shevardnadze, in November. Rustavi-2, a private national television station known for its independent reporting—a rarity in post-Soviet countries—played a pivotal role with its coverage of protesters who were angered by fraudulent parliamentary elections and sought to oust Sheverdnadze. Rustavi-2 endured an intense campaign of harassment during the crisis—the Central Electoral Commission tried to revoke the station's broadcasting license, and unknown assailants attacked the outlet's offices with a grenade launcher. The popular uprising was the region's first anti-corruption revolt, and it highlighted the role independent media can play in promoting government accountability.

ALBANIA

ALBANIA'S CONTENTIOUS POLITICAL ENVIRONMENT and economic underdevelopment continued to make the country a relatively chaotic and difficult place for the independent press in 2003. Journalists faced government pressure, criminal libel lawsuits, arbitrary dismissal by politicized owners, and limited access to basic government information, particularly when investigating official corruption and organized crime. Furthermore, low professional standards, an editorial emphasis on sensationalism, and the financial influence of political parties over many media outlets give journalists little public credibility and often force the press to practice self-censorship.

Albanian media derive much of their income from advertising from state-run firms, and the government continued to use this carrot to divert advertising toward outlets that provided positive coverage of government polices and the ruling Socialist Party.

Prime Minister Fatos Nano's government received favorable coverage from all three national television stations—Albanian State Television, the independent TV Arberia, and the independent TV KLAN—because his ruling Socialist Party retained strong influence over the state broadcaster Radio Television Albania (RTSH) and the broadcast regulatory body, the National Council on Radio and Television (NCRT).

In some cases, the government took a heavy-handed approach toward enforcing media regulations. The NCRT closed the independent broadcaster ALBA TV in August for violating regulations and not paying license fees. According to CPJ sources, because the closure violated legal procedures and was implemented so aggressively, management at other stations feared being shut down, creating a climate of self-censorship.

Intimidation and attacks against journalists are less common than they were in the 1990s, when war was blazing in neighboring Kosovo and the Albanian government was reeling from a national scandal over failed pyramid schemes.

Campaigning for October 12 local elections led to increased political pressure on media outlets, with politicians hurling wild accusations and counteraccusations against each other in the press. There were reports of threats against journalists, financial pressure on media outlets, and a series of lawsuits filed against journalists in the run-up to the poll. The most outrageous incident occurred two days after the elections at a celebration organized by the ruling Socialist Party. Minister of Public Order Luan Rama and his bodyguards beat journalist Ilir Babaramo, editor-in-chief of Vizion Plus TV, because he had helped produce a story about the ministry's poor record in fighting crime. The prime minister dismissed Rama four days later, after an outcry by journalists and human rights and press freedom groups.

On October 1, five human rights and press freedom organizations filed a lawsuit with the Constitutional Court challenging a secret executive gag order issued by Prime Minister Nano in August 2002. The executive order prohibited senior government officials from providing journalists with information about their official activities. The five plaintiffs argued that the order violated domestic and international laws on freedom of expression. During a November 17 hearing on the case, a government representative informed the Constitutional Court that the executive order had been revoked, and the case was immediately closed.

ARMENIA

IN 2003, PRESIDENTIAL AND PARLIAMENTARY ELECTIONS DOMINATED Armenia's political scene. Though President Robert Kocharian managed to retain power, tens of thousands of demonstrators angered by widespread electoral fraud took to the streets in protest before the March runoff, calling for his resignation.

While state television did not cover the mass rallies, it did broadcast one unprecedented event on the eve of the second round of voting: a live debate between the two presidential candidates. Though this was seen as a positive sign, the runoff was marred by fraud, according to U.S. and Western observers.

There were several blows to media freedom in 2003, starting with an April amendment to the Criminal Code making libel a criminal offense punishable by up to three years in prison. The new code also carries harsher punishments for insulting government officials. More disturbing, in December, Parliament passed a new bill that requires media outlets to disclose their sources of information in closed court hearings if it is determined to relate to national security.

But the biggest threat to media freedom was the continued ban on the independent television station A1+. In a country where 85 percent of the population receives its news from television, the A1+ case has become a touchstone for press freedom. Known for its professional standards and harsh criticism of the government, A1+ was yanked off the air in April 2002 in the country's first ever frequency tender, a government procedure that allows for broadcast licenses to be issued (or, in this case, reissued) in an allegedly fair and free process. In an attempt to silence A1+, the president had stacked the National Council on Television and Radio, the government body that oversees broadcast frequencies and licenses, with loyalists who rejected the station's application.

A1+ made several attempts to regain its frequency in a series of tenders, but the government's Broadcasting Commission repeatedly rejected the station's bid in favor of outlets owned by supporters of the president. The first tender of 2003, scheduled for January, was postponed, preventing viewers from accessing A1+ before the presidential elections. While the Broadcasting Commission cited financial concerns and technical reasons for repeatedly rejecting A1+'s bid, many believe that the order came directly from Kocharian.

Armenia's print media enjoy relative freedom but are largely controlled by political parties and wealthy businessmen, which dampens outlets' objectivity. The print press is also plagued by low professional standards. According to IREX ProMedia, a U.S.-based media training organization, journalists in Armenia often take bribes for writing articles.

Meanwhile, the ongoing investigations and trials in two high-profile murder cases captivated the country. In December 2002, the head of Armenian Public Television (APT), Tigran Nagdalian, was shot dead in the capital, Yerevan. A loyal supporter of Kocharian, Nagdalian had been scheduled to testify in the other prominent murder case: the trial of six men accused of gunning down eight high-ranking politicians in Parliament in 1999.

The two cases were linked by political intrigue and speculation. Some families of those murdered in Parliament suggest that Nagdalian was killed because he had information about Kocharian's involvement in the murders. The presidential administration countered with the theory that the opposition killed Nagdalian because he had used his job at APT, the country's most watched TV station, to promote Kocharian and marginalize his rivals. Several months after the murder, the younger brother of a political rival of Kocharian's was arrested for hiring a gunman to kill Nagdalian. Opposition members have condemned the arrest as politically motivated.

AZERBAIJAN

IN JANUARY 2003, PRESIDENT HEYDAR ALIYEV FROZE THE PRINT MEDIA'S debts to the state publishing house through 2005. But that was the only positive development for the Azerbaijani press in what turned out to be a dismal year.

With Aliyev's health failing as 2003 wore on, he began grooming his son Ilham Aliyev to take his place, a move that drew the ire of opposition parties and newspapers. In August, the president appointed his son as prime minister, clearing the way for a transfer of power during presidential elections scheduled for October. Heydar Aliyev passed away in December.

Before he died, Heydar Aliyev managed to keep tight control of his oil-rich nation, including the press. Defamation suits remained a huge problem for the media in 2003. Dozens of defamation lawsuits were filed against independent newspapers throughout the year, according to IREX ProMedia, a U.S.-based media training organization.
In February, libel suits against *Yeni Musavat*, a newspaper associated with the popular opposition party Musavat, resulted in fines of 100,000 euros (US$127,500)—an overwhelming sum for a paper with assets of one-fifth that amount. In a country where local and federal authorities can easily pressure the judicial system, cases against media outlets rarely end in their favor.

Typically, officials use defamation suits to respond to articles implicating them in corruption, which is rife in Azerbaijan. According to Transparency International, an international nonprofit dedicated to combating corruption, Azerbaijan ranked a dismal 95 out of 102 countries on the organization's Corruption Perceptions Index.

In June, the Azerbaijani National Council for Television and Radio adopted new regulations on the use of the state language in the broadcast media, further restricting the use of Russian—the language most older Azerbaijani citizens use.

More blatant forms of harassment followed when the independent press began to focus on Aliyev's failing health. With the government refusing to release any information, many newspapers questioned the president's ability to run the country—a development that pro-government forces saw as a direct assault on Aliyev. These reports were followed by several attacks against journalists. Police officers also detained and beat reporters from opposition newspapers. Violence against the press only increased as the October 15 election neared.

The severity of the Azerbaijani government's abuse of the press did not go unnoticed by Western observers. In a fairly unprecedented September 10 joint statement, the Council of Europe and the Organization for Security and Co-operation in Europe criticized the government for its harassment and intimidation of journalists. The statement specifically expressed concern over "recent attacks against journalists," demanded "a thorough investigation" into the attacks, and asked the authorities to "take all necessary steps to guarantee respect for freedom of the media." The international community also called on Azerbaijan to conduct a free and fair election.

In the run-up to the poll, however, opposition candidates were given little airtime on government-controlled broadcast media—considerably less than Ilham Aliyev. During the election, international observers noted many irregularities, including multiple voting and the stuffing of ballot boxes, as well as omissions from voting lists of those known to support the opposition. In the end, officials declared Ilham Aliyev the victor with 80 percent of the vote.

Pressure from the international community, as well as the presence of international observers, had little effect on security forces during the demonstrations that erupted into violence after the election results were announced. Dozens of journalists were severely beaten and/or detained. The government crackdown was not contained to the capital,

Baku, where the riots occurred, but spread throughout the country. Local election officials who refused to sign falsified voting tally sheets were threatened or arrested, and their families were also subject to reprisals.

In the weeks following the elections, attacks on Azerbaijan's opposition press intensified. Libel suits resumed, resulting in enormous fines and, in some cases, frozen bank accounts. Arrests and intimidation continued. Rauf Arifoglu, the editor of Azerbaijan's largest opposition newspaper, *Yeni Musavat*, was arrested in October and held in prison for the rest of the year while prosecutors investigated his role in the postelection violence. Many opposition newspapers were denied access to the state printing house and distribution system.

Despite these hardships, the opposition press continues to publish in Azerbaijan. *Yeni Musavat*, which already has the highest circulation among newspapers in the Southern Caucasus, increased its numbers even after it was banned from the state printing house and distribution system.

BELARUS

Squeezed by the expansion of NATO and the European Union to the west and tepid relations with Russia to the east, Belarus grew ever more isolated. In the face of that isolation, President Aleksandr Lukashenko continued his assault on the media in 2003, tightening his grip on the impoverished country. Local analysts suspect that Lukashenko's ironfisted approach to the media is an attempt to stifle criticism of his political allies in the run-up to parliamentary elections in 2004, thus ensuring passage of an amendment to the constitution that would allow him to extend his term in office.

Belarus' obedient state media supported Lukashenko's authoritarian policies by discrediting political opponents and arguing that political and media restrictions are necessary to maintain political stability. Loyal judges and security officials punished journalists who questioned state policies, and the politicized bureaucracy charged excessive fees to print and distribute independent newspapers, while channeling budget subsidies, discounts, and tax privileges to the state-run media.

Though criminal libel laws have been in effect since 1999, officials used the statutes for the first time in 2002, targeting journalists who criticized Lukashenko's fraudulent reelection in 2001. Three journalists with independent newspapers—Mikola Markevich and Paval Mazheika of *Pahonya* and Viktar Ivashkevich of *Rabochy*—received corrective labor sentences in 2002 for libeling the president in 2001 in pre-election articles.

Markevich and Mazheika received court-granted early releases in March 2003 after each had served the first six months of their two-and-a-half- and two-year sentences, respectively. Ivashkevich was amnestied in December after serving the first year of his sentence at a corrective labor facility. The independent Belarusian Association of Journalists continued its campaign to decriminalize libel to no avail.

Politically motivated civil libel lawsuits resulting in exorbitant fines have debilitated the media, forcing some outlets, such as the independent newspaper *Nasha Svaboda*, to close. In early 2003, the newspapers *Vecherny Stolin* and *Provintsyyalka* in the western Brest Region were suspended for allegedly libeling local government officials ahead of the March local elections. Both papers remained embroiled in libel lawsuits for much of the year.

In late May, the popular Minsk daily *Belorusskaya Delovaya Gazeta* (*BDG*) was suspended for three months after it received three warnings from the Information Ministry for allegedly defaming Lukashenko and improperly publishing information about court proceedings. *BDG*'s attempts to appeal the suspension were rejected, and independent Belarusian publications that later printed *BDG* articles in their pages were harassed and in some cases suspended. The Moscow-based twice-weekly *Novaya Gazeta* published *BDG* for a time, and it finally resumed publication in Belarus in September.

Tense relations between Lukashenko and Russian President Vladimir Putin over a stalled union proposal (Lukashenko wants a union of two equal states and Putin wants a union in which Belarus is subordinate to Russia) led Lukashenko's government to restrict public access to state-run Russian television and radio broadcasts, one of the few remaining sources of independent news in the country.

In June, the government expelled Pavel Selin, a Minsk correspondent for the Russian NTV television network, because he reported that authorities had interfered with the funeral procession of the celebrated pro-democracy Belarusian author Vasil Bykau. Selin, who has been officially declared persona non grata and banned from entering Belarus for five years, returned to Moscow. In early July, the Belarusian Council of Ministers closed NTV's Minsk bureau.

Belarusian authorities also cracked down on U.S. government–funded organizations providing assistance to local media. In July, the Foreign Ministry refused to extend the accreditations of the International Research and Exchanges Board and Internews Network, forcing them to close their Minsk offices and ending their media training programs.

Lukashenko raised the specter of yet another crackdown on the press when he announced plans to create an autocratic state ideology during his state-of-the-union address in April. The ideology would rely on the media to permeate every aspect of society and act as the "immunity system that protects society from internal and external threats." In the summer and fall, he continued to elaborate on plans to restore Soviet-style propaganda through the media, college lecturers, and a network of state propaganda organizations.

Lukashenko also called for a more repressive new Mass Media Law to punish independent media outlets that do not fit his "ideological" vision. He said that the legislation "should block those that want to manipulate the public opinion and intentionally misinform the population," and that he is "deeply convinced that journalism is a state-oriented profession."

The draft Mass Media Law was kept secret for much of 2003. Copies obtained by journalists in the fall revealed that it would simplify government procedures to shutter media outlets and expand the law's coverage to news Web sites, which have become an alternative source of information and opinion for Belarusians. The law awaited approval by Parliament at year's end.

The July 2000 disappearance of Russian cameraman Dmitry Zavadsky continues to evoke local and international outrage and serves as a chilling reminder of the serious threats that journalists face. Although two former members of Belarus' elite Almaz special forces unit were convicted in 2002 of kidnapping Zadavsky, state prosecutors have failed to investigate allegations that senior government officials may have been involved. CPJ has repeatedly called for an independent international investigation of this case.

In late November 2003, a court in Minsk declared Zavadsky dead at the request of his widow, Svetlana. In mid-December, prosecutors announced they had reopened the Zavadsky investigation about 48 hours before the Council of Europe, a pan-Europe human rights monitoring organization, released a report alleging that high-level government officials were involved in the journalist's disappearance and its subsequent cover-up.

BOSNIA AND HERZEGOVINA

CORRUPTION AND POLITICAL CHAOS IN BOSNIA AND HERZEGOVINA gave journalists many scandals to cover in 2003, from massive fraud at state power companies to illegal weapons sales to Iraq.

Journalists endured a wide array of harassment and abuses, including threatening phone calls, politically motivated tax inspections, retaliatory lawsuits, and physical attacks, most of which were initiated by politicians, businessmen, government officials, and the police. Hopes for greater accountability for press freedom abuses were dashed by the October 2002 general elections, when the three nationalist political parties that led the country into a brutal civil war in the 1990s were all voted back into office at both local and national levels.

Their electoral victories emboldened some nationalists to suppress news reporting they deemed unfavorable. A group of university students linked with the Muslim nationalist Party for Democratic Action (SDA) in the capital, Sarajevo, threatened and harassed journalists from Bosnia and Herzegovina's weekly television news program "60 Minutes" in January for their reporting on a secret training camp run by Iranian intelligence agents during the civil war. Police were posted around the Federation Television (FTV) building for several days to protect the "60 Minutes" staff.

The internationally run Office of the High Representative (OHR), which oversees the implementation of the peace accords in Bosnia and Herzegovina and has legal authority over the country, continued to press ahead with political reforms under the leadership of liberal British politician Paddy Ashdown. Ashdown pressed the ruling nationalist parties to strengthen the central government by integrating the country's two ministates: the Serb-dominated Republika Srpska and the Croat-Muslim dominated Federation.

Many journalists remained skeptical of these new political reforms, since legislation passed in 2001 granting access to government information had still not been implemented. Ashdown's forceful personality alienated many independent journalists in Sarajevo who thought he was working too closely with corrupt nationalist parties that were guilty of genocide and ethnic cleansing.

As part of its broader campaign to centralize state institutions, OHR continued to press for the creation of a national public broadcasting system, as well as two other official broadcasters, FTV and Radio Television Republika Srpska (RTRS). This policy left independent broadcasters such as the Mreza Plus network at a major disadvantage, scrambling for advertising amid a stagnant economy and declining international financial assistance.

The internationally supervised Communications Regulatory Agency continued to strictly monitor and enforce broadcast media regulations. In September, the Federation Intelligence Security Service leaked a transcript to the independent Sarajevo daily *Dnevni Avaz* implicating a prominent reformist politician in a series of explosions that shook Sarajevo during the summer. The leak was seen by many journalists as a smear campaign and an attempt by the new nationalist authorities to discredit a senior official from the previous government.

Impunity for attacks against journalists remained the norm in 2003. No progress was reported in the Republika Srpska police investigation into the October 1999 assassination attempt against Zeljko Kopanja, editor of the daily *Nezavisne Novine*, who lost both legs when a bomb destroyed his car. Kopanja had just published several articles about Serbian war crimes. Despite the country's sluggish economy, *Nezavisne Novine* increased its circulation and advertising revenue in 2003 by continuing to publish hard-hitting news about local politics and war crimes.

Political interference in public radio and television also remained a serious problem at the local and national level. In June, politicians in the northwestern town of Sanki Most ousted Midhat Dedic, the director of the municipal radio station Radio SANA. In October, the Republika Srpska Parliament exceeded its legal authority and tried to gain control of RTRS by passing a resolution demanding that the board of governors, director, and news editors resign. That same month, FTV Director Jasmin Durakovic resigned when the Federation Parliament passed a resolution requiring FTV to broadcast all of Parliament's sessions. According to Durakovic, the resolution amounted to government interference in the editorial independence of a public television station and was a financial burden on the station.

Much of the media remained divided along ethnic lines. The Sarajevo office of IREX ProMedia, a U.S.-based media training organization, held a series of meetings throughout 2003 to encourage four of the country's six journalists' associations to work together to strengthen advocacy for greater press freedom and professional responsibility. The four organizations prepared to establish a state-wide association of journalists.

CROATIA

GRADUAL POLITICAL STABILIZATION IN THE WESTERN BALKANS and the implementation of political reforms required for Croatia to join the European Union by 2007 have led to greater press freedom and media pluralism in the country. However, rivalries in the ruling reformist coalition, a powerful far-right opposition, politicized media owners, and a judiciary in need of reform continued to prevent more balanced reporting by Croatia's lively and influential press.

Physical attacks against journalists have become rarer; in 2003, there were only two reported assaults on media executives. On March 1, a bomb destroyed the car of influential newspaper publisher Nino Pavic in the capital, Zagreb. The bombing occurred after several journalists at Pavic's popular independent weekly *Globus* received threats following a series of articles about organized crime. The second attack occurred on December 17, when Ivan Caleta, owner of the independent national broadcaster Nova TV, was shot in the leg while entering his car in Zagreb. Some journalists linked both incidents to the victims' murky business activities. Police investigations remained inconclusive at year's end.

Croatian Radio Television (HRT) and its two branches—Croatian Television (HTV) and Croatian Radio—made progress in transitioning from a politicized state broadcaster to an autonomous public broadcaster. Economic reforms encouraged greater diversity in the broadcast media, and the commercial success of the independent, national broadcaster NOVA TV and the CCN television network forced HTV's influential news programs to begin competing for viewers. In September, Germany's largest private broadcaster, RTL, won the rights to broadcast nationally on HTV's third channel for the next 10 years.

In 2003, Parliament approved the HRT Law, the Electronic Media Law, the Media Law, and the Access to Information Law, all of which strengthened legal protections for the media and improved access to government information. For the first time, nongovernmental organizations such as the Croatian Helsinki Committee and the Croatian Journalists Association were allowed to comment on early drafts of the laws.

In a misguided effort to curry favor with the United Nations and Western governments, the Croatian government pressured a reporter to provide information about an indicted war crimes suspect. On October 3, just days before a visit to the country by the chief prosecutor of the U.N. War Crimes Tribunal at The Hague, police questioned Ivo Pukanic, editor-in-chief of the independent weekly *Nacional*, about his contacts with Ante Gotovina, an indicted war crimes suspect who is currently in hiding. Pukanic had published an interview with Gotovina in June.

In July, Parliament approved amendments to the Criminal Code that expanded criminal slander and libel provisions. Journalists face up to one year in prison under criminal libel laws. The amendments, which would have required journalists to prove that published information was either true or that they believed it was true, were set to take effect in December. But Parliament repealed them on October 15, pleasing those who feared that the new requirements would have increased self-censorship.

Frustration with poor economic growth led voters to oust Croatia's pro-Western, left-of-center ruling coalition in national elections held in November. The Croatian Democratic Union (HDZ), a nationalist opposition party that ruled Croatia with an iron fist in the 1990s and committed widespread abuses against the press, took the largest share of the vote, forming a minority right-wing government.

Although the HDZ sought to reassure voters during the campaign that it had moved beyond right-wing policies, some journalists were concerned about the future of press freedom. Journalists were particularly alarmed in October when the HDZ's new prime minister, Ivo Sanaders, threatened a journalist from Croatian Radio at an election rally in the eastern city of Osijek. According to press reports, Sanaders was upset by what he said was biased reporting against the HDZ.

GEORGIA

After 11 years in office, President Eduard Shevardnadze and his corruption-ridden government grew increasingly unpopular in 2003. Approval ratings plummeted, culminating in November elections marred by widespread fraud that discredited pro-Shevardnadze forces' claim of victory. Facing escalating protests against the poll, the president resigned on November 23. New presidential and parliamentary elections were scheduled for early 2004.

Throughout 2003, Georgia was consumed by election fever. Although a number of publications present a broad spectrum of views, with little money available to buy newspapers and magazines, most people rely on television as their main source of news. Independent television station Rustavi-2 broadcast the voices and protests of the opposition, thereby strengthening the anti-Shevardnadze movement and helping to bring about the president's resignation.

However, whether the opposition will be an improvement over Shevardnadze remains unclear. The troika of political leaders who temporarily controlled the government until new presidential elections in January 2004 quickly appointed some of their cronies to high-level positions, despite being well-known as reformers. But after criticism from the Liberty Institute, a Tbilisi-based human rights organization that backed the opposition in its showdown with Shevardnadze, the questionable appointees were removed.

Colleagues of slain television journalist Georgy Sanaya, who was murdered in July 2001, were outraged by the verdict in the trial of his accused killer in July 2003. Disregarding arguments that Sanaya's murder was connected to his work, the court convicted the man who gunned him down without searching for those who masterminded the killing. The popular television host was known for both his investigative work and his political talk show on the independent Rustavi-2 television station. His supporters say he was killed because of his efforts to expose government corruption, and to discourage his colleagues at the station from pursuing the same stories.

On the eve of the flawed November elections, the Central Electoral Commission (CEC) attempted to revoke Rustavi-2's license but did not follow through. Some sources speculate that because the station is so popular, the CEC feared sparking additional antigovernment riots with a closure. For years, Rustavi-2 has endured threats, harassment, tax audits, and attacks. In 2003, angry politicians implicated in scandals by the network's famous "60 Minutes" program filed libel suits against the station. Culture Minister Valeri Asatiani filed a US$4.6 million criminal libel suit with the Supreme Court against Rustavi-2 after the station aired a report in April 2000 that linked him to a murder. The Supreme Court also asked the general prosecutor to conduct a criminal inquiry into Rustavi-2's activities because of its aggressive coverage of corruption in the judiciary and police. The court's request appeared to be part of a broader government campaign to harass Rustavi-2 in advance of the November elections.

In a show of increasing independence on the part of the media, after the poll, the state-run Channel 1 TV station, normally a mouthpiece for the Shevardnadze government, began broadcasting the anti-Shevardnadze protests. In response, Shevardnadze criticized the station, and the head of the station resigned. Once the interim government took power in November, the station continued broadcasting. On December 3, a bomb went off at Channel 1 headquarters. The attack was seen as an attempt to destabilize the country ahead of the January 2004 elections.

Other independent media outlets in the provinces, however, were more vulnerable to the whims of local officials eager to silence critics during an election year. In Kutaisi, Georgia's second-largest city, a series of disturbing incidents temporarily silenced the region's only independent radio and television stations. In May, employees at Kutaisi Television suffered from severe gas poisoning. The station, known for criticizing the regional governor, was closed for six days while police investigated the source of the gas leak. Many were convinced that government authorities were to blame, but police concluded it was accidental.

Radical religious groups associated with a fringe element of the Georgian Orthodox Church attacked independent media outlets in 2003. Some of the attacks were sparked by anger over the airing of programs for religious minorities. Dzveli Kalaki, Kutaisi's only independent radio station, was silenced in April after an angry crowd stormed its building and destroyed the station's antenna. In the months prior to the attack, station staff had endured verbal and physical harassment from local Georgian Orthodox extremists who oppose the station's weekly 20-minute program about the country's Catholic minority. While the church distanced itself from such attacks, it made no effort to stop them.

KAZAKHSTAN

President Nursultan Nazarbayev continued his intense persecution of Kazakhstan's independent media in 2003, silencing government critics and sidelining opposition to his autocratic policies and control over the country's billion-dollar oil and gas industries.

Anyone who criticizes the president, his family, and his associates can be criminally prosecuted, and the government's growing persecution of the media has increased self-censorship. Nazarbayev has consolidated his control over the airwaves and newsstands ahead of parliamentary and presidential elections, scheduled for 2004 and 2006, respectively.

Due to his growing military cooperation with the United States and NATO, Nazarbayev has faced no serious international repercussions for his crackdown on the media and the opposition. Kazakhstan has conducted joint military exercises with U.S. forces in its territory and allows the U.S. military to use its airfields for refueling and emergency landings.

Facing a U.S. Department of Justice investigation into allegations that the president and those close to him accepted hundreds of millions of dollars in bribes from American oil companies, Nazarbayev methodically stifled any media coverage that criticized him or his policies. Media outlets that reported on the opposition Democratic Choice of Kazakhstan Party and official corruption in the energy industry are particularly vulnerable to government persecution.

Politicized courts took the lead in persecuting government critics during 2003. In January, a court in the country's financial capital, Almaty, sentenced Sergei Duvanov, a prominent independent journalist who writes for opposition-financed Web sites and edits a human rights bulletin, to three-and-a-half years in prison for allegedly raping a minor. The trial was closed to the public and marred by numerous procedural violations.

Duvanov is known for his criticism of high-level Kazakh officials, including Nazarbayev, and authorities have frequently harassed him in reprisal. His colleagues and defense attorneys maintain that the journalist is innocent, and that Kazakh authorities fabricated the case to muzzle him. The Almaty Regional Court and the Supreme Court both rejected appeals filed by Duvanov's defense team. Independent journalists say Duvanov's imprisonment has increased self-censorship. In late December, a court ruled that Duvanov could serve the rest of his term in a low-security facility near Almaty.

In March, another Almaty court convicted two men of setting fire to the opposition weekly *Delovoye Obozreniye Respublika* in May 2002, sentenced them to three years in prison, and fined them 998,000 tenge (US$6,575). Irina Petrushova, *Delovoye Obozreniye Respublika*'s editor-in-chief and the recipient of CPJ's 2002 International

Press Freedom Award, does not believe that the men prosecuted are responsible for the crime. Rather, she thinks the fire was an attempt by government officials to silence the newspaper's criticism of Nazarbayev and his policies.

Government persecution has forced some journalists like Petrushova to go into exile. Petrushova, who fled the country in 2002 after she was targeted with death threats and lawsuits, now edits her newspaper from Moscow. After a court closed *Delovoye Obozreniye Respublika* in 2002 for its government criticism, Petrushova was forced to change the newspaper's name to *Assandi Times*.

Libel remains a criminal offense in Kazakhstan. Civil libel cases have no statute of limitation, and there is no limit on the fines that can be imposed. In July, an Almaty district court awarded Nazarbayev's son-in-law Rakhat Aliev 300,000 tenge (US$2,000) in a libel case against the *Assandi Times* stemming from an article published in April stating that Aliev had used his political connections to obstruct the activities of business rivals.

Journalists throughout the country continued to face violent reprisals for criticizing government officials. In April, unidentified attackers beat unconscious Maksim Erokhin, editor of the independent newspaper *Rabat* in the southern city of Shimkent, after he published an article about senior government officials building illegal villas. In October, several men beat Andrei Doronin, a correspondent for the independent Almaty daily *Ekspress-K*, near his home and told him to quit journalism after he wrote a series of articles about illegal vodka production

Authorities actively obstructed news and information on the Internet, periodically blocking access to independent and opposition news Web sites such as *Navigator.kz*, *Kub.kz*, and *Eurasia.ru* from the country's main Internet service provider, the state-run Kazakhtelecom.

Authorities also suppress independent reporting by conducting politicized tax audits and police raids, denying accreditation to media outlets, and limiting access to government information and press conferences.

The president's family and pro-government oligarchs control most of the country's private media, including all broadcast media. Nazarbayev's daughter, Dariga, heads the influential Khabar Media Holding Company and chairs the pro-government Congress of Kazakh Journalists. She launched her own political party in October, apparently in preparation for the 2004 parliamentary elections and the 2006 presidential elections. Nazarbayev's term expires in 2006, and his daughter is expected to run to replace him.

The government proposed a new version of the Media Law during the summer that expands restrictions on the independent media and makes it easier for regulators to shutter media outlets for minor violations. Government officials ignored changes proposed by press freedom activists during the fall, and the lower house of Parliament passed the draft Media Law in late December.

KYRGYZSTAN

ONCE REGARDED AS ONE OF CENTRAL ASIA'S more progressive countries, impoverished Kyrgyzstan has become highly repressive when it comes to the press. Despite having cast himself as a liberal when he took office in 1991, in recent years President Askar Akayev has tightened the government's grip on the independent and opposition media.

Senior government officials, including Prime Minister Nikolai Tanaev, have relied on civil and criminal defamation laws to attack media outlets that criticize their policies or produce investigative stories about official corruption. Exorbitant financial penalties imposed by the courts pushed a few media outlets toward financial collapse in 2003.

The independent newspaper *Moya Stolitsa–Novosti*, based in the capital, Bishkek, continued to be the target of a large number of politically motivated lawsuits during 2003. The paper, which is well known for its investigations into high-level corruption, is one of the only publications that openly criticizes the government. After enduring continued legal harassment that resulted in hefty fines, the publication printed its final hard-copy issue on June 13 but shortly thereafter started a print and online version under the name *MSN*.

According to the U.S. government–funded Radio Free Europe/Radio Liberty, in the course of *Moya Stolitsa–Novosti*'s two-year existence in print, the paper faced 31 lawsuits and paid nearly US$90,700 in damages to plaintiffs ranging from politicians to businessmen. The legal actions against the paper began in late 2002, when Prime Minister Tanaev filed a suit in response to a November 26, 2002, article that he said offended his honor and dignity. The article, written by political editor and investigative reporter Rina Prizhivoit, criticized the policies of President Akayev and his inner circle, including Tanaev.

Presidential Press Secretary Abdil Segizbaev denied that the criminal libel lawsuits were politically motivated, claiming that they were merely responses to violations of the law, according to an interview he gave to the London-based Institute for War and Peace Reporting.

Libel suits were the predominant method employed by Kyrgyz authorities to stifle critical voices in 2003. However, there were cases of assaults on journalists. In mid-January in Bishkek, two unidentified assailants attacked *Moya Stolitsa–Novosti* journalist Aleksandra Chernykh, beating her in front of her 11-year-old daughter. Chernykh's colleagues believe that the attack was a warning to the journalist's mother and colleague at the paper, the political editor Prizhivoit.

In late February, Kyrgyz authorities forced Edil Baysalov, an opposition leader and editor of the independent weekly *Demokrat*, to undergo a medical exam and detained him in the hospital for three days. The hospitalization coincided with Baysalov's scheduled appearance at a roundtable discussion in Kyrgyzstan, organized by the local office of the U.S.-based nongovernmental group Freedom House, where he was to discuss voter turnout for the February 2 constitutional referendum.

The referendum, approved by 75 percent of voters, ratified a new constitution put forward by Akayev, as well as an amendment for an extension of his term in office to December 2005. Opposition parties, nongovernmental organizations, and independent journalists questioned the legitimacy of the referendum's results. In addition to omitting any references to press freedom in the new constitution, the document contained vague restrictions on journalists' rights to gather and distribute information.

In September, journalists were alarmed by the death of Ernis Nazalov, of the Bishkek daily *Kyrgyz Ruhu*, whose body was found on the bank of a canal in the southern Kara-Suu District. Nazalov had been investigating government corruption at the time of his death. An incomplete police investigation failed to clarify the circumstances of his death, raising suspicions that it was not accidental.

Ninety-five percent of Kyrgyz journalists polled by the government-sponsored Media Council in the fall of 2003 wanted defamation decriminalized, and they suggested amendments to the existing media law that would protect the dignity and honor of journalists. In mid-December, Akayev forwarded a bill to Parliament that would decriminalize defamation. If approved, the law would require defamation cases to be tried in civil, not criminal, courts. The bill did not specify a maximum amount for the fine to be imposed on convicted journalists and media outlets. While some journalists welcomed the bill, others doubted that it would alleviate the pressure on independent media. Few plaintiffs seek jail terms for journalists; instead, they demand excessive monetary fines that leave news outlets on the brink of financial collapse. At year's end, Parliament had not yet voted on the bill.

On a positive note, in November, Freedom House, which has an office in Bishkek, set up an independent publishing house, ending the state printer Uchkun's monopoly in the capital. The new Freedom House printer is open to both state and independent publications. Uchkun has often refused to print content that officials might consider offensive. According to international observers, the new printer will finally allow opposition papers to publish without fear of censorship or retribution.

MOLDOVA

MOLDOVA HAS EMERGED FROM THE SOVIET ERA with many of the problems that plague other states in the region: an ongoing separatist conflict dividing the nation's ethnic populations, widespread government corruption, financial hardship, and a biased judiciary. Unlike many other former Soviet republics, however, Moldova has neither the natural resources nor the geopolitical importance to make it attractive to foreign investors. Under these harsh conditions, it has been difficult for a free press to develop and flourish.

The Moldovan press can be divided into three categories: state-owned, party-owned, and privately owned. Editorial content usually reflects the views of those holding the purse strings. Since the Communist Party swept back into power in Moldova's 2001 elections, the climate for the country's fledgling independent and opposition media has become more restrictive. The new civil and criminal codes, which went into effect in January 2003, are one example of the government's intent to rein in critical media outlets. Under the Civil Code, there is no longer a cap on the amount an official can win when suing a journalist for libel—a change that could bankrupt a publication with a single lawsuit. And under the new Criminal Code, libel can carry a prison sentence of up to five years.

Throughout 2003, opposition media outlets that published reports on government corruption or topics deemed troublesome by the Communist administration endured police raids, the confiscation of archival material, detentions, and interrogations. Authorities also employed less direct forms of intimidation against the opposition press, such as scaring off advertisers and accusing journalists of taking bribes.

Ongoing attempts to transform the state-run Teleradio-Moldova into a public broadcaster served as a barometer for press freedom in 2003. Under pressure from the Council of Europe, Moldova's Parliament passed a series of amendments to facilitate this transition, including one creating an independent supervisory board. Nevertheless, President Vladimir Voronin still maintains a large measure of control over the station through political interference in its editorial policies. In October, Parliament passed an amendment granting itself the right to close and reorganize Teleradio—a power that may be used, sources say, to fire employees who are not loyal to the ruling Communists.

Despite these government efforts to intimidate Teleradio staff members, many protested government censorship. After the station neglected to broadcast reports of mass demonstrations against censorship in 2002, a group of Teleradio employees walked out in solidarity with opposition journalists.

The conflict between ethnic Russians and Romanians in the country continues to affect the media, as well as Moldova's overall political stability. Sixty-five percent of Moldova's 4.5 million citizens are ethnically Romanian (Moldova was part of Romania before it was annexed by the Soviet Union in 1940), but nearly half of the publications that circulate nationally are in the Russian language. Moldovan is the official state language, and many Moldovans resent plans by Voronin—an ethnic Russian—to reinstate Russian as a state language.

Ethnic tensions are also at the heart of the 10-year-old conflict in the Trans-Dniester region, a separatist enclave largely populated by Russians. Hundreds of Russian troops are still stationed in Trans-Dniester, which the Moldovan government claims as its own.

In January, television broadcasts from Romania restarted, after being banned since August 2002 amid deteriorating relations between Romania and Moldova's pro-Moscow government.

ROMANIA

SINCE THE SOCIAL DEMOCRATIC PARTY (PSD) CAME TO POWER IN 2001, the Romanian government has repeatedly tried to silence its critics in an attempt to stabilize relations with Europe and the United States and thereby secure membership in the European Union (EU) and NATO. Rather than battle the corruption that jeopardizes its status within the international community, the government has opted instead to intimidate media outlets that expose widespread corruption.

Despite these efforts, Romania suffered a setback in late 2002 when EU member states voted to delay its entry into the union. Insufficient progress toward a free press was one of the reasons cited for the postponement. International pressure on Romania to bring its constitution—including media laws—in line with European standards did have some positive effects. Although Parliament stopped short of decriminalizing libel, media advocates welcomed amendments to the Penal Code eliminating prison sentences for libel.

A national referendum passed in October brought Romania's constitution in line with EU standards. Press freedom supporters also welcomed legislation passed in January that removed the national news agency, ROMPRES, from government control. The agency now reports to Parliament rather than the Information Ministry, and its editorial independence is legally guaranteed.

Despite these positive steps, journalists continued to be harassed by individual libel suits that often resulted in heavy fines. In recent years, damage awards have ranged from US$400 to US$20,000—an enormous figure for journalists who earn an average monthly salary of US$130, according to an assessment conducted by IREX-ProMedia, a Washington, D.C.–based media training organization.

Journalists in the provinces are even more vulnerable to government pressure than their colleagues in the capital, Bucharest. Media advocates attribute heavy-handedness by local government officials to the "Berlusconization" of the regional press, referring to a strategy practiced by some local leaders in which they buy up local print, radio, and television stations and exploit their mini media empires for their own business and political gains, just as Italian Prime Minister Silvio Berlusconi has done in Italy.

While intimidation of the press tends to occur in court or through more indirect pressure, physical intimidation is not uncommon. In July, in the northwestern town of Petrosani, unknown assailants attacked Carmen Cosman, a journalist for the independent Bucharest daily *Libera*, and Marius Mitrache, a journalist for *Evenimentul Zilei*, another independent daily also based in Bucharest. According to The Associated Press (AP), the attacks occurred after both journalists had published articles about local government corruption.

In December, several unknown assailants attacked Ino Ardelean, an *Evenimentul Zilei* reporter based in the western city of Timisoara, beating him unconscious. Prior to the assault, Ardelean had written a series of articles linking local politicians from the ruling party to murky business activities.

In 2003, there were also attacks against journalists in the northwestern towns of Sighet and Targu Mures. According to the Media Monitoring Agency, a Bucharest-based press freedom organization, Bucharest District Mayor Marian Vanghelie explicitly told Liviu Vulpe, a journalist for the daily *Adevarul*: "You should not follow me. Otherwise, I will ask my boys to follow you and then I will send someone to put you in the trunk of a car."

Self-censorship is also a problem among state-run and private media outlets. In April, three journalists from Europe FM, Romania's largest private radio station, resigned after accusing their managers of blocking reports criticizing the government, AP reported. This was not an isolated incident, and other broadcast journalists throughout Romania resigned in protest of censorship or reported pressure from managers to support the local government, said the Media Monitoring Agency.

Since the Ceaucescu regime crumbled in 1989, hundreds of newspapers and local independent television and radio stations have emerged, along with several private national television stations. While state-owned television and radio stations are likely to favor the government, private news outlets often reflect the interests of their owners or controlling parties. Indeed, in a February 2003 survey of media professionals cited in a report by the Media Monitoring Agency, 52 percent of all participating editors said they were under pressure to block certain kinds of information. That same month, the government gave the national broadcasting council the right to revoke the licenses of radio and television stations that harm national security or incite social disorder, racial, religious, or sexual discrimination.

In March, the worst fears of Iosif Costinas' colleagues were confirmed when the opposition journalist's body was discovered in a forest near the western city of Timisoara, where he worked. Costinas had been writing a book about organized crime when he disappeared in June 2002. The 62-year-old journalist had also written extensively on government corruption and other sensitive political issues. At year's end, there was no progress reported in the case, and police were still trying to determine the cause of his death.

RUSSIA

RUSSIAN PRESIDENT VLADIMIR PUTIN AND HIS COTERIE of former intelligence officials pressed ahead in 2003 with his vision of a "dictatorship of the law" in Russia to create a "managed democracy." Putin's goal of an obedient and patriotic press meant that the Kremlin continued using various branches of the politicized state bureaucracy to rein in the independent media.

While the independent media continued to provide a certain diversity of views, direct criticism of the president, as well as critical reporting on government corruption or on the war in Chechnya, has become rare since Putin took office in December 1999. A shift from blatant pressures to more subtle and covert tactics, such as politicized lawsuits and hostile corporate takeovers by businessmen with close ties to Putin, has allowed the Kremlin to intimidate or silence critics in the media with minimal impact on the country's international image. Meanwhile, the murder, imprisonment, and harassment of independent journalists throughout Russia's provinces continued in 2003.

U.S. and European governments were largely silent in response to the Kremlin's crackdown on the media. In September, U.S. President George W. Bush shocked even some of his conservative supporters when he called Russia "a country in which democracy and freedom and rule of law thrive."

In early 2003, authorities took advantage of the fear generated by the October 2002 "Nord-Ost" hostage crisis—during which Chechen rebels took over a crowded Moscow theater—by cracking down on media outlets that covered the government's sloppy response to the crisis, which ended with the deaths of 120 civilians when Russian forces stormed the building. In January, officials from the government-controlled gas giant Gazprom dismissed Boris Jordan, director of the national television station NTV, because of the station's aggressive coverage of the hostage crisis. In the following months, senior officials pushed national broadcast media executives to draft a vaguely worded "Anti-Terrorism Convention" committing them to restrict their coverage of terrorism and antiterrorist government operations. The executives signed the measure in April.

The Kremlin also continued to consolidate the national broadcast media under the authority of the state and powerful businesses with links to Putin. Since taking office, Putin and his allies have closed or taken control of all independent national television stations that had previously provided Russia's citizens with alternative sources of news. On June 21, the Media Ministry pulled the independent television station TVS off the air without obtaining a court order and replaced it with Sport TV, a state-run sports channel.

Prior to being pulled off the air, TVS had been paralyzed for months by fierce competition between two groups of rival shareholders led by aluminum tycoon Oleg Deripaska and Anatoly Chubais, a reformist politician and head of Russia's national electricity grid. Deripaska, who has close ties to the Kremlin, finally bought out Chubais in early June but failed to provide funds for the continued operation of the debt-ridden station. TVS Editor-in-Chief Yevgeny Kiselyov accused shareholders of bankrupting the station to please the Kremlin.

The country's remaining national television channels—state-run Rossiya and Channel One and, to a lesser extent, the state-controlled NTV—drifted toward Soviet-style reporting by emphasizing positive news and focusing heavily on Putin's meetings with his

Cabinet and international leaders. Major national television stations portrayed Putin as a stabilizing force following the political upheaval and economic chaos that had characterized President Boris Yeltsin's rule in the 1990s.

The government continued to persecute journalists who exposed corruption and wrongdoing in the country's powerful military, police, and security ministries. Grigory Pasko, a former military reporter for the Pacific Fleet's newspaper *Boyevaya Vakhta*, served two-and-a-half years in prison after being wrongfully convicted for treason in December 2001. The charges against Pasko came after he reported on environmental abuses committed by the military. Pasko was released in January 2003, but authorities denied him a travel passport in March. In August, the Supreme Court refused to hear an appeal challenging his criminal conviction, and a Moscow court upheld the ruling denying him a passport.

Police officers continued to abuse journalists who investigated police activities or criticized law enforcement officials. In February, an Interior Ministry unit in the Chechen capital, Grozny, detained and assaulted Zamid Ayubov, a journalist with the local pro-Russian administration's thrice-weekly *Vozrozhdeniye Chechni*, while he was researching the activities of police units on evening patrols. In May, some 40 police officers fired tear gas and stormed the temporary office of the opposition radio station Krasnaya Armiya in the city of Noyabrsk in the central Ural Region. The attack came days after the station supported an opposition candidate in the May 4 elections. Police officers handcuffed, assaulted, and detained staff members for several hours.

The Kremlin maintained its information embargo on the southern republic of Chechnya, restricting the ability of Russian and foreign correspondents to report independently on the war's devastation. Journalists were required to travel with elaborate police escorts, which, along with the fear of being kidnapped by Chechen rebels, made it difficult to meet and interview citizens or do other independent reporting. During 2003, the Kremlin pressed neighboring Estonia and Lithuania to close the pro-independence Chechen Web site *KavkazCenter.com*. The site changed its Internet service provider several times during 2003 because of lawsuits filed by government officials seeking its closure in response to Russian concerns but continued operating at year's end. Meanwhile, the Media Ministry issued an official warning to the Moscow-based ultranationalist weekly *Zavtra* on February 26 for publishing an interview with an exiled Chechen separatist leader.

Despite a public relations campaign by the Kremlin claiming that life in Chechnya is returning to normal, journalists trying to report on the conflict remain at serious risk. At year's end, police had not reported any progress in investigating the July 2003 disappearance of Ali Astamirov, an Agence France-Presse correspondent. Unknown armed assailants abducted Astamirov in Ingushetia, a southern republic neighboring Chechnya. Prior to his kidnapping, police officers and agents from the Federal Security Service (FSB) had repeatedly harassed Astamirov and obstructed his coverage of the ongoing conflict in Chechnya.

Judges and prosecutors often colluded to shield individuals who harassed journalists. In March, the prosecutor's office in the Siberian city of Nizhnevartovsk cleared a military officer accused of sending death threats to Anna Politkovskaya, a war correspondent covering Chechnya for the Moscow-based newspaper *Novaya Gazeta*. Politkovskaya began receiving threatening e-mails in September 2001 after she wrote an article reporting that the military officer had committed atrocities against civilians in Chechnya.

Only in very rare cases did courts protect journalists from persecution. In July, a district court in the Urals city of Perm acquitted two crime reporters for the local independent newspaper *Zvezda* after the FSB accused them of revealing state secrets in an October 2002 article about a corrupt FSB informant.

Russia's Criminal Code contains defamation laws that are used to stifle critical reporting. German Galkin, the publisher of *Rabochaya Gazeta* and deputy chief editor of *Vecherny Chelyabinsk*, both opposition newspapers in the southern Urals city of Chelyabinsk, was convicted of criminal defamation on August 15, 2003, in a trial that was closed to the public. Galkin was sentenced to one year in a labor camp for allegedly writing anonymous articles for *Rabochaya Gazeta* about misspending by the Chelyabinsk regional administration. In November, after CPJ and other press freedom groups protested Galkin's imprisonment, the Chelyabinsk Regional Court reduced Galkin's sentence to one year of probation, and he was released from prison.

In advance of the December 2003 parliamentary elections and March 2004 presidential elections, the Kremlin continued to tighten already stringent legal and bureaucratic controls over the domestic press. The Parliament passed media legislation in June, which Putin subsequently signed, that grants broad, excessive, and arbitrary authority to the Media Ministry, Central Election Commission (CEC), and regional electoral commissions to close media outlets for printing or broadcasting "biased" political commentary during the elections. While the Supreme Court struck down part of the law in October, many journalists had already turned to self-censorship, and editors curtailed coverage of the election campaigns to protect themselves from legal action.

At the same time, Russian press groups criticized the CEC and regional election commissions for their hypocrisy because they failed to sanction Rossiya and Channel One for improperly promoting pro-Kremlin parties such as United Russia. Government officials who used the state's vast resources to promote Putin's allies also remained untouched. In the end, United Russia and two other pro-Kremlin parties came out on top in the parliamentary elections, guaranteeing Putin a loyal and subservient Parliament. The generally cautious Organization for Security and Co-operation in Europe, a Vienna-based international organization that monitors elections, characterized the poll as "fundamentally distorted" and a "regression in the democratization process."

Regional elections held in Russia's provinces throughout 2003 also favored the Kremlin. Akhmad Kadyrov, a pro-Kremlin candidate in Chechnya's October presidential election, won easily after compliant courts and elections regulators disqualified his most serious competitors.

Despite the Kremlin's success at the polls and in subordinating much of the media, at year's end, authorities continued pressuring journalists, often in underhanded ways. In early November, journalist Pavel Felgenhauer reported that a Kremlin official had mailed documents to his editor at the independent Moscow daily *Moskovsky Komsomolets* calling him a "sympathizer" of Putin's political rival, exiled oligarch Boris Berezovsky. In mid-November, half a dozen of Moscow's prominent editors and media executives from independent media outlets received letters from the Prosecutor General's Office summoning them for immediate questioning about their organizations' finances. The Prosecutor General's Office denied sending the letters.

Even films and books addressing politically sensitive topics were increasingly deemed unacceptable. In October, a Moscow movie theater canceled a Chechnya film festival after being pressured by FSB agents. That same month, *Novaya Gazeta*'s Politkovskaya reported that her invitation to participate in a panel discussion on Chechnya at the Frankfurt Book Fair was withdrawn due to complaints made by Russian authorities. In November, NTV director Nikolai Senkevich canceled a program about Yelena Tregubova, a former Kremlin reporter who wrote a book criticizing the presidential press office for its aggressive management of the media. In December, police and FSB agents seized thousands of copies of a controversial new book implicating the FSB in a series of bombings that struck several Russian cities in 1999.

Journalists in Russia's provinces remained particularly exposed to danger and violence. During 2003, one journalist was killed because of his profession, and a second journalist may have been targeted for his work. In October, Aleksei Sidorov, editor-in-chief of the independent newspaper *Tolyatinskoye Obozreniye* in the Volga River city of Togliatti, was stabbed to death outside his home because of his paper's coverage of organized crime and government corruption. He was the newspaper's second editor-in-chief to be murdered in 18 months. A second journalist, Dmitry Shvets, deputy director of the independent TV-21 station in the northern city of Murmansk, was shot dead outside the station in April, possibly because of TV-21's reporting on a mayoral candidate's links to organized crime.

For years, independent Russian journalists have been murdered with impunity because police, prosecutors, and courts have failed to properly investigate and prosecute these crimes. More than a dozen journalists have been killed in Russia during Putin's four years as president, and none of their murderers has been brought to justice. One of the few cases that has gone to trial during the last decade, the October 1994 assassination of Dmitry Kholodov, a reporter for the independent newspaper *Moskovsky Komsomolets* who had investigated corruption in the Defense Ministry, took six years to go before the courts and has yet to produce a conviction. In May 2003, the Military Collegium of Russia's Supreme Court overturned the June 2002 acquittal of six suspects by the Moscow Circuit Military Court and ordered a retrial. Court hearings resumed in August, and no significant developments in the Kholodov case had been reported by year's end.

SERBIA AND MONTENEGRO

SERBIA'S RULING REFORMIST COALITION, THE DEMOCRATIC OPPOSITION OF SERBIA (DOS), struggled to come to terms with the legacy of corruption and extreme nationalism left by a decade of rule under former Yugoslav President Slobodan Milosevic. Political division in the Federal Republic of Yugoslavia, powerful organized crime groups, and political apathy kept the conflict-ridden DOS coalition on the brink of collapse after the assassination of the prime minister in March.

In February, Serbian officials implemented an agreement made with Montenegrin officials transforming the Federal Republic of Yugoslavia into a loose union called Serbia and Montenegro, with the southern province of Kosovo remaining under temporary U.N. administration.

On March 12, a sniper assassinated Serbian Prime Minister Zoran Djindjic while he was stepping out of his car in front of a government building in the capital, Belgrade. Parliament Speaker Natasa Micic became acting head of the government the same day and immediately imposed a state of emergency authorizing the Culture and Public Information Ministry to restrict media reporting on the situation. A week later, Parliament approved Djindjic ally Zoran Zivkovic as the new prime minister.

During the 42-day state of emergency, government officials cracked down on the former special operations officers and members of the powerful Zemun mafia clan who were formally charged with Djindjic's murder. Culture and Public Information Minister Branilsav Lecic used his broad authority to fine and close media outlets that violated vaguely defined media restrictions in their reporting on the assassination and the state of emergency.

Oversight of the media became increasingly politicized in March, when the Serbian government reappointed former Djindjic propagandist Vladimir "Beba" Popovic to head its Communications Bureau. Popovic relied on threats and politicized lawsuits to intimidate and silence journalists who criticized government policies.

Gordana Susa, the host and editor-in-chief of the popular current affairs television talk show "Press Pretres" (Discussing the Press), said Popovic placed a threatening call to her on the evening of April 18, right after she questioned Deputy Prime Minister Nebojsa Covic during an interview about Popovic's reappointment to the Communications Bureau. Popovic had been ousted from the post in October 2002 following pressure from U.S. diplomats, who were not pleased with his aggressive attempts to control how independent journalists reported on the prime minister. (Popovic resigned from the Communications Bureau in July 2003 after pressure, again from Western diplomats.)

Zeljko Cvijanovic, editor-in-chief of the independent Belgrade daily *Blic News*, resigned from his post in June following a campaign of harassment and intimidation by police and government officials—including Popovic—in retaliation for his reporting on organized crime and government scandals. Throughout 2003, the independent Belgrade radio station B92 remained an outspoken critic of attempts by the government and nationalist politicians to silence independent journalists who criticized government policies.

During the state of emergency, the government rushed several long-delayed amendments to media-related laws through Parliament in what was seen as an effort to avoid public scrutiny and retain political influence over the media.

In March, Parliament passed amendments to the Broadcasting Law, creating a Broadcasting Agency to regulate the distribution of national broadcast frequencies. A scandal erupted in April, when Parliament began selecting candidates for the nine-member supervisory Broadcast Agency Council. According to the Belgrade-based Association of Independent Electronic Media and the Independent Journalists Association of Serbia, three of the government's nominees were inappropriately appointed to the council in violation of various requirements and nomination procedures. Two council members who represented nongovernmental organizations and media associations resigned in protest.

In April, Parliament passed a new draft of the Public Information Law broadening the ability of courts to close media outlets for using vaguely defined "hate speech" and weakening protection for the identity of journalistic sources.

The overall lack of progress in reforming the regulation of broadcast media worked in favor of the government because it allowed private, pro-government television stations like Pink TV and BK TV to retain their national broadcasting licenses. This limited pluralism in the news and inhibited the broader process of democratization.

While the DOS coalition has been far less heavy-handed with the press than former Yugoslav President Milosevic, politicians still believe that they have a right to influence and guide editorial polices of independent outlets. Journalists covering politically sensitive issues remain vulnerable to politically motivated civil and criminal lawsuits, intimidating police interviews, and threatening calls from politicians, businessmen, and clergy because the government has failed to reprimand or prosecute those responsible for harassment.

In some cases, politicians filed lawsuits against journalists. Former Yugoslav President Dobrica Cosic filed a criminal libel lawsuit against Milan Colic, a translator for the independent Belgrade daily *Danas*, because of an October 2001 article that linked Cosic to war crimes committed by the Yugoslav People's Army when he was head of state. Colic is currently living in the Czech Republic, but in October 2003, a court in the northern city of Novi Sad tried him in absentia and sentenced him to three months in prison.

This impunity was compounded by the fact that at year's end, police and prosecutors had made no progress in solving the June 2002 murder of Milan Pantic, a crime reporter for the Belgrade daily *Vecernje Novosti*, and the April 1999 assassination of Slavko Curuvija, editor-in-chief of the independent daily *Dnevni Telegraf*. The public prosecutor responsible for the stalled investigation into Curuvija's murder, Sinisa Simic, was temporarily suspended from his duties in March after the police arrested Deputy Public Prosecutor Milan Sarajlic for being on the payroll of the notorious Zemun mafia gang and for obstructing a number of murder inquiries on their behalf.

Constant infighting in the DOS coalition, as well as its inability to reduce widespread poverty, led to significant political apathy, resulting in three presidential elections in just over a year that were deemed invalid because voter turnout rates were under 50 percent. In November—three years after Milosevic's removal from power—the coalition dissolved itself and set parliamentary elections for December, which saw the biggest share of the vote go to the ultranationalist Serbian Radical Party (SRS), led by an indicted war criminal. In January 2004, a group of pro-democracy parties were struggling to form a coalition government to prevent the SRS from taking power.

In Montenegro, an ongoing debate about the prospect of independence from Serbia and allegations of widespread government corruption dominated the media during 2003. Despite progress in the reform of media legislation, access to basic government information remained difficult, and politicized oversight of the media continued to favor state-run outlets and inhibit independent reporting.

In April, the U.N. International Criminal Tribunal for the Former Yugoslavia (ICTY) charged a journalist for the first time in its history. The ICTY charged Dusan Jovanovic, editor-in-chief of the opposition daily *Dan*, based in Montenegro's capital, Podgorica, with contempt of court after he published the identity of a protected witness in the Milosevic trial. The witness received threatening phone calls after *Dan* revealed the witness's identity. An initial hearing in the case was held in December. If convicted, Jovanovic faces up to seven years in jail and/or a fine of up to US$106,000. Some press freedom groups have argued that Jovanovic should only face financial penalties, and not jail time, for the charge.

In Kosovo, political tensions remained high due to an international crackdown on ethnic Albanian extremists and renewed negotiations with Serbian authorities to determine the final political status of the politically polarized and crime-ridden province. Harassment, political interference, and a lack of access to basic government information continued to plague journalists, who have responded by establishing the Association of Professional Journalists of Kosova and the Association of Independent Media of Kosova to defend their rights.

In July, NATO peacekeeping forces announced that an inquiry was unable to determine whether the Macedonian army or ethnic Albanian rebels were responsible for the March 2001 death of Associated Press Television News journalist Kerem Lawton. Lawton died from shrapnel wounds when a mortar shell struck his car in the village of Krivenik in southern Kosovo.

That same month, the U.N. Interim Administration in Kosovo adopted a new Interim Criminal Code, which retained criminal defamation as an offense punishable by up to one year in prison.

TAJIKISTAN

THE TAJIK MEDIA CONTINUED TO BE HAUNTED IN 2003 by the devastating legacy of the 1992-1997 civil war, which pitted the People's Front, a paramilitary organization led by the current president, Imomali Rakhmonov, against a coalition of Islamic and nationalist groups. Because of widespread poverty—a result of the war, geographic isolation, and a string of natural disasters—reporters often work in run-down offices with outdated equipment. Only a small fraction of the population can afford to buy newspapers or access the Internet. Scared by the murders of dozens of their colleagues and the failure of authorities to solve them, journalists continue to limit their reporting to avoid official harassment and intimidation.

President Rakhmonov nurtured his role as an ally in the United States' "war on terror" to consolidate his rule over the country. Following his December 2002 meeting in Washington, D.C., with U.S. President George W. Bush, Rakhmonov won a controversial constitutional referendum in June that gave him the right to run for two more terms, which could allow him to stay in office until 2020.

Rakhmonov relied on the slavish propaganda from the Soviet-style state media to promote his image. In August, the president basked in two days of constant television coverage of his participation in a conference on potato farming. In October, however, when real news broke about a typhoid outbreak in Tajikistan's capital, Dushanbe, the state-run media delayed covering the epidemic for several weeks until after the end of the Central Asian Games, which were taking place in the city.

A CPJ delegation traveled to Tajikistan in July and encouraged senior officials to combat the culture of fear and self-censorship among the media that lingers from the civil war. The delegation urged officials to investigate and prosecute those responsible for murdering dozens of journalists. CPJ first visited Tajikistan in 1994 and found that both parties to the conflict—President Rakhmonov's People's Front and the United Tajik Opposition—were targeting journalists in reprisal for their work.

Senior officials from the Interior Ministry and the Prosecutor General's Office who met with CPJ eagerly pointed to the October 2002 creation of a special task force of police officers and prosecutors to investigate political murders carried out during the civil war. Journalists, however, expressed skepticism about the government's intentions. They said commanders from the People's Front linked to the killings are now serving in senior posts in the Interior Ministry, the security apparatus, and the Prosecutor General's Office.

CPJ also called on the government to reverse its culture of secrecy by making its activities and deliberations more accessible to journalists and the public. The Foreign Affairs Ministry and Rakhmonov's administration expressed a degree of openness on the issue, but other institutions such as the Broadcasting Commission and the Committee for Radio and Television Broadcasting flatly stated that their activities were not matters of public interest.

A week after the CPJ delegation left Tajikistan, the country's Supreme Court convicted two suspects in the murders of Muhiddin Olimpur, head of the BBC's Persian Service bureau, and Viktor Nikulin, a correspondent with the Russian television network ORT. Both journalists were killed during the civil war in the mid-1990s. The two suspects were sentenced to 15 and 22 years in prison, respectively, for serving as accomplices in the slayings. Journalists welcomed the convictions but said they doubted that the trials represented a larger government commitment to fully investigate the dozens of other murders of journalists.

During the CPJ delegation's visit, Deputy Prosecutor General Azizmat Imomov and Dushanbe Mayor Mahmadsaid Ubaidulloyev, who is also president of Parliament, agreed to respond to formal letters from CPJ regarding unsolved murder cases and criminal defamation laws. By year's end, CPJ had received no response from Ubaidulloyev. In December, however, CPJ received a letter from the Prosecutor General's Office stating that it was unaware of some of the murder cases on CPJ's list and would open inquiries into them.

Government harassment continued to threaten the country's fledgling independent press throughout 2003. Journalists avoided reporting on sensitive political issues such as government corruption, drug trafficking, and organized crime and struggled to obtain basic information from Tajikistan's secretive bureaucracy. Direct criticism of the president and other senior officials remained taboo, and several publications faced retribution after testing the government's limited tolerance for public debate.

In February, Mukhtor Bokizoda, editor of the independent weekly *Nerui Sukhan*, was summoned to the Dushanbe Prosecutor's Office for questioning after publishing an interview with an opposition leader. In December, tax inspectors visited the weekly after a string of articles in 2003 criticized government policies.

During the summer, Internet service providers blocked access to the Web site *Tajikistantimes.ru*, allegedly at the request of officials angered by content that criticized government polices. Authorities denied making the request. In November and December, the state-run printing monopoly Sharki Ozod, which is controlled by the president's administration, refused to print the independent weekly *Ruzi Nav* after it recounted Rakhmonov's ascent to power and criticized excessive perks for government officials.

The government ignored the concerns of the country's independent media in 2003. A letter signed by 29 prominent media executives to the president and Parliament in April requesting desperately needed exemptions from the country's heavy tax and customs duties went unanswered. The government also obstructed the development of private broadcast media by delaying licensing applications, sometimes for several years. In September, the Broadcasting Commission rejected a television broadcasting application made by the media holding company Asia-Plus, citing a lack of technical equipment and qualified personnel. An Asia-Plus executive told CPJ that the government never inspected their equipment or inquired about their personnel.

Even journalists working for the foreign press were not safe from government harassment. Abbas Djavadi, director of the Tajik Service at the U.S. government–funded Radio Free Europe/Radio Liberty, reported in April that officials had recently threatened to close the broadcaster's Dushanbe bureau and revoke its journalists' accreditation for reporting on a forthcoming reshuffling of government ministers, as well as for interviewing a member of an exiled opposition group.

TURKMENISTAN

IN 2003, TURKMENISTAN'S MEGALOMANIACAL DICTATOR, President-for-life Saparmurat Niyazov, continued to tighten his grip on the country's politics, natural resources, and the press.

A wave of political repression against Niyazov's real and imagined opponents followed an alleged assassination attempt against the president on November 25, 2002. The president escaped unharmed, and some Turkmen journalists and opposition activists living in exile have speculated that Niyazov orchestrated the attack himself to create an excuse to persecute sympathizers of the exiled Turkmen opposition.

In the weeks following the alleged assassination attempt, Niyazov arrested government officials and relatives of exiled opposition activists on suspicion of involvement in the attack. In December 2002, state media publicized the suspects' reportedly forced confessions, and in January 2003, dozens of them were sentenced in political show trials to 25 years or life terms in prison.

In April, Niyazov issued a presidential decree revoking a Turkmen-Russian dual-citizenship agreement, making it easier to extradite exiled opposition activists and journalists living in Moscow back to Turkmenistan for prosecution. The decree sent a chill throughout the Turkmen exile community in Moscow. According to press reports, Turkmen officials have asked Russia to extradite Orazmuhammet Yklymov, a Moscow-based journalist for the U.S. government–funded Radio Free Europe/Radio Liberty (RFE/RL), claiming he was linked to the assassination attempt against Niyazov. Turkmen officials have also asked Russian and Swedish officials to extradite opposition activists in connection to the assassination investigation. So far, however, no journalists or opposition figures have been forced to return from exile.

The government uses its control over all Turkmen newspapers, radio and television stations, and the state printing company, Turkmenmetbugat, to promote Niyazov's Soviet-style cult of personality. Political dissent is not tolerated, and the Committee for the Preservation of State Secrets is responsible for prior censorship of the media.

The president personally appoints editors of media outlets, and approval from Niyazov's office is required before newspapers can be printed and the evening news can be broadcast on state television. Self-censorship is ubiquitous; only journalists writing in overseas publications under pseudonyms are safe from intimidation, persecution, torture, and imprisonment.

Access to foreign news and information remains extremely limited. In July 2002, the Communications Ministry began blocking the delivery of Russian publications to Turkmen subscribers and officially terminated their subscriptions a month later. Customs officials check all written material passing through borders and confiscate anything that criticizes the government.

Programming from Russia's state-run Channel One is delayed for a day so that Turkmen officials can examine and censor the content before it airs. Authorities temporarily blocked access to Russian-language cable television in July 2002 and again in September 2003 in response to programming that criticized Turkmenistan. Some people with enough money have installed satellite dishes to circumvent government interference.

The government regularly denies accreditation to journalists working for international media. In March, the State Service for the Registration of Foreigners was established to intensify surveillance of foreign correspondents, who are allowed to visit the country on rare occasions.

Russia's state-run Radio Mayak and RFE/RL do provide alternative sources of information, but citizens say they listen to them in private, at their own risk. Officials refuse to give interviews to RFE/RL, and in December 2002, authorities detained a man interviewed by RFE/RL and sent him to a psychiatric facility for two months.

RFE/RL Turkmen Service journalists working in Moscow and Turkmenistan remained under government surveillance. On September 2, Shanazar Berdyev, a Moscow-based RFE/RL stringer and son of a prominent opposition activist, was attacked and severely injured at the door of his apartment in Moscow by an assailant dressed in a police uniform, according to RFE/RL. On September 11, National Security Ministry agents detained Ashgabat-based RFE/RL stringer Saparmurat Ovezberdiyev for two days, threatened him with 20 years in prison, and injected him several times with an unknown substance, RFE/RL reported.

The online media have fared no better than the rest of the country's press. The state-run TurkmenTelecom is the country's only Internet service provider. Restrictive application procedures, high costs, heavy monitoring of e-mail, and blocked access to a growing list of news and opposition Web sites keep the Internet in the government's choking grasp.

While the rest of the world focused on Iraq and the U.S. "war on terror," Western human rights organizations criticized the United States and its allies for repeatedly overlooking Niyazov's atrocious human rights record in exchange for permission to station troops in Turkmenistan to service cargo planes en route to Afghanistan, and to build a natural-gas pipeline from Turkmenistan to South Asia via Afghanistan.

UKRAINE

THE 2000 MURDER OF INTERNET JOURNALIST GEORGY GONGADZE continued to dog Ukrainian President Leonid Kuchma, who was fighting for political survival in 2003. Gongadze, editor of *Ukrayinska Pravda*, an online publication that often reports on government corruption, disappeared on September 16, 2000. A headless corpse believed to be Gongadze's was found shortly after his disappearance, but the remains were not definitively identified until March 2003.

In 2000, secret tapes were released implicating Kuchma and other high-level government officials in the journalist's disappearance. The tapes, allegedly recorded by a former Kuchma bodyguard, launched the "Kuchmagate" scandal, which became a rallying point for domestic opposition and international criticism. Demonstrators continue to mark the anniversary of Gongadze's disappearance with mass protests calling for the president's resignation, and Western governments, international organizations, and human rights and press freedom groups regularly chastise Ukraine for its lack of progress in investigating the murder.

In May, a former prosecutor was convicted of obstructing justice, forging documents, and planting false evidence at the scene of the crime, but he was immediately amnestied on a technicality. In August, Igor Goncharov, a suspect in the case, died in police custody, and his body was cremated before an autopsy could be conducted. A former police officer, Goncharov headed a criminal gang accused of several murders and kidnappings. Shortly after his death, a Kyiv-based press freedom organization released a letter that Goncharov had written prior to his death accusing senior government officials of ordering Gongadze's murder.

Prosecutors originally dismissed Goncharov's allegations but in September declared some details of his letter true, paving the way for the investigation's first major breakthrough in late October—the arrest of former police officer Oleksander Pukach. Pukach, who had overseen the initial police investigation into Gongadze's death, had been identified in Goncharov's letter as a suspect.

Goncharov's allegations also buoyed Kuchma's opponents in Parliament. Opposition parliamentarian Grigory Omelchenko, who heads the parliamentary commission investigating Gongadze's death, has called on a Kyiv court to launch a criminal case against Kuchma and other officials in connection with Gongadze's murder, adding that there was sufficient evidence to consider them accomplices. Instead, the Supreme Court issued a ruling in December granting Kuchma immunity from crimes committed while in office, the Deutsche Presse Agentur news agency reported.

Many of the officials implicated in Gongadze's murder are currently immune from prosecution. The constitution bars the president from seeking a third term in office, but in December, the Constitutional Court ruled that Kuchma could seek another term. The court decided that Kuchma's first term, which began in 1994, did not count because it preceded the country's first post-Soviet constitution, which was adopted in 1996.

In 2003, a few legislative changes appeared to have strengthened the country's media. Amendments to the Law on Television and Radio passed in May lifted limits on advertising revenues, a change welcomed in the broadcast community. And in April, Kuchma signed a law banning censorship. The law makes it a crime to "deliberately intervene in the professional work of journalists," while limiting financial awards granted in defamation cases. The law also prohibits state and local government agencies from filing defamation lawsuits

While the law is a huge step in theory, media advocates have only cautious praise for the legislation because it has had little effect on government authorities, including their practice of issuing *temniki*, or secret memos used to influence reporting. The memos instruct journalists how to report on politically sensitive issues, such as ongoing scandals, demonstrations, and corruption. Media outlets that do not comply with the instructions are targeted with tax audits, lawsuits, license withdrawals, and other forms of harassment.

Because the majority of Ukrainians get their news from television, controlling the broadcast media is particularly important to the government. Kuchma and his supporters dominate the airwaves through their control of influential national channels. In March, an opposition member of Parliament asked the government Antimonopoly Committee to investigate violations of the Television Ownership Law, which prohibits anyone from owning more than two television channels. Kuchma's son-in-law was among those under scrutiny, but the committee ruled in May that it could neither confirm nor disprove the existence of monopolies.

With a growing number of Ukrainians gaining access to the Internet, online publications are becoming more influential and are therefore more likely to be monitored by authorities. In July, the government put Ukraine's Internet domain under the control of the security service. In January, the prosecutor general tightened accreditation rules for journalists to gain access to government press conferences and other government events by requiring media executives to submit detailed applications on behalf of journalists. These new guidelines make it difficult for freelance and online journalists to work.

The ongoing attacks and harassment of the Ukrainian press has led to a growing sense of solidarity within the media community. Some advocates say that journalists' ability to rally widespread support has restrained officials who might otherwise have cracked down even harder on the press.

UZBEKISTAN

INCREASED INTERNATIONAL AID AND THE PRESENCE OF U.S. TROOPS using Uzbekistan as a base for the "war on terror" have focused new international attention on the country, forcing President Islam Karimov to pay lip service to press freedom. "Today, there are no boundaries to the flow of information, and any attempts to restrict freedom of speech are absolutely pointless and useless," Karimov told journalists at a June 27 celebration of Uzbekistan's Press Day.

With much fanfare, Karimov's government ended prior censorship of newspapers in May 2002, yet the change was almost entirely undermined when the government subsequently pressured editors to censor articles themselves. Some frightened editors even hired the state's former censors to minimize the risk of publishing anything that might be deemed offensive.

In addition, the country's highly centralized government and vigilant security service, along with the police, courts, prosecutors, inspectors, and other state agencies—all of which remain firmly under Karimov's control—engender widespread fear and self-censorship among journalists, who rarely question or debate government policy.

Those who do try to push government limits on censorship receive swift punishment. Uzbekistan remains the leading jailer of journalists in Europe and Central Asia, with five in prison at year's end. In August, Ruslan Sharipov, former head of the Union of Independent Journalists of Uzbekistan (UIJU), was sentenced to five-and-a-half years in jail on spurious charges of sodomy, managing prostitutes, and having sexual relations with minors. Authorities have harassed Sharipov for several years because of critical articles he contributed to the Russian news agency Prima and protest letters he wrote to the president for the UIJU describing police abuses and press freedom violations.

Gayrat Mehliboyev, a freelance journalist who wrote occasionally for the Tashkent newspaper *Hurriyyat*, was sentenced to seven years in prison in February for writing a political commentary about Islam and allegedly sympathizing with a banned Islamic opposition party. Madzhid Abduraimov, a correspondent with the national weekly *Yangi Asr*, was sentenced to 13 years in August 2001 for writing about corruption and remained jailed at year's end. Mukhammad Bekdzhanov, editor of *Erk*, a newspaper published by the banned opposition Erk party; and Yusuf Ruzimuradov, an *Erk* employee, were sentenced to 14 years and 15 years in prison, respectively, in August 1999 for distributing *Erk* and criticizing the government.

In May, the government fired the political editor of Uzbek state television after the station broadcast embarrassing footage of audience members sleeping during a speech Karimov delivered at a conference in the capital, Tashkent. And in March, administration officials dismissed the editor of *Hurriyat* for publishing articles about child poverty and mismanagement in the cotton industry, The Associated Press reported.

State-run and state-funded media dominate the airwaves and newsstands, churning out dreary reports about cotton harvests, recent government decrees, and Karimov's daily meetings. Many citizens prefer to get their news through gossip at the bazaar, the Internet, Russian television, and international radio broadcasts from the BBC and the U.S. government–funded Radio Free Europe/Radio Liberty and Voice of America.

The government makes every effort to block these alternative sources of news by intimidating stringers for foreign media outlets, denying international radio broadcasters access to local frequencies, and blocking access to religious, opposition, human rights, and news Web sites.

In January, the government's monopoly Internet service provider, UzPAK, blocked several Russia-based news Web sites after they posted articles by an anonymous analyst about government corruption in Karimov's inner circle. In February, police arrested freelance journalist Oleg Sarapulov as he left an Internet café in Tashkent and detained him for two days because he had printed several articles from *centralasia.ru*, a Russia-based news Web site that focuses on Central Asia.

Senior government officials often make threatening phone calls to editors outlining political guidelines and editorial instructions for news coverage. Journalists refer to these calls as *telefonaya pravo*, or "law of the telephone." In March, meanwhile, Foreign Minster Sodyk Safaev summoned leading editors to his office to request that they provide pro-U.S. coverage of the war in Iraq, according to the German government–funded broadcasting agency Deutsche Welle. In December, according to the London-based Institute for War and Peace Reporting, the Cabinet issued a decree forcing media outlets to re-register with authorities and subjecting newsletters published by nongovernmental human rights organizations to the same media regulations as newspapers.

The country's politicized and secretive Interagency Coordination Committee, which issues licenses for broadcast outlets, only gives local and regional broadcasting licenses to pro-government businesspeople and organizations that concentrate on entertainment programming. ■

MIDDLE EAST AND NORTH AFRICA

OVERVIEW: MIDDLE EAST AND NORTH AFRICA

by Joel Campagna

War and political violence drew hundreds of journalists to the Middle East in 2003 for what proved to be a series of relentlessly dangerous assignments. The U.S.-led war in Iraq was one of the most heavily covered conflicts in modern history—and one of the deadliest for journalists. Thirteen reporters died from hostile acts, both during and after the conflict, while several more died from illnesses or accidents. The sources of danger were varied and often unpredictable. At least four were killed by U.S. fire, three on the same day, April 8, when the shelling of Baghdad's Palestine Hotel killed two journalists and an air strike on the Baghdad bureau of the Qatar-based broadcaster Al-Jazeera killed another. Four journalists embedded with U.S. troops were killed by Iraqi fire. Still others were killed by land mines or died in suicide bombings.

The postwar environment has proved just as hazardous. Although journalists generally have not been singled out as targets, they have nevertheless had to cope with banditry, crime, firefights, and deliberate attacks against international organizations, leading even the most battle-hardened correspondents to call Iraq the most dangerous assignment they have ever experienced.

Elsewhere in the Middle East, journalists also faced danger. In Israel and the Occupied Territories, including those under the Palestinian National Authority, journalists continued to document violence, often at great peril. Until the Iraq war, the most dangerous place to work as a journalist in the Middle East was the occupied West Bank and Gaza Strip, where journalists have repeatedly braved bombs, bullets, and various forms of harassment from the Israeli army and Palestinian militants since the intifada erupted in 2000. Nearly lost among the headlines from Iraq were the shocking deaths of Associated Press Television News cameraman Nazih Darwazeh and freelance cameraman James Miller. Both men were killed by Israeli army gunfire in the Occupied Territories within a two-week span.

As the Darwazeh and Miller cases demonstrated, Israeli forces' gunfire was a major threat to photojournalists and reporters working in the Occupied Territories. Journalists also had to grapple with tough restrictions on their freedom of movement, which often hampered their ability to cover stories. Israeli soldiers were by no means the only threat. With the Palestinian Authority decimated by Israeli military assaults, Palestinian militias have filled the void, threatening journalists and destroying media equipment.

Despite looming danger and threats of physical harm, correspondents were adept at providing news and information when it mattered most, during a crisis. The war in Iraq was a major turning point for Arab media. Twelve years after the first Gulf War, when all

Joel Campagna is CPJ's senior program coordinator, responsible for the Middle East and North Africa. **Hani Sabra**, research associate for the Middle East and North Africa, contributed to the writing and research of this section. CPJ consultants **Nilay Karaelmas** and **Rhonda Roumani** provided important research on Turkey and Iraq, respectively. **The Open Society Institute** provided emergency funding for the Middle East and North Africa program during the Iraq conflict.

Photo (previous page): A television correspondent reports outside the Palestine Hotel in Iraq's capital, Baghdad, on April 16, 2003. *AP/Hussein Malla* eyes were glued to CNN and its live coverage from Baghdad, a bevy of new Arab satellite news channels were on the ground in 2003, breaking news and captivating viewers. The emergence in recent years of Al-Jazeera, the revamped United Arab Emirates–based Abu Dhabi TV and the pan-Arab Al-Arabiyya demonstrated that despite some weak points, Arab media were a force to be reckoned with in terms of spot news reporting and political debate. Long-established pan-Arab newspapers based in London have also contributed to the mix. Together, these new Arab media have provided varying degrees of uncensored coverage of regional events, serving as a platform for discussion otherwise unavailable in the regional media. Some, most notably Al-Jazeera, have pushed the boundaries of free expression by presenting dissident political views and airing criticism of Arab governments.

But the view beyond pan-Arab television and newspapers was altogether different. Local print and broadcast media have yet to break free from the yoke of government control. Autocratic governments continued to exert tremendous leverage over their national media, stifling the emergence of truly representative, independent news outlets. State ownership of print media is

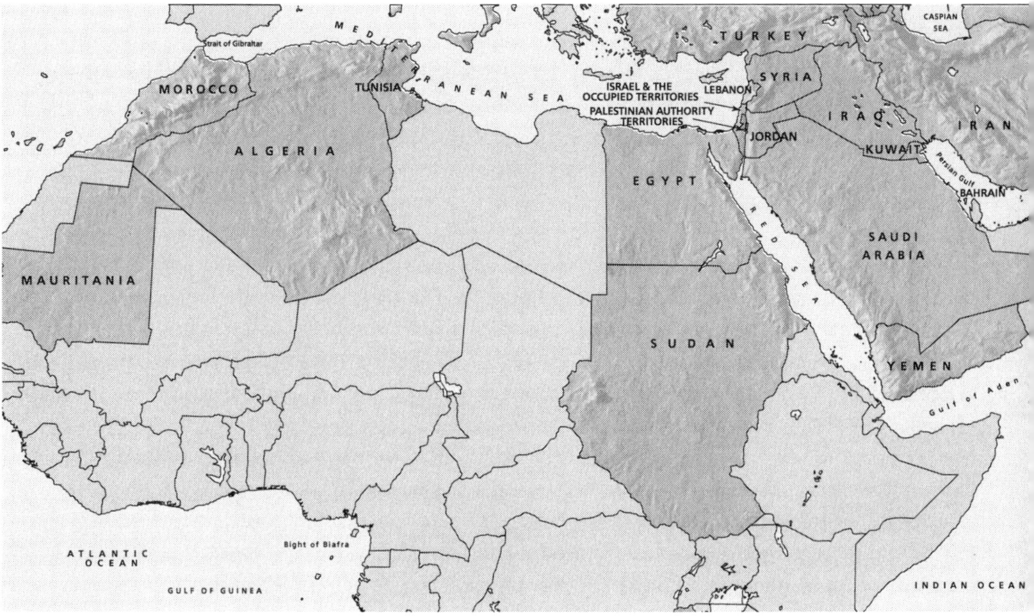

increasingly rare, but authorities in various Arab countries have crafted efficient systems of carrots and sticks to keep journalists in line.

Repressive press laws and penal codes are common throughout the region and provide the legal framework for what journalists can and cannot write. They also give governments broad powers to sanction dissenting media through criminal prosecution, the closure of newspapers, and the detention or imprisonment of journalists.

In Morocco—a country often recognized for its political moderation and relative tolerance for critical media—authorities jailed maverick editor Ali Lmrabet for eight months because of critical articles and cartoons he published about the country's young monarch, King Mohammed VI. Several other journalists were arrested or imprisoned under antiterrorism legislation that was enacted shortly after the multiple suicide bombings that rocked Casablanca in May.

In nearby Tunisia, which operates largely as a police state with little criticism from the West, Internet journalist Zouhair Yahyaoui spent more than 17 months behind bars for his satirical Web postings about the government. He was released in November, just prior to official visits to Tunis by U.S. Secretary of State Colin Powell and French President Jacques Chirac.

The imprisonments of Lmrabet and Yahyaoui were not the only cases of media harassment in the region in 2003. Cognizant of their international image, some governments in the Middle East and North Africa have become less inclined to employ blunt repression against the media. Instead, many use indirect forms of pressure to stifle critical views, such as Saudi Arabia, which has quietly dismissed columnists; Morocco, which has discouraged advertising in hard-hitting newspapers; and Algeria, which controls the printing company many publications use. Cronyism, cash in exchange for coverage, and cozy relationships between editors and officials are also common behind-the-scenes practices that have neutered the media.

The ever present security services of the region continued to vex journalists and impede independent reporting. Security forces harassed journalists and often controlled unions that were ostensibly charged with defending journalists' interests.

The press received a jolt, however, with the toppling of Saddam Hussein's repressive regime in April, which produced an explosion of new media in Iraq, where, for the first time in decades, journalists enjoyed the freedom to publish what they wished. Despite this new openness, there were worrying indicators about the future of media freedom, with U.S. authorities and the new Iraqi Governing Council penalizing local news outlets with closures and detaining and harassing working journalists in the field.

The aftermath of the Iraq war kindled debate about whether Hussein's fall would serve as a catalyst for political reform—and, by extension, greater media freedoms—throughout the region. However, by year's end, governments seemed unprepared to make changes.

Some did take a number of positive steps to expand press freedom during 2003, but they were cosmetic when viewed against overall conditions. For example, while Tunisia approved the country's first privately owned radio station and boasted of its support for a free press, security forces there continued to harass and prosecute independent journalists. In 2002, the tiny archipelago nation of Bahrain licensed the independent daily *Al-Wasat*, but in 2003 the government took the paper's editor to court for violating the country's regressive press law.

Three years ago, Syria licensed the country's first private and party newspapers in 40 years. However, in 2003 authorities closed the country's most independent newspaper, the satirical weekly *Al-Domari*. The Jordanian government announced the imminent licensing of private broadcast media and abolished a controversial press law, but the security forces retained their tight grip on the media, blunting aggressive domestic reporting by keeping close tabs on journalists and monitoring their activities. Saudi Arabia allowed the creation of the country's first journalists' association but cracked down on the press by dismissing writers when they boldly criticized religious militancy in the kingdom.

Amid seemingly insurmountable obstacles, a small group of locally based independent journalists challenged the status quo and offered hope for the future. In Morocco, courageous journalists such as Aboubakr Jamai, editor of the groundbreaking weeklies *Le Journal Hebdomadaire* and *Assahifa al-Ousbouiya*, and jailed editor Lmrabet remained uncompromising in their attempts to hold public officials accountable. Risk-takers such as Tunisian Internet journalist Yahyaoui and other Web-based independent journalists challenged one of the region's most intolerant regimes by continuing to publish online in the face of repeated threats. Despite government reprisals, Saudi journalists tackled taboo topics, such as religious militancy in their country. Other journalists barred from expressing their views in domestic media throughout the region made their voices heard in the growing number of offshore newspapers and satellite channels.

Greater media independence will ultimately go hand in hand with real political reform in the Middle East and North Africa. In the meantime, those outspoken voices that refuse to be silenced will play a pivotal role in laying the foundations of the future of free media.

ALGERIA

WITH ALGERIANS PREPARING FOR THE APRIL 2004 PRESIDENTIAL ELECTION, the government of President Abdelaziz Bouteflika, who has always had a contentious relationship with the media, took steps to restrict press freedom. Since 1990, when the first private newspapers were allowed in Algeria, the media and the government have engaged in a tug-of-war. In 2003, government interference intensified, marked by a campaign of legal harassment and financial pressure on private newspapers.

Authorities have used amendments to the Penal Code passed in 2001 against journalists, who can face prison sentences of up to one year and substantial fines if convicted of defaming the president, the courts, the military, or Parliament.

The government still controls radio and television, which rarely broadcast critical views. But some private newspapers aggressively report on government affairs and the political violence that has plagued the country for more than a decade. Algerian journalists say they are most careful when reporting on the army and the president, although they do criticize Bouteflika's policies. Nonetheless, self-censorship, ideological prejudices, and limited information have restricted coverage of controversial topics such as government human rights abuses, military corruption, and the military's role in national politics. Just how independent the private press really is remains up for debate, and journalists sometimes accuse publications of serving the interests of powerful politicians and military figures. Many journalists work for or have close ties with military intelligence officers, Algerian journalists told CPJ.

Between 1993 and 1996, fifty-eight Algerian journalists were murdered at the height of the country's civil conflict, which pitted the army and security forces against Islamist militants and other armed groups. It is believed that Islamist extremists were behind most of the killings, but many Algerian journalists suspect the government was involved in some as well. According to CPJ research, more journalists were killed in Algeria between 1992 and 2003 than in any other country in the world. The government has not allowed independent or international inquiries into the deaths.

In addition to the journalists killed in the 1990s, journalists Djamel Eddine Fahassi and Aziz Bouabdallah have been missing since 1995 and 1997, respectively, and no progress has been made in finding them. While Algerian authorities deny any responsibility for their disappearances, CPJ investigations have revealed that state security agents likely abducted the journalists.

In August 2003, after several private newspapers ran articles about financial malfeasance committed by top government officials, including the president's brother, the state-owned printer ordered the newspapers *El-Khabar*, *Errai*, *Le Soir d'Algérie*, *Le Matin*, *L'Expression*, and *Liberté* to pay debts owed to it within 72 hours, or they would not be printed. Many journalists believe that the order was an attempt by Bouteflika to muzzle the papers.

While the publications' editors confirmed that they owed money to the printer, they said they had agreed to pay in installments, and that the money demanded was not owed for months. The editors also pointed out that only critical newspapers were targeted, while many others that owed debts to the printer never received the ultimatum.

In September and October, after all the newspapers except *Errai* had paid off their debts to the printer and resumed publication, police began summoning many of the papers' editors, publishers, and journalists, as well as other journalists and editors who had criticized the government. Officers questioned them about articles and cartoons in their publications. Later, many of the journalists were brought before investigating judges and told that they were being investigated for defaming the president. When journalists began ignoring the summonses, police arrested them at their offices and homes. None of the journalists had been charged by year's end, and all had been released from jail.

In November, Algerian courts sentenced a number of journalists to prison. A court in Saida, in southwestern Algeria, sentenced Hassan Bouras, a journalist with the private daily *Al-Jazairi*, to two years in prison and barred him from practicing journalism for five years. Several individuals had sued him for defamation because of articles he wrote in *Al-Jazairi* about the misconduct of local government officials, including a story about their involvement in a real estate scam. Bouras spent several weeks in prison, but he was released just prior to U.S. Secretary of State Colin Powell's visit to the country in early December. Later that month, an appeals court overturned the sentence and the ban but ordered Bouras to pay fines and damages of 110,000 Algerian dinars (US$1,500).

Also in November, columnist Sid Ahmed Semiane, who lives in France, was sentenced in absentia to six months in jail in retaliation for a column he had written in 2002 criticizing the Ministry of Defense, which sued him for defamation as well. His case was awaiting an appeal at year's end. In November, Farid Alilat, editor of the French-language daily *Liberté*, was handed a four-month suspended prison sentence after being convicted of insulting the president in a recent article about high-level government corruption. Alilat and another journalist at the paper were also fined a crippling sum, but the case was awaiting an appeal at year's end.

Journalists say that obtaining a license for a new publication remains difficult, with some applications approved while others languish with no response. Some journalists have accused the authorities of blocking new titles that could be politically controversial. Nonetheless, at least four new publications have appeared recently: *Le Jour D'Algerie*, a French-language daily; *Al-Akhbar*, an Arabic-language daily; and two French-language weeklies, *Le Débat* and *La Dépêche*. Other license applications have also been approved, and the papers should be appearing on newsstands shortly.

Foreign journalists working in Algeria also face obstacles. The government sometimes monitors what they report, curtails their freedom of movement, and even censors their work. Many journalists are forced to be accompanied by government security escorts, which authorities say ensures journalists' safety. Journalists, however, contend the escorts are intended to control their work and limit whom they meet.

In the summer of 2003, government officials contacted foreign news outlets in the capital, Algiers, and barred them from covering the July 2 release of Ali Belhadj and Abassi Madani, leaders of the banned Islamic Salvation Front (FIS) who were sentenced to prison in 1992. The state-run French television stations France 2 and France 3 and the private French station TF1 ignored the orders and fed a tape of Belhadj's release to Paris from their hotel. After the footage aired on French television, police went to the hotel and confiscated the journalists' equipment. The TF1 team left the country July 3, before officials drafted an expulsion order, while Algerian authorities accompanied the France 2 and France 3 journalists to the airport that day.

BAHRAIN

A NEW PRESS LAW IMPLEMENTED BY THE GOVERNMENT IN OCTOBER 2002 imposes harsh restrictions on the press, undermining the limited democracy that was introduced in this tiny Persian Gulf archipelago after elections that year.

The law includes an assortment of restrictions and stipulates fines, prison terms, or closure of publications for those that violate them. Newspapers must obtain the approval of the information minister and the Cabinet before being allowed to publish. It is prohibited to criticize the king and Islam, insult the heads of Arab or Islamic countries, incite "sectarian hatred," or publish "false information" or any news that harms "national unity." The information minister can keep both local and foreign publications out of the country if they are deemed to break the law, and he can also seek court-ordered closures of newspapers and refer journalists to court for prosecution. Parliament was expected to review the law and possibly make amendments, but lawmakers had not done so by year's end.

In the meantime, authorities applied the law in at least three cases. In March, prosecutors charged editor Mansour al-Jamri and reporter Hussein Khalaf, both with the independent daily *Al-Wasat*, with violating a government-imposed media blackout surrounding the arrests of three alleged members of a terrorist cell. The journalists face up to six months in prison and a 1,000 dinar (US$2,650) fine if convicted, according to the paper's lawyer.

In September, Radhi al-Musawi, a member of the local political group National Democratic Action Society, was briefly detained and charged with defaming a government tourism agency employee. The employee had been accused of corruption in the group's newsletter, *Al-Democrati.*

Editor-in-chief Anwar Abdul Rahman and reporter Mariam Ahmed, both of the Arabic daily *Akhbar al-Khaleej*, were tried on charges of defaming several judges of an Islamic religious court. The case came after their newspaper ran a report in May about a Bahraini woman who staged a hunger strike outside the Justice Ministry after losing custody of her two daughters in the court.

In late October, all three cases were temporarily frozen when Bahrain's Constitutional Court was asked to rule on the constitutionality of certain articles of the Press Law and the Penal Code, under which the journalists were charged. The court ruled that the journalists can be prosecuted under the laws. All three cases were pending at year's end.

While most private newspapers are pro-government, the daily *Al-Wasat*, founded in 2002, has established itself as an independent paper by approaching political stories with a critical eye. In December, the new weekly *Al-Ahd* hit newsstands but staunchly toed the government line, according to local journalists.

Bahraini newspapers take special care to avoid certain topics, such as criticism of the king, high-level government corruption, divisions between Shiite and Sunni Muslims, and aggressive political commentary. Editors told CPJ that direct pressure is common, including phone calls from officials who "advise" them how to cover sensitive stories or ask them not to report on them at all. The information minister, however, described the calls as "meetings for exchanging information, not imposing orders."

The government remains the country's sole Internet provider. In the past, authorities have blocked access to a number of political sites—including those of opposition groups—claiming that they incite "sectarianism" and contain "offensive content." The government has also imposed restrictions on reporters from foreign news organizations. Journalists from Qatar's Al-Jazeera satellite channel remained barred from working in the country a year after officials prevented the station from covering local elections in May 2002. Authorities had accused Al-Jazeera of harming Bahrain, encouraging violence, and spreading "false news to its viewers."

EGYPT

EGYPT BOASTS MANY NATIONAL, PARTY, INDEPENDENT, AND OPPOSITION PUBLICATIONS that feature some of the Arab world's best-known commentators. But over the years, the government has alternated between crackdowns on the media and periods of relative openness.

For Egyptian journalists, self-censorship is the norm because violating the country's stringent press laws can land them in prison. Although some positive press freedom developments occurred in 2003, including more freedom to criticize authorities and cover sensitive stories, some topics remained off-limits—including the army, the judiciary, and the security services.

In general, journalists avoid criticizing President Hosni Mubarak, but in 2003, smaller, opposition-party newspapers were able to criticize Mubarak's son, Gamal, who is playing a more visible role in Egypt's public life. Weekly opposition papers such as *Al-Arabi*, the Nasserist Party's paper, published several critical columns regarding the possibility that Gamal, now the secretary for policy in his father's ruling National Democratic Party, may become the next president.

Much of the new criticism has appeared in smaller, lower-circulation party papers or in independent papers because authorities see these publications as less of a threat compared with mainstream national dailies. While many journalists are pleased by the critical voices in some opposition papers, they said the professional standards of these publications are low.

Journalists still faced legal threats in 2003. In June, Egypt's highest court, the Court of Cassation, upheld the convictions of Mostafa Bakry and his brother Mahmoud Bakry, editor-in-chief and deputy editor-in-chief, respectively, of the weekly newspaper *Al-Osboa*. The two men were sentenced to one year in prison each in 1998 for libeling Mohamed Abdel Aal, head of Egypt's suspended Social Justice Party. The case stemmed from articles the journalists wrote in 1996 in the opposition daily *Al-Ahrar*, which Mostafa Bakry was editing at the time, accusing Abdel Aal of financial misconduct. The journalists were imprisoned on June 2, 2003, and spent about three weeks in jail before the prosecutor ordered their release when Abdel Aal was sentenced to prison on charges similar to those mentioned in *Al-Ahrar*.

The political situation in Egypt was volatile prior to the U.S.-led war in Iraq, and many antiwar activists were arrested during protests, where journalists were sometimes harassed. Journalists also said that during the war, editors of the mainstream national newspapers, which maintain close relations with government authorities and whose editors are appointed by President Mubarak, instructed journalists about their coverage and what issues to avoid.

In June, authorities suspended the small Takaful Party newspaper *Al-Sada*. Editor Yasser Barakat told CPJ that agents from State Security Investigation called in Essam Abdel Razek, the president of the paper's board of directors and head of the party, for questioning the day the paper was suspended. Barakat said that although no exact reason was given for the suspension, agents cited the paper's harsh criticism of the United States and Israel.

Foreign newspapers are also at the mercy of the Egyptian government. The London-based pan-Arab daily *Al-Quds Al-Arabi*, which often harshly criticizes the Egyptian regime, was banned in Egypt in late August, according to the paper's editor-in-chief, Abdel Bari Atwan. Atwan said that although he never received an official explanation, he believes that the ban came in response to an opinion piece that criticized the possibility of Gamal Mubarak becoming president.

Several private satellite television channels are available in Egypt, such as the popular Dream TV, which was established in late 2001. While they broadcast mostly entertainment, some news shows feature discussions and debates on political issues. The channels are subject to Egyptian censors, and some shows and segments have been restricted for going too far. Journalists say that access to satellite and cable television is increasing in

Egypt, and that regional pan-Arab stations like Abu Dhabi Television and Al-Jazeera were popular among viewers, especially before and during the war in Iraq.

IRAN

THE DEATH IN DETENTION OF IRANIAN-CANADIAN FREELANCE PHOTOGRAPHER ZAHRA KAZEMI in July punctuated a year of ongoing state repression against dissident media. Newspaper closures continued, as did the arrest, prosecution, and imprisonment of journalists.

The press crackdown further added to popular disappointment with Iran's two-term president, Mohammed Khatami, whose attempts at social and political reform have been thwarted by the entrenched conservative establishment that controls most of the country's main levers of power. Conservative-controlled courts continued to sanction and harass the media in 2003.

Kazemi's death made international headlines and sparked a diplomatic row between Iran and Canada. Kazemi, a contributor to *Recto Verso*, a Montreal-based magazine, and the London-based photo agency Camera Press, was detained on June 23 while taking photographs outside Tehran's Evin Prison. She was taken to Baghiatollah Hospital after being held in government custody for nearly two weeks. She died at the hospital on July 10.

Initially, Iranian officials maintained that Kazemi had died of a stroke, but on July 16, Vice President Mohammed Ali Abtahi announced that the cause of death was a "brain hemorrhage resulting from beatings." A government inquiry released in late July concluded that Kazemi died as a result of a skull fracture likely caused by a blow to her head. The conservative and pro-reform factions that have vied for influence within the state apparatus appeared at odds over Kazemi's death as new revelations were countered with denials and efforts to cover up the details.

In late July, authorities prevented an independent autopsy by burying Kazemi in Iran against the wishes of family members in Canada who had sought to repatriate the body. Canada responded by withdrawing its ambassador to Iran. In the ensuing months, several agents from the Intelligence Ministry were arrested in connection with Kazemi's death, but by October just one—Mohammed Reza Aghdam Ahmadi—remained in jail. His trial was ongoing at year's end. A parliamentary commission report released in November said that members of the Iranian judiciary had been holding Kazemi in custody when she was beaten, making it unlikely, according to journalists and reformist politicians, that those responsible for her death will be brought to justice.

Judicial authorities closed or suspended several pro-reform newspapers in 2003. In January, Iran's Special Court for Clergy closed the leading reformist daily *Hayat-e-No*, and authorities detained its editor, Alireza Eshraghi, and two other journalists after the paper reprinted a 1930s American cartoon depicting U.S. President Franklin D. Roosevelt squashing a Supreme Court justice with his thumb. The cartoon triggered outrage among religious conservatives because the judge was thought to resemble former Iranian revolutionary leader Ayatollah Khomeini. Also in January, a court indefinitely suspended the popular reformist daily *Bahar* after it ran stories about funding for state television and the alleged financial improprieties of a charitable society run by senior religious officials. In September, another reformist daily, *Yas-e-No*, was shuttered for 10 days after it refused to reprint an article it had run by Tehran prosecutor and press nemesis Saeed Mortazavi about jailed political activist Abbas Abdi. Mortazavi complained that his article had not been displayed prominently enough in the newspaper the first time it was published.

Dozens of newspapers have been suspended or closed since April 2000, when Supreme Leader Ayatollah Ali Khamenei publicly lashed out against reformist publications, triggering a judicial crackdown on the press.

Government forces have routinely detained, questioned, and brought criminal charges against journalists in response to news coverage and opinions deemed provocative by the conservative establishment. In July, authorities detained Iraj Jamshidi, editor of the daily newspaper *Asia*, after he published a photograph of Maryam Rajavi, who heads the Iranian opposition group the People's Mujahedeen. The government closed *Asia*, and at year's end Jamshidi remained in jail.

At the end of 2003, at least three journalists were imprisoned in Iran for their work, in addition to several activists and dissident intellectuals who had formerly worked in the media. In February, the government freed Emaddedine Baghi, a maverick investigative journalist who was jailed in May 2000 for publishing articles about the role of Intelligence Ministry agents in the 1998 murders of several Iranian intellectuals and dissidents. In December, a revolutionary court handed him a suspended one-year prison sentence in a separate case but did not make clear on what charges the journalist had been convicted.

The government used other levers of control against the print media. The Supreme Council for National Security, which comprises President Khatami and other top state officials, frequently censors sensitive political news. For example, in May, the council barred the media from reporting on a petition signed by more than 100 reformist members of Parliament calling on Ayatollah Khamenei to stop blocking political reforms.

The Internet, particularly in the form of Web logs, has become an increasingly important forum for journalists, political activists, and intellectuals. Web access in Iran has largely been unregulated, but in 2003, the government followed through on threats made in previous years that it would begin to censor content. In May, the government ordered local Internet services providers to begin filtering pornographic material, as well as certain opposition news sites. According to local and international press reports, the conservative-controlled Supreme Cultural Revolutionary Council has ordered tens of thousands of sites to be blocked.

Sensitive to the growing influence of the Internet as a platform for political ideas, the government arrested Internet journalist Sina Motallebi on April 20, apparently in response to critical content on his Web site *Rooznegar.com*. He was released in May.

Iranians have also turned to satellite television as a source of independent news. Local television and radio remain state-owned and under the influence of conservative elements of the regime. Though technically banned, satellite dishes are widespread. The government has accused U.S.-based Iranian satellite news channels of fomenting student demonstrations and political unrest and took measures to jam their broadcasts during 2003. In January, the Council of Guardians, a conservative body that ensures laws conform to Islamic principles, rejected a parliamentary proposal to make limited satellite programming legally available to the public.

IRAQ

THE U.S.-LED WAR IN IRAQ PROVED EXTREMELY DANGEROUS FOR JOURNALISTS. More than a dozen lost their lives reporting there in 2003, and many seasoned war correspondents have called the postwar environment the most risky assignment of their lives. With the demise of Saddam Hussein's repressive regime, Iraqi media have flourished, but news organizations faced potentially restrictive new media regulations, as well as harassment from U.S. and Iraqi authorities.

While the Bush administration geared up for a military assault in 2002 and early 2003 to unseat Saddam Hussein, news organizations prepared to cover one of the biggest stories in years. Journalists braced for a range of possible dangers, including the prospect of Baghdad-based reporters being used as "human shields" or being taken hostage by the Iraqi government. There were major concerns that Saddam Hussein might use chemical or biological weapons, which would have not only jeopardized the local population but also those covering the front lines. Many journalists expressed fears about banditry and random violence in the chaos that might ensue following the collapse of the Iraqi regime. Journalists were also apprehensive about whether the Pentagon, which had sharply limited press access to previous conflicts in Grenada, Panama, the first Gulf War, and Afghanistan, would censor reporting and keep the press at bay.

But the Pentagon's plan to embed some 600 journalists with U.S. troops proved to be advantageous for both media organizations and the military. Soon after the war began on March 20, networks captivated viewers with dramatic images of U.S. tanks rolling through the Iraqi desert and firefights between U.S. and Iraqi forces. Embedded reporters covered the battle of Baghdad, U.S. air strikes on the city, and Hussein's garish palaces. They also produced a number of stories that embarrassed U.S. forces, such as *Washington Post* reporter William Branigin's account of an incident in which U.S. soldiers killed 10 Iraqi civilians at a checkpoint in central Iraq, refuting the military's claim that troops had fired warning shots that went unheeded. Also noteworthy was Dexter Filkins' story in *The New York Times* describing a U.S. soldier who mistakenly shot an Iraqi woman and then remarked: "I'm sorry. But the chick got in the way." Other stories described how armed Iraqis inflicted damage on U.S. Apache helicopters, forcing them to retreat, and how U.S. Army units were running out of food because supply lines had come under Iraqi attack.

Before the war began, embedded journalists raised concerns about whether they would face unreasonable restrictions. Embedded reporters were required to sign ground rules containing a host of vaguely worded provisions that could have easily been used to limit or censor reporting. In most cases, these formal restrictions were not enforced. However, some commanders did impose unreasonable embargoes on stories, expel a handful of reporters for alleged security breaches, and bar some from covering sensitive topics, such as a *Los Angeles Times* reporter who was told to refrain from reporting on extensive damage to a group of Apache helicopters, even though reporters with other units reported the details.

The close quarters shared by journalists and troops inevitably blunted reporters' critical edge. There were also limits on what types of stories reporters could cover, since the ground rules barred journalists from leaving their unit. "[The] access could be suffocating and blinding," noted the *Los Angeles Times*' David Zucchino, who was embedded with the 101st Airborne. "Often I was too close, or confined, to comprehend the war's broad sweep. I could not interview survivors of Iraqi civilians killed by U.S. soldiers or speak to Iraqi fighters trying to kill Americans. I was not present when Americans died at the hands of fellow soldiers in what the military calls 'frat,' for fratricide. I had no idea what ordinary Iraqis were experiencing. I was ignorant of Iraqi government decisions and U.S. command strategy."

News organizations also covered the war with independent, non-embedded reporters, or "unilaterals," as the Pentagon termed them. These journalists faced a multitude of hazards and restrictions, limiting the reporting from non-U.S. military perspectives.

The Pentagon frowned on the presence of unilateral reporters in Iraq. Officials repeatedly warned that the military could not guarantee their safety and urged them to avoid the country. Once hostilities began, Kuwaiti authorities systematically prevented non-embedded reporters from entering southern Iraq by enforcing a 75-mile (120-kilometer) "military exclusion zone" established in mid-February in the northern third of the country where U.S. troops were based. Those journalists wishing to travel to the border were required to obtain official approval from the Kuwaiti government, although in practice, few were granted approval. One Reuters correspondent told CPJ that if journalists managed to cross the border, they could work freely. But he said U.S. and British military authorities often would not speak to them or allow them into military bases.

In some cases, however, unilateral journalists faced outright harassment from U.S. forces. On March 25, U.S. troops detained two Israeli and two Portuguese journalists near Baghdad and accused them of being spies. According to the journalists, soldiers assaulted one of the men, Portuguese reporter José Castro, who was thrown to the ground and kicked in the ribs. In a separate incident, U.S. troops detained *Christian Science Monitor* reporter Phillip Smucker and escorted him out of southern Iraq to Kuwait on March 27, accusing him of revealing the location of a nearby military unit during a CNN telephone interview. (Smucker's editors pointed out that the unit's position had previously been revealed in other U.S. media.) He was marched away at gunpoint and denied contact with his newspaper and family for two days. Troops threatened to detain the journalist again when he re-entered Iraq a few days later.

Unilateral reporters who did manage to get into Iraq remained partly dependent on U.S. and coalition troops for security and supplies. In several instances, troops provided support to unilateral journalists and allowed them to accompany U.S. troops. Many journalists stayed away from the front lines altogether because of the fighting. The death of ITV News correspondent Terry Lloyd—who was killed after his car came under U.S. and Iraqi gunfire in southern Iraq in the first days of the war—made some non-embedded journalists more cautious. But there were other incidents in which non-embedded journalists came under fire, were nearly killed on the battlefield, or were detained after stumbling across Iraqi forces.

The 200 or so journalists who stayed in Baghdad to cover the start of the war faced similar challenges. Operating mainly from hotels, foreign correspondents worked under close Iraqi government supervision, with authorities assigning reporters minders who shadowed their moves. In many cases, the fear of expulsion further deterred hard-hitting reporting. Iraqi officials detained, threatened, or otherwise intimidated several reporters.

Shortly after the war began, Iraqi authorities detained four reporters on suspicion of espionage. Freelance photographer Molly Bingham; Johan Rydeng Spanner, a freelance photographer with the Danish daily *Jyllands Posten*; and correspondent Matthew McAllester and photographer Moises Saman, both with the U.S.-based daily *Newsday*, were taken from the Palestine Hotel and held for eight days in Bagdhad's Abu Ghraib Prison. The journalists were eventually released following an intensive international campaign on their behalf.

The war in Iraq raised public awareness about the risks journalists face to report the news. By year's end, 13 journalists had been killed by hostile acts, while six others died of ailments or in accidents. Two more media workers—ITV News cameraman Fred Nerac and translator Hussein Othman—have been missing since late March, when they were caught in the crossfire incident in southern Iraq that killed ITV's Terry Lloyd.

The bloodiest day of the war for journalists was April 8, when two separate attacks by U.S. forces killed three journalists and injured several others. In the first attack, a U.S. warplane struck an electricity generator outside the Baghdad bureau of the Qatar-based satellite channel Al-Jazeera, killing reporter Tareq Ayyoub. The attack occurred in an area of heavy fighting, although Al-Jazeera noted that it had provided the Pentagon with the coordinates of its offices weeks before the incident. The nearby office of Abu Dhabi TV also came under U.S. fire at the time. In October, a U.S. military spokesman acknowledged to CPJ that no investigation into the incident was ever launched.

In the second incident later that day, a U.S. tank fired a shell at the Palestine Hotel, which housed most foreign correspondents in Baghdad, killing cameramen Taras Protsyuk of Reuters and José Couso of Spanish television channel Telecinco. U.S. troops claimed that they were responding to hostile fire emanating from the hotel. A CPJ investigative report published in May concluded that the shelling of the hotel, while not deliberate, was avoidable since U.S. commanders knew that journalists were in the hotel but failed to relay this information to soldiers on the ground.

On August 12, U.S. Central Command (Centcom) issued a news release summarizing the results of its investigation into the incident, which determined that the tank unit that opened fire on the hotel did so "in a proportionate and justifiably measured response." Centcom called the shelling "fully in accordance with the Rules of Engagement." While Centcom's summary was mostly consistent with CPJ's findings, it failed to address one of the conclusions in CPJ's report: U.S. commanders knew that journalists were in the Palestine Hotel but failed to convey this knowledge to forces on the ground. CPJ has urged Centcom to make the full report public, but a Centcom spokesperson told CPJ on August 13 that the report is classified. At press time, CPJ was still waiting for the Defense Department to respond to Freedom of Information Act (FOIA) requests related to both April 8 attacks.

In covering postwar Iraq, journalists have confronted an assortment of hazards, including bomb attacks, shootings, carjackings, holdups, and abductions. Traveling to Iraq from Jordan and Kuwait carried risks of armed assault by well-organized bandits who prowl the main roads. Western correspondents, who stand out and can be mistaken for coalition personnel or foreigners in general, were particularly vulnerable.

In September, a small explosive device detonated outside the Al-Aike Hotel in central Baghdad, where NBC News had based its Iraq operations. The blast shattered windows, killed a hotel security guard, and slightly injured NBC News soundman David Moodie, who was one of about a dozen NBC employees in the hotel at the time. In November, the Palestine and Sheraton hotels, which continued to house large numbers of journalists, came under rocket attack, though no one was seriously hurt.

Also in November, unidentified gunmen in southern Iraq opened fire on a convoy of Portuguese journalists, wounding Maria João Ruela, a reporter with the television channel Sociedade Independente de Comunicação. Reporter Carlos Raleiras, who works for the Portuguese radio station TSF, was abducted by the assailants but was freed 36 hours later.

The conduct of U.S. troops has exacerbated the tenuous security situation for journalists in Iraq. On August 17, soldiers shot and killed veteran Reuters cameraman and former CPJ International Press Freedom Award recipient Mazen Dana while he filmed a U.S. tank convoy outside Abu Ghraib Prison near Baghdad. U.S. soldiers said they mistook his camera for a rocket-propelled grenade (RPG) launcher. Dana had secured permission from U.S. forces to film in the area, and, according to eyewitnesses, there was no fighting in the area when the journalist was shot.

On September 22, the U.S. military announced that it had concluded its investigation into Dana's killing, and a Centcom spokesman told CPJ that while the journalist's death was "regrettable," the soldiers "acted within the rules of engagement." No further details were provided, and the results of the investigation have not been made public. Observers have frequently pointed out that although a soldier might mistake a camera for an RPG at a long distance, a camera would be clearly visible from the estimated 55 yards (50 meters) at which Dana was hit. In October, CPJ filed a FOIA request with the Department of Defense seeking information about Dana's killing and the subsequent classified military investigation. In December, U.S. Central Command said it would provide CPJ in 2004 with a "redacted copy" of the classified report on Dana's killing.

Journalists who approached or worked near U.S. troops encountered other forms of harassment. Many described incidents in which they were briefly detained, roughed up, had warning shots fired over their heads, or had their film or equipment confiscated. In August, U.S. soldiers detained Associated Press (AP) photographer Karim Kadim and his driver, Mohammed Abbas, near Abu Ghraib Prison. Both men were handcuffed, forced to stand in the sun for three hours, and denied water and the use of a telephone while soldiers kept their guns pointed at them, even though the journalist had told the troops they were members of the press. A U.S. military officer later apologized to the journalists and told AP's Baghdad bureau that their arrest was a "misunderstanding."

In July, U.S. forces detained Said Abu Taleb and Soheil Kareemi, two journalists with Iranian State Television who, according to their colleagues, were in Iraq working on a documentary for Iran's Channel 2 television. U.S. forces arrested the journalists after they were seen filming near a U.S. military outpost. At the time of the arrests, the Coalition Provisional Authority (CPA), the U.S.-led interim authority in Iraq, said the two were being held for committing "security violations," and that they were "not acting in a journalistic capacity when they were arrested." They were released in November and allowed to return to Iran. The British Foreign Office later admitted that, "It was unfortunate that these two journalists were caught up in the stringent security regime currently in place in Iraq."

Al-Jazeera reported that its correspondents were arrested on multiple occasions while covering the aftermath of guerrilla attacks on U.S. troops. U.S. forces accused Arab satellite channels Al-Jazeera and Al-Arabiyya of having prior knowledge of attacks on coalition troops—a charge that both stations deny. U.S. officials also continued to launch other harsh invectives against both stations, labeling them as anti-coalition, among other things.

Following the downing of a U.S. Army helicopter by guerrillas in the Iraqi town of Fallujah in early November, U.S. troops confiscated the camera of Knight Ridder photographer David Gilkey, of *The Detroit Free Press*, and erased all of his photographs.

In November, representatives of 30 U.S. and international media organizations signed a letter to Pentagon spokesman Larry DiRita stating that they had "documented numerous examples of U.S. troops physically harassing journalists and, in some cases, confiscating or ruining equipment, digital camera discs, and videotapes." Pentagon officials acknowledged the organizations' concerns and said that they had reissued guidance to field commanders and public affairs officers in the region that journalists should be allowed to do their jobs.

Since the fall of Baghdad, new Iraqi media outlets have exploded on the scene, with dozens of partisan and independent newspapers being published after decades of state control under Saddam Hussein. The quality of the journalism is uneven, but a number of respected publications have emerged. The CPA, which inherited the old Iraqi broadcasting infrastructure, operates a nationwide television station, Al-Iraqiyya, as well as two radio stations and a newspaper.

In an attempt to regulate nascent Iraqi media outlets and rein in what it viewed as inflammatory material, the CPA implemented a controversial anti-incitement decree in June that empowered occupation authorities to close newspapers and detain, fine, or imprison journalists. Specifically, the order bars incitement to violence against individuals, religious sects, and the CPA and prohibits any support for the return of the Baath Party to power in Iraq. The CPA closed the publication *Al-Mustqaillah*, which had cited the calls of Islamic clerics for the death of "spies" who cooperate with U.S. troops. The clerics said killing spies was a religious duty. There were also reports of U.S. forces raiding or closing other local media outlets.

While the Iraqi media are freer than ever, the CPA and the U.S.-appointed Iraqi Governing Council have made several attempts to sanction the press. In September, the council barred Arabic satellite broadcasters Al-Jazeera and Al-Arabiyya from covering official press conferences and from entering official buildings for two weeks. Council spokesmen said the decision came because the channels incite "sectarian differences in Iraq," "political violence," and the murders of council and U.S. coalition members. Officials also said the broadcasters failed to disclose information about pending attacks on U.S. troops, but it is unclear what specific broadcasts prompted the sanctions.

In November, the council closed the Iraq offices of Al-Arabiyya after it aired an audiotape on November 16 purportedly of Saddam Hussein urging Iraqis to resist the U.S.-led occupation. Jalal Talabani, a member of Iraq's Governing Council who ordered the closure, said in an op-ed published in *The Washington Post* several days later that the ban was "temporary," and that the broadcaster was only barred from transmitting footage from Iraq via satellite and could continue newsgathering. He said the penalty was instituted because Al-Arabiyya had incited violence by airing the tape.

Because satellite dishes were banned under Hussein's rule, Iraqis have voraciously bought dishes, giving citizens a wide range of international and Arabic programming. The Internet, although beyond the financial reach of most Iraqis, is available to those who can afford it.

ISRAEL AND THE OCCUPIED TERRITORIES (INCLUDING THE PALESTINIAN AUTHORITY TERRITORIES)

THE ISRAELI ARMY CONTINUED TO IMPERIL REPORTERS and restrict their work in the occupied West Bank and Gaza Strip, making the area one of the most complicated and dangerous assignments for journalists in the Middle East. During 2003, two journalists were shot and killed by Israel Defense Forces (IDF) fire. Others encountered harsh treatment at checkpoints or had to contend with army-imposed limits on their movements.

As in previous years, the press freedom climate in the Occupied Territories changed depending on the conflict. With fewer armed clashes between Israelis and Palestinians in 2003 than during the first two years of the second intifada, which began in 2000, journalists say that working in the territories has become in some ways less dangerous. However, conditions remain violently unpredictable.

Within two weeks in late April and early May, Israeli forces shot dead two cameramen, bringing to six the number of journalists killed by Israeli fire since 2000. On April 19, Associated Press Television News cameraman Nazih Darwazeh was shot in the West Bank city of Nablus while covering clashes between Palestinian youths and Israeli troops. Darwazeh was filming an Israeli tank stranded at the corner of an alleyway when an Israeli soldier took a position on one knee near the tank and fired a single shot at where Darwazeh and several colleagues were standing, about 11 to 22 yards (10 to 20 meters) away. Darwazeh, who was wearing a fluorescent jacket marked "Press," was hit in the head and died instantly, according to eyewitnesses. (See CPJ's Web site, *www.cpj.org*, for more details.)

The IDF maintains that troops had been rescuing the stranded tank when they were attacked with stones, and that "explosive devices and shots were fired from the crowd." Journalists said that although gunfire and clashes had occurred nearby, none took place in the alley at the time of the shooting. Despite eyewitness accounts and video footage, the IDF argues that it cannot say who fired the shot that killed Darwazeh. The IDF says it is conducting an investigation into the incident but has yet to make public any results.

Thirteen days later, on May 2, British freelance cameraman and film director James Miller was fatally shot in Rafah, in the Gaza Strip. An award-winning documentary filmmaker, Miller was with a crew filming an HBO documentary about the Israeli-Palestinian conflict. When they attempted to leave the area that evening, Miller and several crew members came under fire while they tried to identify themselves as journalists to Israeli troops in armored personnel carriers about 109 yards (100 meters) away. The journalists, who were wearing jackets and helmets marked "TV," shined a flashlight on a white flag they were holding and shouted at the troops. As they approached, Miller was hit in the neck by one of several rounds that were fired, and he later died of his injuries. The Israeli army said troops in the area returned fire after being attacked with rocket-propelled grenades. Army officials claimed that Miller was struck by a bullet from behind, suggesting that he may have been hit by Palestinian fire.

A detailed investigation sponsored by Miller's colleagues, family, and friends and conducted by British security consultant Chris Cobb-Smith of the security company Chiron Resources Limited, however, concluded that IDF soldiers "consciously and deliberately targeted" Miller and his crew. The report noted that the area where Miller's crew was operating had been quiet for about an hour before he was killed. Prior to that time, only sporadic gunfire was heard, but not in the journalists' vicinity. According to the report, it is reasonable to assume that the IDF troops heard the crew calling to them, and that they were aware of the crew's presence. At year's end, an Israeli military police investigation into the incident was under way. The IDF's investigation into the shooting has not been made public.

The military's previous record of investigating such incidents does not bode well for the official inquiries launched into the deaths of Darwazeh and Miller. Over the years, the army has failed to conduct thorough investigations into cases where journalists have been wounded or killed by IDF gunfire, let alone punish those responsible for the attacks. The same can be said for troops who physically attack or otherwise mistreat journalists in the field.

A number of such incidents occurred during 2003 in the West Bank and Gaza Strip. In January, Israeli border police in Nablus assaulted Nasser Ishtayeh, of The Associated Press, and Jaafar Ishtayeh, of Agence France-Presse. (The two are distant relatives.) Troops punched and threatened the journalists when they attempted to photograph Israeli border police who had forced two Palestinian youths to ride on the hood of a moving jeep. The journalists claimed that the troops were using the two as "human shields" to deter attacks from stone-throwing youths.

The army closed a number of Palestinian radio and television stations in late January. On January 30, troops entered the building housing the private, Hebron-based Al-Nawras TV and Al-Marah Radio and ordered the stations closed without providing a reason, according to staff members. Troops also shuttered the private Al-Majd TV a few hours later after soldiers asked the staff if they had contacts with the militant organizations Hamas and Islamic Jihad. An IDF spokesman said the stations were closed "based on information of broadcasting and distribution of incitement to terror." In October, troops briefly raided the Ramallah office of the Qatar-based Al-Jazeera satellite news channel during a larger sweep of a nearby mosque.

Since the second intifada began in September 2000, journalists trying to report from the West Bank and Gaza Strip have experienced sharp limits on their freedom of movement. The Israeli army has created a web of checkpoints throughout the West Bank and has sealed off towns and cities with large barriers. Moving from town to town can be a logistical headache or, depending on the security situation or the whims of individual soldiers, impossible. Since the army reoccupied most West Bank towns in April 2002, it increased the number of roadblocks and has regularly imposed curfews on Palestinian cities, which has also curtailed reporting.

Today, only a few Israeli journalists venture into the Occupied Territories because of army restrictions and safety concerns. The few who do go must sign a waiver absolving the army of responsibility for their safety. Foreign journalists are generally not required to sign waivers.

It is extremely difficult for Palestinian journalists to work in the Occupied Territories. In January 2002, Israel's Government Press Office (GPO) suspended the accreditation of most Palestinian journalists from the territories, including those who work with foreign media outlets. Because GPO press cards help facilitate journalists' movement through army checkpoints, news organizations complain that the measure has hurt their ability to cover the territories since many employ Palestinian stringers and fixers. During 2003, Israeli forces detained several Palestinian journalists working during curfews because, without GPO press cards, they were unable to prove they were accredited journalists.

Foreign correspondents say they have experienced increased hostility from some Israeli officials who accuse international media outlets of bias or unfair coverage of Israel. Journalists cite the GPO's accreditation suspension as one result of that hostility, but there were other examples. In June, Israel ceased all official cooperation with the BBC after the network aired a documentary about Israel's arsenal of unconventional weapons. The government said officials would not give interviews to the BBC and would make it difficult for BBC reporters to get accreditation and work visas. In April, security authorities at Ben Gurion Airport detained two French journalists from TV channel Canal Plus and held them overnight. The journalists had arrived to work on a story about international peace activists in the Occupied Territories, some of whom were shot and wounded by Israeli troops.

The Foreign Press Association of Israel (FPA) and foreign correspondents cited numerous other examples of foreign journalists who endured protracted delays, interrogations, and the confiscation of their equipment at various ports of entry into Israel. Some foreign media workers also encountered excessive bureaucracy while attempting to secure residency visas.

In November, the GPO announced new administrative guidelines for press accreditation that included a provision requiring the country's internal security service, Shin Bet, to vet all journalists seeking accreditation. The new regulation appeared to give the GPO and Israeli security authorities broad discretion to deny applications based on vague or unsubstantiated security concerns. After vocal protest from Israeli press groups and the FPA, the guidelines were quietly scrapped in November.

Israel's Hebrew-, Arabic-, and English-language press are mostly free, but government and military officials can censor media outlets if authorities deem certain news—such as troop buildups and death counts—harmful to the country's security interests. Journalists, however, have the option of appealing such censorship to the High Court of Justice. Most media can circumvent restrictions by attributing sensitive stories to foreign news outlets, whose information is not subject to censorship.

Israeli journalists objected in January when Attorney General Elyakim Rubinstein subpoenaed the cell phone records of *Ha'aretz* journalist Baruch Kra. The subpoena came as part of a criminal investigation to determine the source of a leak Kra received about an undercover government criminal inquiry into a questionable loan to Prime Minister Ariel Sharon's sons from a family friend. The phone records were obtained and officials eventually fingered the source of the leak—a state prosecutor who is now facing prosecution herself.

PALESTINIAN AUTHORITY TERRITORIES

Journalists operating in areas under the control of Yasser Arafat's Palestinian National Authority (PNA) faced several obstacles in 2003, but overt press freedom abuses by the

PNA have diminished as its power has faded. For years, the PNA and its various security apparatuses have routinely harassed the local media by arresting, intimidating, and censoring those who publish dissenting views. However, with the PNA weakened by repeated Israeli military assaults and the IDF's reoccupation of most of the West Bank, the authority's ability to impose control has been greatly reduced.

Palestinian journalists said they received fewer phone calls in 2003 from officials pressuring them to change their reporting. As a result, some journalists were more likely to criticize Palestinian authorities. Nonetheless, the mainstream Palestinian media engage in self-censorship because of the close financial or political ties they have with Palestinian officials.

Authorities still crack down on the media, particularly in the Gaza Strip, where Palestinian institutional control has long been concentrated. In January, Palestinian security forces detained Saifeddin Shahin, the Gaza correspondent for the Qatar-based satellite channel Al-Jazeera, for several hours. They questioned him about an Al-Jazeera news bulletin during which a news anchor conducted a telephone interview with a man claiming to be a member of the Al-Aqsa Martyrs Brigade who said the group was responsible for a recent suicide bombing. The caller also criticized the PNA.

In July, when Palestinian groups and Israel reached a temporary cease-fire, the Palestinian Information Ministry warned print and broadcast editors to tone down their political coverage. Specifically, editors were warned to avoid interviews with armed militants not under PNA control, to avoid overly nationalistic editorializing, and to support the cease-fire.

While the PNA's weakness limited official interference in the press in 2003, it created other potential threats to journalists, because armed groups and political factions now have more power. On September 13, five armed masked men stormed the Ramallah offices of the Dubai-based satellite news channel Al-Arabiyya and destroyed office equipment. The assailants, who identified themselves as members of the Al-Aqsa Martyrs Brigade, a militant group loosely linked to Arafat's Fatah organization, told the staff to stop working from the office. The journalists said the men never gave a reason for the attack, but staff members believe that the attack may have come in retaliation for Al-Arabiyya's recent reports on internal struggles in the PNA, including control over security services and the role of the Palestinian prime minister.

The PNA controls the official Palestine TV and Voice of Palestine radio, which reflect PNA views. Private Palestinian broadcast stations have proliferated across the West Bank and Gaza Strip during the last decade but have endured financial hardship, closure by Israeli and Palestinian forces, and the destruction of their facilities by the Israeli army.

JORDAN

THE NEW GOVERNMENT OF PRIME MINISTER FAISAL AL-FAYEZ, formed in October 2003, pledged to improve basic freedoms in Jordan. But if the last two years are any indication, the task will be formidable.

Since 2001, Jordan has witnessed a sharp erosion of liberties, chief among them press freedom. After King Abdullah II dissolved Parliament in June 2001, the government of then Prime Minister Ali Abou al-Ragheb enacted by fiat more than 200 "temporary laws," including restrictive Penal Code amendments with harsh new penalties for the media. The amendments, adopted shortly after the September 11, 2001, attacks on the United States under the guise of combating terrorism, allowed the government to jail and fine journalists and close publications that violate a number of broadly defined offenses.

In a surprise but welcome move, the government repealed the most restrictive amendment in April, apparently in response to local and international protest, but it was not soon enough. Several journalists and one opposition figure had already been detained, prosecuted, or investigated for their outspokenness.

In January 2003, officials detained three journalists from the weekly *Al-Hilal* after the paper published an article purporting to describe the sexual relations between the Prophet Muhammad and his wife Aisha. Editor-in-Chief Nasser Qamash, Managing Editor Roman Haddad, and writer Mohannad Mubaidin were sentenced in early February to prison terms ranging from two to six months for publishing "false rumors," "insulting the dignity of the state," and causing instability. The court retroactively banned *Al-Hilal* for two months beginning January 16, when the State Security Court prosecutor had initially halted the magazine's publication. On February 18, the court converted the prison sentences against Qamash and Haddad into fines, and both men were released. Mubaidin, the article's author, served out a six-month sentence.

In September, the general prosecutor banned the September 23 issue of the private weekly *Al-Wihda*. Staffers said the ban came after editors refused to comply with the prosecutor's demand that certain articles be removed before the paper appeared on newsstands. One editor said the authorities objected in particular to an article alleging that political detainees had been tortured in custody. In October, security agents ordered the newspaper to remove a cartoon from its galleys that depicted Prime Minister al-Faisal and Foreign Minister Marwan Musher as cooperating with the U.S. occupation of Iraq. The paper replaced it with another cartoon and printed the issue.

The country's powerful internal security service remains one of the greatest impediments to independent media in the country. Agents frequently exert backdoor pressure on newspapers through admonishing phone calls or warnings. The security service also enlists journalists to keep close tabs on their colleagues.

With the U.S.-led war in Iraq looming in February, newspapers failed to cover the controversial presence of U.S. troops in Jordan or even the deployment of Patriot missile batteries to protect the country against a possible missile attack by Saddam Hussein. Publications also played down or avoided coverage of antiwar demonstrations in the capital, Amman. In February, the editor of the leading pro-government daily *Al-Rai* told *The Washington Post* that he was not afraid of government reprisals against his paper because he was so heavily censoring its pages.

Foreign journalists in Jordan fared better than their local counterparts. In the months before the Iraq war, hundreds of reporters descended on Amman in hopes of securing Iraqi visas or, once hostilities began, of crossing the border to Baghdad. Most foreign correspondents experienced few difficulties reporting from the country and in many cases praised the government for accommodating them. Before the war, the government designated the area along the Iraqi border a closed military zone, and there were reports that Jordanian forces briefly detained some Western journalists for filming there. After the fall of Saddam Hussein's regime, most reporters were able to cross the border without incident.

The Qatar-based satellite channel Al-Jazeera, which was banned in Jordan in 2002 for airing a program during which a guest poked fun at King Abdullah's limited knowledge of classical Arabic, was allowed to resume broadcasting in March 2003.

In December, the government created a new licensing system for private radio and television stations, ending the state's monopoly on broadcast media. The regulations for news stations were not entirely clear at press time, but the government-appointed Audio Visual Commission, which said it was already reviewing license requests, retains veto power over all applications. Licensing fees are expensive, between 25,000 and 100,000 Jordanian dinars (US$35,000 and US$140,000) for television. Radio and TV stations wanting to cover news and political issues are required to pay 50 percent above the normal licensing fees. At year's end, it remained unclear which stations would receive licenses.

KUWAIT

IN THE LEAD-UP TO THE U.S.-LED WAR IN IRAQ, HUNDREDS OF INTERNATIONAL JOURNALISTS assembled in Kuwait, the main launching pad for the U.S. invasion. Although journalists were able to report freely within the country, those seeking to cross the border into Iraq encountered stiff resistance from the Kuwaiti military.

In mid-February, the Kuwaiti government declared a 75-mile (120-kilometer) "military exclusion zone" in the northern third of the country where U.S. troops were based. Journalists wishing to travel toward the border were required to have a special permit from the Interior Ministry, which often proved difficult to obtain.

Once hostilities commenced in late March, Kuwaiti authorities prevented non-embedded reporters from entering southern Iraq. As a result, many remained in Kuwait or went on official trips to southern Iraq with the U.S. military. The latter often turned out to be less than optimal for independent newsgathering. "To show up with a Humvee with machine guns on top, and guys in flak jackets and helmets, completely changes the dynamic when you try to talk to people," ABC News reporter John Donvan told *The Washington Post* during a trip to southern Iraq.

Some journalists managed to sneak past checkpoints and gain entry to Iraq. Others camped out at Bedouin farms along the Kuwait-Iraq DMZ before the war started and were able to make their way north once the fighting began.

Inside Kuwait, restrictions on the media were less dramatic. As war approached, Kuwaiti journalists speculated that the government might impose martial law and, with it, press censorship. CPJ articulated these concerns in meetings with Kuwaiti officials in February in the capital, Kuwait City. In the end, such measures never materialized. The Information Ministry, however, issued a directive barring journalists from filming Kuwaiti troops in the streets, and reporters complained about the lack of access to Kuwaiti officials.

More troubling, the ministry warned journalists, under the threat of criminal penalties, not to file stories for Israeli media. The move was apparently precipitated by the presence of a number of dual-national Israeli reporters who had arrived on non-Israeli passports to cover events. Absent from the mix of foreign media was the Qatar-based broadcaster Al-

Jazeera, which remained banned from Kuwait one year after authorities closed its local bureau because its reports were allegedly "biased" against the country.

Kuwait's relatively robust print press maintained its critical edge in war coverage and other domestic issues throughout 2003. Unfortunately, however, the country's press law can serve as a deterrent to coverage of sensitive topics. For instance, under the law, it is prohibited to subject "the person of the emir to criticism," and the government can suspend newspapers and jail journalists for "tarnishing public morals," "disparaging God [and] the prophets," "violating the national interest," or "creating divisions among people."

On June 8, Kuwait's Council of Ministers filed a lawsuit against Mohammad al-Jasem, editor of the leading daily *Al-Watan*, accusing the journalist of "object[ing] to the rights and powers of the emir publicly." The charges, punishable by up to five years in prison, stemmed from a speech al-Jasem made on June 7 at a campaign gathering for a parliamentary candidate. During the speech, al-Jasem criticized official misconduct in Kuwait's electoral process. Al-Jasem said he actually made no mention of the emir, and he believes that the charges against him were prompted by his stand against a restrictive draft press law and criticism of Kuwaiti officials in his newspaper. The incident triggered international protests, and authorities dropped the original charge. However, they replaced it with a new one of insulting the prime minister and ruling family, which also carries the possibility of imprisonment. On December 28, the court dismissed the case, citing procedural errors on the part of the prosecution. The verdict could be appealed within 20 days of the ruling, but nothing had been filed by year's end.

Kuwaiti editors have strongly criticized the changes to the press law proposed by the government in 2002. The amendments would empower state prosecutors to suspend newspapers on the recommendation of the Information Ministry and place a cap on the number of newspapers that can be licensed. The amendments have remained bogged down in Parliament for more than a year, and it was unclear when they might be debated.

In other developments, Kuwait's High Court commuted the death sentence handed down on March 11 against police officer Khaled al-Azmi, who was convicted of murdering Hidaya Sultan al-Salem, owner and editor of the weekly magazine *Al-Majales*. Al-Salem was shot in March 2001 on her way to work in what her lawyers and the government said was retribution for an *Al-Majales* article that allegedly insulted the women of al-Azmi's tribe. However, some Kuwaiti journalists believe that al-Azmi may have killed al-Salem because of a personal dispute. Al-Azmi, who never admitted to the crime, is now serving a life sentence.

In December, Kuwait's press corps was rattled by another act of violence when a letter bomb, postmarked Beirut, Lebanon, arrived at the offices of Ahmed Jarallah, editor of the daily *Al-Siyassah*. The package exploded, slightly injuring Jarallah's secretary. The motive and source of the bombing was unclear, though the paper was critical of "political and religious fanatics in the Arab world," said Jarallah.

Meanwhile, two journalists remained in official custody in Kuwait. Ibtisam Berto Sulaiman al-Dakhil and Fawwaz Muhammad al-Awadi Bessisso, were jailed for life in June 1991 for working with the collaborationist newspaper *Al-Nida'*, which was published under the Iraqi occupation of Kuwait. Kuwait's emir pardoned the journalists in 2002, but they remained in jail because Bessisso, a stateless Palestinian, is not a citizen of any country and Al-Dakhil, a naturalized Kuwaiti citizen from Iraq, lost her citizenship as a result of her conviction. Efforts were still under way to identify a country willing to accept them. Since 1996, some 15 *Al-Nida'* journalists have been released, many by royal decree, and all have been deported.

Kuwait's government owns and controls all radio and television stations in the country. The Information Ministry periodically issues directives to Internet service providers to filter "immoral" content and some political content.

LEBANON

LEBANESE MEDIA FEATURE DIVERSE OPINIONS, AGGRESSIVE QUESTION-AND-ANSWER television programs with government officials, and lively criticism of authorities and policies. In addition, the prevalence of satellite dishes gives Lebanese citizens access to other Arab and international TV stations.

Nonetheless, self-censorship remains a problem because authorities and editors are quick to clamp down on journalists who cross unstated boundaries on sensitive topics. The press avoids harsh criticism of the president, political and business corruption, and Lebanon's relationship with Syria, which posts some 20,000 troops in Lebanon and plays a significant role in the country's politics.

Libel is still a criminal offense punishable by prison, though no journalists have been jailed in the last several years. However, in March, a state prosecutor opened an investigation into columnist Akl Aweet, of the independent daily *Al-Nahar*, after he wrote a column titled, "Letter to God." In the column, Aweet, a Christian, asked God to prove his existence by halting Israel's subjugation of Palestinians and the U.S. war against Iraq. His article elicited an angry response from some Muslim religious leaders, who said the article was an offense to religion. The prosecutor also contended that the article was harmful to religion. Though Aweet was called in for questioning, the investigation was later dropped. Journalists say cases like Aweet's increase self-censorship.

The government tolerates some criticism of Syria's military presence in Lebanon, as long as it appears in publications that do not reach a mass audience. Low-circulation papers, ones that are not published in Arabic, or those that have already been branded opposition papers can be more daring in their coverage than mainstream papers.

Many prominent politicians own shares in private broadcasters and publications, including Prime Minister Rafiq Hariri, who owns both the daily newspaper *Al-Mustaqbal* and Future Television. Because such media outlets often reflect politicians' positions, journalists complain that they often cannot report freely.

Murr Television (MTV) and Radio Mount Lebanon (RML) remained off the air in 2003 following their September 2002 closure on charges that the stations, owned by Christian opposition politician Gabriel Murr, violated a prohibition against airing propaganda during elections. By April 2003, all legal efforts to overturn the closure had been exhausted. Murr, who was an opposition member of Parliament at the time his stations were shuttered, was stripped of his parliamentary seat in November 2002 by the Constitutional Council, Lebanon's highest legal body. The council ruled that Murr had unfairly benefited from the "propaganda" of his channel during the elections. Some observers suspect the 2002 closure of MTV was partly due to its harsh criticism of Syria's military presence in Lebanon.

In January, the Telecommunications Ministry cut the satellite link of the private television station New Television just before it was to air a program that criticized Saudi Arabia. According to press reports, the order came from Prime Minister Hariri, who has Saudi citizenship, made his personal fortune in Saudi Arabia, and maintains strong ties with the Saudi ruling elite. The station resumed broadcasting four days later, following the intervention of President Emile Lahoud.

In December, intelligence agents questioned New Television owner Tahsin Khayyat and accused him of harming Lebanon's foreign relations and collaborating with Israel, according to news reports. He was released the next day without charge, but two weeks later, Information Minister Michel Samaha barred the station from broadcasting news for two days, saying it broke the law by airing "subjective" news. According to local sources, the action came after the station mentioned the names of two high-level Lebanese and Syrian security officials in a news report about a Sudanese colleague whose residency visa had been rejected.

Journalists who want to cover the southern Ein al-Hilweh Palestinian refugee camp, which was the site of frequent fighting between Palestinian factions during 2003, do so at great risk. The Lebanese army and police do little to regulate the camp, where violent shoot-outs and killings occur often. In May, Agence France-Presse photographer Mahmoud Zayyat was struck in the foot by shrapnel from a bullet while he and several other journalists were covering a clash between two Palestinian groups.

According to press reports, in June, assailants fired two rockets from the trunk of a car at the building housing Prime Minister Hariri's Future Television and Orient Radio. No one was injured in the attack, which damaged the building. A previously unknown Islamic group, which identified itself as Ansar Allah, initially took responsibility for the attack. A few days later, however, Interior Minister Elias Murr told the daily *Al-Safir* that Asbat al-Ansar, a Palestinian group based in the Ein al-Hilweh refugee camp, was behind the attack. By year's end, the motive for the attack was still unclear, and no one had been arrested.

MAURITANIA

In 2003, Mauritania's press remained subject to the whims of the Interior Ministry, which continued to use the country's broadly defined, restrictive press law to stifle independent reporting. For years, Article 11 of the law has been the state's strongest weapon against the press. The article grants the Interior Ministry the power to suspend any newspaper that, among other things, "harms general interests" or "touches upon Islamic principles." Journalists complain that when a publication is banned, specific reasons are rarely provided.

Although journalists are rarely jailed for their work, Article 11 stipulates that offending journalists can be imprisoned for up to a year for violating the press law. The threat of sanctions further solidifies the self-censorship already prevalent among journalists, who avoid negative coverage of the president, the military, and foreign governments that maintain close ties with Mauritania.

Mauritanian journalists worked amid a climate of uncertainty in 2003, highlighted by a June coup attempt against President Maaouya Ould Sid Ahmed Taya, who has ruled for 19 years. Journalists said that in the months following the coup attempt, authorities were less tolerant of dissent and more apt to use the law to silence criticism.

In July, the government banned an issue of *Le Rénovateur*, a French-language bimonthly that has been a victim of Article 11 on numerous occasions. According to press reports, *Le Rénovateur*'s editor said the ban was imposed because of an article about the decrease in the black-market value of the Mauritanian currency. The Interior Ministry also banned Arabic- and French-language versions of the private weekly *Le Calame* in July and August because of an interview with Ahmad Ould Daddah, one of President Ould Taya's main opponents in the November presidential election. And in September, the Interior Ministry banned an issue of the Arabic weekly *Assahafa*. Its editors believe that the move came because the paper ran a political advertisement for opposition candidates before the official campaign period had begun.

Authorities banned the Islamist-leaning weekly newspaper *Raya* in June a few days prior to the coup attempt. The ban against the paper, which the authorities accused of incitement, took place as part of a government crackdown on Islamist activists.

Legal restrictions make it nearly impossible to establish a daily newspaper. For instance, editors are required to give five copies of each issue to the Interior Ministry and then wait for approval, which is often subject to long delays. Because of the uncertainty in knowing how long approval will take, editors say it is not financially feasible to establish a daily publication.

Newspaper circulations are small in Mauritania, and editors say that high production costs are reflected in high newsstand prices. As a result, publications are only available to a small portion of the population. According to one editor, newspapers are rarely available outside the capital, Nouakchott, and high production costs mean that only a few papers publish on a regular basis. Low levels of literacy further erode the print media's influence. Broadcast media remain firmly under state control.

MOROCCO

THE MULTIPLE SUICIDE BOMBINGS THAT ROCKED CASABLANCA on May 16, killing 44 people, triggered a government clampdown on the local media and further dimmed hopes that 40-year-old King Mohammed VI would institute greater press freedoms. In the aftermath of the attacks, the government ordered at least four newspapers closed and detained or imprisoned five journalists. Known for its relative tolerance of dissenting media, Morocco nonetheless held two journalists behind bars in 2003 for their work.

Days after the bombings, Parliament enacted a harsh antiterrorism law that granted authorities broad powers to arrest journalists and close publications. As a result of this new law, on June 5, authorities detained veteran editor Mustafa Alaoui of the weekly *Al-Ousboua* after his paper ran a communiqué issued by an Islamist group claiming responsibility for some of the Casablanca bombings. The communiqué, described by some journalists as dubious in its authenticity, alleged that Moroccan security forces had been aware of a pending terrorist attack in the country. Later that month, Alaoui was given a one-year suspended prison sentence and freed. A three-month ban on the paper was also suspended.

On June 12, three journalists—editors Mohammed al-Herd and Abdel Majid Ben Taher, of the Oujda-based weekly newspaper *Al-Sharq*, and Mustapha Qashnini, editor of the Oujda-based weekly *Al-Hayat Al-Maghribiya*—were detained and charged with extolling terrorist acts. The charges came in response to an article by a Moroccan Islamist in *Al-Hayat Al-Maghribiya* and reprinted in *Al-Sharq* that discussed the history of the Islamist movement in Morocco and its alleged relationship with the country's intelligence services.

In August, al-Herd was sentenced to three years in prison, while Ben Taher and Qashnini were each sentenced to a year in prison. At year's end, Ben Taher and Qashnini were free pending appeal, while al-Herd remained in prison. The court also suspended both weeklies from publication for three months.

The most publicized of the government's retaliatory strikes against the media, however, was the trial and imprisonment of maverick editor Ali Lmrabet, who owns and edits the French-language weekly *Demain* and its Arabic-language sister publication, *Douman*. In a case launched earlier in 2003 before the Casablanca attacks, Lmrabet was convicted and jailed on May 21, five days after the bombings. A court found him guilty of "insulting the king," "undermining the monarchy," and "challenging the territorial integrity of the state." He was sentenced to four years (later reduced on appeal to three years) in prison and fined 20,000 Moroccan dirhams (US$2,000). The court also ordered his two weeklies closed.

Lmrabet angered officials with a series of articles and cartoons that tackled two of the most politically sensitive issues in Morocco: the monarchy and the country's disputed sovereignty over Western Sahara. The articles included an interview with Abdullah Zaazaa, an opponent of Morocco's monarchy who called for the self-determination of the people of Western Sahara; a satirical photomontage that included a photo from King Mohammed VI's wedding; an article about the royal court's finances; and a cartoon that criticized public displays of reverence to the monarchy. During 2003, Lmrabet launched separate hunger strikes to protest his persecution. (Lmrabet and *Al-Sharq*'s al-Herd were released in early January 2004 after King Mohammed pardoned them along with several dozen other prisoners.)

Lmrabet was charged under Morocco's new Press Code, which Parliament approved in March 2002. Under the new law, journalists can be sentenced to three to five years in jail for defaming the monarchy, Islam, or challenging Morocco's right to possess Western Sahara. The government retains the power to revoke publication licenses or confiscate and suspend papers deemed to threaten public order.

Lmrabet's imprisonment, in addition to other journalists' detentions and newspaper closures throughout 2003, sparked condemnation from the Moroccan press and international human rights groups. In June, a CPJ delegation met with the Moroccan ambassador to the United States, Aziz Mekouar, in Washington, D.C., and called for the immediate release of all imprisoned journalists. Members of the U.S. Congressional Human Rights Caucus wrote letters of concern to Mekouar, and in October, CPJ briefed the U.S. Helsinki Commission in Washington, D.C., on the deteriorating press freedom situation in the country.

While the state's clampdown on the media intensified after the Casablanca attacks, the implementation of new restrictive measures had been going on for some time. In fact, in the months before the May attacks, authorities harassed or intimidated reporters in a number of unrelated incidents. On April 11, a group of unidentified men assaulted *Douman* reporter Mohamed Benouna in Settat, a town about 65 miles (104 kilometers) south of Casablanca, after he wrote an article alleging that the governor of Settat had granted a concession for the sale of alcohol in the province to Andre Azoulay, the royal adviser for economic and financial matters. The assailants beat Benouna and stripped him of his pants, telling him never to write about the governor again.

In a separate case, journalist Maria Mokrim, with the independent weekly *Al-Ayyam,* told CPJ that she received a series of threatening phone calls on her mobile phone in March regarding an article she had penned about the Moroccan secret service. On one occasion, she received a call while in a taxi from a man describing himself as "one of the people that you dared insult." Moments later as she exited the taxi, the journalist was assaulted by a man with a large stick.

Foreign media that operate in the country are targets of occasional government pressure. In March, state-owned Moroccan public television temporarily barred the Qatar-based satellite television channel Al-Jazeera from using its facilities to feed broadcasts to Al-Jazeera's headquarters in Doha after it completed a report on demonstrations in the capital, Rabat, against the U.S.-led war in Iraq.

Morocco still boasts a number of feisty party papers and a few truly independent ones. Among the most independent are the groundbreaking weekly newspaper *Le Journal Hebdomadaire* and its sister publication, *Assahifa al Ousbouiya*. Since they were founded in the late 1990s under the names *Le Journal* and *Assahifa*, the papers have boldly staked out new terrain in Moroccan journalism through tough investigative reporting on government corruption, corporate impropriety, and taboo political topics. In November, CPJ honored the papers' publisher, Aboubakr Jamai, with an International Press Freedom Award in recognition of his commitment to independent news coverage amid repeated government interference. Since their founding, both of Jamai's papers have been closed and reopened under their current names, and Jamai has been the target of government-inspired lawsuits for exposés on state corruption. In addition to these overt measures, officials have also attempted to pressure businesses not to advertise in Jamai's publications.

SAUDI ARABIA

Since the September 11, 2001, attacks on the United States, Saudi Arabia's rigid press has exhibited spurts of uncharacteristic independence, reporting on once taboo topics such as crime, unemployment, and even the problem of religious militancy in the kingdom. However, these welcome displays of openness in one of the region's most restricted press corps have been greeted with disapproval by Saudi officials, who have sought to rein in the press.

This dynamic was on display again in 2003. This time the main catalyst for revitalized press coverage was the shocking May 12 suicide bombings that struck the capital, Riyadh, killing more than two dozen people. Some Saudi newspapers actively covered the government's subsequent crackdown on suspected Islamist militants. Several journalists responded with editorials that criticized Saudi society and discussed the problem of religious extremism, corruption, and the absence of basic liberties. Journalists who raised these difficult issues found themselves caught between the government and religious militants, both of which sought to silence them.

One such case involved Jamal Khashoggi, editor of the daily *Al-Watan*. Government officials removed Khashoggi from his post in May in response to his paper's increasingly provocative editorial stance against religious militancy in the country. Some columns and cartoons in the paper appeared to ascribe blame for the May attacks to the religious establishment and religious fanatics who breed intolerance. Prior to Khashoggi's dismissal, religious conservatives had complained to Saudi officials about the newspaper's coverage, and one cleric urged readers to boycott *Al-Watan*.

In July, the Information Ministry banned writer Hussein Shobokshi from publishing his weekly newspaper column in the daily *Okaz*. Although it was unclear what triggered the ban, Shobokshi had written a critical column on July 1 in which he imagined waking up one day in a country where the government showed accountability to the public, citizens could vote in elections, and women could drive. Shobokshi said the column triggered a huge public response, including death threats against him.

In late August, the Information Ministry barred newspapers from carrying the work of Wajeha al-Huwaider, who wrote for *Al-Watan* and the English-language daily *Arab News*. The ban came in response to an al-Huwaider column from late May that discussed some Saudis' disillusionment with their country and the tendency to look to the United States for solutions to problems.

Throughout 2003, CPJ received unconfirmed reports of several other writers who were banned from the press, along with cases of Saudi religious clerics who issued edicts calling for the death of dissidents and reformists who expressed unorthodox views in the media.

Reprisals were not limited to dismissals or verbal threats. In December, Saudi journalist Mansour Nogaidan, of the daily *Al-Riaydh*, described in *The New York Times* how he had been ordered by a religious court to receive 75 lashes for articles "calling for freedom of speech and criticizing Wahhabism, Saudi Arabia's official religious doctrine." According to Nogaidan, he refused to report to the police to accept his punishment.

These repressive measures highlighted just how difficult a place Saudi Arabia is for independent-minded journalists to work. Although newspapers in the kingdom are privately owned, the government wields tremendous influence. The Information Ministry approves the hiring of editors and can dismiss them at will. Newspapers receive generous state subsidies, and government guidelines on how to cover political news are still the norm. Despite the more provocative coverage in recent months, papers are still relatively tame. Editors avoid criticizing the ruling family and official policies, as well as reporting on anything that might be interpreted as critical of Islam.

In a positive development in February, the government approved the creation of a journalists' association aimed at representing the interests of media professionals. Journalists welcomed the move but expressed doubts that the group would become an assertive advocate for greater press freedoms.

Despite government attempts to control what Saudis read or watch, citizens have proved skillful at finding independent sources of news. The country has one of the highest penetration rates for satellite television, and many Saudis have access to a wide range of international programming, including Arabic-language news stations. Activists and other citizens can criticize the government by calling in to talk shows on Arab satellite channels. Some exchange views and advocate for political reforms on the Internet, which made its official debut in the kingdom in 1999. Domestic Internet service is heavily restricted, with the government using a filtering system that blocks morally and politically objectionable material. Thousands of sites are banned. Enforcement of Web censorship is erratic, however, and can be circumvented by savvy Web users. Some Saudis also bypass state controls by dialing into service providers outside the country.

Using Internet sites, chat rooms, cell phones, and text messaging to relay breaking news across the kingdom is becoming increasingly popular. The London-based Movement for Islamic Reform in Arabia (MIRA) has an Internet site that it uses to keep its followers abreast of political developments. In 2002, the group launched a radio station, Al-Islah, which is broadcast from London and can be heard by satellite. Al-Islah and the group's Web site were used to organize public demonstrations that occurred across the country in October. According to MIRA, the Saudi government jammed its radio broadcasts during the demonstrations. MIRA also established a satellite television station but reported that it lost service for undetermined reasons.

Foreign media continue to face numerous barriers in Saudi Arabia. The government censors foreign publications before they enter the country, blacking out articles deemed morally or politically objectionable and barring distribution of publications. Foreign journalists able to obtain visas have reported that they could move freely around the country, though they suspected that the government may have monitored their movements and phone calls.

Those who report unfavorably about the country may be barred from it. For instance, the government refused to allow the Qatar-based Arabic language satellite station Al-Jazeera to cover the annual Muslim pilgrimage to Mecca, known as the hajj. An Al-Jazeera crew was also barred for no specific reason from covering a February meeting of defense and foreign ministers of the Gulf Cooperation Council.

SUDAN

With more than a dozen private dailies and one government daily, Sudan's print press is surprisingly diverse. Though some private papers are pro-government, many report aggressively on government policies. The state controls all television and radio stations.

Rebel leaders and the Sudanese government moved closer in 2003 to an agreement to end their bloody 20-year civil war. Over the years, the government's main concern regarding the media has been to control what is written about the war. Negative accounts of the government's role in the conflict can result in an array of punishments under the country's restrictive press law. Journalists covering the conflict have had to contend with pressures from government security officials, who have made harassing phone calls, detained journalists, and confiscated publications.

According to local journalists, the government still objects to negative portrayals of the military. However, in August, President Omar al-Bashir announced an end to security censorship—which means that the security services can no longer question journalists, confiscate publications, or direct newspaper coverage, though they can ask prosecutors to sanction the media. Since this announcement, the daily opinion pages have become livelier. Journalists now regularly conduct interviews with the rebel Sudan People's Liberation Army (SPLA) leader John Garang. The press also regularly interviews Dr. Hasan al-Turabi, an ex-Parliament speaker and former close ally of the president who was released from house arrest in October. Al-Turabi was arrested on charges of committing crimes against the state in 2001 because he negotiated with the SPLA.

Enforcement of the press law is mainly the responsibility of a government agency called the National Press Council (NPC). Over the years, the NPC has usually punished press law violators by suspending the offending newspaper for a few days. Newspapers can be suspended for anything from criticizing the government to publishing articles considered harmful to public morals. The NPC is composed of journalists, Parliament members, and presidential appointees.

The English-language *Khartoum Monitor*, a small-circulation daily that has frequently endured government pressure, was not spared in 2003. In March, the security services briefly detained *Khartoum Monitor* reporter Edward Lado Terso for an article he had written claiming that the history of Islam in Sudan was not always peaceful.

Two months later, a Khartoum criminal court suspended the *Khartoum Monitor* for two months. The paper was originally charged with inciting hatred by allegedly misquoting the Quran, said Nhial Bol, the paper's editor. But during the trial, the judge produced a document that purported to prove that the *Monitor* had not paid a fine levied on it by a court in January 2002. Bol said an appeals court had overturned the fine. Following the court's decision to suspend the paper, Bol received a letter from the NPC claiming that the suspension was due to the original charge of misquoting the Quran.

The day after the *Monitor* reopened in July, another Khartoum criminal court suspended the paper's license because it had allegedly published false information. The charges stemmed from a series of articles about the existence of slavery in southern Sudan. In late August, an appeals court rescinded the suspension ruling, but before the paper could reopen, the prosecutor for crimes against the state interjected and ordered that the paper remain closed while he investigated the publication for what he called threats to national stability. The prosecutor general intervened in October and allowed the *Monitor* to reopen and resume publishing. In late November, however, the prosecutor for crimes against the state reimposed the suspension pending further investigation. According to the government, the newspaper "rebels against all that could bring stability to this homeland, and its continuation does not serve peace and causes a threat to society and an outstanding threat to the individual."

The prosecutor for crimes against the state, who is under the authority of the Justice Ministry and handles terrorism cases and trials of government opponents, was behind the suspension of three other private dailies: *Alwan*, *Al-Azminah*, and *Al-Ayam*. *Alwan* was suspended for a month in early September after the prosecutor said the paper's reports had incited violence against the government but gave no specifics. The pro-government *Al-Azminah* was suspended in late September after it published an article saying that the Popular Defense Forces, an Islamist militia allied with the army, would be disbanded under an agreement between the government and rebels. The paper began publishing again in

October. The independent daily *Al-Ayam* was suspended for six days in November and indefinitely in early December. The prosecutor accused the paper of publishing false information about fighting between rebels and the army.

Al-Sahafa, one of Sudan's more popular dailies, ran into trouble with authorities in 2003. Security agents twice detained without charge Youssef al-Bashir Moussa, a contributor to *Al-Sahafa* who is based in western Sudan's Darfur State, where the army and rebels have clashed. Both of his detentions came after he wrote articles about the civil war. On July 28, the day after Moussa was detained the second time, security forces confiscated an issue of the paper. The issue contained an article about talks between rebels and the government in Darfur at a time when the level of fighting in the state had intensified. In October, the NPC suspended *Al-Sahafa* for three days after the paper ran an advertisement for Ethiopian Airlines that mentioned the wine served on its flights. The NPC took issue with the newspaper for advertising alcohol, which is banned in Sudan.

In December, security forces closed the office of the pan-Arab satellite channel Al-Jazeera and detained its correspondent Islam Salih for about five days. According to Al-Jazeera, Sudanese authorities had complained that Salih's reporting was biased against Sudan and wanted him replaced.

SYRIA

ALTHOUGH SYRIAN OFFICIALS CONTINUED TO PAY LIP SERVICE to their support for more open media discourse in the country, in practice they failed to exhibit a willingness to tolerate independent news outlets in 2003.

President Bashar al-Assad's first months in office in 2000 witnessed important press freedom gains that included the launching of private and party-run newspapers and the emergence of a more assertive state-run press. But these developments were undermined by a subsequent government crackdown on dissent and pro-democracy activism that had blossomed following Bashar's ascent to power. In 2003, the appointment of Prime Minister Muhammad Naji al-Otari did not improve matters, and now the situation for the press does not differ greatly from the heavily censored, pro-regime media that prevailed under Bashar's ironfisted father, the late Hafez al-Assad.

In April, *Al-Domari,* a satirical weekly owned by renowned political cartoonist Ali Farzat, ceased publication under government pressure, including the state-owned printing press's refusal to print the paper, attempts by state officials to review issues before their distribution, and, according to Farzat, government pressure on advertisers to withhold ads from his paper. Farzat resumed publishing *Al-Domari* in July, but the state-controlled distributor refused to circulate the paper, forcing *Al-Domari* staff to distribute issues on their own. Soon thereafter, the government canceled *Al-Domari*'s license, saying it had violated the country's press law by not publishing for three consecutive months. The decision to close the newspaper was apparently triggered by the unprecedented boldness of the paper's last issue, which featured articles criticizing the country's repressive press law and the overall lack of press freedom in Syria.

The controversial press law under which *Al-Domari* was closed demonstrates the government's intent to keep the emergence of independent media in check. The law, issued in

2001, enables the government to suspend newspapers for up to six months for publishing "falsehoods" and "fabricated reports" and allows the prime minister to revoke the licenses of repeat offenders. Violators can also be jailed for one to three years and fined between 500,000 and 1 million lira (US$9,500 and US$18,900).

The government took some symbolic steps to promote a freer press. For instance, in July, the pan-Arab London-based daily *Al-Hayat* reported that the government formed a committee charged with encouraging greater diversity of voices in the state-run press. The paper also reported that authorities permitted distribution of a Lebanese-licensed newspaper run by Syrians that contained a blunt assessment of the country's press freedom record.

However, with few exceptions this spirit of tolerance failed to translate into improved news coverage. State papers remained bland and unflinchingly supportive of the regime. Other private and party newspapers that have won permission to launch in recent years are politically toothless. In 2002, the government took the auspicious step of licensing private radio stations. A handful has since been launched, but they are barred from airing news or political programming. Television remains state controlled.

Although local media struggle under state-imposed limits, Syrians have chipped away at the wall of fear erected under Hafez al-Assad's 30-year authoritarian rule, and today some citizens publicly express views that would have landed them in jail previously. Lebanese newspapers and other pan-Arab media remain the preferred forum for Syrians to conduct open political discussion and voice criticism of the government. Syrian dissidents have appeared on programs on satellite channels such as Qatar's Al-Jazeera.

The government relented in two press freedom cases in 2003. In late May, Syrian officials released jailed journalist Ibrahim Hemaidi, the Damascus bureau chief of *Al-Hayat*. Hemaidi was detained on December 23, 2002, after writing an article discussing the government's alleged preparations for a possible influx of Iraqi refugees in the event of a U.S.-led attack on Iraq. He was charged with "publishing false information," which carries a sentence of up to three years in jail if convicted. The case was still pending, though authorities did not appear eager to pursue it. And in July, a military court dismissed a case against lawyer Haithem Maaleh, director of the Human Rights Society in Syria, and four others charged with distributing unauthorized copies of a human rights magazine.

The government is the sole Internet provider and restricts access to politically sensitive content. Local human rights groups reported cases during 2003 of Syrians who were arrested for passing on politically sensitive news and information abroad via e-mail.

TUNISIA

SINCE PRESIDENT ZINE AL-ABDINE BEN ALI SEIZED POWER in 1987, Tunisian authorities have crafted a nearly perfect system to censor and suppress the media. The few courageous voices remaining in the country succeed in circumventing these controls mainly by publishing on the Internet, but Tunisian authorities do not hesitate to block their Web sites, harass them, and even imprison them. Ben Ali's 16-year reign is almost certain to continue; the government held a referendum in May 2002 in which officials said 99.52 percent of voters approved constitutional changes that will allow him to run for a fourth term as president in 2004. Opposition figures and other critics called the referendum a sham.

Tunisia has escaped the kind of criticism heaped on other repressive regimes in the region, partly because of the shortsightedness of its allies—Europe and the United States—who tend to focus on Tunisia's economic successes. During his state visit to Tunisia's capital, Tunis, in December, U.S. Secretary of State Colin Powell did mildly prod the government when he said that the "world is looking for more political pluralism and openness and a standard openness that deals with journalists being able to do their work." His remaining public comments, however, were largely laudatory.

Tunisian newspapers are by and large private. But independent journalists say that editors must remain loyal to Ben Ali, resulting in hagiographic coverage of the president and his policies.

Those who don't toe the official line are dealt with swiftly and severely. Over the years, the government has prosecuted dissenting reporters and banned newspapers. Critical journalists have been dismissed from their jobs, denied accreditation, put under police surveillance, assaulted, and prevented from leaving the country. Regularly published opposition papers are uncritical and belong to government-sanctioned opposition parties, which receive state subsidies.

In addition to co-opting private newspapers, the state dominates the broadcast media. In November, however, President Ben Ali announced the establishment of the country's first private radio station, Radio Mosaique FM. According to press reports, the station airs mainly music with some news and is run by a former journalist with close ties to the regime.

The government censors the Web for politically objectionable material and has lashed out at online critics. In an apparent attempt to deflect scrutiny of its poor rights record, the government released jailed cyberjournalist Zouhair Yahyaoui on November 18, weeks before U.S. Secretary of State Powell and French President Jacques Chirac visited Tunis. Yahyaoui, who edited and published the online journal *TUNeZINE* (*www.tunezine.com*), had been in prison since June 2002, after he was arrested and sentenced to 28 months in jail on charges of intentionally publishing false information and using stolen communication lines to post his Web site. (In July 2002, an appeals court reduced the sentence to 24 months.)

Material posted on *TUNeZINE* included a mock referendum ridiculing the May 2002 referendum and an open letter to Ben Ali from Mokhtar Yahyaoui, the journalist's uncle and a dissident judge, who complained about the lack of independence in the judiciary.

During his detention, Yahyaoui staged numerous hunger strikes to protest his prison conditions. His lawyers and family members told CPJ that his reading and writing materials were confiscated, and that prison guards tampered with his food.

During 2003, the Tunisian Embassy in Washington, D.C., ignored CPJ's repeated requests to discuss Yahyaoui's case and that of another jailed journalist, Hammadi Jebali, who has been in prison since 1991. In October, CPJ gave an informational briefing to the U.S. Helsinki Commission in Washington, D.C., on Tunisia's appalling press freedom record.

In 2003, the government put more pressure on Internet journalists. In September, the Tunisian Customs Bureau summoned Naziha Rejiba, an editor of the online publication *Kalima*, which is hosted abroad and blocked inside the country by Tunisian authorities, for questioning following her return from Europe. Rejiba, who is also known as Om

Zied, was charged with violating currency exchange laws for giving 170 euros (US$200) to the friend of an acquaintance when she returned to the capital, Tunis. Rejiba's colleagues insist that she did not violate currency laws, which are designed to punish people who funnel large amounts of undeclared foreign currency into Tunisia. It is common for Tunisian authorities who are unhappy with a journalist's writing to find another reason to harass the journalist, and *Kalima*'s staff have faced harassment for years. Rejiba was given an eight-month suspended prison sentence on November 18—the same day that Yahyaoui was released from prison.

According to Rejiba's colleagues, the case against her stemmed from her writing about the government's poor human rights record, as well as an appearance she made on a now defunct Paris-based satellite channel, Al-Hiwar, during which she criticized shopkeepers who display photos of Ben Ali.

Officials carefully screen foreign publications and confiscate issues when they enter the country if they contain articles that criticize the Tunisian government. The government has frequently harassed journalists and activists when they express critical views in the foreign media. In the summer of 2003, in anticipation of the 2004 presidential election, Parliament adopted an amendment to the Electoral Code that prohibits individuals from supporting or criticizing candidates on foreign or domestic broadcast media. Violators of the law are subject to a crippling fine of 25,000 Tunisian dinars (US$20,000).

TURKEY

IN AN EFFORT TO MEET EUROPEAN UNION CRITERIA FOR MEMBERSHIP, Turkey continued in 2003 to rewrite laws that restrict press freedom. That effort has improved the country's spotty press freedom record, but many impediments remain. Journalists continued to face criminal prosecution for their work, although the number of jailed journalists has drastically declined in recent years, from dozens in the mid-1990s to at least five in 2003.

In June, Parliament passed a reform bill repealing the infamous Article 8 of the antiterror law. For years, Article 8, which outlaws "separatist propaganda," was used to prosecute and jail dozens of journalists and writers sympathetic to the country's Kurdish minority or Kurdish nationalist ideas. The reform bill also formally permits private television and radio stations to use the Kurdish language, which was previously banned in the broadcast media. To the surprise of many, reform-minded President Ahmet Necdet Sezer vetoed the bill, arguing it could "create important dangers to the existence of the Turkish state and the indivisible unity of the state with its country and people." Parliament, however, overrode the veto.

The reform bill was the latest in a series of legislative initiatives since 2002 that have loosened legal strictures on freedom of expression. However, prosecutors continued to use the laws that remain on the books to bring suits against journalists and writers, particularly those who criticized the army and judiciary, or who wrote critically about sensitive political issues, such as the struggle of the country's Kurdish minority for greater cultural rights or the role of Islam in politics and society. The Turkish Human Rights Foundation, a local nongovernmental organization, reported that the number of such prosecutions during the first six months of 2003 had decreased from the previous year but still stood at well over 1,000 cases. More encouragingly, however, the report noted that the number of convictions had dropped about 50 percent.

Some of the government's legal reforms give Turkish prosecutors and judges greater leeway to dismiss or acquit cases. Application, however, was uneven, and the spirit of the reforms did not always filter through to the judicial system, as was evidenced by new prosecutions undertaken in 2003.

In October, Sinan Kara, a muckraking journalist in the southwestern town of Datcha, began serving a one-year prison term for allegedly threatening bodyguards of the son of former Prime Minister Tansu Ciller. According to Kara's lawyer, Mert Ciller's bodyguards attacked the journalist in 2000 when he tried to photograph Mert Ciller. Kara's lawyer maintains that the charges against his client were fabricated, and that witnesses for the prosecution provided dubious testimony. Local politicians and businessmen have targeted Kara with several lawsuits over his reporting on local government. Officials have frequently harassed the journalist through petty administrative measures. In 2002, for example, Kara served jail time for failing to comply with a press law requiring newspaper publishers to send two copies of each issue to the governor's office.

In October, the trial of editor Mehmet Emin Sert and journalists Emin Karaca and Dogan Ozguden, who lives in exile in Belgium, resumed. They stood accused of insulting the Turkish army in articles in the daily *Turkiya'de ve Avrupa'da* in 2002 that accused the army of murdering leftists in the 1960s. The journalists face possible prison time and/or fines if convicted. The trial was ongoing at year's end.

In May, an appeals court upheld the 2002 conviction of publisher Abdullah Keskin on charges of disseminating "separatist propaganda." Two months later, the government formally abolished the law under which he was convicted. Keskin had published a Turkish-language edition of former *Washington Post* reporter Jonathan Randal's book about the Kurds, *After Such Knowledge, What Forgiveness? My Encounters in Kurdistan*. A State Security Court sentenced Keskin to six months in prison, which was later converted to a fine of about US$500. Prosecutors objected to passages in the book that referred to "Kurdistan."

The number of journalists imprisoned in Turkey continued to drop in 2003, with at least five in jail at year's end. Most were imprisoned for involvement with the publications of outlawed leftist or pro-Kurdish political groups. At the height of the government's conflict with Kurdish insurgents in the mid-1990s, dozens of journalists were imprisoned.

Turkey's airwaves host a multitude of private radio and television stations that opened in the mid-1990s. However, the government has established a highly restrictive regime for regulating them. The Supreme Radio and Television Board (RTUK) is the main body that oversees broadcasting and continues to dole out punitive suspensions to stations that air violent, sensational, or politically controversial programming. During 2003, RTUK closed dozens of stations. In July, RTUK imposed a one-month ban on five stations owned by media mogul Cem Uzan in response to Uzan's on-air criticism of Prime Minister Recep Tayyip Erdogan. Uzan had lambasted the government's decision to annul a contract with power supply plants he owns.

A controversial law passed in 2002 subjects Internet content to Turkey's laws governing freedom of expression. In October 2003, a Turkish court closed the news sites *Ekmek ve Adalet* and *Ozgur Politika* because they "insulted Turkish armed forces," according to the Web site Bianet. The court provided no further details.

Before the U.S.-led war in Iraq began, about 300 foreign journalists converged on the southeastern border town of Silopi, Turkey, to cover northern Iraq. As in previous years, the government prohibited journalists from crossing the border without a Turkish government escort. In one case, Turkish authorities asked two U.S. journalists—Donald Bartletti, a photographer for the *Los Angeles Times*, and Alan Weeks, a freelance cameraman for the U.S.-based ABC television—to leave the country in early March after they were caught in a forbidden area while trying to cross the border into Iraq without the required escort. The journalists were held overnight and released the next day after paying a fine of about US$50 each.

YEMEN

THE EMERGENCE OF OUTSPOKEN PRIVATE AND PARTY NEWSPAPERS FOLLOWING the unification of North and South Yemen in 1990 has set the country apart from many of its neighbors in the Persian Gulf, where the press remains tightly controlled. Yemeni papers are notably opinionated and not shy about confronting the government. But the government's record on press freedom has been uneven. In the last 13 years, several government crackdowns have led to the arrest or prosecution of independent journalists and the closure of their newspapers.

In 2003, there were fewer cases of overt government harassment of journalists compared with previous years. However, journalists were still hampered by the threat of legal action and other forms of state reprisal, and, as a result, self-censorship remained an issue.

Though not employed against the media as in past years, Yemen's 1990 Press Law remained a formidable threat in 2003. The law bars criticism of the president and lists a wide range of vaguely worded offenses that can land a journalist in court and prison. For example, Article 103 prohibits journalists and editors from publishing articles that "cause tribal, sectarian, racial, regional or ancestral discrimination" or "undermine public morals or prejudices the dignity of individuals or personal freedoms."

In March, three journalists from the pan-Arab Nasserist party newspaper, *al-Wihdawi*—Editor-in-Chief Ali al-Saqaf and two reporters, Ahmed Said Nasser and Abdel Aziz Ismail—received four-month suspended prison sentences after they were convicted of harming relations between Yemen and Saudi Arabia. Al-Saqaf said the case was brought against the paper after the Saudi government complained to the Yemeni Information Ministry. He added that the proceedings were vague, and that the judge never specified what law the journalists had violated. The paper had published several articles critical of Saudi Arabia, including one that said that although Yemen has a reputation for being home to Islamist extremists, Saudi Arabia is responsible for funding them.

In November, the government introduced a bill in Parliament that would compel journalists to join the Yemeni press association to legally practice journalism in the country. The bill also required news organizations to contribute 3 percent of their advertising revenue to support the association's activities. Yemeni journalists and CPJ protested the bill, which was withdrawn from Parliament in early December.

Still, many independent journalists—including those working for foreign media outlets—noticed improvements in the government's willingness to allow coverage of major events, particularly developments in the battle against religious extremists. In 2002, the Information Ministry issued a directive ordering journalists not to cover events in provinces where clashes between government forces and Islamist groups were occurring, but in 2003, journalists said they were allowed to cover freely such clashes in the Hatat Mountains. In some cases, authorities even facilitated coverage. For example, the Defense Ministry had journalists accompany troops in an embed-type program, and ministry officials made themselves available to journalists for questions. Opposition journalists, however, complained that the government gave preferential treatment to journalists described as being close to the government.

One independent editor told CPJ that the government's change of heart was due to the fact that most major newspapers have supported the government's war against extremists, and that the government hoped to increase its credibility by being more transparent.

Human rights issues, such as prisoners' rights, were also covered with greater regularity and aggressiveness by independent and opposition party newspapers, local journalists said. In describing the improved press climate, one Yemeni editor gave the example of an article in a government paper about defective pesticides produced in Yemen. The story led Saudi Arabia to suspend imports of Yemeni produce and pesticides, and the president publicly criticized the journalist who wrote the story. While the journalist could have faced a government lawsuit in previous years, nothing came of the incident.

Yemen has one of the lowest literacy rates in the region, and the government controls television and radio, which is where most Yemenis get their news. Many journalists complain that the quality of television news is poor. Amat al-Aleem Alsoswa, Yemen's human rights minister (a newly created post that also handles press freedom issues), told CPJ in a meeting in New York in September that even though the government controls TV and radio, there is nothing in Yemeni law that precludes individuals from applying for licenses to start a private radio or television station. One Yemeni journalist said that while this is technically true, there are no guidelines on how to establish a private television or radio station. He said that he sent a letter to the Information Ministry several years ago stating that he intended to open a radio station and asking procedural questions. He had yet to receive a response at year's end. ■

36 JOURNALISTS KILLED IN 2003

CPJ DOCUMENTED THE CASES OF 36 JOURNALISTS who were killed for their work in 2003. An analysis of this alarming death toll is included in the introduction to this book on page 10.

The number of journalists killed in the line of duty each year is probably the world's most frequently cited press freedom statistic. CPJ thoroughly investigates each report of a journalist killed to determine whether the journalist was targeted because of his or her profession. Those caught in crossfire while covering conflict are included along with journalists singled out for assassination. We define journalists as those who cover the news or comment on public affairs in print, in photographs, on radio, on television, or online. Reporters, writers, editors, publishers, and directors of news organizations are all included. We do not classify a case as confirmed until we are sure that the death was related to the victim's journalistic work.

When the motive for a journalist's murder is unclear but there is reason to suspect that it was related to the journalist's profession, CPJ classifies that death as "motive unconfirmed" and includes it on a separate list. CPJ then continues to investigate the crime. CPJ documented 12 "motive unconfirmed" cases in 2003. They are described beginning on page 237. With regard to both lists, CPJ continues to press for official investigations of the killings, as well as for the apprehension and punishment of the perpetrators.

JOURNALISTS KILLED: MOTIVE CONFIRMED

BRAZIL: 2

NICANOR LINHARES BATISTA
Rádio Vale do Jaguaribe, June 30, 2003
Limoeiro do Norte

Nicanor, radio host and owner of Rádio Vale do Jaguaribe, based in the city of Limoeiro do Norte, in the northeastern state of Ceará, was killed by at least two unidentified gunmen at around 8 p.m. while he was recording his daily show "Encontro Político" (Political Encounter) at his station's studios.

According to the daily *Diário do Nordeste,* which is based in Fortaleza, the capital of Ceará State, a sound operator who witnessed the murder said the gunmen came into the studio, shot Nicanor several times at close range, and fled on a motorcycle. Nicanor was taken to Limoeiro do Norte's public hospital and pronounced dead on arrival.

The Fortaleza daily *O Povo* reported that "Encontro Político," broadcast weekdays from 11:30 a.m. to 2 p.m., was one of the most popular radio shows in the region. According to *O Povo*, Nicanor was considered a controversial journalist whose hard-hitting commentaries had angered many local politicians and public officials.

Ceará State parliamentary deputy Paulo Duarte was quoted in *Diário do Nordeste* as saying that he had heard about a plot to kill Nicanor, and that the journalist had received threats. According to Duarte, Nicanor had scheduled a July 1 meeting with him and another state government official to discuss his safety.

Several members of Nicanor's family who gave testimony to the police believe that he was killed for his journalism, *O Povo* reported. The journalist's wife told *Diário do Nordeste* that Nicanor had received threats before he bought the radio station in 2001 but had not received any recently.

According to the news agency Agência Nordeste, police said that Nicanor's murder may have been a contract killing, and that the journalist had many enemies because of the critical reports that aired on his station.

In October, the Ceará State Public Prosecutor's Office identified a judge from the neighboring state of Pernambuco and his wife, Limoeiro do Norte's mayor, as the people who ordered Nicanor's murder. Under Brazilian law, federal and state prosecutors—not local prosecutors—deal with criminal cases against public officials, and they have yet to bring formal charges against the suspects.

Luiz Antônio da Costa
Época, July 23, 2003
São Bernardo do Campo

Da Costa, a photographer with the weekly *Época*, was killed while on assignment in the city of São Bernardo do Campo, São Paulo State.

The 36-year-old photographer, who was known professionally as La Costa, and *Época* reporter Alexandre Mansur were covering the occupation by homeless families of an empty lot belonging to a Volkswagen auto factory in São Bernardo do Campo. The homeless families, who numbered in the thousands and had been organized by the Movement of Homeless Workers (MTST), had been camping at the site since July 19 to demand housing and jobs from the state and federal governments.

At around 3 p.m., while MTST leaders were talking to the journalists, three men who had just robbed a nearby gas station entered the campsite brandishing handguns. One of them shot da Costa in the chest at close range. The journalist was then taken to the São Bernardo Municipal Hospital but died shortly after.

Based on eyewitness testimony and several pictures taken at the scene of the shooting by photographer André Porto, of the newspaper *Agora São Paulo*, police were able to identify da Costa's suspected attackers, two of whom were captured on July 30.

The same day, police announced that one of the suspects had confessed to shooting da Costa accidentally while aiming at his camera, *Época* reported. The suspect also told police that the three men thought da Costa had taken pictures of the robbery at the gas station. The police believe that da Costa was targeted deliberately, according to *Época*.

Época is owned by Editora Globo S.A., part of the giant media group Organizações Globo.

CAMBODIA: 1

Chou Chetharith
Ta Prum, October 18, 2003, Phnom Penh

Chetharith, a deputy editor of the royalist FUNCINPEC party's Ta Prum radio station, was killed by a gunman riding on the back of a motorcycle while the journalist was on his way to work in the capital, Phnom Penh.

According to witnesses interviewed by Agence France-Presse, Chetharith, 37, was shot in the head at point-blank range in broad daylight. Local sources tell CPJ that Ta Prum is known for its critical reporting of Cambodian Prime Minister Hun Sen, and that the station's director, Noranarith Anandayath, is an adviser to FUNCINPEC party chief Prince Norodom Ranaridhh.

The day before the shooting, the prime minister criticized Ta Prum in the English-language *Cambodia Times*, accusing the station of insulting his leadership.

Chetharith's murder came ahead of scheduled three-way talks between the FUNCINPEC party, the opposition Sam Rainsy Party, and the ruling Cambodian People's Party (CPP). The talks were canceled after the journalist's killing. They had been aimed at ending a political stalemate following the July 27 elections, when Hun Sen and his CPP failed to garner a two-thirds majority of the vote. By law, the CPP was required to form a coalition with opposition parties but refused to do so.

In early December, Police Commissioner Heng Pov told the Cambodian Center for Human Rights (CCHR) that although police have identified possible suspects in Chetarith's murder, they do not have enough evidence to make any arrests. The CCHR conducted an in-depth investigation into the killing and concluded that Chetarith was killed because of his work as a journalist.

COLOMBIA: 4

Luis Eduardo Alfonso Parada
Radio Meridiano-70, March 18, 2003
Arauca

Alfonso, a 33-year-old radio news host, was shot to death at 4:55 a.m. by two gunmen in the town of Arauca, near the Venezuelan border, while he tried to enter his office at Radio Meridiano-70. Two men were waiting for him there and fled on a motorcycle after the attack, said an Arauca Department police spokesperson.

The journalist, who had been threatened previously by members of a right-wing paramilitary army, was also a freelance reporter for Colombia's most widely read daily, *El Tiempo*.

In June 2002, presumed paramilitary gunmen shot and killed the owner of Radio Meridiano-70, Efraín Varela Noriega. Varela had alerted listeners to the presence of paramilitary fighters in the region days before he was assassinated.

Alfonso co-hosted several news shows broadcast during the day. Since October, he had been covering armed conflict in Arauca Department as a freelance reporter for *El Tiempo*, said Álvaro Sierra, an editor at the daily. The conflict, which pits leftist rebels against rival paramilitary combatants and the government, is almost 40 years old.

Alfonso lambasted all sides of the conflict but was particularly critical of the paramilitary United Self-Defense Forces of Colombia (AUC), said Miguel Ángel Rojas, who worked with Alfonso at Radio Meridiano-70. Rojas said Alfonso frequently reported in great detail on paramilitary activity in the region. "He didn't hold back at all," said Rojas. "I think that's what compromised him."

Fearing for his life, Alfonso fled for the capital, Bogotá, soon after Varela was killed, said Jorge Enrique Meléndez, an *El Tiempo* reporter and a friend of Alfonso's who spoke to him hours before he was killed.

In Bogotá, Alfonso received about US$320 from a government protection program for journalists to help support him while he sought refuge. Alfonso returned to Arauca six weeks later.

In November 2002, Alfonso's name was one of about 100 that appeared on a list distributed in the town of Arauca by paramilitary fighters, who threatened to kill the people on the list unless they "reformed," said Meléndez. In the weeks before his death, however, Alfonso had told friends and colleagues that he no longer feared for his life.

Guillermo Bravo Vega
Alpevisión Radio, April 28, 2003, Neiva

Bravo, a 65-year-old investigative journalist with the regional Alpevisión Radio, was shot dead at around 8 p.m. by an unidentified gunman who sneaked into his house in the southern town of Neiva, Huila Department. Bravo died while he was being driven to a local hospital, state police chief Col. Jairo Rolando Delgado said.

The journalist was shot once in the head and twice in the neck. The gunman escaped on the back of a motorcycle driven by another unknown individual. As of December, no arrests had been made, said Delgado.

Bravo, who directed the morning program "Hechos y cifras" (Facts and Figures) for Alpevisión, had frequently accused municipal and departmental government officials of mishandling public funds. Bravo also published an occasional newsletter focused on economics and finance called *Eco Impacto* (Eco Impact).

Authorities, who believe that Bravo may have been assassinated for denouncing public officials on his program, are investigating reports that he was killed by a professional assassin hired by government officials, said Pedro Moreno, director of intelligence for the Administrative Department for Security in Huila. Moreno declined to give more details.

According to a friend of Bravo's, two weeks before he was killed, a man approached the journalist at his house and warned him to leave town. The man told Bravo that he had been paid 2 million Colombian pesos (US$700) to kill him. Authorities have not been able to confirm the report.

Known for his investigative reporting, Bravo won Colombia's Simón Bolívar National Journalism Award in 1979. Ricardo Areiza, editor-in-chief of the Neiva-based daily *Diario del Huila*, said that Bravo had received death threats a month before his murder. "He said that he was going to be killed, and I believe that his assassination is related to his work," Areiza added.

Bravo was also well known as a left-leaning politician. He served as a departmental lawmaker in Huila for more than two decades and was recently a candidate for mayor of Neiva, according to an April 30 report published in *El Tiempo*, Colombia's leading daily.

Jaime Rengifo Revero
Olímpica Radio, April 29, 2003, Maicao

Rengifo, a 48-year-old host for Radio Olímpica, was shot dead at around 6 a.m. by an unidentified gunman in the hallway of a hotel where the journalist lived in the northern town of Maicao, La Guajira Department, according to local authorities.

The journalist was shot five times in the back while he was walking to his room at Hotel Venecia after drinking a cup of coffee in the lobby. The gunman, who had checked into the hotel under a false name the day before, fled on a motorcycle, said state police chief Col. Heriberto Naranjo.

As of December, authorities had not made any arrests, Naranjo told CPJ. Officials continue to investigate reports that Rengifo was killed for comments made during his weekly morning program on Radio Olímpica, "Periodistas en acción" (Journalists in action).

Rengifo frequently criticized state security forces for failing to bring security to the region and also accused local politicians of corruption, said James Vargas, the station's production director. Leftist guerrillas and rival right-wing paramilitary forces fighting in the country's decades-long civil conflict all operate in the lawless region.

Vargas said Rengifo had received death threats in the past. A month before the journalist was killed, someone scrawled the message "Death to Jaime Rengifo" on the side of a building in Maicao. Rengifo was also the publisher of an infrequently published newspaper called *El Guajiro Quincenario* (The Guajiro Biweekly).

JUAN CARLOS BENAVIDES ARÉVALO
Manantial Estéreo, August 22, 2003
Puerto Caicedo

Benavides, a 29-year-old host for the community radio station Manantial Estéreo, was shot dead when the vehicle in which he was traveling was fired on at a checkpoint reportedly guarded by members of the Revolutionary Armed Forces of Colombia (FARC) near the town of Puerto Caicedo, in southern Colombia.

Benavides died at about 6:15 p.m., after being shot when his driver decided to elude the checkpoint. The journalist hosted the morning radio program "Panorama Informativo" (News Outlook) on Manantial Estéreo, which is run by the Roman Catholic Diocese of Putumayo Department, in the town of Sibundoy.

Also in the car was Jaime Conrado Juajibioy Cuarán, 24, who worked on Benavides' program. Juajibioy was seriously injured in the attack and was taken to a hospital for treatment, according to CPJ sources.

According to local press reports, the rebels who shot at the vehicle were FARC members. However, government forces, right-wing paramilitary militias, and drug lords—in addition to the FARC—are also known to control checkpoints in the region.

On September 3, the Colombian military reported that two FARC rebels who had allegedly shot Benavides were killed in a confrontation with the army. Army officials said the rebels had set up a checkpoint in the area where the journalist was killed, the Bogotá-based daily *El Espectador* reported.

Benavides and Juajibioy were traveling with a group including local politicians from Sibundoy to the town of Puerto Asís, where they had planned to cover a meeting between Colombian President Álvaro Uribe and regional leaders. At the meeting, Uribe said that FARC rebels had been trying to attack him during his visit there, The Associated Press reported.

GUATEMALA: 1

HÉCTOR RAMÍREZ
Noti7 and Radio Sonora, July 24, 2003
Guatemala City

Ramírez, a reporter for Guatemala's Noti 7 television station and Radio Sonora, died from a heart attack after fleeing from attackers who were beating him while he was covering protests in the capital, Guatemala City, according to autopsy results.

On July 24, riots erupted across Guatemala City after the Supreme Court's July 20 decision granting two opposition parties an injunction temporarily barring former dictator Efraín Ríos Montt from running for president in the November 9 elections. A later ruling allowed Ríos Montt to run in the poll, which he lost.

Supporters of Ríos Montt's political party, the Guatemalan Republican Front (FRG), attacked other journalists in different areas of the capital, sources told CPJ. "It was crazy, the mob was completely out of control," Haroldo Sánchez, news director for Guatevisión television station, told CPJ. According to CPJ sources, government authorities and the National Police did little to control the protesters.

In August, Ramírez's family filed a criminal complaint against President Alfonso Portillo Cabrera, several government ministers, Ríos Montt, and high-ranking FRG officials, accusing them of being responsible for the journalist's death.

In an October meeting with a CPJ delegation, Marco Antonio Cortez, the Attorney General Office's special prosecutor for crimes against journalists and trade unionists, told CPJ that he had asked the Supreme Court to initiate preliminary proceedings (*antejuicios*) against President Portillo, Ríos Montt, and other high-ranking government officials to determine if their immunity can be lifted so they can be tried as private citizens. At year's end, the proceedings had not yet begun.

INDIA: 1

Parvaz Mohammed Sultan
News and Feature Alliance
January 31, 2003, Srinagar

Sultan, editor of the independent newswire service News and Feature Alliance (NAFA), which is based in Srinagar, the summer capital of Jammu and Kashmir State, was shot dead by an unidentified gunman.

Two men entered Sultan's office at around 5:30 p.m., according to news reports. After a brief conversation with Sultan, one of the men shot him in the head. The Associated Press (AP) reported that the killer used a pistol with a silencer. No one stopped the assailants from leaving the premises, which is located in the press enclave in central Srinagar.

Though Sultan was rushed to the hospital, doctors declared the journalist dead within minutes of his arrival, police told the AP.

Sultan, 36, was known as an independent journalist who had worked for several local Urdu-language dailies during his career. In addition to running NAFA, he contributed investigative stories and columns to the Urdu-language newspaper *Chattan*, one of the oldest newspapers in Kashmir.

Journalists working in the disputed territory of Kashmir, which both India and Pakistan claim, have long been vulnerable to attack by various parties to the conflict. Sultan's colleagues told CPJ that though they were not aware of any specific threats against the journalist, wire service agencies such as NAFA are under constant pressure to carry statements issued by competing political and militant groups.

Police blamed the murder on militant groups but have not yet conducted a thorough investigation. No group claimed responsibility for Sultan's murder, and many of the leading militant organizations, including Hezb-ul Mujahedeen, condemned the murder, as did the All Parties Hurriyat Conference, the main separatist alliance.

INDONESIA: 1

Ersa Siregar

Rajawali Citra Televisi, December 29, 2003
Aceh

Siregar, a senior reporter with private Indonesian channel Rajawali Citra Televisi (RCTI), was shot and killed during a gun battle between Indonesian military forces and separatist rebels in the war-torn Aceh Province, according to RCTI chief editor Derek Manangka. Aceh military spokesman Lt. Col. Firdaus Komarno told Agence France-Presse that the firefight broke out when Indonesian soldiers came across a group of rebels in the area. Siregar's body and the body of a rebel fighter were found later.

According to news reports, the rebels accused the military of executing Siregar. In response, the military has claimed that the rebels were using the journalist as a human shield.

Siregar, 52, was kidnapped on June 29 by rebels from the Free Aceh Movement, known by its Indonesian acronym GAM, along with cameraman Ferry Santoro, their driver, and two Indonesian officers' wives who were sharing a ride with the journalists to the town of Lhokseumawe in northern Aceh. The RCTI crew had been reporting on the military offensive in Aceh, which was launched on May 19 to crush the long-running rebel insurgency. On July 3, a spokesman for the rebels announced that the group was being held on suspicion of working for the Indonesian military (TNI).

GAM later dropped that accusation, but various attempts to secure the release of the hostages during the last six months have failed. On July 6, TNI Cmdr. Gen. Endriartono Sutarto set a deadline of July 8 for GAM to release the hostages or face military attack. That same day, Imam Wahyudi, an editor at RCTI, and nine other journalists were allowed to meet with Siregar and reported that Siregar and Santoro were in good health. After GAM failed to meet the July 8 deadline, military officials questioned Wahyudi and the other journalists who had met with Siregar about how they were able to contact GAM and locate their base.

Further negotiations between the military and the rebels stalled over the rebels' demands for a seven-day cease-fire and that the military not be involved in the transfer of the hostages. TNI rejected the demands and proposed instead the creation of a battle-free zone where the hostages could be transferred from GAM control. Meanwhile, on October 4, the *Jakarta Post* reported that Siregar was suffering from deteriorating health, including coughing up blood.

On November 5, Indonesian security minister Susilo Bambang Yudhoyono ordered the military to start an operation to locate the hostages, accusing GAM of being "a terror group which takes reporters and innocent civilians hostage."

On December 19, the driver was released unharmed. RCTI cameraman Ferry Santoro and the two officers' wives are still missing.

IRAN: 1

Zahra Kazemi

Freelance, July 10, 2003, Tehran

Kazemi, an Iranian-Canadian freelance photographer, died in Tehran's Baghiatollah Hospital after being transferred from government custody. Kazemi, a contributor to the Montreal-based magazine *Recto Verso* and the London-based photo agency Camera Press, was detained on June 23 while taking photographs of the families of detainees outside Tehran's Evin Prison. She was held for nearly two weeks before being transferred to the hospital in a coma.

During subsequent weeks, officials tried to cover up the circumstances of Kazemi's death. Initially, Iranian officials maintained that the journalist had died of a stroke, and that she had complained of poor health while she was detained. On July 16, Iranian Vice President Mohammad Ali Abtahi announced that Kazemi had died from a "brain hemorrhage resulting from beatings." Foreign Minister Kamal Kharrazi later backed away from the statement, saying the journalist may have died from an "accident." A government inquiry released in late July concluded that Kazemi died as a result of a skull fracture likely caused by a blow to her head.

Authorities prevented an autopsy by burying Kazemi's body in Iran against the wishes of her family in Canada. The Canadian government responded by withdrawing its ambassador to Tehran. In the ensuing months, several agents from the Intelligence Ministry were arrested in connection with Kazemi's death, but as of early November, only one remained in jail—Mohammed Reza Aghdam Ahmadi. His trial was ongoing at year's end.

A parliamentary commission report released in November said that members of the Iranian judiciary had been holding Kazemi in custody when she was beaten, making it unlikely, according to journalists and reformist politicians, that those responsible for her death will be brought to justice.

IRAQ: 13

Terry Lloyd
ITV News, March 22, 2003
Near Al-Zubayr

Lloyd, a veteran correspondent with ITV News, was confirmed dead on March 23 by the British TV network ITN, which produces ITV News. The previous day, he had disappeared after coming under fire while driving to the southern Iraqi city of Basra.

Two others disappeared with Lloyd, cameraman Fred Nerac and translator Hussein Othman. They remain missing.

The three men, along with cameraman Daniel Demoustier, were traveling in two marked press vehicles in the town of Iman Anas, near Al-Zubayr, when they came under fire, ITN reported. According to Demoustier, the car he and Lloyd had been driving had been pursued by Iraqi troops who may have been attempting to surrender to the journalists. Demoustier reported that the incoming fire to their vehicles likely came from U.S. or British forces in the area.

Demoustier, who was injured when the car he was driving crashed into a ditch and caught fire, managed to escape. He said he did not see what happened to Lloyd, who was seated next to him, or to the other crew members. Lloyd's body was recovered in a hospital in Basra days later.

An investigative article published in *The Wall Street Journal* in May indicated that Lloyd's SUV and another vehicle belonging to his colleagues came under fire from U.S. Marines. The article cited accounts from U.S. troops who recalled opening fire on cars marked "TV." Soldiers also said they believed that Iraqi suicide bombers were using the cars to attack U.S. troops.

The *Journal* article cited a report from a British security firm commissioned by ITN to investigate the incident saying that Lloyd's car was hit by both coalition and Iraqi fire; the latter most likely came from behind the car, possibly after the vehicle had crashed.

The report concluded that "[t]he Iraqis no doubt mounted an attack using the ITN crew as cover, or perhaps stumbled into the U.S. forces whilst attempting to detain the ITN crew." The report also speculated that the missing men—Nerac and Othman, who were last seen by Demoustier in another car being stopped by Iraqi forces—might have been pulled out of their car before it came under fire from coalition forces, and then Iraqi forces used the SUV to attack the coalition forces.

In April, Nerac's wife approached U.S. Secretary of State Colin Powell at a NATO press conference, and he promised to do everything in his power to find out what had happened to the missing men. In late May, Centcom said that it was investigating the incident, while the British Ministry of Defense promised to open an inquiry.

In September, London's *The Daily Mirror* newspaper reported the testimony of an Iraqi man named Hamid Aglan who had allegedly tried to rescue the wounded Lloyd in a civilian minibus. Aglan told the newspaper that he had picked up a lightly wounded Lloyd, who had suffered only a shoulder injury, and attempted to take him to a hospital in Basra when the minibus came under fire from a U.S. helicopter, killing Lloyd. The paper reported that the bus was also carrying wounded Iraqi soldiers.

An ITN spokesperson told CPJ that a number of elements of Aglan's story are not consistent with ITN's own investigation. She said an autopsy revealed that Lloyd had suffered two serious wounds that likely resulted from Iraqi and U.S. fire. She said that after he was wounded, an Iraqi civilian in a minibus had picked up Lloyd and tried to take him to a hospital in Basra. The minibus later came under U.S. attack. "It was a gunshot to the bus and [Terry] was probably in the bus," she said. ITN investigators believe that either wound that Lloyd sustained would have been fatal.

PAUL MORAN

Freelance, March 22, 2003, Gerdigo

Moran, a freelance cameraman on assignment for the Australian Broadcasting Corporation (ABC), was killed in a suicide bombing when a man detonated a car at a checkpoint in northeastern Iraq. Another Australian journalist, ABC correspondent Eric Campbell, was injured in the incident.

Michael Ware, *Time* magazine's northern Iraq correspondent and a witness to the incident, told his editor, Howard Chua-Eoan, that several foreign journalists were standing outside a checkpoint on the edge of Gerdigo, a town in northern Iraq near Halabja, interviewing people who were leaving the town in the wake of a U.S. cruise missile bombardment that began on March 21 and continued until the next day.

U.S. missiles were targeting strongholds of Ansar al-Islam, a militant group that the United States designates as a terrorist organization. The area where the journalists were conducting interviews was reportedly under the control of the Patriotic Union of Kurdistan (PUK), a rival of Ansar al-Islam that had just taken over the area.

At around 3 p.m., a taxi drove to the checkpoint near PUK soldiers and Moran, and the driver then detonated his vehicle. Most of the other journalists had just left the scene. Moran, who was filming at the time, was standing only a few feet from the checkpoint and was killed immediately. Campbell was injured by shrapnel.

Chua-Eoan said it appeared that the bomber was targeting the PUK soldiers, not the journalists. According to The Associated Press, at least four other people were killed in the bombing. Militants from Ansar al-Islam are believed to be responsible for the attack.

Chua-Eoan told CPJ that foreign journalists in northern Iraq had recently received warnings from U.S. State Department and Kurdish intelligence officials that Ansar al-Islam may target members of the media, as well as the hotel where most journalists are staying, the Sulaymaniyeh Palace.

Kaveh Golestan
Freelance, April 2, 2003, Kifri

Golestan, an Iranian freelance cameraman on assignment for the BBC, was killed in northern Iraq after stepping on a land mine, the BBC confirmed.

Golestan accidentally detonated the mine when he exited his car near the town of Kifri, John Morrissey of the BBC's foreign desk told CPJ. The cameraman was traveling as part of a four-person BBC crew that included Tehran, Iran, bureau chief Jim Muir, producer Stuart Hughes, and translator Rabeen Azad. Hughes' foot was injured and later treated by U.S. military medics. Muir and the translator suffered light cuts, Morrissey said.

Golestan, who was also a well-known still photographer, had worked frequently with the BBC out of its Tehran bureau.

Michael Kelly
Atlantic Monthly and *The Washington Post*
April 3, 2003, Outside Baghdad

Kelly, editor-at-large of the *Atlantic Monthly* and a columnist with *The Washington Post*, was killed while traveling with the U.S. Army's 3rd Infantry Division just south of the Baghdad airport, according to a statement from *The Washington Post*.

According to press reports, when the humvee in which Kelly was riding came under Iraqi fire, the soldier driving the vehicle tried to evade the attack, and the jeep ran off the road and rolled into a canal. Both Kelly and the driver drowned.

Kelly, who had previously served as the editor of *The New Republic* and the *National Journal*, was the first U.S. journalist killed while covering the war.

Christian Liebig
Focus, April 7, 2003, Outside Baghdad

Liebig, a reporter for the German weekly magazine *Focus*, died in an Iraqi missile attack while accompanying the U.S. Army's 3rd Infantry Division south of the capital, Baghdad. Both Liebig and Julio Anguita Parrado, a Spanish journalist also killed in the incident, were embedded with the division, according to Agence France-Presse.

According to *Focus* editor-in-chief Helmut Markwort, the two men had decided not to travel with the unit to Baghdad, believing they would be safer at the base. Two U.S. soldiers were also killed during the attack, and 15 were injured. Liebig, 35, had worked for *Focus* since 1999.

Julio Anguita Parrado
El Mundo, April 7, 2003, Outside Baghdad

Parrado, a correspondent for the Spanish daily *El Mundo*, died in an Iraqi missile attack while accompanying the U.S. Army's 3rd Infantry Division south of the capital, Baghdad. Both Parrado and Christian Liebig, a German journalist for *Focus* magazine who was also killed in the incident, were embedded with the division, according to Agence France-Presse.

According to *Focus* editor-in-chief Helmut Markwort, the two men had decided not to travel with the unit to Baghdad, believing they would be safer at the base. Two U.S. soldiers were also killed during the attack, and 15 were injured. Parrado was the second *El Mundo* correspondent to have been killed in conflict in almost two years: Correspondent Julio Fuentes died after gunmen ambushed his convoy in Afghanistan in 2001.

Tareq Ayyoub
Al-Jazeera, April 8, 2003, Baghdad

Ayyoub, a Jordanian national working with the Qatar-based satellite channel Al-Jazeera, was killed when a U.S. missile struck the station's Baghdad bureau, which was located in a two-story villa in a residential area near the Iraqi Information Ministry and the former presidential palace compound of Saddam Hussein. Al-Jazeera cameraman Zouhair Nadhim, who was outside on the building's roof with Ayyoub, was injured in the blast, which targeted a small electric generator outside the building.

Centcom maintains that U.S. forces were responding to enemy fire in the area and that the Al-Jazeera journalists were caught in the crossfire. Al-Jazeera correspondents deny that any fire came from their building.

The attack occurred during heavy fighting around the bureau in an area that housed government buildings targeted by U.S. and coalition forces. Al-Jazeera officials pointed out that the U.S. military had been given the bureau's exact coordinates weeks before the war began.

In an April 8 letter to U.S. Defense Secretary Donald Rumsfeld, CPJ protested the bombing and called for an immediate investigation. In October, a Centcom spokesman confirmed to CPJ that no investigation into the incident has been conducted.

The incident occurred around dawn, after intense anti-aircraft fire began in the area. Talk show host and producer Maher Abdullah, a five-year Al-Jazeera veteran who had been in Baghdad for two weeks at the time, told CPJ that planes began flying low in the area at around 6 a.m.

The crew went up to the roof of the building to report but retreated because they deemed it unsafe. According to Abdullah, the crew realized moments later that their still camera had been knocked out of position and now faced the Ministry of Information building, which Iraqi authorities had explicitly warned the crew not to film. Assistant cameraman Zoheir Nadhim returned to the roof with Ayyoub to adjust the camera.

When Ayyoub and Nadhim went upstairs, Abdullah heard a plane fly so low it that sounded like it was going to crash into the building. At that point, a missile struck Al-Jazeera's small generator, which was located outside the building at ground level just below where Ayyoub was believed to have been at the time. Two Al-Jazeera correspondents said that while they suspect that the strike caused his death, he could have been killed by other ordnance.

Another plane passed low about 15 minutes later and fired another missile, which struck across the road about 50 feet (15 meters) from the front door, blowing it off the hinges, according to Abdullah.

Raed Khattar, a cameraman for Abu Dhabi TV who, at the time, was outside on the nearby roof of Abu Dhabi TV's office, saw what was likely the first missile because his office was between the plane and Al-Jazeera's office, he told CPJ.

Moments later, Abu Dhabi TV staff on the roof came under machine gun fire from a U.S. tank on the nearby Jumhuriyya Bridge, and one of their three unmanned cameras was struck by a shell, staff told CPJ. The three-story building was marked with a large banner labeled "Abu Dhabi TV."

In a statement issued hours after the incident, Centcom in Doha, Qatar, said that, "According to commanders on the ground, Coalition forces came under significant enemy fire from the building where the Al-Jazeera journalists were working and consistent with the right of self-defense, Coalition forces returned fire. Sadly an Al-Jazeera correspondent was killed in this exchange."

Abdullah noted that until that morning anti-aircraft fire in the area had been sporadic. Days before April 8, Abdullah saw manned Iraqi anti-aircraft positions in the general vicinity—some 220 yards (200 meters) away on the opposite side of the generator, but not immediately near the office. However, on April 11, he discovered one abandoned anti-aircraft gun about 44 yards (40 meters) away from the bureau. Journalists from Abu Dhabi TV told CPJ that Al-Jazeera's bureau was located near a villa used by former Iraqi Information Minister Muhammad Said *Sahhaf*.

Just before the war, CPJ obtained a copy of the February 24, 2003, letter that then Al-Jazeera Managing Director Mohammed Jasem al-Ali had sent to Pentagon spokeswoman Victoria Clarke specifying the coordinates of the bureau.

Al-Jazeera also maintains that the night before the strike, al-Ali had received explicit assurances from U.S. State Department official Nabeel Khoury in Doha, Qatar, that the bureau was safe and would not be targeted. Abdullah told CPJ, "The coordinates were actually given four months in advance to the Pentagon, and we were assured that we would not be hit under any circumstances. ... We would never be targeted, that was the assurance."

In an e-mail reply to CPJ, Khoury, who said he did not recall the exact date of his meeting with Al-Jazeera, said, "I doubt very much that I assured anybody's safety in a war zone." He added that he did tell the station "what we had been telling all diplomats and civilians, that whereas our troops would do their utmost not to hurt civilians, there was no way to guarantee anyone's safety in a war zone."

In its April 8 letter to U.S. Secretary of Defense Donald Rumsfeld, CPJ also noted that, "The attack against Al-Jazeera is of particular concern since the station's offices were also hit in Kabul, Afghanistan, in November 2001. The Pentagon asserted, without providing additional details, that the office was a 'known Al-Qaeda facility,' and that the U.S. military did not know the space was being used by Al-Jazeera."

CPJ is still waiting for the Defense Department to fulfill a Freedom of Information Act request related to the April 8, 2003, incident CPJ filed in May.

José Couso
Telecinco, April 8, 2003, Baghdad

Couso, a cameraman for the Spanish television station Telecinco, died after a U.S. tank fired a shell at the Palestine Hotel in Baghdad, Iraq's capital, where most journalists in the city were based during the war. At around 12 p.m., a shell hit two hotel balconies where several journalists were monitoring a battle in the vicinity. Taras Protsyuk, a Ukrainian cameraman for Reuters, was also killed in the attack.

Agence France-Presse reported that Couso was hit in his jaw and right leg. He was taken to Saint Raphael Hospital, where he died during surgery.

Directly after the attack, Maj. Gen. Buford Blount, commander of the U.S. Army's 3rd Infantry Division, confirmed that a single shell had been fired at the hotel from a tank in response to what he said was rocket and small arms fire from the building. Journalists at the hotel deny that any gunfire had emanated from the building.

A CPJ report concluded that the shelling of the hotel, while not deliberate, was avoidable since U.S. commanders knew that journalists were present in the hotel and were intent on not hitting it. The report called on the Pentagon to conduct a thorough and public investigation into the incident.

On August 12, U.S. Central Command (Centcom) issued a news release summarizing the results of its investigation into the incident. The report concluded that the tank unit that opened fire on the hotel did so "in a proportionate and justifiably measured response." It called the shelling "fully in accordance with the Rules of Engagement."

Centcom offered some detail—consistent with CPJ's investigation—that the tank opened fire at what it believed was an Iraqi "spotter" directing enemy fire at U.S. troops. The release also explained that "one 120mm tank round was fired at the suspected enemy observer position. ... It was only some time after the incident that A Company became aware of the fact that the building they fired on was the Palestine Hotel and that journalists at the hotel had been killed or injured as a result."

However, the news release failed to address one of the conclusions in CPJ's report: That U.S. commanders knew that journalists were in the Palestine Hotel but failed to convey this knowledge to forces on the ground.

Centcom's results, which were summarized in the release, appeared to back away from earlier charges by U.S. military officials that the tank unit was responding to hostile fire emanating from the hotel. Yet, despite considerable testimony to the contrary from several journalists in the hotel, Centcom maintains "that the enemy used portions of the hotel as a base of operations and that heavy enemy activity was occurring in those areas in and immediately around the hotel."

In addition, the news release failed to provide other specific information, such as how the decision to target the hotel was made.

CPJ has urged Centcom to make the full report available, but a Centcom spokesperson told CPJ the report is classified. CPJ is still waiting for the Defense Department to fulfill a Freedom of

Information Act request related to the April 8, 2003, incident filed in May.

TARAS PROTSYUK
Reuters, April 8, 2003, Baghdad

Protsyuk, a cameraman for Reuters, died after a U.S. tank fired a shell at the Palestine Hotel in Baghdad, Iraq's capital, where most journalists in the city were based during the war. At around 12 p.m., a shell hit two hotel balconies where several journalists were monitoring a battle in the vicinity. José Couso, a cameraman for the Spanish television station Telecinco, also died in the attack.

Agence France-Presse reported that Protsyuk died of wounds to his head and stomach. He had worked for Reuters since 1993, covering conflicts in Bosnia, Kosovo, Chechnya, and Afghanistan.

Directly after the attack, Maj. Gen. Buford Blount, commander of the U.S. Army's 3rd Infantry Division, confirmed that a single shell had been fired at the hotel from a tank in response to what he said was rocket and small arms fire from the building. Journalists at the hotel denied that any gunfire had emanated from the building.

A CPJ report concluded that the shelling of the hotel, while not deliberate, was avoidable since U.S. commanders knew that journalists were present in the hotel and were intent on not hitting it. The report called on the Pentagon to conduct a thorough and public investigation into the incident.

On August 12, U.S. Central Command (Centcom) issued a news release summarizing the results of its investigation into the incident. The report concluded that the tank unit that opened fire on the hotel did so "in a proportionate and justifiably measured response." It called the shelling "fully in accordance with the Rules of Engagement."

Centcom offered some detail—consistent with CPJ's investigation—that the tank opened fire at what it believed was an Iraqi "spotter" directing enemy fire at U.S. troops. The release also explained that "one 120mm tank round was fired at the suspected enemy observer position. ... It was only some time after the incident that A Company became aware of the fact that the building they fired on was the Palestine Hotel and that journalists at the hotel had been killed or injured as a result."

However, the news release failed to address one of the conclusions in CPJ's report: That U.S. commanders knew that journalists were in the Palestine Hotel but failed to convey this knowledge to forces on the ground.

Centcom's results, which were summarized in the release, appeared to back away from earlier charges by U.S. military officials that the tank unit was responding to hostile fire emanating from the hotel. Yet, despite considerable testimony to the contrary from several journalists in the hotel, Centcom maintains "that the enemy used portions of the hotel as a base of operations and that heavy enemy activity was occurring in those areas in and immediately around the hotel."

In addition, the news release failed to provide other specific information, such as how the decision to target the hotel was made.

CPJ has urged Centcom to make the full report available, but a Centcom spokesperson told CPJ the report is classified. CPJ is still waiting for the Defense Department to fulfill a Freedom of

Information Act request related to the April 8, 2003, incident filed in May.

Richard Wild
Freelance, July 5, 2003, Baghdad

Wild, a 24-year-old British freelance cameraman who was working in Baghdad, died after an unidentified assailant approached him and shot him in the head at close range on a street near the city's Natural History Museum.

Wild, who had previously worked at Britain's ITN as a picture researcher, went to Iraq with aspirations of being a war reporter. Some press reports stated that Wild was not carrying a camera or wearing any clothing that would have identified him as a journalist at the time of the shooting. One of Wild's colleagues in Baghdad, British TV producer Michael Burke, told newspapers that Wild was working on a story about looting at the museum. While some speculated that he may have been mistaken for a member of the U.S. military, the motive for the murder remains unclear. CPJ considers that Wild was killed in action while working.

Jeremy Little
NBC News, July 6, 2003, Fallujah

Little, an Australian freelance soundman working for the U.S.-based television network NBC, was injured in a grenade attack in the Iraqi town of Fallujah on June 29 while embedded with U.S. troops. He died of "post-operative complications," according to a statement from NBC News. Little, 27, was embedded with the U.S. 3rd Infantry Division for NBC News and had been receiving treatment at a military hospital in Germany.

Mazen Dana
Reuters, August 17, 2003, Outside Baghdad

Dana, a veteran conflict cameraman for Reuters news agency, was killed by machine gun fire from a U.S. tank near the capital, Baghdad. Dana was struck in the torso while filming near Abu Ghraib Prison, outside Baghdad, in the afternoon. He had been reporting with a colleague near the prison after a mortar attack had killed six Iraqis there the previous night. The soldier in the tank who fired on Dana did so without warning, while the journalist filmed the vehicle approaching him from about 55 yards (50 meters).

U.S. military officials said the soldier who opened fire mistook Dana's camera for a rocket-propelled grenade (RPG) launcher. There was no fighting taking place in the area, and the journalists had been operating in the vicinity of the prison with the knowledge of U.S. troops near the prison gates.

In an August 18 letter to U.S. Secretary of Defense Donald H. Rumsfeld, CPJ protested the shooting, stating that it raised "serious questions about the conduct of U.S. troops and their rules of engagement."

On September 22, the U.S. military announced that it had concluded its investigation into the incident. A spokesman for U.S. Central Command (Centcom) in Iraq told CPJ that while Dana's killing was "regrettable," the soldier "acted within the rules of engagement." No further details were provided. The results of the investigation have not been made public. A Centcom spokesman said other details of the report are classified.

Dana's soundman, Nael Shyioukhi, who witnessed the incident, told CPJ that he and Dana arrived at the prison with their driver, Munzer Abbas, in the late afternoon. According to Shyioukhi, several journalists were also in the area. Shyioukhi said that after a short while Dana suggested that they approach the prison gates to begin filming. At one point, Dana identified himself to a U.S. soldier as a journalist from Reuters and asked if a spokesman was available to comment on camera about the attack the previous night. The soldier replied that he could not comment, and no spokesmen were available. Dana then asked the soldier if he and Shyioukhi could film the prison from a nearby bridge. According to Shyioukhi, the soldier politely told them they were welcome to do so.

After filming from the bridge, located between 330 and 660 yards (300 and 600 meters) from the prison, Dana and Shyioukhi, who were wearing jeans and T-shirts, packed their equipment in their car and began to head off for the Reuters office. As they approached the main road to the prison, Dana noticed a convoy of tanks approaching and told Abbas to stop so he could film it. According to Shyioukhi, he and Dana were not apprehensive because the area was calm, and it was apparent that U.S. troops were in complete control. Neither Dana nor Shyioukhi were wearing flak jackets, and their car was not marked press.

Dana exited the car and set up his blue, canvas-encased camera with a white microphone facing the tanks while Shyioukhi lit a cigarette. Shyioukhi said Dana filmed for about 10 seconds when suddenly, without warning, several shots rang out from the lead tank, which was approximately 55 yards (50 meters) away.

Shyioukhi ducked for cover then heard Dana scream and place his hand on his stomach, which was bleeding profusely. Shyioukhi said that within moments of the shooting, approximately six U.S. soldiers, including the one who shot Dana, surrounded them. Shyioukhi recounted that the soldier who shot Dana screamed at Shyioukhi to "stand back."

A doctor arrived in an armored personnel carrier (APC) after about 10 minutes and tried to stop the bleeding. The APC took Dana back to the prison complex for treatment and to evacuate him to a hospital.

U.S. military spokesman Col. Guy Shields called Dana's death a "tragic incident" and promised to do everything to avoid a similar incident in the future. When questioned by London's *Independent* about the rules of engagement for U.S. troops, Shields said, "I can't give you details on the rules of engagement, but the enemy is not in formations, they are not wearing uniforms. During wartime firing a warning shot is not a necessity. There is no time for a warning shot if there is potential for an ambush."

Some journalists at the scene questioned how troops could mistake the camera for a weapon. According to experts who train war correspondents, although one might easily mistake a camera for an RPG launcher at a distance, a camera would be clearly visible from 55 to 110 yards (50 to 100 meters)—the distance at which Dana was hit.

In December, CPJ received an update to a Freedom of Information Act request filed about the incident with the Defense Department. In the update, Centcom said it was preparing a response in Baghdad, which would include a "redacted copy" of the classified report written about Dana's death. Centcom said it expects the redaction process to take "at least two months."

Ahmed Shawkat
Bilah Ittijah, October 28, 2003, Mosul

Shawkat, editor of the weekly *Bilah Ittijah* (Without Direction), was shot and killed by one or more gunmen at his office in Mosul. According to press reports, a gunman and an accomplice followed the journalist to the roof of his office in the afternoon. One local journalist told CPJ that Shawkat was on the roof making a call from his satellite telephone when he was shot.

CPJ continues to investigate the case. But based on current research, CPJ believes that Shawkat was killed for his work as a journalist.

Sources report that Shawkat's writing often criticized Islamists, Islam, the former regime of Saddam Hussein, and the U.S-led occupation. According to one local journalist who has followed the case, Shawkat had recently written a piece that questioned whether Arabic was the language of heaven.

Shawkat's daughter, Roaa, who also works at *Bilah Ittijah*, told CPJ in an e-mail that her father had received several verbal threats warning him to close the newspaper, as well as one written threat a few months before his death. *The Washington Post* reported on November 16 that Shawkat's son, Sindbad, said the written threat accused Shawkat of being a Zionist guilty of colluding with infidels. The *Post* reported that Sindbad had warned his father not to write about foreign Islamist extremists in Iraq.

According to the local journalist, Shawkat was confronted in his office a few days prior to his shooting by several men with long beards—sometimes a sign of religiosity in Muslim countries. The journalist told CPJ that a man who has an office in the same building as the paper told investigators that he saw the same bearded men fleeing the scene after Shawkat was shot. The journalist said that both local and regional police were investigating the case, but that the regional police have ended their investigation and closed the case file for lack of evidence. The journalist said that an employee of the paper, whom Roaa also mentioned in her e-mail to CPJ as being a suspect in the case, was released by police, also for lack of evidence.

ISRAEL AND THE OCCUPIED TERRITORIES: 2

Nazih Darwazeh
Associated Press Television News
April 19, 2003, Nablus

Darwazeh, a cameraman for The Associated Press Television News (APTN), was shot and killed by Israeli forces in the West Bank city of Nablus while filming clashes between Palestinian youths and Israeli troops at around 9 a.m., according to Palestinian journalists who witnessed the incident. Video footage of the attack, reviewed by CPJ, appears to corroborate their accounts.

The shooting occurred after clashes erupted in Nablus when Israeli forces entered the city's downtown area in tanks, searching for an alleged Palestinian suicide bomber. Clashes broke out in several locations near the city's center, involving youths throwing stones and Molotov cocktails at Israeli troops. Some Palestinian gunmen were also observed firing guns, according to press accounts.

At the time that Darwazeh was shot, he had been filming an Israeli tank stranded at the corner of an alleyway.

Darwazeh and several other Palestinian journalists were standing by a door in the alleyway. A few minutes before Darwazeh was killed, Reuters cameraman Hassan Titi filmed a group of Palestinian youths running down the alley away from the stranded tank. Titi and Reuters photographer Abed Qusini, who were standing near Darwazeh, said that an Israeli soldier crouched under the tank and quickly fired a single shot at the journalists from a distance of about 11 to 22 yards (10 or 20 meters). Darwazeh was struck in the back of the head and died instantly.

Titi and Qusini said there were no clashes or gunfire in the alley at the time, although there had been some Palestinian gunfire in the vicinity earlier. The AP reported that gunfire may have struck near the tank at around the same time, but that it likely came from a different direction than where Darwazeh was standing.

Maj. Sharon Feingold, a spokeswoman for the Israel Defense Forces (IDF), was quoted by the AP as saying that Israeli troops had been rescuing the stranded tank when they were attacked with stones, and "explosive devices and shots were fired from the crowd." Despite eyewitness accounts and video footage, the IDF said that it was unclear who fired the shot that killed Darwazeh.

Darwazeh and his colleagues were clearly identified as members of the press, based on the testimony of those at the scene and the video footage of the events. In fact, Darwazeh was wearing a fluorescent jacket marked "Press," and before the shooting, the journalists said they shouted loudly in both English and Hebrew that they were with the media.

The IDF says it is investigating the incident but has not released any details.

James Miller
Freelance, May 2, 2003, Rafah

Miller, a British freelance cameraman and film director with U.K.-based Frostbite Films, was fatally shot in the Gaza Strip. An award-winning documentary filmmaker, the journalist was with a crew in the town of Rafah in southern Gaza near the Egyptian border filming an HBO documentary on the Israeli-Palestinian conflict. That evening, he and his four-person crew were in a Palestinian home filming the army's demolition of houses in the area that the Israeli army alleged contained tunnels used to smuggle arms.

According to published testimonies of eyewitnesses and an Associated Press Television News cameraman who was filming in the same house, the incident occurred between 11 p.m. and 11:30 p.m., when the group decided to leave. Miller, his producer Saira Shah, and translator Abdul Rahman Abdullah attempted to identify themselves to the Israeli troops in the area while they were leaving. The Israel Defense Forces (IDF) troops were in armored personnel carriers (APCs) about 330 feet (100 meters) away from the house where the journalists had been filming.

The journalists were wearing jackets and helmets marked "TV." Abdullah waved a white flag while Miller used a flashlight to illuminate the flag. As they approached the APCs, the journalists shouted "Hello," and then a shot was fired. The journalists yelled that they were British journalists, and a second shot was fired immediately after. In video footage of the incident, it appears that the second shot hit Miller, who was struck in the neck. Several more shots followed.

An Israeli army spokesman was quoted as saying that troops in the area returned fire after being fired on by rocket-propelled grenades (RPGs). Later, the army said that Miller was struck by a bullet from behind, claiming that he may have been hit by Palestinian fire.

A detailed onsite investigation sponsored by Miller's colleagues, friends, and family and conducted by Chris Cobb-Smith, of the British security company Chiron Resources Limited (*www.chiron-resources.com*), concluded that Miller and his crew "were consciously and deliberately targeted by the IDF soldiers." The report added that it is not clear "whether this action is a deliberate policy by the IDF or whether this incident is a result of ill discipline and malicious intent by the junior soldiers." A copy of the investigation is available at a Web site hosted by James Miller's family, *www.justice4jamesmiller.com.*

According to the investigation, the area where Miller's crew was operating was quiet for about an hour before he was killed. Prior to that time, witnesses heard only sporadic gunfire, but not in the journalists' vicinity. The report concluded that the IDF must have known that the journalists were in the area.

After viewing the video taken of the incident, Cobb-Smith discounted the IDF's claim that RPG fire had occurred before the troops opened fire on the journalists and observed that the shots were fired without warning. Based on the trajectory of the bullets fired, as well as the unanimous testimony of eyewitnesses who said the fire came from the direction of the APC's, Cobb-Smith also disagrees with suggestions from Israeli officials that the shots came from behind the crew.

As of press time, an Israeli military police investigation into the incident was under way, and the IDF's investigation had not been made public.

IVORY COAST: 1

JEAN HÉLÈNE
Radio France Internationale
October 21, 2003, Abidjan

Hélène, correspondent for Radio France Internationale (RFI) in Ivory Coast's commercial capital, Abidjan, was shot by a police officer in the evening outside the national police headquarters in central Abidjan while waiting to interview detained opposition activists who were being released, according to local and international press reports.

After Hélène's family, RFI, and the France-based press freedom group Reporters Without Borders applied in France to become civil parties in the case, a French public prosecutor began conducting an investigation into the murder. Under French law, French authorities have jurisdiction in the case because the victim was French. Although the French and Ivoirian inquiries are legally separate, officials have been cooperating. France and Ivory Coast have a bilateral treaty on judicial cooperation dating back to Ivoirian independence.

The day Hélène was killed, he was waiting in his car in front of the headquarters when the officer walked over and asked what he was doing, according to press reports. The journalist said he was waiting to talk to opposition party members. The officer then went into the building, came back out, and fired two shots, hitting Hélène in the head and killing him instantly.

Although the motive for the killing is unknown, the assassination occurred against a background of anti-French sentiment since Ivory Coast plunged into civil war and crisis in September 2002. France has troops in the country and helped broker a peace agreement signed in Paris in January 2003. The international—and especially French—media have also come under attack from the local press since the crisis began.

Jérome Bouvier, director of RFI's French-language services, told CPJ that the climate for foreign journalists had been extremely difficult but seemed to have improved in the months before the killing. "That's what makes it even more shocking," he said. " It happened in the center of the city, in front of an official building full of people in uniform."

Hélène had been covering Africa for RFI for more than 10 years, including conflicts in Rwanda and Somalia. He was known for his rigor, independence, and calm. In one of many tributes, French President Jacques Chirac described Hélène as "a great professional who died doing his job in the service of providing information about the Africa he knew so well."

On January 22, 2004, a military court in Abidjan sentenced Ivoirian police officer Sgt. Théodore Séry Dago to 17 years in prison for Hélène's murder. The officer was also fined 500,000 CFA francs (US$960), stripped of his rank in the national police, and barred from voting or leaving his home province for 10 years. The tribunal ordered the Ivoirian State to pay 137 million CFA francs (US$263,850) in damages to Hélène's heirs.

NEPAL: 1

Gyanendra Khadka

Rastriya Samachar Samiti
September 7, 2003
Jyamire, Sindhupalchowk

Khadka, 35, a journalist with the state-owned news agency Rastriya Samachar Samiti (RSS), was brutally murdered in Nepal's eastern Sindhupalchowk District by a group of suspected Maoist rebels.

According to RSS, the rebels took Khadka away from a school where he taught part time and led him to a nearby field, where they tied his hands to a pole and slit his throat. No motive is known for his murder, but during Nepal's 7-year-old civil war, both rebels and government security forces have targeted journalists. Local journalists believe that the rebels killed Khadka because he was a journalist.

Khadka is the first journalist to be killed in Nepal since the rebels broke a cease-fire agreement with government forces in August. His murder came amid intensified violence in the country, as well as increased attacks on journalists.

Khadka's murder has outraged the journalistic community in Nepal. A group of at least 30 journalists gathered to peacefully protest the killing on September 11, but police dispersed them and detained them briefly for defying a ban on demonstrations.

PAKISTAN: 1

Fazal Wahab

Freelance, January 21, 2003, Mingora

Wahab, a freelance writer, was shot and killed by unidentified gunmen while he was sitting in a roadside shop in Manglawar Bazaar, near the resort town of Mingora in northwestern Pakistan. The shopkeeper and his young assistant also died in the attack.

Wahab, who lived in Mingora, had published several books in Urdu and in Pashto—the language spoken in the border region of Pakistan and parts of neighboring Afghanistan—that criticized local religious leaders and Islamic militant organizations.

Local journalists and human rights activists told CPJ that Wahab had been receiving threats for years in response to his writings. Although they do not know who is responsible for his murder, his colleagues believe that he was targeted for his work.

Among Wahab's most controversial works was a book titled *Mullah Ka Kirdar* (The Mullah's Role), which analyzed the Islamic clergy's involvement in politics. He had also recently completed a manuscript about Osama bin Laden and the Taliban.

During the last decade, a militant group known as Tehrik Nifaz Shariat-e-Mohammadi (Movement for the Enforcement of Islamic Law) has gained strength in Mingora and the surrounding Malakand Region. Wahab's writings and outspoken opposition to radical and militant strains of Islam made him particularly vulnerable to attack.

PHILIPPINES: 5

Apolinario "Polly" Pobeda
DWTI-AM radio, May 17, 2003
Lucena City, Quezon

At about 6:00 a.m., two unidentified gunmen stopped radio host Pobeda while he rode his motorcycle to work in Lucena City, Quezon Province, and shot him repeatedly, according to Philippine press reports. Pobeda suffered seven gunshot wounds, including one to his head. He was brought to a hospital, where he was declared dead on arrival.

On Pobeda's radio program "Nosi Balasi" (Who Are They?), which he co-hosted on DWTI-AM, the journalist often criticized corrupt local officials. *The Philippine Daily Inquirer* reported that Pobeda was particularly outspoken against Lucena City Mayor Ramon Talaga, whom the journalist had accused of being involved in the local drug trade.

Pobeda had received repeated anonymous death threats, including one about a month before his murder, according to his wife, Rowena Morales.

On May 22, police arrested brothers Eric and Eulogio Patulay as suspects in the murder. An eyewitness to the crime had identified them as the triggermen, according to local police. Press reports said the Patulay brothers were bodyguards of Romano Talaga, Ramon Talaga's son, although Romano Talaga claimed they had just acted as his "guides" when he traveled. Both the Patulays and Ramon Talaga denied any involvement in Pobeda's murder. A third suspect remains at large.

Pobeda's colleagues and family members say he was murdered for his work. "My husband was killed because he exposed the wrongdoing of the government," Rowena Morales told the Center for Media Freedom and Responsibility, a Manila-based press freedom organization.

Bonifacio Gregorio
Dyaryo Banat, July 8, 2003, La Paz, Tarlac

Gregorio, a reporter and columnist for the weekly *Dyaryo Banat*, in La Paz, a town in the central Tarlac Province, was talking to a colleague on a cell phone in front of his house when an unidentified gunman shot him in the head three times at close range. According to news reports, the gunman was likely a professional killer who fled the scene on foot. Gregorio was rushed to La Paz District Hospital before being transferred to Ramos General Hospital, where he was pronounced dead on arrival.

Local journalists believe that Gregorio, 55, was killed for his journalistic work. Before joining the newspaper, Gregorio served for nine years as chief of Caramutan, a *barangay*, or village, in La Paz. During his three years as a columnist for *Dyaryo Banat*, Gregorio wrote many critical articles about officials in La Paz, including Mayor Dionisio Manuel. Shortly before Gregorio's death, the journalist had accused Manuel of building a cemetery without following local regulations. In interviews with local newspapers, Manuel has denied having anything to do with Gregorio's death.

While police have formed a special task force to solve Gregorio's murder, and Tarlac governor Jose Yap Sr. has publicly urged police to find the killer and prosecute him, no arrests have been made.

Noel Villarante
DZJV Radio and *Laguna Score*
August 19, 2003, Santa Cruz, Laguna

Villarante, of DZJV Radio and the local newspaper *Laguna Score*, was shot and killed by a gunman outside his house in Santa Cruz City in central Laguna Province. After being shot once, Villarante ran inside his home. While his relatives helped him outside again to get to a hospital, the gunman shot Villarante twice in the head, killing him instantly.

Villarante was known for his critical reports on allegedly corrupt local officials and drug traffickers. An editor of *Laguna Score* told journalists he believes that Villarante was murdered in reprisal for his work, and that the reporter had received numerous death threats in the past.

On August 26, police in Laguna announced that they had arrested Senando Palumbarit, identified in press reports as a civilian police agent, as a suspect in Villarante's murder. The National Bureau of Investigation said that Palumbarit's arrest was based on a police sketch of the suspect. Palumbarit has denied any involvement in the murder.

Local journalists have expressed concerns that the investigation into Villarante's killing has not been conducted in a thorough and impartial manner, and that Palumbarit's arrest is part of a police effort to protect high-profile individuals who may be responsible for killing the journalist. Soon after the murder, Santa Cruz Police Chief Superintendent Renato Paras told *The Philippine Daily Inquirer* that investigators were hesitant to reveal too many details about the case because high-profile individuals could be behind the killing.

Soon after Villarante's murder, police ransacked his house and confiscated a number of articles he had written, according to the *Philippine Star* newspaper. Villarante's sister told the *Star* that during the search, officers treated her family and her deceased brother as criminal suspects. The regional police superintendent has ordered an investigation into the incident.

Rico Ramirez
DXSF Radio, August 20, 2003
Agusan del Sur

Police found the body of Ramirez, a commentator for DXSF Radio, on the side of the road in San Francisco, a town in the southern province of Agusan del Sur. Authorities did not announce the murder until September 2 but offered no explanation for the two-week delay.

Police said that Ramirez had been shot once in the back, but that the investigation was hindered by the fact that there were no witnesses. According to *The Philippine*

Daily Inquirer, Ramirez had reported on corruption, drug trafficking, and official wrongdoing by local politicians.

A DXSF Radio manager told the Manila-based Center for Media Freedom and Responsibility that Ramirez could have been killed "because of his recent exposés on the crime and drug syndicates operating in the area." Police also told journalists that he was likely killed by drug traffickers he had exposed on air.

Juan "Jun" Pala
DXGO Radio, September 6, 2003
Davao City

Unidentified gunmen riding a motorcycle shot Pala, a commentator on DXGO Radio, while he was walking home with a bodyguard and a friend in Davao City. The journalist, who suffered nine gunshot wounds, was pronounced dead on arrival at the San Pedro Hospital, according to the Manila-based Center for Media Freedom and Responsibility (CMFR). His companions sustained minor injuries.

In the 1980s, Pala was known for his fiery criticisms of communist rebel groups. At that time, he also served as a spokesperson for an anticommunist vigilante group. In recent years, his radio show has focused more on exposing corruption among local politicians, according to CMFR and press reports.

Pala had repeatedly been targeted for attack before his death. On April 29, unidentified gunmen opened fire on a taxi carrying the journalist, wounding him in the buttocks. Since that attack, Pala aired his show, "Isumbong Mo Kay Pala" (Tell Pala), from his home, according to CMFR.

Following Pala's murder, President Gloria Macapagal Arroyo ordered the Philippine National Police to form a task force to investigate all recent murders of journalists.

RUSSIA: 1

Aleksei Sidorov
Tolyatinskoye Obozreniye, October 9, 2003
Togliatti

Sidorov, editor-in-chief of the independent daily *Tolyatinskoye Obozreniye*, was murdered in Togliatti, a city on the Volga River 600 miles (960 kilometers) east of the capital, Moscow.

Sidorov was the second editor-in-chief of *Tolyatinskoye Obozreniye* to be murdered in the last two years. His predecessor, Valery Ivanov, was shot at point-blank range in April 2002.

According to local press reports, two unidentified assailants stabbed Sidorov several times in the chest late in the evening while he was approaching the apartment building in Togliatti where he lived with his family. The assailants fled after stabbing Sidorov, and the editor died in his wife's arms after she heard his call for help and came down to the entrance of their building.

Journalists at *Tolyatinskoye Obozreniye*—a newspaper known for its investigative reporting on organized crime, government corruption, and shady corporate deals in the heavily industrialized city of Togliatti—are convinced the murder came in retaliation for Sidorov's work.

"All of our investigative work was supervised by Aleksei," a journalist at *Tolyatinskoye Obozreniye* told CPJ. Another journalist at the paper told CPJ that Sidorov had received unspecified threats in retaliation for his work.

Government officials initially agreed that Sidorov's murder appeared to be a contract killing in retaliation for his work. But a week after the killing, officials began offering conflicting explanations about the motive for the murder. On October 16, the local head of the Interior Ministry, Vladimir Shcherbakov, said Sidorov was stabbed after refusing to give a stranger a sip of some vodka he had supposedly been drinking, the independent Moscow daily *Gazeta* reported.

That same day, Deputy Prosecutor General Vladimir Kolesnikov said the murder was related to "the journalist's professional activity," the independent Moscow daily *Kommersant* reported. But the next day, he switched his story, calling the murder "an act of hooliganism," the ITAR-TASS news agency reported.

According to the local press reports, Samara's Deputy Prosecutor General Yevgeny Novozhylov said that an intoxicated welder from one of the local factories, Yevgeni Maininger, stumbled upon Sidorov that evening and murdered him after a brief argument. Local police detained Maininger on October 12 and charged him with murder on October 21 after he confessed to the killing.

Journalists at Sidorov's paper say they are skeptical, especially because Maininger misidentified the location where the journalist had been stabbed outside his apartment.

Maininger's wife disputed the confession, pointing out a number of inconsistencies in his statement—including errors in the description of the clothes Maininger was wearing that evening and the time he left his home—and said she believed that he was being set up, the independent Moscow daily *Kommersant* reported.

In early November, Maininger retracted his statement, saying investigators had forced him to confess. Prosecutors in Togliatti, however, insist that Maininger is guilty of the murder.

SOMALIA: 1

Abdullahi Madkeer
DMC Radio, January 24, 2003, Baidoa

Madkeer, a journalist with DMC Radio, was accidentally shot in the stomach by members of the Rahanweyn Resistance Army (RRA) militia while covering the reopening of Baidoa Airport in the southwest of the country, according to the Somali Journalists' Network (SOJON) and the Action Alert Group, a press freedom organization. He was taken to a hospital and died that day after doctors refused to operate on him because he was HIV positive.

The shooting occurred while militia belonging to the RRA faction of Shaykh Adan Madobe fired on the airport crowd to drive them back from an aircraft with a cargo of the narcotic khat. The airport had just reopened after months of war between rival RRA factions in the region.

SOJON quoted Madkeer's father as saying that there has been no investigation into his son's death because of civil war and lawlessness in Baidoa Region. According to SOJON, Madkeer's death has left his family destitute.

Madkeer's station, DMC Radio, has since been forced to close after local fighters from RRA factions requisitioned the stations' offices.

JOURNALISTS KILLED: MOTIVE UNCONFIRMED

COLOMBIA: 3

Oscar Salazar Jaramillo
Radio Sevilla, March 10, 2003, Sevilla

Salazar, owner of Radio Sevilla in the Valle del Cauca Department in southwestern Colombia, was found dead in his apartment in the town of Sevilla at 9:30 a.m. with several stab wounds in his chest, stomach, and abdomen, according to a police bulletin.

Salazar, 74, hosted a one-hour radio program broadcast on Saturdays called "Sevilla in Seven Days" and was also the founder and owner of the station, said Wilson Rendón, a station employee. Salazar's apartment, where he lived alone, is located above the station.

On his radio program, Salazar gave commentary on politics, sports, and community news and discussed issues on air with listeners who called. He had served as a congressman and a state deputy but did not hold a political position at the time of his death, said Rendón. Salazar had recently criticized local politicians for not fulfilling campaign promises and ignoring constituents' needs. However, he did not criticize any politicians by name, said Rendón.

Although Rendón said he was unaware of threats against Salazar's life, a relative of Salazar's, Rafael Salazar, told local reporters that the journalist had been threatened with death shortly before he was killed for opinions expressed on the air.

A spokesman for the Valle Department police said there was no evidence that Salazar had been robbed, and that authorities are investigating rumors that he was killed in reprisal for the views he expressed on his program. No arrests have been made, and investigators have not established a motive for the murder.

Leftist rebels and right-wing paramilitary fighters are all active in the region. The rival groups and the Colombian government are embroiled in a decades-long civil war. Salazar founded Radio Sevilla, part of the Caracol Radio network, 49 years ago.

José Emeterio Rivas
Radio Calor Estéreo, April 6, 2003
Barrancabermeja

Rivas, a 44-year-old journalist for Radio Calor Estéreo, was killed by unidentified gunmen. Police found the journalist's bullet-ridden body on April 7 on a road outside the town of Barrancabermeja, Santander Department, in northeastern Colombia.

He had four bullet wounds, according to local police commander Col. Jorge Gil. Lying next to him was the body of Paolo César Montesinos, a 22-year-old university student whom authorities believe was also killed with Rivas. It is not yet clear why the two men were together.

Rivas hosted a controversial morning program on Radio Calor Estéreo called "Fuerzas Vivas" (Live Forces). In the weeks before his death, Rivas had publicly accused the town's mayor of corruption and collaboration with members of the Central Bolívar Block of the right-wing paramilitary United Self-Defense Forces of Colombia (AUC), said Carolina Sánchez, spokeswoman for Colombia's Attorney General's Office.

On July 11, the office issued arrest warrants for the mayor, Julio César Ardila, and three high-level officials in his office identified as Abelardo Rueda Tobón, Juan Pablo Ariza Castañeda, and Fabio Pajón Lizcano, who were arrested that day. Ardila gave himself up on September 17.

Sánchez said it is believed that the four men may have hired paramilitary members to kill Rivas. The four town officials appealed their arrests, and in late October a prosecutor found that there was not enough evidence to keep Rueda, Ariza, and Lizcano in custody. Ardila remains in jail on charges of collaborating with paramilitary forces.

Authorities have also issued arrest warrants for three leaders of the Central Bolívar Block in connection with the killing. Sánchez said one of the men has been captured. Another was killed before authorities reached him, and the third is in hiding. Sánchez declined to discuss whether investigators believe that Rivas was killed for his journalistic work.

Before he was killed, Rivas had been assigned a 24-hour police escort through a protection program for journalists run by the Interior Ministry after receiving numerous death threats, said Gil.

The escort was not with Rivas when he was shot. The journalist had told police that he didn't want the bodyguard to be with him during the weekend, allegedly because he was planning to attend a secret meeting with paramilitary fighters in the region, Gil said.

Although Rivas never told police he had planned to meet with the paramilitaries, a man who refused to identify himself called police two days before the journalist's death and warned that the paramilitaries were going to kill him during a meeting he had scheduled with them. When police relayed the message to Rivas, he assured them that he was planning to stay home all weekend, said Gil.

According to CPJ sources, Rivas was a very controversial figure. "Rivas was very involved in politics and had a lot of enemies. It will be difficult to establish the reasons of his murder," Enrique Fuentes, a member of Barrancabermeja's Journalists Association, told CPJ.

Rivas worked as a public official for the local city council years ago and was a candidate for the Colombian Senate in November 2002, according to local press reports.

"It is a complicated case," said Janeth Montoya, a reporter with the Barrancabermeja-based *Vanguardia Liberal*. "The motives are not really clear at this time," she added.

Several people in the region had recently complained to police that Rivas had threatened to denounce them on the radio unless they paid him money. Gil said officials from the Public Prosecutor's Office in Santander were investigating the extortion claims.

Sánchez said she wasn't aware of those claims.

William Soto Cheng
Telemar, December 18, 2003, Buenaventura

Soto, a 46-year-old journalist with the local television station Telemar, was shot dead by two unknown gunmen in the city of Buenaventura, Valle del Cauca Department, in western Colombia.

At around 3:30 p.m., two men riding on a motorcycle shot Soto three times at close range while he was near the Telemar offices, where he hosted the news program "Litoral Pacífico" (Pacific Coast) four times a week and the sports show "Deportes en Acción" (Sports in Action) once a week. Soto died at the scene.

According to CPJ sources, during the October 26 municipal elections, Soto said on his show that police and military forces were responsible for irregularities in the tally of votes. Soto also accused the local police chief of corruption. Sources said that after the journalist made the accusations, he admitted he was wrong and apologized after being threatened with criminal charges.

Manuel Barrantes, a reporter with Cascajal Estéreo radio station and vice president of the local press organization Unión de Periodistas de Buenaventura, told CPJ that Soto was a very controversial figure. Although Barrantes said he did not know of any direct threats against Soto, he said the journalist had expressed his intention of leaving Buenaventura in the near future because of unspecified pressures from his job.

Soto's wife, Doralba Soto, who worked with him as a camerawoman, told CPJ that she was not aware of any threats against her husband. According to her, Soto was not investigating corruption of local security forces or municipal authorities.

Adonai Cárdenas Castillo, local correspondent for the Cali-based newspaper *El País*, said that since Soto had many enemies in Buenaventura because of his controversial reporting, it is difficult to establish a motive.

A few months ago, Soto threatened to denounce a local official on his television show unless the official gave Soto government advertising, a source told CPJ. The sources also said that before his murder, Soto had threatened to denounce the local water utility for malfeasance unless the manager canceled a debt Soto owed.

On December 23, Buenaventura Mayor Jaime Mosquera Borja announced the arrest of two individuals suspected of carrying out the crime. The mayor refused to speculate about the motives of the murder.

HONDURAS: 1

Germán Antonio Rivas
Corporación Maya Visión
November 26, 2003, Santa Rosa de Copán

Rivas, owner of the local TV station Corporación Maya Visión-Canal 7, was murdered outside his station's studios in the western city of Santa Rosa de Copán, near the border between Honduras, Guatemala, and El Salvador.

The murder occurred at around 6:30 p.m., several minutes before his station's news program was about to begin, according to local news reports. When Rivas exited his car, an unidentified gunman shot him in the head and fled.

The police suspect that several accomplices were waiting for the hit man in a car, according to the Tegucigalpa daily *El Heraldo*. Police are pursuing several possible motives in the investigation, including that Rivas was killed for his journalistic work. Authorities have identified three individuals who allegedly committed the murder, but arrest warrants for the suspects have not yet been issued, the Tegucigalpa daily *La Prensa* reported.

In addition to his duties as owner of Corporación Maya Visión, Rivas was the director of the daily news program "CMV Noticias" (CMV News). The program, which is broadcast between 6 p.m. and 7:30 p.m., also airs on radio station Estéreo Maya Visión, which Rivas and his wife own.

Before he was murdered, Rivas survived a shooting on February 24. That evening, unidentified assailants attacked the journalist outside his house when he arrived home after finishing his station's daily news program, he told CPJ after the incident. When Rivas exited the car to open the garage door, the attacker, who was hidden, fired a single shot and fled. The shot missed Rivas, hitting the pavement. Rivas then went into his house and called the police, who arrived about 20 minutes later. Officers examined the area but left soon because it became too dark to search. Two people, including a neighborhood guard, witnessed the attack.

The next day, Rivas and the neighborhood guard looked for evidence, found a gun that appeared to have been used in the shooting, and turned it over to police. Officers told Rivas it was a .30-caliber weapon. They sent it to a lab in the capital, Tegucigalpa, for ballistic tests. The test results were never announced, and the weapon used in the attack remains in a Tegucigalpa lab.

The journalist told CPJ he believed that the attack was linked to his journalistic work and cited several sensitive stories that his station had covered. In September 2002, the station's investigative journalism team reported on the smuggling of coffee and cattle from Honduras to Guatemala. (The segment was dropped in December 2002 after the sponsor canceled its contract.) The station has also extensively covered local neighborhood associations that have denounced a local mining company for spilling cyanide into Copán Department's Lara River. The night of the February attack, Rivas said, the station reported that the Honduran government had ordered the mining company to pay a fine of 1 million lempiras (US$60,000).

Félix Molina, deputy coordinator of the Honduran freedom of expression organization Comité para la Libertad de Expresión, said that although the station's crime reporting was not very aggressive, the fact that it covered crime at all could have provoked retaliation.

Rivas, who said he had no enemies, did not have any particular suspects for the February shooting. The day after the attack, he filed a complaint with the General Department of Criminal Investigations, part of the Ministry of Security. Rivas complained that the police had not offered the protection he requested.

INDIA: 1

Parmanand Goyal
Punjab Kesari, September 18, 2003, Kaithal

Goyal, a journalist with the daily newspaper *Punjab Kesari*, was shot and killed by three unidentified assailants at his home in Kaithal, Haryana, north of the capital, Delhi, according to local press reports. CPJ is investigating the motives behind his murder.

According to India's *The Tribune* newspaper, Goyal's son Naveen Rinku answered the door at Goyal's home, where three men asked to speak with his father. Rinku told Goyal about the visitors and asked the men to wait in the backyard. *The Tribune* reported that Rinku claimed to have overheard the men threatening his father to stop writing about a local political figure and the police. Soon after, Goyal was found wounded in the backyard, and his assailants fled the scene. Goyal was rushed to the hospital but was pronounced dead on arrival, according to press reports.

Goyal had been arrested on corruption charges in May and was released on bail earlier this month. His family says that the charges against him were false.

Goyal was the district president of the Haryana Union of Journalists. Local journalists, outraged by the murder, gathered on September 19 for a moment of silence in his memory and to call for an investigation into his murder.

INDONESIA: 1

Mohamad Jamal

TVRI, Date unknown, Banda Aceh

Jamal, 30, a cameraman for the Indonesian state broadcast network TVRI, was kidnapped on May 20 by unidentified gunmen at his office in Banda Aceh, the administrative center of strife-torn Aceh Province. Though the journalist was abducted on May 20, just one day after the launch of a major Indonesian military offensive to crush the separatist rebellion in Aceh, it is not clear why he was targeted.

A military spokesman told Reuters news agency that Jamal's body was found in a river on June 17. Other witnesses said that Jamal's eyes and mouth had been covered with duct tape, his hands bound with a nylon cord, and that a noose lashed to a boulder was tied around his neck, according to Reuters.

Indonesia's military has denied any involvement in Jamal's murder and accused him of being sympathetic to the Free Aceh Movement GAM rebels, according to the Alliance of International Journalists, Indonesia's oldest independent journalists' organization. The motive behind Jamal's kidnapping and murder remains unknown, but CPJ continues to investigate the incident.

IVORY COAST: 1

Kloueu Gonzreu

Ivoirian Press Agency, Date unknown
Toulépleu

The body of Ivoirian journalist Kloueu Gonzreu, 51, who worked for the state-owned Ivoirian Press Agency and the Red Cross, was found in March near the western town of Toulépleu, on the border of Liberia, by a team from the Red Cross. His body was found with those of his 19-year-old son and two local Red Cross volunteers.

The victims reportedly disappeared on January 11. Local journalists told CPJ at the time they believed that Gonzreu had been kidnapped and killed by Liberian mercenaries fighting for the Ivoirian government, and that his death could have been linked to his work as a journalist. The pro-government newspaper *Notre Pays*, in its January 30 edition, had accused him of "voicing sympathy with the rebellion."

However, the circumstances of his death remain murky, and some have also raised the possibility that he was killed in crossfire during an upsurge of fighting in early 2003 between government and rebel forces there. Because Toulépleu is remote with no government authority ruling it, no inquiry has been conducted.

JAPAN: 1

Satoru Someya

Freelance, Date unknown, Tokyo

On September 12, police found Someya's body near a pier in Tokyo Bay. The exact time of his death is unknown, although an autopsy determined that Someya had been dead for one to two weeks, according to Japanese press reports. Police are considering several motives behind the murder, including his journalism and problems with debt. CPJ continues to investigate the case.

Someya's body was wrapped in a weighted chain, his hands were tied with rope, and he had eight stab wounds in his back and two gashes in his head, according to police reports. Someya had been missing since September 5, when he last spoke by phone with a magazine editor.

Someya, 38, reported for various magazines about organized crime in Tokyo under the pen name Kuragaki Kashiwabara. In July, he published a book titled *Kabukicho Underground* about Chinese criminal groups operating in Kabukicho, Tokyo's notorious red light district.

The motive for Someya's murder is unclear. In the postscript to *Kabukicho Underground*, the journalist wrote that he might be in danger because of his investigations, according to press reports. On November 22, police detained two men who work in the locksmith industry in connection with the murder. The two men were seen in a restaurant with Someya shortly before he disappeared. In 2002, Someya wrote an investigative report about the locksmith industry, and police said he had encountered problems with the suspects about both the contents of his report and debts he had incurred during the course of the project.

KYRGYZSTAN: 1

Ernis Nazalov
Kyrgyz Ruhu, September 15, 2003
Kara-Suu

The body of Nazalov, a journalist for the independent Bishkek daily *Kyrgyz Ruhu*, was found early in the morning on the bank of an irrigation canal in Kara-Suu District near the southern region of Osh, according to local press reports.

Police in Kara-Suu District initially opened a criminal inquiry into the 26-year-old journalist's death but closed it after they said autopsy reports showed Nazalov had drowned, local CPJ sources reported.

While Nazalov's journalism had focused on cultural and social issues, his family and colleagues suspect that his death may have been related to his recent investigation of corrupt senior government officials in the Osh regional administration.

The Bishkek-based Bureau for Human Rights and the Rule of Law reported that it took Nazalov's father an entire month to obtain a copy of the autopsy report, which listed numerous wounds and injuries found on the journalist's body and suggested they could have been inflicted prior to death.

The human rights group also noted that police never interviewed the last person to see Nazalov prior to his death, a friend who had left a wedding Nazalov attended the night before with the journalist and then abruptly moved to Bishkek.

Nazalov's colleagues point out that a group of unidentified assailants had attacked and robbed Nazalov on the night of August 26 in the city of Osh, stealing sensitive documents about the Osh regional administration, as well as other personal belongings.

The Interior Ministry in the Osh Region opened an investigation into the case after local police in Kara-Suu District closed their inquiry, but no progress has been reported.

PHILIPPINES: 1

Nelson Nadura
Radio DYME, December 2, 2003
Masbate City

Nadura, a commentator for Radio DYME in the Philippine's central Masbate City, was shot dead at about 8:30 a.m. by two unidentified gunmen. The attack occurred while Nadura was on his motorcycle leaving the radio station after his daily broadcast, according to press reports and the Center for Media Freedom and Responsibility, a Manila-based press freedom organization. He died immediately from multiple gunshot wounds to the chest. Six empty shells and a slug were found on the scene. The suspects fled on foot.

The motive behind Nadura's killing is unclear, and police are conducting an investigation. Nadura, 42, hosted a morning talk show on political affairs called "Opinyon Publiko" (Public Opinion), during which he criticized local officials. A former member of the communist rebel group New Peoples Army, Nadura was amnestied in 1998 after surrendering to the government. He later started working as a radio commentator. At the time of his death, he was president of the Union of Print and Broadcast Journalists of Masbate.

On December 3, President Gloria Macagapal Arroyo condemned Nadura's murder, stating, "These attacks against members of the press shall not go unpunished." Since the return of democracy in the Philippines in 1986, more than 40 journalists have been murdered there for their work. None of these murders has been solved.

RUSSIA: 1

Dmitry Shvets
TV-21 Northwestern Broadcasting
April 18, 2003, Murmansk

Shvets, the 37-year-old deputy director-general of the independent television station TV-21 Northwestern Broadcasting in the northern Russian city of Murmansk, was shot dead outside the station's offices.

An unknown assailant shot Shvets several times at approximately 5 p.m. in front of witnesses and escaped in a getaway car that was waiting nearby. Shvets died instantly.

Shvets was well-known in Murmansk, not only for running the television station but also for his political activism and a number of commercial interests. Although he had not worked as a journalist in many years, Shvets remained in a managerial position and on the station's board of directors. According to press reports and the Moscow-based Center for Journalism in Extreme Situations, he influenced the station's editorial policy, and TV-21's reporting often reflected his political persuasions.

The Murmansk media covered Shvets' murder widely and actively speculated about the possible motive. Shvets' colleagues said TV-21 had received multiple threats for its critical reporting on several influential politicians, including Andrei Gorshkov, a candidate in the city's mayoral race.

Several weeks before Shvets' murder, Gorshkov had threatened TV-21 journalists several times after they broadcast a tough interview with him.

TV-21 news editor Svetlana Bokova told CPJ that at the time of his death, Shvets was using his contacts at the police and prosecutor's office to investigate the mayoral candidate's links to organized crime.

Police continue to investigate various motives behind the murder, including Shvets' political, commercial, and journalistic activities at TV-21. Shvets' colleagues maintain that he was killed in retaliation for TV-21's critical reporting on local politics.

Bokova told CPJ that, during the murder investigation, police have requested videotapes with critical reports broadcast by TV-21 during the last two years.

THAILAND: 1

Surapong Ritthi
Freelance, February 11, 2003
Patong Beach

Freelance journalist Surapong, 43, was shot dead at around 3:00 a.m. while leaving a grocery store on Rat-U-Thit Road in Patong Beach, a popular tourist destination in southern Phuket Province, according to local journalists. A lone gunman shot him twice in the back of the head at close range.

The *Phuket Gazette*, a local English-language newspaper, reported that the owner of the grocery store "told the police that the killer was a large man with pale skin in a yellow T-shirt."

Surapong worked as a local stringer in Phuket for the national newspaper *Thai Rath*, the regional newspaper *Siang Tai*, and the independent, national television station Channel 3. He also owned several businesses in Phuket, including a bar and restaurant and a shrimp farm, according to the Thai Journalists Association.

Police said that in his capacity as a reporter, Surapong would likely have been aware of illegal dealings in the area, and that they are investigating many possible motives behind the killing. One focus of the police inquiry is Surapong's reporting on illicit activities at a Patong Beach nightclub, a story that local journalists say may have led to the reporter's murder. Surapong had reported that the nightclub featured nude dancers, prompting a police raid that resulted in the bar's closure.

Several of the journalist's colleagues in Phuket believe that Surapong may have been killed in reprisal for his reporting, but other colleagues say he was probably killed because of an unspecified "personal conflict." The motive behind the murder remains unconfirmed. ■

JOURNALISTS IN PRISON IN 2003

136 journalists in prison as of December 31, 2003

THERE WERE 136 JOURNALISTS IN PRISON AROUND THE WORLD at the end of 2003 who were jailed for practicing their profession. The number is the same as last year. An analysis of the reasons behind this is contained in the introduction on page 10.

At the beginning of 2004, CPJ sent letters of inquiry to the heads of state of every country on the list below requesting information about each jailed journalist. Readers are encouraged to add their voices to CPJ's by writing directly to the heads of state, whose names and addresses can be found at *www.cpj.org*.

This list represents a snapshot of all the journalists who were incarcerated at midnight on December 31, 2003. It does not include the many journalists who were imprisoned and released throughout the year; accounts of those cases can be found at *www.cpj.org*.

A word about how this list is compiled: In totalitarian societies where independent journalism is forbidden, CPJ often defends persecuted writers whose governments view them as political dissidents rather than as journalists. This category would embrace the samizdat publishers of the former Soviet Union and the wall-poster essayists of the pre-Tiananmen period in China. We also include political analysts, human rights activists, and others who were prosecuted because of their written or broadcast work.

We consider any journalist who is deprived of his or her liberty by a government to be imprisoned. Journalists remain on this list until we receive positive confirmation that they have been released. In some cases, we have received reports that a journalist was killed in government custody. One example is Nepalese journalist Krishna Sen, who was arrested by government forces in Nepal on May 20, 2002, and has not been heard from since. We keep Sen on this list as a way of holding the Nepalese government accountable for his fate.

Journalists who either disappear or are abducted by nonstate entities, including criminal gangs, rebels, or militant groups, are not included on the imprisoned list. Their cases are classified as "missing." CPJ documented four such cases in 2003. Details are available on CPJ's Web site.

ALGERIA: 2

Djamel Eddine Fahassi, Alger Chaîne III
Imprisoned: May 6, 1995

Fahassi, a reporter for the state-run radio station Alger Chaîne III and a contributor to several Algerian newspapers, including the now banned weekly of the Islamic Salvation Front, *Al-Forqane*, was abducted near his home in the al-Harrache suburb of the capital, Algiers, by four well-dressed men carrying walkie-talkies. According to eyewitnesses who later spoke with his wife, the men called out Fahassi's name and then pushed him into a waiting car. He has not been seen since, and Algerian authorities have denied any knowledge of his arrest.

Prior to Fahassi's "disappearance," Algerian authorities had targeted him on at least two occasions because his writing criticized the government. In late 1991, he was arrested after an article in *Al-Forqane* criticized a raid conducted by security forces on an Algiers neighborhood. On

January 1, 1992, the Blida Military Court convicted him of disseminating false information, attacking a state institution, and disseminating information that could harm national unity.

He received a one-year suspended sentence and was released after five months. On February 17, 1992, he was arrested a second time for allegedly attacking state institutions and spreading false information. He was transferred to the Ain Salah Detention Center in southern Algeria, where hundreds of Islamic suspects were detained in the months following the cancellation of the January 1992 elections.

In late January 2002, Algerian Ambassador to the United States Idriss Jazairy responded to a CPJ query, saying a government investigation had not found those responsible for Fahassi's abduction. The ambassador added that there was no evidence of state involvement.

Aziz Bouabdallah, *Al-Alam al-Siyassi*
Imprisoned: April 12, 1997

Bouabdallah, a reporter for the daily *Al-Alam al-Siyassi*, was abducted by three armed men from his home in the capital, Algiers. According to Bouabdallah's family, the men stormed into their home and, after identifying the journalist, grabbed him, put his hands behind his back, and pushed him out the door and into a waiting car. An article published in the daily *El-Watan* a few days after his abduction reported that Bouabdallah was in police custody and was expected to be released soon.

In July 1997, CPJ received credible information that Bouabdallah was being held in Algiers at the Châteauneuf detention facility, where he had reportedly been tortured. But Bouabdallah's whereabouts are currently unknown, and authorities have denied any knowledge of his abduction.

In late January 2002, Algerian Ambassador to the United States Idriss Jazairy responded to a CPJ query, saying a government investigation had not found those responsible for Bouabdallah's abduction. The ambassador added that there was no evidence of state involvement.

BANGLADESH: 1

Salah Uddin Shoaib Choudhury, *Blitz*
Imprisoned: November 29, 2003

Choudhury, editor of the weekly tabloid *Blitz*, was arrested by security personnel at Zia International Airport in the capital, Dhaka, on suspicion of antistate activities and espionage while on his way to Israel to participate in a conference with the Hebrew Writers Union.

Intelligence agents interrogated Choudhury at the airport and confiscated his luggage, according to *The Daily Star*. Choudhury's home was also raided, *The Independent* newspaper reported.

According to *The Daily Star*, the journalist was suspected of having links to an Israeli intelligence agency and had been under surveillance for several months before his arrest. Choudhury has denied the charges, *The Independent* reported.

On December 17, the Chief Metropolitan Magistrate Court denied Choudhury's request for bail, and police formally charged him with violating passport regulations, which carries a maximum sentence of six months, according to Choudhury's family. Bangladesh has no formal relations with Israel, and travel to Israel is illegal for Bangladeshi citizens.

Two other charges of antistate activities are being prepared against the journalist by Bangladesh's Home Ministry for alleged involvement in "anti-religious activities," according to Choudhury's family.

CPJ is investigating the motives behind Choudhury's detention. He was traveling to address a writers' symposium in Tel Aviv titled "Bridges Through Culture" and was scheduled to speak about "the role of media in establishing peace," according to the conference organizer. Choudhury would have been the first journalist from Bangladesh to address such a group in Israel.

Choudhury was affiliated with the Israel-based International Forum for Literature and Culture of Peace, a non-profit organization dedicated to promoting world peace. He recently wrote about the rise of al-Qaeda in Bangladesh.

BURMA: 10

U Win Tin, freelance
Imprisoned: July 4, 1989

U Win Tin, former editor-in-chief of the daily *Hanthawati* and vice chairman of Burma's Writers Association, was arrested and sentenced to three years of hard labor on the spurious charge of arranging a "forced abortion" for a member of the opposition National League for Democracy (NLD). One of Burma's most well-known and influential journalists, U Win Tin helped establish independent publications during the 1988 student democracy movement. He was also a senior leader of the NLD and a close adviser to opposition leader Daw Aung San Suu Kyi.

In 1992, he was sentenced to an additional 10 years for "writing and publishing pamphlets to incite treason against the State" and "giving seditious talks," according to a May 2000 report by the Defense Ministry's Office of Strategic Studies. On March 28, 1996, prison authorities extended U Win Tin's sentence by another seven years after they convicted him, along with at least 22 others, of producing clandestine publications—including a report describing the horrific conditions at Rangoon's Insein Prison to the U.N. special rapporteur for human rights in Burma.

U Win Tin was charged under Section 5(e) of the Emergency Provisions Act for having "secretly published anti-government propaganda to create riots in jail," according to the Defense Ministry report. His cumulative sentence is, therefore, 20 years of hard labor and imprisonment.

Now 73 years old, the veteran journalist is said to be in extremely poor health after years of maltreatment in Burma's prisons—including a period when he was kept in solitary confinement in one of Insein Prison's notorious "dog cells," formerly used as kennels for the facility's guard dogs. He suffers from spondylitis, a degenerative spine disease, as well as a prostate gland disorder and hemorrhoids. The journalist has had at least two heart attacks and spent time in the hospital for treatment twice in 2002: once following a hernia operation, and again in connection with a heart ailment.

U Win Tin remained in the prison ward of the Rangoon General Hospital at the beginning of 2003, but representatives from Amnesty International and the United Nations were allowed to visit him there. The Amnesty International group saw him on February 5, 2003, for about an hour and reported that although U Win Tin's health seemed to have stabilized, he was suffering from urinary problems. On March 21, 2003, U.N. Special Human Rights Envoy to Burma Paulo Sergio Pinhiero also spent an hour visiting with U Win Tin in the hospital.

According to a report in *Le Monde*, a Burmese army officer asked U Win Tin to sign a document in early 2003 that would have freed him from prison if he agreed to stop his political work, but the journalist refused.

If he is forced to complete his full 20-year sentence, U Win Tin will not eligible for release from prison until July 2009.

Ohn Kyaing, freelance
Thein Tan, freelance
Imprisoned: September 6, 1990

On September 7, 1990, Col. Than Tun, Burma's deputy chief of military intelligence, announced at a press conference that Ohn Kyaing and Thein Tan were among six leaders of the opposition National League for Democracy (NLD) arrested on the previous day, according to international news reports.

On October 19, 1990, the Information Committee of the junta (then known as the State Law and Order Restoration Council and later renamed the State Peace and Development Council) announced at a press conference that Ohn Kyaing and Thein Tan "had been sentenced to seven years imprisonment by a military tribunal for inciting unrest by writing false reports about the unrest, which occurred in Mandalay on 8 August 1990," according to the BBC's translation of a state radio broadcast.

The Mandalay "unrest" the committee referred to involved the military's killing of four pro-democracy demonstrators. Government troops fired on protesters—who were commemorating the democracy rallies of August 8, 1988, during which hundreds were shot dead, including two monks and two students.

Ohn Kyaing, who also uses the name Aung Wint, is the former editor of the newspaper *Botahtaung* and one of Burma's most prominent journalists. He retired from *Botahtaung* in December 1988 to become more involved in the pro-democracy movement, according to the PEN American Center. In 1990, Ohn Kyaing was elected to Parliament for the NLD, representing a district in Mandalay. (The results of the elections, which the NLD won, were never honored by the military junta.) A leading intellectual, he continued to write. Thein Tan, whose name is sometimes written as Thein Dan, is also a freelance writer and political activist associated with the NLD.

PEN reported that in mid-1991, Ohn Kyaing received an additional sentence of 10 years in prison under the 1950 Emergency Provisions Act for his involvement in drafting a pamphlet for the NLD titled "The Three Paths to Power." Thein Tan also received an additional 10-year sentence, according to Amnesty International, presumably for the same reason.

In a list of Burmese political prisoners published in April 2001, Amnesty International reported that the sentences of both men were reduced to 10 years on January 1, 1993. However, Ohn Kyaing and Thein Tan remained in prison at the end of 2003. Ohn Kyaing was jailed at Taungoo Prison, and Thein Tan was jailed at Thayet Prison, according to the Thailand-based Assistance Association for Political Prisoners in Burma.

Maung Maung Lay Ngwe, *Pe-Tin-Than*
Imprisoned: September 1990

Maung Maung Lay Ngwe was arrested and charged with writing and distributing publications that "make people lose respect for the government." The publications were titled, collectively, *Pe-Tin-Than* (Echoes). CPJ believes that he may have been released but has not been able to confirm his legal status or find records of his sentencing.

Sein Hla Oo, freelance
Imprisoned: August 5, 1994

Sein Hla Oo, a freelance journalist and former editor of the newspaper *Botahtaung*, was arrested along with dissident writer San San Nwe on charges of contacting antigovernment groups and spreading information damaging to the state. On October 6, 1994, Sein Hla Oo was sentenced to seven years in prison. San San Nwe and three other dissidents, including a former UNICEF worker, received sentences ranging from seven to 15 years in prison on similar charges.

Officials said the five had "fabricated and sent anti-government reports" to diplomats in foreign embassies, foreign radio stations, and foreign journalists. Sein Hla Oo, elected in 1990 to Parliament representing the National League for Democracy (NLD), had been imprisoned previously for his political activities.

Though San San Nwe was granted an early release in July 2001 along with 10 other political prisoners associated with the NLD, Sein Hla Oo remained in jail. He was held at Myitkyina Prison, according to the Thailand-based Assistance Association for Political Prisoners in Burma.

Though Sein Hla Oo's sentence should have expired in August 2001, he is now being forced to serve the remainder of an earlier 10-year prison sentence, issued by a military court in Insein Prison in March 1991, according to his wife, Shwe Zin. Authorities had arrested Sein Hla Oo in August 1990 along with several other NLD members but released him under an amnesty order in April 1992. Shwe Zin told the Oslo-based opposition radio station Democratic Voice of Burma in an interview that her husband had signed a document in October 2001 agreeing to abide by Article 401 of the Criminal Procedure Code, which allows prisoners' sentences to be suspended if they pledge not to engage in activities that threaten public order.

Aung Htun, freelance
Tha Ban, freelance
Imprisoned: February 1998

Aung Htun, a writer and activist with the All Burma Federation of Student Unions, was arrested in February 1998 for writing a seven-volume book documenting the history of the Burmese student movement. He was sentenced to a total of 17 years in prison, according to a joint report published in December 2001 by the Thailand-based Assistance Association for Political Prisoners in Burma and the Burma Lawyers Council. Aung Htun was sentenced to three years for allegedly violating the 1962 Printer and Publishers Registration Act, seven years under the 1950 Emergency Provisions Act, and another seven years under the 1908 Unlawful Associations Act. He is jailed at Tharawaddy Prison.

In April 1998, the All Burma Students Democratic Front announced that five others were also prosecuted for contributing to the books, including journalist Tha Ban, a former editor at *Kyemon* newspaper and a prominent Arakanese activist. Tha Ban, whose name is sometimes written as Thar Ban, was sentenced to seven years in prison. He is being held at Insein Prison.

In August 2002, the human rights group Amnesty International issued an urgent appeal on behalf of Aung Htun and Tha Ban, saying that both journalists required immediate medical attention. Amnesty reported that Aung Htun "has growths on his feet which require investigation, is unable to walk, and suffers from asthma," and that Tha Ban's eyesight has "seriously deteriorated." According to the BBC, Tha Ban was allowed to undergo surgery for his failing eyesight in November 2003.

Aung Pwint, freelance
Thaung Tun, freelance
Imprisoned: October 1999

Aung Pwint, a videographer, editor, and poet, and Thaung Tun, an editor, reporter, and poet better known by his pen name Nyein Thit, were arrested separately in early October 1999. CPJ sources said they were arrested for making independent video documentaries that portrayed "real life" in Burma, including footage of forced labor and hardship in rural areas. Aung Pwint worked at a private media company that produced videos for tourism and educational purposes, but he also worked with Thaung Tun on documentary-style projects. Their videotapes circulated through underground networks.

The military government had prohibited Aung Pwint from making videos in 1996 "because they were considered to show too negative a picture of Burmese society and living standards," according to Human Rights Watch, which awarded Aung Pwint a Hellman-Hammett grant in 2001. A notable poet, he has also written under the name Maung Aung Pwint.

The two men were tried together, and each was sentenced to eight years in prison, according to CPJ sources. Aung Pwint was initially jailed at Insein Prison but was later transferred to Tharawaddy Prison, according to CPJ sources. Thaung Tun was jailed at Moulmein Prison, according to the Thailand-based Assistance Association for Political Prisoners in Burma.

Zaw Thet Htway, *First Eleven*
Imprisoned: July 17, 2003

Zaw Thet Htway, screenwriter and editor of the popular sports monthly *First Eleven*, was arrested with four other *First Eleven* journalists, all of whom were soon released, when military intelligence officers raided the magazine's offices in the capital, Rangoon. According to exile groups, the officers beat Zaw Thet Htway during the arrest.

On November 28, Zaw Thet Htway and eight other individuals, including a lawyer and a member of an opposition party, were charged with high treason and sentenced to death at a special court in Burma's notorious Insein Prison. Although death sentences are rarely carried out in Burma, according to exiled Burmese journalists, the harsh sentence was intended to send a strong warning to journalists inside the country.

The eight other defendants who were sentenced to death had also been arrested in mid-July. According to The Associated Press (AP), the government accused all nine of plotting to overthrow Burma's ruling junta, and of being involved with pro-democracy leader Aung San Suu Kyi's opposition National League for Democracy (NLD) party.

In June, *First Eleven* had received a government warning after it published an article that month questioning how grant money from the international community for the development of soccer in the country had been spent, according to *The Irrawaddy*, a Bangkok-based news magazine run by exiled Burmese journalists.

In a statement released soon after the arrests, the government denied that Htway was arrested because of his work as a journalist and said he was detained "on a totally different subject" but did not provide further details, according to the AP.

The journalist's arrest came amid a crackdown by Burma's ruling military junta that began on May 30, when pro-democracy leader Aung San Suu Kyi was arrested along with as many as 17 other NLD members.

Htway spent several years in jail in the 1990s because of his work with the Democratic Party for a New Society, a banned political party now operating in exile. Family members told Agence France-Presse that he has also been accused of being in contact with "unlawful elements" in the party. The AP reported that his wife, Khine Cho, was not allowed in the court for the sentencing, but that she plans to appeal the conviction.

CHINA: 39

Chen Renjie, "Ziyou Bao"
Lin Youping, "Ziyou Bao"
Imprisoned: July 1983

In September 1982, Chen, Lin, and Chen Biling wrote and published a pamphlet titled "Ziyou Bao" (Freedom Report), distributing about 300 copies in Fuzhou, Fujian Province. They were arrested in July 1983 and accused of making contact with Taiwanese spy groups and publishing a counterrevolutionary pamphlet. According to official government records of the case, the men used "propaganda and incitement to encourage the overthrow of the people's democratic dictatorship and the socialist system." In August 1983, Chen Renjie was sentenced to life in prison, and Lin Youping was sentenced to death with reprieve. Chen Biling was sentenced to death and later executed.

Hu Liping, *Beijing Ribao*
Imprisoned: April 7, 1990

Hu, a staff member of *Beijing Ribao* (Beijing Daily), was arrested and charged with "counterrevolutionary incitement and propaganda" and "trafficking in state secrets," according to a rare release of information on his case from the Chinese Ministry of Justice in 1998. The Beijing Intermediate People's Court sentenced him to 10 years in prison on August 15, 1990. Under the terms of his original sentence, Hu should have been released in 2000, but CPJ has been unable to obtain information about his legal status.

Chen Yanbin, *Tieliu*
Imprisoned: September 1990

Chen and Zhang Yafei, both university students, were arrested and charged with counterrevolutionary incitement and propaganda for publishing *Tieliu* (Iron Currents), an underground publication about the 1989 crackdown at Tiananmen Square. Several hundred mimeographed copies of the publication were distributed. Chen was sentenced to 15 years in prison and four years without political rights after his release. Zhang was sentenced to 11 years in prison and two years without political rights after his release. However, Zhang was freed on January 6, 2000, after showing "genuine repentance and a willingness to reform." In September 2000, the Justice Ministry announced that Chen's sentence had been reduced by three months for good behavior.

Liu Jingsheng, freelance
Imprisoned: May 28, 1992

Liu was arrested and charged with "organizing and leading a counterrevolutionary group and spreading counterrevolutionary propaganda." He was sentenced to 15 years in prison after being tried secretly in July 1994.

Liu had belonged to labor and pro-democracy groups, including the Liberal

Democratic Party of China, the Free Labor Union of China, and the Chinese Progressive Alliance, and had written articles supporting the 1989 pro-democracy demonstrations. During the Democracy Wall movement in 1979, Liu co-edited the pro-democracy journal *Tansuo* (Explorations) with dissident Wei Jingsheng.

Court documents stated that Liu was involved in organizing and leading antigovernment and pro-democracy activities. Prosecutors also accused him and other dissidents who were tried on similar charges of writing and printing political leaflets that were distributed in June 1992, during the third anniversary of the Tiananmen Square demonstrations. Liu has had his sentence reduced three times for good behavior by a total of one year and eight months. In May 2002, on the 10th anniversary of her husband's arrest, Liu's wife, Jin Yanming, wrote an account of his imprisonment, trial, and security officials' subsequent harassment of her family. The document was distributed online.

Wu Shishen, Xinhua News Agency
Ma Tao, *Zhongguo Jiankang Jiaoyu Bao*
Imprisoned: November 6, 1992

Wu, an editor for China's state news agency, Xinhua, was arrested for allegedly leaking an advance copy of President Jiang Zemin's 14th Communist Party Congress address to a journalist from the now defunct Hong Kong newspaper *Kuai Bao* (Express). His wife, Ma, editor of *Zhongguo Jiankang Jiaoyu Bao* (China Health Education News), was arrested on the same day and accused of acting as Wu's accomplice. The Beijing Municipal Intermediate People's Court held a closed trial and on August 30, 1993, sentenced Wu to life imprisonment for "illegally supplying state secrets to foreigners." Ma was sentenced to six years in prison. According to the terms of her original sentence, Ma should have been released in November 1998, but CPJ has been unable to obtain information on her legal status.

Fan Yingshang, *Remen Huati*
Sentenced: February 7, 1996

In 1994, Fan and Yang Jianguo printed more than 60,000 copies of the magazine *Remen Huati* (Popular Topics). The men had allegedly purchased fake printing authorizations from an editor of the *Journal of European Research* at the Chinese Academy of Social Sciences, according to official Chinese news sources. CPJ was unable to determine the date of Fan's arrest, but on February 7, 1996, the Chang'an District Court in Shijiazhuang City sentenced him to 15 years in prison for "engaging in speculation and profiteering." Authorities termed *Remen Huati* a "reactionary" publication. Yang escaped arrest and was not sentenced.

Hua Di, freelance
Imprisoned: January 5, 1998

Hua, a permanent resident of the United States, was arrested while visiting China and charged with revealing state secrets. The charge is believed to stem from articles that Hua, a scientist at Stanford University, had written about China's missile defense system.

On November 25, 1999, the Beijing No. 1 Intermediate People's Court held a closed trial and sentenced Hua to 15 years in prison, according to the Hong Kong–based Information Center for Human Rights and Democracy. In March 2000, the Beijing High People's Court overturned Hua's conviction and ordered that the case be retried. This judicial reversal was extraordinary, particularly for a high-profile political case. Nevertheless, in April 2000, the Beijing State Security Bureau rejected a request for Hua to be released on medical parole; he suffers from a rare form of male breast cancer.

On November 23, 2000, after a retrial, the Beijing No. 1 Intermediate People's Court issued a slightly modified verdict, sentencing Hua to 10 years in prison. News of Hua's sentencing broke in February 2001, when a relative gave the information to foreign correspondents based in Beijing. In late 2001, Hua was moved to Tilanqiao Prison in Shanghai, according to CPJ sources.

Liu Xianli, freelance
Imprisoned: March 1998

The Beijing Intermediate Court found writer Liu guilty of subversion and sentenced him to four years in prison, according to a report by the Hong Kong–based Information Center for Human Rights and Democracy.

Liu was imprisoned for attempting to publish a book on Chinese dissidents, including Xu Wenli, one of China's most prominent political prisoners and a leading figure in the China Democracy Party. In December 1998, Xu was himself convicted of subversion and sentenced to 13 years in prison. On December 24, 2002, Xu was released on medical parole and deported to the United States.

According to the terms of his original sentence, Liu should have been released in March 2002, but CPJ has been unable to obtain information on his legal status.

Gao Qinrong, Xinhua News Agency
Imprisoned: December 4, 1998

Gao, a reporter for China's state news agency, Xinhua, was jailed for reporting on a corrupt irrigation scheme in drought-plagued Yuncheng, Shanxi Province. Xinhua never carried Gao's article, which was finally published on May 27, 1998, in an internal reference edition of the official *People's Daily* that is distributed only among a select group of party leaders. But by fall 1998, the irrigation scandal had become national news, with reports appearing in the Guangzhou-based *Nanfang Zhoumo* (Southern Weekend) and on China Central Television. Gao's wife, Duan Maoying, said that local officials blamed Gao for the flurry of media interest and arranged for his prosecution on false charges.

Gao was arrested on December 4, 1998, and eventually charged with crimes including bribery, embezzlement, and pimping, according to Duan. On April 28, 1999, he was sentenced to 13 years in prison after a closed, one-day trial. He is being held in a prison in Qixian, Shanxi Province, according to CPJ sources.

In September 2001, Gao wrote to Mary Robinson, then the U.N. high commissioner for human rights, and asked her to intercede with the Chinese government on his behalf. Gao has received support from several members of the Chinese People's Political Consultative Conference of the National People's Congress, who issued a motion at its annual parliamentary meeting in March 2001 urging the Central Discipline Committee and Supreme People's Court to reopen his case. But by the end of 2003, there had been no change in his legal status.

Yue Tianxiang, *Zhongguo Gongren Guancha*
Imprisoned: January 1999

The Tianshui People's Intermediate Court in Gansu Province sentenced Yue to

10 years in prison on July 5, 1999. The journalist was charged with "subverting state power," according to the Hong Kong–based Information Center for Human Rights and Democracy. Yue was arrested along with two colleagues—Wang Fengshan and Guo Xinmin—both of whom were sentenced to two years in prison and have since been released. According to the Hong Kong–based daily *South China Morning Post*, Yue, Guo, and Wang were arrested in January 1999 for publishing *Zhongguo Gongren Guancha* (China Workers' Monitor), a journal that campaigned for workers' rights.

With help from Wang, Yue and Guo started the journal after they were unable to get compensation from the Tianshui City Transport Agency following their dismissal from the company in 1995. All three men reportedly belonged to the outlawed China Democracy Party, a dissident group, and were forming an organization to protect the rights of laid-off workers. The first issue of *Zhongguo Gongren Guancha* exposed extensive corruption among officials at the Tianshui City Transport Agency. Only two issues were ever published.

Wu Yilong, *Zaiye Dang*
Imprisoned: April 26, 1999
Mao Qingxiang, *Zaiye Dang*
Zhu Yufu, *Zaiye Dang*
Xu Guang, *Zaiye Dang*
Imprisoned: June 1999

Wu, an organizer for the banned China Democracy Party (CDP), was detained by police in Guangzhou on April 26, 1999. Mao, Zhu, and Xu, also leading CDP activists, were reportedly detained sometime around June 4, the 10th anniversary of the brutal crackdown on pro-democracy demonstrations in Tiananmen Square. The four were later charged with subversion for, among other things, establishing a magazine called *Zaiye Dang* (Opposition Party) and circulating pro-democracy writings online.

On October 25, 1999, the Hangzhou Intermediate People's Court in Zhejiang Province conducted what *The New York Times* described as a "sham trial." On November 9, 1999, all four journalists were convicted of subversion. Wu was sentenced to 11 years in prison. Mao was sentenced to eight years; Zhu, to seven years; and Xu, to five years.

In December 2002, Mao was transferred to a convalescence hospital after his health had sharply declined as a result of being confined to his cell. Zhu, who has also been confined to his cell and forbidden from reading newspapers, was placed under tightened restrictions in 2002 after refusing to express regret for his actions, according to the New York–based advocacy group Human Rights in China.

Zhang Ji, freelance
Imprisoned: October 1999

Zhang, a student at the University of Qiqihar in Heilongjiang Province, was charged on November 8, 1999, with "disseminating reactionary documents via the Internet," according to the Hong Kong–based Information Center for Human Rights and Democracy.

Zhang had allegedly distributed news and information about the banned spiritual movement Falun Gong. He was arrested sometime in October 1999 as part of the Chinese government's crackdown on the sect.

Using the Internet, Zhang reportedly transmitted news of the crackdown to Falun Gong members in the United States and Canada and also received reports from abroad, which he then circulated among practitioners in China. Before Zhang's arrest, Chinese authorities had increased Internet surveillance in their efforts to crush Falun Gong.

Huang Qi, Tianwang Web site
Imprisoned: June 3, 2000

Public security officials came to Huang's office and arrested him for articles that had appeared on the Tianwang Web site, which he published. In January 2001, he was charged with subversion.

On August 14, 2001, the Chengdu Intermediate Court in Sichuan Province held a closed trial after postponing the trial date several times. On May 9, 2003, almost two years after the trial, the court sentenced Huang Qi to five years in prison and one subsequent year without political rights. Huang was sentenced under Articles 69, 103, and 105 of the Criminal Law, which cover the crimes of "splitting the country" and subversion.

In October 1998, Huang and his wife, Zeng Li, launched Tianwang (*www.6-4tianwang.com*), a missing-persons search service based in Chengdu, Sichuan Province. The site soon became a forum for users to publicize abuses of power by local officials and to post articles about a variety of topics, including the June 4, 1989, military crackdown on peaceful demonstrations in Tiananmen Square, the independence movement in the Xinjiang Uighur Autonomous Region, and the banned spiritual group Falun Gong.

In December 1999, Huang published an investigative report about labor abuses committed against workers whom the Sichuan provincial government had sent abroad. While several domestic newspapers subsequently investigated and published stories on the case, authorities in Chengdu began threatening Huang and repeatedly interrogated him about his reporting.

Huang has been beaten in prison and has tried to commit suicide, according to an open letter he wrote from prison in February 2001 that was published on the Tianwang site. His family members, including his wife and young son, have only been allowed to visit Huang once, in November 2003.

Huang's family was not notified of his sentencing hearing and only learned of Huang's conviction after Zeng Li called the court. On May 18, 2003, Huang Qi appealed his sentence, pointing out that China's constitution guarantees the right to freedom of speech and of the press. Huang's trial had been postponed several times throughout 2001 in an apparent effort to deflect international attention from China's human rights practices during the country's campaign to host the 2008 Olympic Games. (Two of the trial delays—on February 23 and June 27—coincided with important dates in Beijing's Olympics bid.)

Xu Zerong, freelance
Imprisoned: June 24, 2000

Xu was arrested in the city of Guangzhou and held incommunicado for 19 months before being tried by the Shenzhen Intermediate Court in January 2002. He was sentenced to 10 years in prison on charges of "leaking state secrets," and to an additional three years on charges of committing "economic crimes."

Xu, an associate research professor at the Institute of Southeast Asian Studies at Zhongshan University in Guangzhou, has written several freelance articles about China's foreign policy and co-founded a Hong Kong–based academic journal,

Zhongguo Shehui Kexue Jikan (China Social Sciences Quarterly). Xu is a permanent resident of Hong Kong.

Chinese officials have said that the "state secrets" charges against Xu stem from his use of historical materials for his academic research. In 1992, Xu photocopied four books published in the 1950s about China's role in the Korean War, which he then sent to a colleague in South Korea, according to a letter from the Chinese government to St. Antony's College, Oxford University. (Xu earned his Ph.D. at St. Antony's College, and since his arrest, college personnel have actively researched and protested his case.) The Security Committee of the People's Liberation Army in Guangzhou later determined that these documents should be labeled "top secret."

The "economic crimes" charges are related to the "illegal publication" of more than 60,000 copies of 25 books and periodicals since 1993, including several books about Chinese politics and Beijing's relations with Taiwan, according to official government documents.

Some observers believe that the charges against Xu are more likely related to an article he wrote for the Hong Kong–based *Yazhou Zhoukan* (Asia Weekly) newsmagazine revealing clandestine Chinese Communist Party support for Malaysian communist insurgency groups. Xu was arrested only days before the article appeared in the June 26, 2000, issue. In the article, Xu accused the Chinese Communist Party of hypocrisy for condemning the United States and other countries for interfering in China's internal affairs by criticizing its human rights record. "China's support of world revolution is based on the concept of 'class above sovereignty'… which is equivalent to the idea of 'human rights above sovereignty,' which the U.S. promotes today," Xu wrote.

Xu's family has filed an appeal, which was pending at the end of 2003.

Guo Qinghai, freelance
Imprisoned: September 15, 2000

Guo was arrested after posting numerous essays on overseas online bulletin boards calling for political reforms in China. In essays posted under the pen name Qing Song, Guo covered a variety of topics, including political prisoners, environmental problems, and corruption. In one essay, Guo discussed the importance of a free press, saying, "Those who oppose lifting media censorship argue that it will negatively influence social stability. But according to what I have seen ... countries that control speech may be able to maintain stability in the short term, but the end result is often violent upheaval, coup d'états, or war."

On April 3, 2001, the Cangzhou Intermediate People's Court in Hebei Province tried Guo on subversion charges. On April 26, he was sentenced to four years in prison. Sentencing papers cited 27 articles that Guo had written between October 1999 and September 2000 as evidence, including one titled "Be An Eternal Opponent," which advocated Western-style democracy, according to prosecutors.

Guo, who worked in a bank, also wrote articles for Taiwanese newspapers. He was a friend and classmate of writer Qi Yanchen, who was sentenced to four years in prison on subversion charges just four days after Guo's arrest. One of Guo's last online essays appealed for Qi's release. Qi Yanchen was freed from prison in April 2003.

Liu Weifang, freelance
Imprisoned: October 2000

Liu was arrested sometime after September 26, 2000, when security officials from the Ninth Agricultural Brigade District, in the Xinjiang Uighur Autonomous Region, came to his house, confiscated his computer, and announced that he was being officially investigated, according to an account that Liu posted online. His most recent essay is dated October 20, 2000.

Liu had recently posted a number of essays criticizing China's leaders and political system in Internet chat rooms. The essays, which the author signed either with his real name or with the initials "lgwf," covered topics such as official corruption, development policies in China's western regions, and environmental issues. The articles are available online at *http://liuweifang.ipfox.com.*

"The reasons for my actions are all above-board," Liu wrote in one essay. "They are not aimed at any one person or any organization; rather, they are directed at any behavior in society that harms humanity. The goal is to speed up humanity's progress and development." The official *Xinjiang Daily* characterized Liu's work as "a major threat to national security." According to a June 15, 2001, report in the *Xinjiang Daily*, the Ninth Agricultural Brigade District's Intermediate People's Court had sentenced Liu to three years in prison.

Jiang Weiping, freelance
Imprisoned: December 4, 2000

Jiang, a freelance journalist, was arrested after he published a number of articles in the Hong Kong–based magazine *Qianshao* (Frontline), a Chinese-language monthly focusing on mainland affairs, revealing corruption scandals in northeastern China.

Jiang wrote the *Qianshao* articles, which were published between June and September 1999, under various pen names. His coverage exposed several major corruption scandals involving high-level officials. Notably, Jiang reported that Shenyang Vice Mayor Ma Xiangdong had lost nearly 30 million yuan (US$3.6 million) in public funds gambling in Macau casinos. Jiang also revealed that Liaoning provincial Governor Bo Xilai had covered up corruption among his friends and family during his years as Dalian mayor.

Soon after these cases were publicized in *Qianshao* and other Hong Kong media, central authorities detained Ma. He was accused of taking bribes, embezzling public funds, and gambling overseas and was executed for these crimes in December 2001. After Ma's arrest, his case was widely reported in the domestic press and used as an example in the government's ongoing fight against corruption. However, in May 2001, Jiang was indicted for "revealing state secrets."

The Dalian Intermediate Court held a secret trial in September 2001. On January 25, 2002, the court formally sentenced Jiang to eight years in prison on charges including "inciting to subvert state power" and "illegally providing state secrets overseas." This judgment amended an earlier decision to sentence Jiang to nine years. During the January sentencing, Jiang proclaimed his innocence and told the court that the verdict "trampled on the law," according to CPJ sources. Jiang immediately appealed his sentence to the Liaoning Province Higher People's Court. On December 26, 2002, the court heard the appeal and, while upholding Jiang's guilty verdict, reduced his sentence to six years, according to the California-based Dui Hua Foundation, which has been in direct contact with the Chinese government about the case. A court official told The Associated Press that, "We just thought that his criminal records were not as serious as previously concluded."

According to CPJ sources, Jiang has a serious stomach disorder and has been denied medical treatment. Jiang's wife and daughter have not been allowed to see or speak with him in the three years since his arrest. His wife, Li Yanling, has been repeatedly interrogated and threatened since her husband's arrest. In March 2002, the local public security bureau brought her in for questioning and detained her for several weeks.

An experienced journalist, Jiang had worked until May 2000 as the northeastern China bureau chief for the Hong Kong–based newspaper *Wen Hui Bao*. He contributed freelance articles to *Qianshao*. In the 1980s, he worked as a Dalian-based correspondent for Xinhua, China's official news agency.

In November 2001, CPJ honored Jiang with its annual International Press Freedom Award. In February 2002, CPJ sent appeals to Chinese President Jiang Zemin from almost 600 supporters—including CBS news anchor Dan Rather, civil rights leader Jesse Jackson, and former U.S. Ambassador to China Winston Lord—demanding Jiang's unconditional release. That month, U.S. President George W. Bush highlighted Jiang's case in meetings with Jiang Zemin during a state visit to China.

Lu Xinhua, freelance
Imprisoned: March 10, 2001

Lu was arrested in Wuhan, Hubei Province, after articles he had written about rural unrest and official corruption appeared on various Internet news sites based overseas. On April 20, 2001, he was charged with "inciting to subvert state power," a charge frequently used against journalists who write about politically sensitive subjects. Lu's trial began on September 18. On December 30, 2001, he was sentenced to four years in prison.

Yang Zili, Yangzi de Sixiang Jiayuan Web site
Xu Wei, *Xiaofei Ribao*
Jin Haike, freelance
Zhang Honghai, freelance
Imprisoned: March 13, 2001

Yang, Xu, Jin, and Zhang were detained on March 13 and charged with subversion on April 20. On May 29, 2003, the Beijing Intermediate Court sentenced Xu and Jin to 10 years in prison each on subversion charges, while Yang and Zhang were sentenced to eight years each on similar charges.

The four were active participants in the Xin Qingnian Xuehui (New Youth Study Group), an informal gathering of individuals who explored topics related to political and social reform and used the Internet to circulate relevant articles.

Yang, the group's most prominent member, published a Web site, Yangzi de Sixiang Jiayuan (Yangzi's Garden of Ideas), which featured poems, essays, and reports by various authors on subjects such as the shortcomings of rural elections. Authorities closed the site after Yang's arrest.

When Xu, a reporter with *Xiaofei Ribao* (Consumer Daily), was detained on March 13, 2001, authorities confiscated his computer, other professional equipment, and books, according to an account published online by his girlfriend, Wang

Ying. Wang reported that public security officials also ordered *Xiaofei Ribao* to fire Xu. The newspaper has refused to discuss his case with reporters, according to The Associated Press.

The Beijing No. 1 Intermediate People's Court tried all four on September 28, 2001. Prosecutors focused predominately on the group's writings, including two essays circulated on the Internet called "Be a New Citizen, Reform China" and "What's to Be Done?" According to the indictment papers, these articles demonstrated the group's intention "to overthrow the Chinese Communist Party's leadership and the socialist system and subvert the regime of the people's democratic dictatorship." In November 2003, the Beijing Supreme People's Court rejected an appeal filed by a lawyer for Yang, Xu, Jin, and Zhang. In the appeal, the defense noted that three key witnesses who testified for the prosecution against the four men have since retracted their original testimony.

Liu Haofeng, freelance
Imprisoned: March 2001

Liu was secretly arrested in Shanghai in mid-March 2001 while conducting research on social conditions in rural China for the dissident China Democracy Party (CDP). On May 16, 2001, Liu was sentenced to "re-education through labor," a form of administrative detention that allows officials to send individuals to labor camps for up to three years without trial or formal charges.

After Liu's arrest, friends and family were not informed of his whereabouts, and CDP members say they only found out what had happened to him when they received news of his sentence in August 2001.

Sentencing papers issued by the Shanghai Re-education Through Labor Committee cited several alleged offenses, including a policy paper and an essay written by Liu that were published under different pen names on the CDP's Web site. The essay focused on the current situation of China's peasants. The committee also accused Liu of trying to form an illegal organization, the China Democracy Party Joint Headquarters, Second Front.

The journalist had previously worked as an editor and reporter for various publications, including the magazine *Jishu Jingji Yu Guanli* (Technology, Economy, and Management), run by the Fujian Province Economic and Trade Committee, and *Zhongguo Shichang Jingji Bao* (China Market Economy News), run by the Central Party School in the capital, Beijing. Beginning in 1999, he worked for Univillage, a research organization focusing on rural democratization, and managed its Web site. He was working as a freelance journalist at the time of his arrest.

Wang Jinbo, freelance
Imprisoned: May 2001

Wang, a freelance journalist, was arrested in early May 2001 for e-mailing essays to overseas organizations arguing that the government should change its official view that the 1989 protests in Tiananmen Square were "counterrevolutionary." In October 2001, Wang was formally charged with "inciting to subvert state power." On November 14, the Junan County Court in Shandong Province held a closed trial; only the journalists' relatives were allowed to attend. On December 13, 2001, Wang was sentenced to four years in prison.

Wang, a member of the banned China Democracy Party, had been detained several times in the past for his political activities. In February 2001, days before the International Olympic Committee (IOC) visited Beijing, he was briefly taken into custody after signing an open letter calling on the IOC to pressure China to release political prisoners. A number of Wang's essays have been posted on various Internet sites. One, titled "My Account of Police Violations of Civil Rights," describes his January 2001 detention, during which police interrogated him and held him for 20 hours with no food or heat after he signed an open letter calling for the release of political prisoners.

Tao Haidong, freelance
Imprisoned: July 9, 2002

Tao, an Internet essayist and pro-democracy activist, was arrested in Urumqi, the capital of the Xinjiang Uighur Autonomous Region, and charged with "incitement to subvert state power." According to the Minzhu Luntan (Democracy Forum) Web site, which had published Tao's recent writing, his articles focused on political and legal reform. In one essay, titled "Strategies for China's Social Reforms," Tao wrote that "the Chinese Communist Party and democracy activists throughout society should unite to push forward China's freedom and democratic development or else stand condemned through the ages."

Previously, in 1999, Tao was sentenced to three years of "re-education through labor" in Xi'an, Shaanxi Province, according to the New York–based advocacy group Human Rights in China, because of his essays and his work on a book titled *Xin Renlei Shexiang* (Imaginings of a New Human Race). After his early release in 2001, Tao began writing essays and articles and publishing them on various domestic and overseas Web sites.

In early January 2003, the Urumqi Intermediate Court sentenced Tao to seven years in prison.

Zhang Wei, *Shishi Zixun, Redian Jiyao*
Imprisoned: July 19, 2002

Zhang was arrested and charged with illegal publishing after producing and selling two underground newspapers in Chongqing, in central China. According to an account published on the Web site of the Chongqing Press and Publishing Administration, a provincial government body that governs all local publications, beginning in April 2001, Zhang edited two newspapers, *Shishi Zixun* (Current Events) and *Redian Jiyao* (Summary of the Main Points), which included articles and graphics he had downloaded from the Internet.

Two of Zhang's business associates, Zuo Shangwen and Ou Yan, were also arrested on July 19, 2002, and indicted for their involvement with the publications. Zuo printed the publications in neighboring Sichuan Province while Ou managed the publications' finances. At the time of their arrests, police confiscated 9,700 copies of *Shishi Zixun*.

The official account of their arrests stated that the two publications had "flooded" Chongqing's publishing market. The government declared that "the political rumors, shocking 'military reports,' and other articles in these illegal publications misled the public, poisoned the youth, negatively influenced society and sparked public indignation." Zhang, Zuo, and Ou printed more than 1.5 million copies of the publications and sold them in Chongqing, Chengdu, and other cities.

On December 25, 2002, the Yuzhong District Court in Chongqing sentenced Zhang to six years in prison and fined him 100,000 yuan (US$12,000), the amount that police said he had earned in profits from the publications. Zuo was sentenced to five years and fined 50,000 yuan (US$6,000), while Ou was sentenced to two years in prison.

Chen Shaowen, freelance
Imprisoned: August 2002

Chen, a freelance writer, was arrested on suspicion of "using the Internet to subvert state power," according to a September 14, 2002, report in the official *Hunan Daily*. The article did not give the date of Chen's arrest, although Boxun News, an overseas online news service, reported that he was arrested on August 6, 2002.

Chen, who lives in Lianyuan, Hunan Province, has written numerous essays and articles for various overseas Chinese-language Web sites, including the online magazine *Huang Hua Gang* and *Minzhu Luntan* (Democracy Forum). According to his biography on the Minzhu Luntan Web site (*asiademo.org*), Chen's essays covered topics including China's unemployment problem, social inequalities, and flaws in the legal system.

The *Hunan Daily* article accused Chen of "repeatedly browsing reactionary websites ... sending in numerous articles of all sorts, fabricating, distorting and exaggerating relevant facts, and vilifying the Chinese Communist Party and the socialist system." The report stated that Chen had published more than 40 articles on overseas "reactionary" Web sites. Chen is still under investigation, and it is not clear whether he has been formally charged.

Jae Hyun Seok, freelance
Imprisoned: January 17, 2003

Freelance photojournalist Seok was arrested by Chinese police while photographing two groups of about 60 North Korean refugees in Yantai, Shandong Province, who were trying to board two fishing boats bound for Cheju Island, South Korea, and Sasebo Island, Japan. Officers also arrested the refugees and a South Korean aid worker.

Seok, a South Korean national, was filming the boatlift as part of a journalistic project documenting the plight of North Korean refugees in China, according to his friends and colleagues who spoke with him shortly before he was arrested. Seok regularly works for *The New York Times* and other publications but was working independently at the time of his arrest.

Soon after Seok was detained, a Chinese Foreign Ministry spokesperson acknowledged that two South Koreans were arrested with the refugees, but she did not confirm their identities. "They are suspected of smuggling or organizing smuggling activities and now are in criminal detention," she said.

On May 22, a Yantai court sentenced Seok to two years in prison on charges of human trafficking. On December 19, a court in Shandong Province rejected an appeal filed by Seok and upheld his original sentence. The appeal hearing, which was originally set for June 2003, was postponed until mid-July and then further delayed without explanation.

According to CPJ sources, while in prison, Seok has suffered from a skin infection on his face, as well as other medical problems.

In recent years, hundreds of thousands of North Koreans have fled to China to escape severe food shortages and political repression. China considers the refugees economic migrants and regularly repatriates them to North Korea, where they often face imprisonment or other types of persecution. As a part of the Chinese government's crackdown on North Korean refugees, authorities have harassed journalists who report on their plight.

Cai Lujun, freelance
Imprisoned February 21, 2003

Cai was arrested at his home in Shijiazhuang, Hebei Province. In October 2003, the Shijiazhuang Intermediate People's Court sentenced him to three years in prison on charges of subversion.

Cai, 35, had used pen names to write numerous essays distributed online calling for political reforms. His articles included "Political Democracy Is the Means; A Powerful Country and Prosperous Citizenry Is the Goal," "An Outline for Building and Governing the Country," and "The Course of Chinese Democracy."

Following the November 2002 arrest of Internet essayist Liu Di, Cai Lujun began to publish online essays under his own name calling for Liu's release and expressing his political views. (Liu was released on November 28, 2003.)

Luo Changfu, freelance
Imprisoned March 13, 2003

Public security officials arrested Luo from his home in Chongqing municipality and charged him with "subversion." On November 6, 2003, the Chongqing Number One Intermediate Court sentenced him to three years in prison.

Luo, 40, is an unemployed factory worker. Before his arrest, he had actively campaigned for the release of Internet essayist Liu Di, who was arrested in November 2002 and released on bail a year later. Luo had written a series of articles calling for Liu's release and protesting the Chinese government's censorship of online speech. His essays also called for political reforms in China.

In the 1980s, Luo was sent to a re-education-through-labor camp for three years for his dissident activities, according to the New York–based organization Human Rights in China.

Yan Jun, freelance
Imprisoned: April 2003

Yan disappeared in Xi'an, Shaanxi Province, in April 2003, and his family members did not know his whereabouts until May 9, when public security officials notified them that Yan had been charged with subversion.

On December 8, 2003, the Xi'an Intermediate People's Court sentenced Yan to two years in prison in a trial that lasted 20 minutes, his mother said.

Yan, a high school biology teacher, had published several essays online advocating political reforms, freedom of expression, and a free press. His articles also called for the release of Zhao Ziyang, the former general secretary of the Communist Party who has been under house arrest in Beijing since he expressed support for pro-democracy demonstrators in 1989, according to the Information Center for Human Rights and Democracy. He also expressed support for independent labor unions and workers' rights. Yan had created a Web site where he posted his writing.

In July 2003, Yan's mother told journalists that he had been sent to the hospital after being beaten in prison.

Luo Yongzhong, freelance
Imprisoned: June 14, 2003

Luo, who has written numerous articles that have been distributed online, was detained on June 14 in Changchun, Jilin Province. On July 7, he was formally arrested. On October 14, the Changchun Intermediate Court sentenced him to three years in prison and two years without political rights upon his release, which is scheduled for June 13, 2006.

In sentencing papers, which have been widely distributed online, the court stated that between May and June 2003, Luo wrote several essays that "attacked the socialist system, incited to subvert state power, and created a negative influence on society." Several specific articles were cited as evidence, including "At Last We See the Danger of the Three Represents!"—a reference to a political theory formulated by former President Jiang Zemin, and "Tell Today's Youth the Truth about June 4," a reference to the military crackdown on peaceful pro-democracy protesters in June 1989. According to the court papers, the articles were published on online forums including Shuijing Luntan (Crystal) Web site.

Luo, who has a crippled leg, has also written a number of articles advocating the rights of disabled people.

Du Daobin, freelance
Imprisoned October 28, 2003

At about 4:00 p.m. on October 28, Internet essayist Du Daobin was arrested and brought to the Public Security Bureau in Xiaogan District, Yingcheng, Hubei Province, according to writer Liu Xiaobo, who first published news of Du's arrest online. Later that day, police came to Du's house and confiscated his computer, books, and copies of his writings.

When Du's wife asked police why he had been arrested, the officer responded, "We have spoken to Du Daobin several times, but he did not listen. He has already crossed the line." According to Liu, the officer also warned his wife against telling foreign journalists about the arrest.

On November 12, officials from the Xiaogan Public Security Bureau delivered a formal arrest warrant to Du's house, which stated that he was being held on charges of "incitement to subvert state power" and that he was detained in the Xiaogan Number One Detention Center. Du's wife has not been allowed to visit him.

Before his arrest, Du had been a prolific writer who distributed his essays online. Many of his essays offered commentary about official policies or social issues in China. In one essay, titled "Media Discipline is Greater Than the Constitution," Du argued that the Propaganda Bureau's stringent regulation of the media is unconstitutional. He called on Chinese citizens, especially journalists, to "exercise our innate right to disobey arbitrary power, to actively support all suppressed media, to reject the voices of the Party's 'mouthpieces,' and to fight against the tyranny of the Propaganda Bureau." His writing was published on several Chinese-language news sites, including *Dajiyuan* (Epoch Times, *www.dajiyuan.com*) and Minzhu Luntan (Democracy Forum, *www.asiademo.org*), both of which are based outside China.

Du was deeply affected by the arrest of fellow Internet journalist Liu Di, a 23-year-old college student, who was detained in Beijing on November 7, 2002. After Liu Di's arrest, Du vigorously called for her release and co-organized an online campaign to show solidarity by taking a series of actions, including spending one day in a darkened room to symbolically "Accompany Liu Di in Prison." He also wrote a number of essays supporting Liu Di, who was released on bail on November 28, 2003.

Kong Youping, freelance
Imprisoned December 13, 2003

Kong, an essayist and poet, was arrested in Anshan, Liaoning Province. He had written articles online that supported democratic reforms and called for a reversal of the government's "counterrevolutionary" ruling on the pro-democracy demonstrations of 1989, according to the Hong Kong–based Information Center for Human Rights and Democracy.

Kong's essays included an appeal to democracy activists in China that stated, "In order to work well for democracy, we need a well-organized, strong, powerful and effective organization. Otherwise, a mainland democracy movement will accomplish nothing." Several of his articles and poems were posted on the Minzhu Luntan (Democracy Forum, *www.asiademo.org*) Web site.

In 1998, Kong served time in prison after he became a member of the Liaoning Province branch of the China Democracy Party, an opposition party. At the end of 2003, Kong had not yet been tried.

CUBA: 29

Alejandro González Raga, freelance
Imprisoned: March 18, 2003

González Raga, an independent freelance journalist based in central Camagüey Province, is one of 29 independent Cuban journalists who were detained in March in a massive government crackdown on the independent media and political opposition.

His one-day summary trial was held in early April behind closed doors. He was tried under Article 91 of the Penal Code, which imposes lengthy prison sentences or death for those who act against "the independence or the territorial integrity of the State." On April 7, the Camagüey Provincial Tribunal announced he had been sentenced to 14 years in prison.

The journalist remained imprisoned in the provincial headquarters of the State Security Department until April 24, when he was sent to Canaleta Prison in central Ciego de Ávila Province.

Alfredo Pulido López, El Mayor
Imprisoned: March 18, 2003

Pulido López, the director of the independent news agency El Mayor in central Camagüey Province, is one of 29 independent Cuban journalists who were detained in March in a massive government crackdown on the independent media and political opposition.

His one-day summary trial was held in early April behind closed doors. He was tried under Article 91 of the Penal Code, which imposes lengthy prison sentences or death for those who act against "the independence or the territorial integrity of the State." On April 7, the Camagüey Provincial Tribunal announced he had been sentenced to 14 years in prison.

The journalist remained imprisoned in the provincial headquarters of the State Security Department until April 24, when he was sent to Combinado del Este Prison in western Ciudad Habana Province, hundreds of miles from his home.

Edel José García Díaz, Centro Norte del País
Imprisoned: March 18, 2003

García Díaz, the Havana-based director of the independent news agency Centro Norte del País, is one of 29 independent Cuban journalists who were detained in March in a massive government crackdown on the independent media and political opposition.

His one-day summary trial was held in early April behind closed doors. He was tried under Law 88 for the Protection of Cuba's National Independence and Economy, which imposes up to 20 years in prison for committing acts "aimed at subverting the internal order of the Nation and destroying its political, economic, and social system." On April 7, the Havana Provincial Tribunal announced he had been sentenced to 15 years in prison.

The journalist remained imprisoned in the Havana headquarters of the State Security Department until April 24, when he was sent to Boniato Prison in eastern Santiago de Cuba Province.

Iván Hernández Carrillo, Patria
Imprisoned: March 18, 2003

Hernández Carrillo, a journalist with the independent news agency Patria in western Matanzas Province, is one of 29 independent Cuban journalists who were detained in March in a massive government crackdown on the independent media and political opposition.

His one-day summary trial was held in early April behind closed doors. He was tried under Law 88 for the Protection of Cuba's National Independence and Economy, which imposes up to 20 years in prison for committing acts "aimed at subverting the internal order of the Nation and destroying its political, economic, and social system." On April 7, the Matanzas Provincial Tribunal announced he had been sentenced to 25 years in prison.

The journalist remained imprisoned in the provincial headquarters of the State Security Department until April 24, when he was sent to Holguín Provincial Prison in eastern Holguín Province, hundreds of miles from his home.

On August 15, Hernández Carrillo joined imprisoned journalists Adolfo Fernández Saínz and Mario Enrique Mayo Hernández in a 13-day hunger strike to demand adequate food and medicine.

On October 18, prison officials placed him in a punishment cell for complaining about feeling ill. To protest his treatment, Hernández Carrillo began a hunger strike that ended in early November.

Jorge Olivera Castillo, Havana Press
Imprisoned: March 18, 2003

Olivera Castillo, the Havana-based director of the independent news agency Havana Press, is one of 29 independent Cuban journalists who were detained in March in a massive government crackdown on the independent media and political opposition.

His one-day summary trial was held in early April behind closed doors. He was tried under Law 88 for the Protection of Cuba's National Independence and Economy, which imposes up to 20 years in prison for committing acts "aimed at subverting the internal order of the Nation and destroying its political, economic, and social system." On April 7, the Havana Provincial Tribunal announced he had been sentenced to 18 years in prison.

The journalist remained imprisoned in the Havana headquarters of the State Security Department until April 24, when he was sent to Guantánamo Provincial Prison in eastern Guantánamo Province, hundreds of miles from his home. In June, the People's Supreme Tribunal, Cuba's highest court, dismissed his appeal for annulment (*recurso de casación*) and upheld his conviction.

José Gabriel Ramón Castillo, Instituto Cultura y Democracia Press
Imprisoned: March 18, 2003

Ramón Castillo, director of the independent news agency Instituto Cultura y

Democracia Press, is one of 29 independent Cuban journalists who were detained in March in a massive government crackdown on the independent media and the political opposition.

His one-day summary trial was held in early April behind closed doors. He was tried under Article 91 of the Penal Code, which imposes lengthy prison sentences or death for those who act against "the independence or the territorial integrity of the State." On April 7, the Santiago de Cuba Provincial Tribunal announced he had been sentenced to 20 years in prison.

The journalist remained imprisoned in the provincial headquarters of the State Security Department until April 24, when he was sent to Santa Clara Provincial Prison in central Villa Clara Province, hundreds of miles from his home.

José Luis García Paneque, Libertad
Imprisoned: March 18, 2003

García Paneque, director of the independent news agency Libertad in eastern Las Tunas Province, is one of 29 independent Cuban journalists who were detained in March in a massive government crackdown on the independent media and political opposition.

His one-day summary trial was held in early April behind closed doors. He was tried under Article 91 of the Penal Code, which imposes lengthy prison sentences or death for those who act against "the independence or the territorial integrity of the State." On April 7, the Las Tunas Provincial Tribunal announced he had been sentenced to 24 years in prison.

The journalist remained imprisoned in the provincial headquarters of the State Security Department until mid-April, when he was sent to El Típico Prison in Las Tunas Province. In May, he was sent to Guamajal Prison in central Villa Clara Province, hundreds of miles from his home. In August, he was transferred to Santa Clara Provincial Prison, also in Villa Clara.

Julio César Gálvez Rodríguez, freelance
Imprisoned: March 18, 2003

Gálvez Rodríguez, a Havana-based independent freelance journalist, is one of 29 independent Cuban journalists who were detained in March in a massive government crackdown on the independent media and political opposition.

His one-day summary trial was held in early April behind closed doors. He was tried under Law 88 for the Protection of Cuba's National Independence and Economy, which imposes up to 20 years in prison for committing acts "aimed at subverting the internal order of the Nation and destroying its political, economic, and social system." On April 7, the Havana Provincial Tribunal announced he had been sentenced to 15 years in prison.

The journalist remained imprisoned in the Havana headquarters of the State Security Department until April 24, when he was sent to Santa Clara Provincial Prison in central Villa Clara Province, hundreds of miles from his home.

Léster Luis González Pentón, freelance
Imprisoned: March 18, 2003

González Pentón, an independent journalist based in central Villa Clara Province, is one of 29 independent Cuban journalists who were detained in March in a massive government crackdown on the independent media and political opposition.

His one-day summary trial was held in early April behind closed doors. He was tried under Article 91 of the Penal Code, which imposes lengthy prison sentences or death for those who act against "the independence or the territorial integrity of the State." On April 7, the Villa Clara Provincial Tribunal announced he had been sentenced to 20 years in prison.

The journalist remained imprisoned in the provincial headquarters of the State Security Department until April 24, when he was sent to Kilo 8 Prison in central Camagüey Province, hundreds of miles from his home. In November, he was transferred to Kilo 7 Prison, also in Camagüey.

Miguel Galván Gutiérrez, Havana Press
Imprisoned: March 18, 2003

Galván Gutiérrez, a journalist with the independent news agency Havana Press, is one of 29 independent Cuban journalists who were detained in March in a massive government crackdown on the independent media and political opposition.

His one-day summary trial was held in early April behind closed doors. He was tried under Article 91 of the Penal Code, which imposes lengthy prison sentences or death for those who act against "the independence or the territorial integrity of the State." On April 7, the Havana Provincial Tribunal announced he had been sentenced to 26 years in prison.

The journalist remained imprisoned in the Havana headquarters of the State Security Department until April 24, when he was sent to Agüica Prison in western Matanzas Province, hundreds of miles from his home. In June, the People's Supreme Tribunal, Cuba's highest court, dismissed his appeal for annulment (*recurso de casación*) and upheld his conviction.

Omar Rodríguez Saludes, Nueva Prensa Cubana
Imprisoned: March 18, 2003

Rodríguez Saludes, director of the independent news agency Nueva Prensa Cubana, is one of 29 independent Cuban journalists who were detained in March in a massive government crackdown on the independent media and political opposition.

His one-day summary trial was held in early April behind closed doors. He was tried under Article 91 of the Penal Code, which imposes lengthy prison sentences or death for those who act against "the independence or the territorial integrity of the State." On April 7, the Havana Provincial Tribunal announced he had been sentenced to 27 years in prison.

The journalist remained imprisoned in the Havana headquarters of the State Security Department until April 24, when he was sent to Kilo 8 Prison in central Camagüey Province, hundreds of miles from his home. In December, he was transferred to Nieves Morejón Prison in central Sancti Spíritus Province.

Pedro Argüelles Morán, Cooperativa Avileña de Periodistas Independientes
Imprisoned: March 18, 2003

Argüelles Morán, director of the independent news agency Cooperativa Avileña de Periodistas Independientes in central Ciego de Ávila Province, is one of 29 independent Cuban journalists who were detained in March in a massive government crackdown on the independent media and political opposition.

His one-day summary trial was held in early April behind closed doors. He was tried under Law 88 for the Protection of Cuba's National Independence and Economy, which imposes up to 20 years in prison for committing acts "aimed at subverting the internal order of the Nation and destroying its political, economic, and social system." On April 7, the Ciego de Ávila Provincial Tribunal announced he had been sentenced to 20 years in prison.

The journalist remained imprisoned in the provincial headquarters of the State Security Department until April 24, when he was sent to Santa Clara Provincial Prison in central Villa Clara Province, about 100 miles (160 kilometers) from his home.

Ricardo González Alfonso, freelance
Imprisoned: March 18, 2003

González Alfonso, an independent freelance journalist and Cuba correspondent for the Paris-based press freedom organization Reporters Without Borders, is one of 29 independent Cuban journalists who were detained in March in a massive government crackdown on the independent media and political opposition.

His one-day summary trial was held in early April behind closed doors. He was tried under Article 91 of the Penal Code, which imposes lengthy prison sentences or death for those who act against "the independence or the territorial integrity of the State." On April 7, the Havana Provincial Tribunal announced he had been sentenced to 20 years in prison.

The journalist remained imprisoned in the Havana headquarters of the State Security Department until April 24, when he was sent to Kilo 8 Prison in Camagüey Province, hundreds of miles from his home. In June, the People's Supreme Tribunal, Cuba's highest court, dismissed his appeal for annulment (*recurso de casación*) and upheld his conviction.

González Alfonso is also the president of the independent journalists' association Sociedad de Periodistas Manuel Márquez Sterling, founded in May 2001. His house, which was used as the association's office, was raided on March 18.

In November, González Alfonso, who was earlier put in solitary confinement for seven months, was transferred to a cell with common criminals, who have harassed him. The journalist has suffered from high blood pressure and on November 18 had to be taken to a hospital, where doctors found two lumps in his throat and recommended their removal. While in the hospital, the journalist's personal belongings were stolen. According to his wife, independent journalist Álida Viso Bello, González Alfonso was scheduled to return to the hospital on December 19 to have the lumps removed, but the appointment was postponed until January 8, 2004.

González Alfonso went on a hunger strike on December 8, 2003, to demand his transfer to another unit within the prison where he can be with other political prisoners, said Viso Bello. As punishment for the strike, prison officials placed González Alfonso in a small cell with no running water that was lit 24 hours a day. He remained in the cell until late December.

On December 17, Viso Bello met with her husband for an hour in the presence of a prison official. Viso Bello, who did not expect to be allowed to see her husband, believes that she was able to meet with him because prison officials thought she could convince him to stop his hunger strike. González Alfonso halted the hunger strike on December 24, after prison authorities met his demands, Viso Bello told CPJ.

Víctor Rolando Arroyo Carmona, Unión de Periodistas y Escritores de Cuba Independientes (UPECI)
Imprisoned: March 18, 2003

Arroyo Carmona, a journalist with the independent news agency Unión de Periodistas y Escritores de Cuba Independientes (UPECI) in western Pinar del Río Province, is one of 29 independent Cuban journalists who were detained in

March in a massive government crackdown on the independent media and political opposition.

His one-day summary trial was held in early April behind closed doors. He was tried under Article 91 of the Penal Code, which imposes lengthy prison sentences or death for those who act against "the independence or the territorial integrity of the State." On April 7, the Pinar del Río Provincial Tribunal announced he had been sentenced to 26 years in prison.

Arroyo Carmona remained imprisoned in the provincial headquarters of the State Security Department until late April, when he was sent to Guantánamo Provincial Prison in eastern Guantánamo Province, hundreds of miles from his home.

Adolfo Fernández Saínz, Patria
Imprisoned: March 19, 2003

Fernández Saínz, a journalist with the independent news agency Patria, is one of 29 independent Cuban journalists who were detained in March in a massive government crackdown on the independent media and political opposition.

His one-day summary trial was held in early April behind closed doors. He was tried under Law 88 for the Protection of Cuba's National Independence and Economy, which imposes up to 20 years in prison for committing acts "aimed at subverting the internal order of the Nation and destroying its political, economic, and social system." On April 7, the Havana Provincial Tribunal announced he had been sentenced to 15 years in prison.

The journalist remained imprisoned in the Havana headquarters of the State Security Department until April 24, when he was sent to Holguín Provincial Prison in eastern Holguín Province, hundreds of miles from his home. In June, the People's Supreme Tribunal, Cuba's highest court, dismissed his appeal for annulment (*recurso de casación*) and upheld his conviction.

On August 15, Fernández Saínz joined imprisoned journalists Mario Enrique Mayo Hernández and Iván Hernández Carrillo in a 13-day hunger strike to demand adequate food and medicine.

Two months later, on October 18, Fernández Saínz and Mayo Hernández joined four other jailed dissidents in a hunger strike to protest the treatment of Hernández Carrillo, who was placed in a punishment cell after complaining about feeling ill. The strike ended in early November.

As punishment for his involvement in the hunger strike, Fernández Saínz was transferred to another unit within the same prison.

Alfredo Felipe Fuentes, freelance
Imprisoned: March 19, 2003

Fuentes, an independent freelance journalist based in western Habana Province, is one of 29 independent Cuban journalists who were detained in March in a massive government crackdown on the independent media and political opposition.

His one-day summary trial was held in early April behind closed doors. He was tried under Article 91 of the Penal Code, which imposes lengthy prison sentences or death for those who act against "the independence or the territorial integrity of the State." On April 7, the Havana Provincial Tribunal announced he had been sentenced to 26 years in prison.

The journalist remained imprisoned in the Havana headquarters of the State Security Department until April 24, when he was sent to Guamajal Prison in central Villa Clara Province, hundreds of miles from his home.

Carmelo Díaz Fernández, Agencia de Prensa Sindical Independiente de Cuba
Imprisoned: March 19, 2003

Díaz Fernández, director of the independent news agency Agencia de Prensa Sindical Independiente de Cuba, is one of 29 independent Cuban journalists who were detained in March in a massive government crackdown on the independent media and political opposition.

His one-day summary trial was held in early April behind closed doors. He was tried under Article 91 of the Penal Code, which imposes lengthy prison sentences or death for those who act against "the independence or the territorial integrity of the State." On April 7, the Havana Provincial Tribunal announced he had been sentenced to 16 years in prison.

The journalist remained imprisoned in the provincial headquarters of the State Security Department until April 24, when he was sent to Guanajay Prison in western Habana Province.

Fabio Prieto Llorente, freelance
Imprisoned: March 19, 2003

Prieto Llorente, an independent freelance journalist based in western Isla de la Juventud Special Municipality, is one of 29 independent Cuban journalists who were detained in March in a massive government crackdown on the independent media and political opposition.

His one-day summary trial was held in early April behind closed doors. He was tried under Law 88 for the Protection of Cuba's National Independence and Economy, which imposes up to 20 years in prison for committing acts "aimed at subverting the internal order of the Nation and destroying its political, economic, and social system." On April 7, the Isla de la Juventud Special Tribunal announced he had been sentenced to 20 years in prison.

The journalist remained jailed at police headquarters in Nueva Gerona, the capital of Isla de la Juventud, until early May, when he was sent to Guanajay Prison in western Habana Province, about 100 miles (160 kilometers) from his home.

Héctor Maseda Gutiérrez, Grupo de Trabajo Decoro
Imprisoned: March 19, 2003

Maseda Gutiérrez, a journalist with the independent news agency Grupo de Trabajo Decoro, is one of 29 independent Cuban journalists who were detained in March in a massive government crackdown on the independent media and political opposition.

His one-day summary trial was held in early April behind closed doors. He was tried under Article 91 of the Penal Code, which imposes lengthy prison sentences or death for those who act against "the independence or the territorial integrity of the State"; and under Law 88 for the Protection of Cuba's National Independence and Economy, which imposes up to 20 years in prison for committing acts "aimed at subverting the internal order of the Nation and destroying its political, economic, and social system." On April 7, the Havana Provincial Tribunal announced he had been sentenced to 20 years in prison.

The journalist remained imprisoned in the Havana headquarters of the State Security Department until April 24, when he was sent to Manacas Prison in central Villa Clara Province, hundreds of miles from his home. In June, the People's Supreme Tribunal, Cuba's highest court, dismissed his appeal for annulment (*recurso de casación*) and upheld his conviction.

In May, he was transferred to La Pendiente Prison, also in Villa Clara Province. In July, the journalist's wife, Laura Pollán, told CPJ that he had been diagnosed with scabies and other skin rashes triggered by the conditions in the prison. Pollán said that prison authorities would not allow her to bring clean sheets and medicines to her husband.

José Ubaldo Izquierdo, Grupo de Trabajo Decoro
Imprisoned: March 19, 2003

Ubaldo Izquierdo, a journalist with the independent news agency Grupo de Trabajo Decoro in western Habana Province, is one of 29 independent Cuban journalists who were detained in March in a massive government crackdown on the independent media and political opposition.

His one-day summary trial was held in early April behind closed doors. He was tried under Article 91 of the Penal Code, which imposes lengthy prison sentences or death for those who act against "the independence or the territorial integrity of the State." On April 7, the Havana Provincial Tribunal announced he had been sentenced to 16 years in prison.

The journalist remained imprisoned in the Havana headquarters of the State Security Department until April 24, when he was sent to Kilo 5 1/2 Prison in western Pinar del Río Province, hundreds of miles from his home. In June, the People's Supreme Tribunal, Cuba's highest court, dismissed his appeal for annulment (*recurso de casación*) and upheld his conviction.

Juan Carlos Herrera Acosta, Agencia de Prensa Libre Oriental
Imprisoned: March 19, 2003

Herrera Acosta, a journalist with the independent news agency Agencia de Prensa Libre Oriental in eastern Guantánamo Province, is one of 29 independent Cuban journalists who were detained in March in a massive government crackdown on the independent media and political opposition.

His one-day summary trial was held in early April behind closed doors. He was tried under Law 88 for the Protection of Cuba's National Independence and Economy, which imposes up to 20 years in prison for committing acts "aimed at subverting the internal order of the Nation and destroying its political, economic, and social system." On April 7, the Guantánamo Provincial Tribunal announced he had been sentenced to 20 years in prison.

The journalist remained imprisoned in the provincial headquarters of the State Security Department until April 24, when he was sent to Boniato Prison in eastern Santiago de Cuba Province.

On August 31, Herrera Acosta joined imprisoned journalists Manuel Vázquez Portal and Normando Hernández González and other jailed dissidents at Boniato Prison in a hunger strike that lasted one week. As punishment for his involvement in the strike, Herrera Acosta was transferred to Kilo 8 Prison in central Camagüey Province, hundreds of miles from his home. In November, he was transferred to Kilo 7 Prison, also in Camagüey.

Manuel Vázquez Portal, Grupo de Trabajo Decoro
Imprisoned: March 19, 2003

Vázquez Portal, a writer and journalist with the independent news agency Grupo de Trabajo Decoro, is one of 29 independent Cuban journalists who were detained in March in a massive government crackdown on the independent media and political opposition.

His one-day summary trial was held in early April behind closed doors. He was tried under Law 88 for the Protection of Cuba's National Independence and Economy, which imposes up to 20 years in prison for committing acts "aimed at subverting the internal order of the Nation and destroying its political, economic, and social system." On April 7, the Havana Provincial Tribunal announced he had been sentenced to 18 years in prison.

The journalist remained imprisoned in the Havana headquarters of the State Security Department until April 24, when he was sent to Boniato Prison in eastern Santiago de Cuba Province, hundreds of miles from his home.

In May, Vázquez Portal wrote a prison diary, which was later smuggled out of prison, describing the harsh conditions in Boniato Prison. In recognition of the efforts by Cuban independent journalists to disseminate news in a climate of harsh government repression, CPJ honored Vázquez Portal with one of its International Press Freedom Awards in November.

On August 31, Vázquez Portal joined imprisoned journalist Normando Hernández González and other jailed dissidents at Boniato Prison in a hunger strike that lasted one week. As punishment for his involvement in the strike, Vázquez Portal was transferred to Aguadores Prison.

From November 9 to November 16, Vázquez Portal held another hunger strike to support other jailed journalists and dissidents who in October began a hunger strike at Holguín Provincial Prison.

Mario Enrique Mayo Hernández, Félix Varela
Imprisoned: March 19, 2003

Mayo Hernández, the director of the independent news agency Félix Varela, is one of 29 independent Cuban journalists who were detained in March in a massive government crackdown on the independent media and political opposition.

His one-day summary trial was held in early April behind closed doors. He was tried under Article 91 of the Penal Code, which imposes lengthy prison sentences or death for those who act against "the independence or the territorial integrity of the State." On April 7, the Camagüey Provincial Tribunal announced he had been sentenced to 20 years in prison.

The journalist remained imprisoned in the provincial headquarters of the State Security Department until April 24, when he was sent to Holguín Provincial Prison in eastern Holguín Province.

On August 15, Mayo Hernández joined imprisoned journalists Adolfo Fernández Saínz and Iván Hernández Carrillo in a 13-day hunger strike to demand better food and adequate medical attention.

Two months later, on October 18, Fernández Saínz and Mayo Hernández joined other jailed dissidents in another hunger strike to protest the treatment of Hernández Carrillo, who was placed in a punishment cell after complaining about feeling ill. As punishment for his involvement in the strike, Mayo Hernández was sent to Mar Verde Prison in neighboring Santiago de Cuba Province.

Mijaíl Bárzaga Lugo, Agencia Noticiosa Cubana
Imprisoned: March 19, 2003

Bárzaga Lugo, a journalist with the independent news agency Agencia Noticiosa Cubana, is one of 29 independent Cuban journalists who were detained in March in a massive government crackdown on the independent media and political opposition.

His one-day summary trial was held in early April behind closed doors. He was tried under Law 88 for the Protection of Cuba's National Independence and Economy, which imposes up to 20 years in prison for committing acts "aimed at subverting the internal order of the Nation and destroying its political, economic, and social system." On April 7, the Havana Provincial Tribunal announced he had been sentenced to 15 years in prison.

The journalist remained imprisoned in the Havana headquarters of the State Security Department until April 24, when he was sent to Santa Clara Provincial Prison in central Villa Clara Province, hundreds of miles from his home.

Normando Hernández González, Colegio de Periodistas Independientes de Camagüey (CPIC)
Imprisoned: March 19, 2003

Hernández González, director of the independent news agency Colegio de Periodistas Independientes de Camagüey (CPIC), is one of 29 independent Cuban journalists who were detained in March in a massive government crackdown on the independent media and political opposition.

His one-day summary trial was held in early April behind closed doors. He was tried under Article 91 of the Penal Code, which imposes lengthy prison sentences or death for those who act against "the independence or the territorial integrity of the State." On April 7, the Camagüey Provincial Tribunal announced he had been sentenced to 25 years in prison.

The journalist remained imprisoned in the provincial headquarters of the State Security Department until April 24, when he was sent to Boniato Prison in eastern Santiago de Cuba Province, hundreds of miles from his home.

On August 31, Hernández González joined imprisoned journalist Manuel Vázquez Portal and other jailed dissidents at Boniato Prison in a hunger strike that lasted one week. As punishment for his involvement in the strike, Hernández González was sent to Kilo 5 1/2 Prison in western Pinar del Río Province, on the opposite end of the island.

Omar Ruiz Hernández, Grupo de Trabajo Decoro
Imprisoned: March 19, 2003

Ruiz Hernández, a journalist with the independent news agency Grupo de Trabajo Decoro in central Villa Clara Province, is one of 29 independent Cuban journalists who were detained in March in a massive government crackdown on the independent media and political opposition.

His one-day summary trial was held in early April behind closed doors. He was tried under Article 91 of the Penal Code, which imposes lengthy prison sentences or death for those who act against "the independence or the territorial integrity of the State." On April 7, the Villa Clara Provincial Tribunal announced he had been sentenced to 18 years in prison.

The journalist remained imprisoned in the provincial headquarters of the State Security Department until April 24, when he was sent to Boniato Prison in eastern Santiago de Cuba Province, hundreds of miles from his home.

Oscar Espinosa Chepe, freelance
Imprisoned: March 19, 2003

Espinosa Chepe, a Havana-based independent freelance journalist, is one of 29 independent Cuban journalists who were detained in March in a massive government crackdown on the independent media and political opposition.

His one-day summary trial was held in early April behind closed doors. He was tried under Article 91 of the Penal Code, which imposes lengthy prison sentences or death for those who act against "the independence or the territorial integrity of the State"; and under Law 88 for the Protection of Cuba's National Independence and Economy, which imposes up to 20 years in prison for committing acts "aimed at subverting the internal order of the Nation and destroying its political, economic, and social system." On April 7, the Havana Provincial Tribunal announced he had been sentenced to 20 years in prison.

The journalist remained imprisoned in the Havana headquarters of the State Security Department until April 24, when he was sent to Guantánamo Provincial Prison in eastern Guantánamo Province, hundreds of miles from his home. In June, the People's Supreme Tribunal, Cuba's highest court, dismissed his appeal for annulment (*recurso de casación*) and upheld his conviction.

The 62-year-old journalist suffers from several severe medical conditions, including cirrhosis, hepatitis, liver failure, and high blood pressure. According to his wife, independent journalist Miriam Leiva, while in prison, Espinosa Chepe has had blood in his stools, anemia, and parasites.

Due to his liver conditions—which Leiva says had been under control before his detention and imprisonment—and other ailments that have been exacerbated in jail, the journalist has been in and out of hospitals. In July, he was transferred to Boniato Prison, where, despite his poor health, he spent eight days in solitary confinement.

On August 7, Espinosa Chepe became ill and was taken to the Carlos J. Finlay Military Hospital in Havana, where he remained at year's end.

Pablo Pacheco Ávila, Cooperativa Avileña de Periodistas Independientes
Imprisoned: March 19, 2003

Pacheco Ávila, a journalist with the independent news agency Cooperativa Avileña de Periodistas Independientes, is one of 29 independent Cuban journalists who were detained in March in a massive government crackdown on the independent media and political opposition.

His one-day summary trial was held in early April behind closed doors. He was tried under Law 88 for the Protection of Cuba's National Independence and Economy, which imposes up to 20 years in prison for committing acts "aimed at subverting the internal order of the Nation and destroying its political, economic, and social system." On April 7, the Ciego de Ávila Provincial Tribunal announced he had been sentenced to 20 years in prison.

The journalist remained imprisoned in the provincial headquarters of the State Security Department until April 24, when he was sent to Agüica Prison in western Matanzas Province, hundreds of miles from his home.

Raúl Rivero, Cuba Press
Imprisoned: March 20, 2003

Rivero, a prominent independent journalist, writer, and director of the independent news agency Cuba Press, is one of 29 independent Cuban journalists who were detained in March in a massive government crackdown on the independent media and political opposition.

His one-day summary trial was held in early April behind closed doors. He was tried under Article 91 of the Penal Code, which imposes lengthy prison sentences or death for those who act against "the independence or the territorial integrity of the State." On April 7, the Havana Provincial Tribunal announced he had been sentenced to 20 years in prison.

The journalist remained imprisoned in the Havana headquarters of the State Security Department until April 24, when he was sent to Canaleta Prison in central Ciego de Ávila Province, hundreds of miles from his home. In June, the People's Supreme Tribunal, Cuba's highest court, dismissed his appeal for annulment (*recurso de casación*) and upheld his conviction.

ERITREA: 17

Zemenfes Haile, *Tsigenay*
Imprisoned: January 1999

Sometime in early 1999, Haile, founder and manager of the private weekly *Tsigenay*, was detained by Eritrean authorities and sent to Zara Labor Camp in the country's lowland desert. Authorities accused Haile of failing to complete the National Service Program, but sources told CPJ that the journalist completed the program in 1994.

Near the end of 2000, Haile was transferred to an unknown location, and friends and relatives have not seen or heard from him since. CPJ sources in Eritrea believe that Haile's continued detention is part of the government's general crackdown on the press, which began in September 2001.

According to Eritrean sources, in 2003, the government claimed that Haile was performing his national service requirement.

Ghebrehiwet Keleta, *Tsigenay*
Imprisoned: July 2000

Keleta, reporter for the private weekly *Tsigenay*, was kidnapped by security agents on his way to work sometime in July 2000 and has not been seen since. The reasons for Keleta's arrest remain unclear, but CPJ sources in Eritrea believe that Keleta's continued detention is part of the government's general crackdown on the press, which began in September 2001.

Selamyinghes Beyene, *Meqaleh*
Imprisoned: Fall 2001

Beyene, reporter for the independent weekly *Meqaleh*, was arrested sometime in the fall of 2001 and has been missing since. CPJ was unable to confirm the reasons for his arrest, but Eritrean sources believe that his detention is part of the government's general crackdown on the press, which began in September 2001.

According to Eritrean sources, in 2003, the government claimed that Beyene was performing his national service requirement.

Amanuel Asrat, *Zemen*
Imprisoned: September 2001
Medhanie Haile, *Keste Debena*
Imprisoned: September 18, 2001
Yusuf Mohamed Ali, *Tsigenay*
Mattewos Habteab, *Meqaleh*
Imprisoned: September 19, 2001
Temesken Ghebreyesus, *Keste Debena*
Said Abdelkader, *Admas*
Imprisoned: September 20, 2001
Dawit Isaac, *Setit*
Seyoum Fsehaye, freelance
Imprisoned: September 21, 2001
Dawit Habtemichael, *Meqaleh*
Imprisoned: on or about September 21, 2001
Fesshaye "Joshua" Yohannes, *Setit*
Imprisoned: September 27, 2001

Beginning September 18, 2001, Eritrean security forces arrested at least 10 local journalists. Two others fled the country. The arrests came less than a week after authorities abruptly closed all privately owned newspapers, allegedly to safeguard national unity in the face of growing political turmoil in the tiny Horn of Africa nation.

International news reports quoted presidential adviser Yemane Gebremeskel as saying that the journalists could have been arrested for avoiding military service. Sources in the capital, Asmara, however, say that at least two of the detained journalists, freelance photographer Fsehaye and Mohamed Ali, editor of *Tsigenay*, are legally exempt from national service. Fsehaye is reportedly exempt because he is an independence war veteran, while Mohamed Ali is apparently well over the maximum age for military service.

CPJ sources in Asmara maintain that the suspension and subsequent arrests of independent journalists were part of a full-scale government effort to suppress political dissent in advance of December 2001 elections, which the government canceled without explanation.

On March 31, 2002, the 10 jailed reporters began a hunger strike to protest their continued detention without charge, according to local and international sources. In a message smuggled from inside the Police Station One detention center in Asmara, the journalists said they would refuse food until they were either released or charged and given a fair trial. Three days later, nine of the strikers were transferred to an undisclosed detention facility. According to CPJ sources, the 10th journalist, Swedish national Isaac, was sent to a hospital, where he was treated for post-traumatic stress disorder, a result of alleged torture while in police custody.

During a July 2002 fact-finding mission to Asmara, a presidential official told a CPJ delegation that only "about eight" news professionals were being held in detention facilities, whose locations he refused to disclose.

Hamid Mohammed Said, Eritrean State Television
Saidia Ahmed, Eritrean State Television
Saleh Aljezeeri, Eritrean State Radio
Imprisoned: February 15, 2002

During a July 2002 fact-finding mission to the capital, Asmara, CPJ delegates confirmed that around February 15, Eritrean authorities arrested Said, a journalist for the state-run Eritrean State Television (ETV); Ahmed, a journalist with the Arabic-language service of ETV; and Aljezeeri, a journalist for Eritrean State Radio. All three remained in government custody at the end of 2003.

The reasons for their arrests are unclear, but CPJ sources in Eritrea believe that their continued detention is related to the government's general crackdown on the press, which began in September 2001.

Aklilu Solomon, Voice of America
Imprisoned: July 8, 2003

On June 27, Solomon, stringer for the U.S. government–funded Voice of America (VOA) news service based in the capital, Asmara, was stripped of his press accreditation by Eritrean authorities after he reported on the families of soldiers who had died during Eritrea's 1998-2000 war with Ethiopia. Solomon's report that the families were anguished over the soldiers' deaths contradicted state media coverage, which claimed that the families had celebrated when the government publicly announced their relatives' deaths, according to the VOA. Authorities said that Solomon's reporting was biased and designed to "please the enemy."

On July 8, Eritrean security officers arrested Solomon at his home and took him away to an undisclosed location. Government officials later said that Solomon had been taken to Sawa Military Training Camp to complete his mandatory national military service. According to the VOA, however, Solomon had documents proving that he had already completed a part of his service and was exempt from the rest for medical reasons. Eritrean authorities told the VOA that they were reviewing the documents in question.

Sources in Asmara told the VOA that Eritrean police returned to Solomon's home shortly after his arrest, cut his phone line, and confiscated his tape recorder and tapes.

ETHIOPIA: 1

Tewodros Kassa, *Ethiop*
Imprisoned: mid-May 2002

On July 7, 2002, Kassa, former editor-in-chief of the Amharic-language weekly *Ethiop*, was sentenced to two years in prison on two counts of violating Ethiopia's restrictive Press Proclamation No. 34 of 1992 in three articles published in *Ethiop* in 1997. At the time of his conviction, Kassa had already been in jail since mid-May 2002 for missing a court hearing related to the charges.

The first charge, "disseminating false information that could incite people to political violence," stemmed from two stories. The first reported that the ruling Ethiopian People's Revolutionary Democratic Front (EPRDF) had fired personnel at the Debre Zeit air force base who previously worked for the former regime of Mengistu Haile Mariam and replaced them with pro-EPRDF workers; the second article alleged that unidentified individuals had failed in an attempt to bomb a popular hotel in the capital, Addis Ababa.

The second charge, "defamation," resulted from another 1997 article in *Ethiop*, which alleged that a private investment company specializing in natural-resource development had connections in the EPRDF government. According to a source at *Ethiop*, Kassa was charged even after the newspaper complied with a government order forcing the publication to print a letter of apology.

IRAN: 3

Akbar Ganji, *Sobh-e-Emrooz, Fath*
Imprisoned: April 22, 2000

Ganji, a leading investigative reporter for the now defunct reformist daily *Sobh-e-Emrooz* and a member of the editorial board of the now defunct, pro-reform daily *Fath*, was arrested and prosecuted in both Iran's Press Court and Revolutionary Court.

The case in the Press Court stemmed from Ganji's investigative articles about the 1998 killings of several dissidents and intellectuals that implicated top intelligence officials and former President Hashemi Rafsanjani. In the Revolutionary Court, Ganji was accused of making propaganda against the Islamic regime and threatening national security in comments he made at an April 2000 conference in Berlin on the future of the reform movement in Iran.

The status of the case in the Press Court remained unclear at the end of 2003, but on January 13, 2001, the Revolutionary Court sentenced Ganji to 10 years in prison, followed by five years of internal exile. In May 2001, after Ganji had already served more than a year in prison, an appellate court reduced his punishment to six months.

The Iranian Justice Department then appealed that ruling to the Supreme

Court, arguing that the appellate court had committed errors in commuting the original 10-year sentence. The Supreme Court overturned the appellate court's decision and referred the case to a different appeals court. On July 16, 2001, that court sentenced Ganji to six years in jail. According to the state news agency IRNA, the ruling was "definitive," meaning that it cannot be appealed.

Iraj Jamshidi, *Asia*
Imprisoned: July 6, 2003

Jamshidi, editor of the economic daily *Asia*, was arrested by Iranian authorities, who also closed his newspaper. Both actions occurred after Jamshidi's newspaper published a photograph of Maryam Rajavi, leader of the opposition group People's Mujahadeen. Iranian authorities have released no details as to why they are detaining him, and it is unclear whether any formal charges have been levied against Jamshidi, who remained in prison at year's end.

Alireza Ahmadi, *Asia*
Imprisoned: July 2003

Ahmadi, an editor with the economic daily *Asia*, was arrested by Iranian authorities in July, sometime after his *Asia* colleague Iraj Jamshidi was detained on July 6. The arrests occurred after *Asia* published a photograph of Maryam Rajavi, leader of the opposition group People's Mujahadeen. The U.S. government–funded Radio Farda reported in December that the journalist was held in solitary confinement and quoted the journalist's sister as saying she believed that her brother was jailed for articles he wrote about corruption in the Tehran Stock Exchange. Iranian authorities have not yet released details as to why they detained Ahmadi, and it is unclear whether any formal charges have been made against him.

On January 8, 2004, the journalist was released. Attempts by CPJ to contact Ahmadi after his release were unsuccessful.

KAZAKHSTAN: 1

Sergei Duvanov, *Prava Cheloveka v Kazakhstane i Mire*
Imprisoned: October 27, 2002

Duvanov, a prominent 49-year-old journalist known for his criticism of Kazakh authorities, was arrested on suspicion of raping a minor. The journalist was officially charged on November 6, 2002.

Duvanov denied the rape accusation, saying it was a government effort to discredit him. The charges came just as Duvanov was preparing to leave for the United States, where he was scheduled to give a series of talks at Washington, D.C.– and New York–based think tanks about political conditions in Kazakhstan.

Shortly after his arrest, Duvanov went on a hunger strike to protest his detention. He ended the strike after 13 days, when prison authorities began to force-feed him. His trial, which began on December 24, 2002, ended on January 28, 2003. Duvanov was convicted and sentenced to three-and-a-half years in prison.

Duvanov's defense team appealed the conviction, but the appeal was rejected by the Almaty Regional Court in March 2003, and by the Supreme Court in November 2003.

Duvanov, who wrote for opposition-financed Web sites and was the editor-in-chief of a bulletin published by the Almaty-based Kazakhstan Bureau for Human Rights and the Rule of Law, is known for his biting criticism of Kazakhstan's political system and high-level officials, including Kazakh President Nursultan Nazarbayev. Authorities have frequently harassed him in reprisal for his work.

On the evening of August 28, 2002, three unknown assailants beat and stabbed Duvanov in the stairwell of his apartment building, saying of his work, "If you carry on, you'll be made a total cripple."

On July 9, 2002, the General Prosecutor's Office charged him with "infringing the honor and dignity of the president"—a criminal offense punishable by a fine or a maximum three-year prison sentence—after he accused President Nazarbayev of corruption in an article. Authorities later dropped that criminal case against him without any explanation.

On December 29, 2003, the Kapchagay District Court ruled that Duvanov could serve the rest of his term in a low-security labor camp and would be transferred to the facility in January 2004.

KUWAIT: 2

Ibtisam Berto Sulaiman al-Dakhil, *Al-Nida'*

Fawwaz Muhammad al-Awadi Bessisso, *Al-Nida'*

Imprisoned: June 1991

Bessisso and al-Dakhil were sentenced to life in prison for their work with *Al-Nida'*, a newspaper that Iraqi authorities launched during Iraq's occupation of Kuwait in 1990. At the end of 2002, they were the last remaining imprisoned journalists in Kuwait, which jailed 17 reporters and editors for their work with *Al-Nida'* following the Gulf War, charging them with collaboration.

The two jailed journalists were reportedly tortured during their interrogations. Their trial, which began on May 19, 1991, in a martial-law court, failed to meet international standards of justice. In particular, prosecutors failed to refute the journalists' defense that they had been forced to work for the Iraqi newspaper.

On June 16, 1991, the journalists were sentenced to death. Ten days later, following international protests, all martial-law death sentences were commuted to life imprisonment. The other 15 journalists were freed gradually starting in 1996, most on the occasion of Kuwaiti Emir Sheikh Jaber al-Ahmed al-Sabah's annual prisoner amnesties in February.

In 2002, the emir pardoned Bessisso and al-Dakhil. But because Bessisso is not a citizen of any country, no nation is willing to accept him as a refugee. Al-Dakhil, a naturalized Kuwaiti citizen from Iraq, lost her citizenship as a result of her conviction and is also awaiting deportation. Both are currently being held in Kuwaiti jails while they try to find countries of residence.

MOROCCO: 2

Ali Lmrabet, *Demain, Douman*

Imprisoned: May 21, 2003

Lmrabet, the owner and editor of two weeklies, the French-language *Demain* and its Arabic-language sister publication, *Douman*, was jailed on May 21 after a court in the capital, Rabat, convicted him of "insulting the king," "undermining the monarchy," and "challenging the territorial integrity of the state." He was sentenced to four years in prison (later reduced on appeal to three years) and fined 20,000 Moroccan dirhams (US$2,000). The court also ordered the two weeklies closed.

Lmrabet's conviction stemmed from articles and cartoons published in the two magazines, including an interview with Abdullah Zaazaa, an opponent of Morocco's monarchy who called for the self-determination of the people of Western Sahara; a satirical photomontage that included a photo from King Mohammed VI's wedding; an article about the royal court's finances; and a cartoon that criticized public displays of reverence to the monarchy.

Lmrabet was released in early January 2004 after King Mohammed VI pardoned him and several dozen other prisoners.

Mohammed al-Herd, *Al-Sharq*
Imprisoned: June 12, 2003

Al-Herd, editor of the Oujda-based weekly newspaper *Al-Sharq*, was detained on June 12 along with two other journalists—*Al-Sharq* Editor Abdel Majid Ben Taher and Mustapha Qashnini, editor of the Oujda-based weekly *Al-Hayat Al-Maghribiya*—under Morocco's new antiterrorism law and later charged with "extolling the actions that comprise terrorism." Ben Taher and Qashnini were released in July, but al-Herd remained in jail at year's end.

The charges against all three men stemmed from an article published in the May 5-20 edition of the weekly *Al-Hayat Al-Maghribiya* by an Islamist activist that was reprinted on June 5 in *Al-Sharq*. In the article, the author discussed the history of the Islamist movement in Morocco and its alleged relationship with the country's intelligence services. The article criticized the Moroccan intelligence services for doing the "dirty work" of the U.S. Central Intelligence Agency.

On August 4, al-Herd, Ben Taher, and Qashnini were convicted. Al-Herd was sentenced to three years in prison, while Ben Taher and Qashnini were each sentenced to a year in prison. Ben Taher and Qashnini remained free pending appeal, while al-Herd began serving his sentence immediately. The court also suspended both weeklies for three months.

Al-Herd was freed in early January 2004 after King Mohammed VI pardoned him and several dozen other prisoners. The cases against Ben Taher and Qashnini were also dropped under the pardon.

NEPAL: 3

Krishna Sen, *Janadisha*
Imprisoned: May 20, 2002

Sen, the editor of *Janadisha*, a publication closely associated with the Maoist rebels, was arrested by police under the provisions of a sweeping antiterrorism ordinance introduced in November 2001 that criminalized any contact with or support for Maoist rebels.

The journalist's arrest was widely reported in the local press. However, after news reports emerged in late June 2002 that Sen may have been killed while in police custody, a government-appointed commission said it found no evidence that he had ever been detained. Officials have since denied responsibility for Sen's disappearance.

Because Sen's body has not been recovered and no credible investigation has been undertaken to determine his status, CPJ holds the government accountable for his fate.

Dhana Bahadur Magar, Federation of Nepalese Journalists
Imprisoned: November 18, 2003
Bhai Kaji Ghimire, *Samadristi*
Imprisoned: December 3, 2003

Magar, a central council member of the Federation of Nepalese Journalists (FNJ) and secretary of the FNJ's Kathmandu office, was last seen running an errand in the afternoon of November 18, according to the FNJ. Local press freedom groups suspect that security forces took Magar into custody.

Security forces also detained Ghimire, managing director of the monthly *Samadristi*, while he was on his way to work on his motorcycle, according to the Kathmandu-based Center for Human Rights and Democratic Studies, a press freedom group. His whereabouts are unknown.

In the wake of the government's August 27 broken cease-fire agreement with Maoist rebels, many journalists were targeted and detained by security forces. While the majority of journalists were held briefly and then released, Magar and Ghimire were still being detained at undisclosed locations at year's end. No known charges have been filed against them.

NIGER: 1

Maman Abou, *Le Républicain*
Imprisoned: November 5, 2003

Police officers arrested Abou, director of the private weekly newspaper *Le Républicain*, at the newspaper's offices in the capital, Niamey. He was transferred to Central Prison in Niamey the same day.

On November 7, Abou was sentenced to six months in prison for criminal defamation at a closed, secret trial. Neither Abou nor his lawyers were present at the trial, according to Abou's colleagues. The journalist was also ordered to pay two fines, one of 300,000 CFA francs (US$530), and another of 10 million CFA francs (US$17,560).

The sentence stemmed from a July article in *Le Républicain* that accused several government ministers of using unauthorized treasury funds to pay for government contracts. The article alleged that several contracts had been awarded to government supporters without allowing competitive bidding, according to *Le Républicain* staff. The newspaper also published several documents, allegedly from the Public Treasury, along with the article. Following the article's publication, Prime Minister Hama Amadou announced on state television that he would pursue defamation charges against *Le Républicain*, according to local journalists.

After the sentence was delivered, Abou was transferred from Central Prison in Niamey to a prison in the town of Say, about 30 miles (50 kilometers) south.

On December 23, after the defamation charge against Abou had been appealed, Niamey's Correctional Court amended the journalist's sentence, changing it from six months in prison to a suspended sentence of four months. The fines were also reduced to 100,000 (US$190) and 2 million CFA francs (US$3,780), respectively.

However, Abou was kept in prison under so-called preventive detention on a second charge of complicity in stealing and possessing confidential government documents. The possession charge falls under the country's criminal code and can carry a sentence of several years in prison, according to local journalists.

On January 6, 2004, an appeals court granted Abou a provisional release, and he was freed from jail. His lawyer said he could soon be summoned for hearings on the possession charges.

PAKISTAN: 4

Munawar Mohsin, *The Frontier Post*
Imprisoned: January 29, 2001

Police in Peshawar arrested Mohsin and four colleagues from *The Frontier Post* after the newspaper published a letter to the editor titled "Why Muslims Hate Jews," which included derogatory references to the Prophet Mohammed.

Although the newspaper's senior management claimed that the letter was inserted into the copy by mistake and apologized for failing to stop its publication, district officials responded to complaints from local religious leaders by closing the paper and ordering the immediate arrest of seven staff members on blasphemy charges. In Pakistan, anyone accused of blasphemy is subject to immediate arrest without due process; those convicted may be sentenced to death.

On July 8, 2003, a court in Northwest Frontier Province convicted Mohsin of blasphemy and sentenced him to life in prison. The court's ruling said that Mohsin had "intentionally and willfully committed an offense."

Mohsin is the only journalist from *The Frontier Post* who remains in prison. (Two of the journalists charged in the case immediately went into hiding and were never arrested. The other four were eventually released on bail.) Mohsin, who was working as the newspaper's subeditor, admitted responsibility for publishing the letter, which he says he had not read carefully. He told *The New York Times* that he "could never think of abusing our Holy Prophet" but confessed that, having recently completed a drug rehabilitation program, his mind may have been slightly addled. Mohsin is imprisoned in Peshawar Central Jail.

Marc Epstein, *L'Express*
Jean-Paul Guilloteau, *L'Express*
Khawar Mehdi Rizvi, freelance
Imprisoned: December 16, 2003

Officers from the Federal Investigation Agency (FIA) arrested Epstein and Guilloteau, a reporter and a photographer, respectively, for the French newsmagazine *L'Express*, at their hotel in Karachi and charged them with visa violations under Pakistan's Foreigners Act for traveling to the southwestern city of Quetta without permission. The French journalists went there in December 2003 with Rizvi, a freelance journalist who was working as their guide, to research a story about Taliban activity in the western area of Pakistan that borders the country of Afghanistan.

Epstein and Guilloteau only had visas to travel to Karachi, Lahore, and Islamabad, and authorities threatened that they would also be charged with taking pictures of "prohibited areas." Pakistan's government began limiting foreigners' access to the western areas of Quetta and Peshawar in 2002, after skirmishes started along the Afghan border, according to international news reports.

The French journalists were released from Karachi Central Prison on December 24, but their passports were confiscated, and they remained under house arrest at year's end while awaiting a verdict in their case.

On January 10, 2004, Epstein and Guilloteau pleaded guilty to the charges of visa violations and received six-month prison sentences. The judge in the case, Nuzhat Ara Hakvi, suspended the sentence for one week and ordered the journalists to pay a fine of 200,000 rupees (US$3,500) each, according to their lawyer, Nafees Siddique. On appeal on January 12, 2004, the two journalists' sentences were waived, and they were allowed to return to France.

Pakistani authorities initially denied that they were holding Rizvi, a reporter with 10 years' experience working for local newspapers and international media outlets, but local journalists and press freedom groups were confident that Rizvi was in government custody because he disappeared on the same day the French journalists were arrested. Footage and interviews of the journalist in custody were shown several times on the state-owned channel PTV.

Rizvi's family filed a motion of habeas corpus on December 30, 2003, at the Sindh High Court in an attempt to free him, but in court FIA officials denied arresting or detaining the journalist.

In an interview with *The New York Times* on January 11, 2004, however, Interior Ministry spokesman Abdur Rauf Chaudry confirmed that security agencies were holding Rizvi, and that he was being interrogated. Chaudry also said that Rizvi would only be allowed to appear in court "when it is essential" and refused to say which security agencies were interrogating Rizvi because it would be "premature."

TUNISIA: 2

Hamadi Jebali, *Al-Fajr*
Imprisoned: January 1991

On August 28, 1992, a military court sentenced Jebali, editor of *Al-Fajr*, the now defunct weekly newspaper of the banned Islamic Al-Nahda Party, to 16 years in prison. He was tried along with 279 other individuals accused of belonging to Al-Nahda. Jebali was convicted of "aggression with the intention of changing the nature of the state" and "membership in an illegal organization."

During his testimony, Jebali denied the charges and presented evidence that he had been tortured while in custody. Jebali has been imprisoned since January 1991, when he was sentenced to one year in prison after *Al-Fajr* published an article calling for the abolition of military courts in Tunisia. International human rights groups monitoring the mass trial concluded that the proceedings fell far below international standards of justice.

Abdullah Zouari, *Al-Fajr*
Imprisoned: August 17, 2003

Zouari, a journalist with the now defunct weekly *Al-Fajr* of the banned Islamic Al-Nahda Party, was sentenced on October 8 to 13 months in prison on two charges: violating administrative controls enacted after his release from a previous prison sentence and defamation. CPJ views his current jailing as a part of a pattern of harassment against the journalist, who was released from prison in 2002 after spending 11 years behind bars for belonging to the Al-Nahda Party.

On August 17, 2003, authorities detained Zouari in Ben Guerdane, a market town near Zarzis in southern Tunisia, after he met with a group of local and international human rights activists.

In October, a court ruled that Zouari had violated administrative controls barring him from leaving Zarzis, although the charge is widely viewed as a pretext to harass the journalist, according to Tunisian human rights activists.

During the October court proceedings, the court also convicted Zouari of defamation. An employee of a cybercafé sued Zouari for defaming her during an argument in April when she barred Zouari—apparently under pressure from Tunisian officials, according to the journalist's colleagues—from accessing the Internet.

Previously, on August 28, 1992, a military court sentenced Zouari to 11 years in prison. He was tried along with 279 other individuals accused of belonging to Al-Nahda. International human rights groups monitoring the trial concluded that it fell far below international standards of justice.

TURKEY: 5

Burhan Gardas, *Mucadele*
Imprisoned: March 23, 1995

Gardas, the Ankara bureau chief for the now banned weekly socialist magazine *Mucadele*, was prosecuted several times beginning in 1994. Court records state that Gardas was arrested on January 12, 1994, at his office and charged with violating Article 168/2 of the Penal Code. During a search of the premises, police reportedly found four copies of "news bulletins" of the outlawed organization Devrimci Sol (also known as Dev Sol).

During the trial, the prosecution claimed that police also found banners with left-wing slogans, along with photographs of Devrimci Sol militants who had been killed in clashes with government security forces. The prosecution also claimed that Gardas shouted antistate slogans during his arrest, and that he was using *Mucadele*'s office for Devrimci Sol activities.

Gardas denied all the charges. His attorney argued that the illegal publications were part of the magazine's archive, and that Gardas had been tortured in prison, submitting a medical report to prove the allegation. On May 14, 1994, Gardas was released pending his trial's outcome.

While awaiting the verdict in the 1994 prosecution, Gardas was arrested on March 23, 1995, when police raided the office of the successor to *Mucadele*, the weekly socialist magazine *Kurtulus*, for which he was also the Ankara bureau chief. Officials said he had violated Article 168/2 of the Penal Code because of his alleged membership in Dev Sol. During the raid, police seized three copies of *Kurtulus* "news bulletins" and six *Kurtulus* articles discussing illegal rallies.

Court documents from his second trial, which was held at the Number 2 State Security Court of Ankara, reveal that the prosecution's evidence against Gardas consisted of his refusal to talk during a police interrogation—allegedly a Devrimci Sol policy—and his possession of publications that the prosecution contended were the mouthpieces of outlawed organizations. In addition, Ali Han, an employee at the Ankara bureau of *Kurtulus*', testified that Gardas was a Devrimci Sol member. Gardas denied the claim, and his lawyer argued that the journalist client had the constitutional right to remain silent during police interrogations.

On July 4, 1995, the Number 1 State Security Court of Ankara sentenced Gardas to 15 years in prison on the 1994 charge. In 1996, he was convicted and sentenced to an additional 15 years for the second set of charges.

Erdal Dogan, *Alinteri*
Imprisoned: July 10, 1995

Dogan, an Ankara reporter for the now banned socialist weekly *Alinteri*, was arrested and later charged under Article 168/2 of the Penal Code for allegedly belonging to the outlawed Turkish Revolutionary Communist Union (TIKB).

According to the trial transcript, the prosecution argued that the TIKB published *Alinteri*. The case against Dogan was based on the following evidence:

(1) a photograph of Dogan, taken at a 1992 May Day parade, allegedly showing him standing underneath a United Revolutionary Trade Union banner;

(2) a photograph of Dogan taken on the anniversary of a TIKB militant's death;

(3) a photograph allegedly showing Dogan attending an illegal demonstration in the capital, Ankara;

(4) a statement of an alleged member

of the TIKB who claimed that Dogan belonged to the organization.

The defense argued that the incriminating statement was invalid because it had been extracted under torture. Dogan's lawyer told CPJ that the photograph from the militant's memorial was blurry, and Dogan testified in court that he had attended the May Day parade in his capacity as a journalist. He was convicted, sentenced to 12 years and six months in prison, and jailed in Bursa Prison.

Sadik Celik, *Kurtulus*
Imprisoned: December 23, 1995

Celik, Zonguldak bureau chief for the now banned leftist weekly *Kurtulus*, was detained and charged with violating Article 168/2 of the Penal Code for allegedly belonging to the outlawed Revolutionary People's Liberation Party-Front (DHKP-C).

The prosecution claimed that the DHKP-C published *Kurtulus*, and that Celik's position with the magazine proved he was a member of the group. Celik was accused of conducting "seminars" for the DHKP-C at the magazine's office, propagandizing for the organization, transporting copies of the magazine from Istanbul to Zonguldak by bus, and organizing the magazine's distribution in Zonguldak. The prosecution also stated that Celik's name appeared in a document written by a DHKP-C leader. (It is not clear whether the document was introduced as material evidence.)

The prosecution claimed that Celik's refusal to speak while in police custody proved his guilt. The defense argued that the prosecution could not substantiate any of its claims. Celik acknowledged having distributed the magazine in his capacity as *Kurtulus*' bureau chief. He said that he had held meetings in the office to discuss the magazine's affairs. The defense presented the statements of two *Kurtulus* reporters to corroborate Celik's statements. On October 17, 1996, Celik was sentenced to 12 years and six months in prison.

Memik Horuz, *Ozgur Gelecek, Isci Koylu*
Imprisoned: June 18, 2001

Horuz, editor of the leftist publications *Ozgur Gelecek* and *Isci Koylu*, was arrested and later charged with "membership in an illegal organization," a crime under Article 168/2 of the Penal Code. Prosecutors based the case against Horuz on interviews he had allegedly conducted with leftist guerrillas in *Topcam*, which *Ozgur Gelecek* later published in 2000 and 2001. The state also based its case on the testimony of an alleged former militant who claimed that the journalist belonged to the outlawed Marxist-Leninist Communist Party. Horuz was convicted on June 18, 2002, and sentenced to 12 years and six months in prison.

Sinan Kara, *Datca Haber*
Imprisoned: October 27, 2003

Kara, publisher of the weekly *Datca Haber* in the southwestern town of Datcha, began serving a one-year prison term for allegedly threatening the bodyguards of Mert Ciller, son of former Prime Minister Tansu Ciller. According to Kara's lawyer, the bodyguards attacked the journalist when he tried to photograph Mert Ciller in 2000. But after Kara filed a complaint with the police, the bodyguards claimed that Kara had threatened them and later sued the journalist. Kara's lawyer maintains that the charge against his client was fabricated, and that the witnesses produced by Mert Ciller's entourage provided dubious testimony. Kara is in Ula Prison.

Local politicians and businessmen have targeted Kara with several lawsuits for his reporting on local government, according to Turkish media reports. Officials have frequently harassed the journalist through petty administrative measures. In 2002, for example, Kara served jail time for failing to comply with a press law requiring newspaper publishers to send two copies of each issue to the governor's office.

UZBEKISTAN: 5

Muhammad Bekjanov, *Erk*
Yusuf Ruzimuradov, *Erk*
Imprisoned: March 15, 1999

Bekjanov, editor of *Erk*, a newspaper published by the banned opposition Erk party, and Ruzimuradov, an employee of the paper, were sentenced to 14 years and 15 years in prison, respectively, at an August 1999 trial in the capital, Tashkent.

They were convicted for publishing and distributing a banned newspaper containing slanderous criticism of President Islam Karimov, participating in a banned political protest, and attempting to overthrow the regime. In addition, the court found them guilty of illegally leaving the country and damaging their Uzbek passports.

Both men were tortured during their six-month pretrial detention in the Tashkent City Prison. Their health has deteriorated as a result of prison conditions.

According to human rights activists in Tashkent, Bekjanov was transferred on November 27, 1999, to "strict-regime" Penal Colony 64/46 in the city of Navoi in central Uzbekistan. He has lost considerable weight and, like many prisoners in Uzbek camps, suffers from malnutrition. Local sources have informed CPJ that Ruzimuradov is being held in "strict-regime" Penal Colony 64/33 in the village of Shakhali near the town of Karshi.

In May 2003, the 49-year-old Bekjanov was interviewed for the first time since his imprisonment by a local correspondent for the London-based Institute for War and Peace Reporting (IWPR) and a local stringer for The Associated Press (AP). The interview took place in the Tashkent Prison Hospital, where he was being treated for tuberculosis, which he contracted while in detention.

Bekjanov described daily torture and beatings that resulted in a broken leg and loss of hearing in his right ear, according to IWPR. The journalist and opposition activist said he intends to resume his political activities after he is released from prison in 2012. "I will do what I used to do," Bekjanov told the AP.

Madzhid Abduraimov, *Yangi Asr*
Imprisoned: August 1, 2001

Abduraimov, a correspondent with the national weekly *Yangi Asr*, was convicted of extortion and sentenced to 13 years in prison. In a January 15, 2001, article in *Yangi Asr*, Abduraimov charged that Nusrat Radzhabov, head of the Boysunsky District grain production company Zagotzerno, had misappropriated state funds and falsified documents. Abduraimov also accused the businessman of killing a 12-year-old in a car accident and alleged that Radzhabov's teenage son was part of a group that had beaten and raped a 13-year-old boy.

Radzhabov claims that Abduraimov asked him for money and threatened to publish more accusations unless he was paid. According to the London-based Institute for War and Peace Reporting (IWPR), Radzhabov tried to sue Abduraimov for slander but dropped the suit after a local prosecutor's investigation confirmed the facts in the article.

Authorities arrested Abduraimov and accused him of receiving a US$6,000 bribe. He and a witness quoted by the IWPR claimed that a man threw the money into the back seat of his car immediately before police stopped his vehicle, searched it, and arrested him.

Abduraimov was held in Termez Regional Police Department jail until his trial began in Termez City Court on July 4, 2001.

According to Abduraimov, the court proceedings were influenced by local officials who objected to his reporting on corruption in the oil business. His request for a change of venue was not granted. He refused to attend the hearings and was sentenced in absentia.

Abduraimov is known for his investigative reporting and critical stance toward local law enforcement bodies and authorities. The journalist and his family have been persecuted for several years with threatening phone calls, while his son was reportedly beaten by police and sentenced to four months in jail for disorderly conduct. Supporters say Abduraimov was most likely framed, and it is not known where he is being held.

Gayrat Mehliboyev, freelance
Imprisoned: July 24, 2002

Mehliboyev was arrested at a bazaar in the capital, Tashkent, for allegedly participating in an antigovernment rally protesting the imprisonment of members of the banned Islamist opposition party Hizb ut-Tahrir. When police searched Mehliboyev's bed in a local hostel, they allegedly found banned religious literature that prosecutors later characterized as extremist in nature, according to international press reports.

Mehliboyev, who was unemployed at the time, admitted in court that he had studied the ideas of Hizb ut-Tahrir but denied possessing the religious material police allegedly found in the hostel where he was staying.

He had written several articles on religious issues for the government-funded Tashkent newspapers *Hurriyat* and *Mohiyyat* during 2001 and graduated from the journalism faculty at Tashkent State University in 2002, according to local press reports.

Mehliboyev was held in pretrial detention for more than six months. His trial began on February 5, 2003, at the Shaikhantaur Regional Court in Tashkent, The Associated Press (AP) reported.

Prosecutors presented as evidence of Mehliboyev's alleged religious extremism a political commentary he had written for the April 11, 2001, edition of *Hurriyat*.

The article questioned whether Western democracy should be a model for Uzbekistan and said that religion was the true path to achieving social justice. Prosecutors claimed that the article contained ideas from Hizb ut-Tahrir.

A Tashkent-based representative of Human Rights Watch monitored the trial and told CPJ that several times during the proceedings, Mehliboyev said he was beaten in custody, but the court ignored his comments.

Mehliboyev's brother, Shavkat, also said the defendant, who was beaten and tortured in police custody, was forced to confess to having connections to Hizb ut-Tahrir.

The Shaikhantaur Regional Court sentenced the 23-year-old Mehliboyev to seven years in prison on February 18, 2003, after convicting him of anticonstitutional activities, participating in extremist religious organizations, and inciting religious hatred, according to local and international press reports.

Ruslan Sharipov, Union of Independent Journalists of Uzbekistan
Imprisoned: May 26, 2003

Police arrested Sharipov, 25, on May 26 in the capital, Tashkent, and charged him with sodomy, having sexual relations with minors, and managing prostitutes, according to local and international press reports.

Sharipov, who is openly gay, denied the charges, saying that authorities had threatened him with torture to get a confession. According to a report by the U.N. special rapporteur on torture, who visited Uzbekistan in 2002 to inspect several prisons, physical abuse of prisoners is a "systematic" problem in the country. Furthermore, international human rights organizations report that Uzbek authorities commonly use fabricated criminal charges to silence government critics.

Police and the security service have threatened and harassed Sharipov for several years because of critical articles he has written for the Russian news agency Prima and for the Union of Independent Journalists of Uzbekistan's Web site (*www.uiju.org*) describing police abuses and press freedom violations. Many of Sharipov's articles were published on the Internet in English, making them far more accessible to an international audience than articles written by other Uzbek journalists and human rights activists.

Two of Sharipov's colleagues, Oleg Sarapulov and Azamat Mumankulov, who were arrested with him but were later released, told human rights activists that authorities had intimidated them in an effort to force them to testify against Sharipov, The Associated Press (AP) reported.

While homosexuality remains a criminal offense and gays face regular police harassment in Uzbekistan, prosecution of such cases is rare. As a result, local journalists and human rights activists suspect that the charges against Sharipov were an effort to silence his criticism of authorities.

Numerous irregularities have been reported in Sharipov's trial, which began on July 23, 2003, behind closed doors at the Mirzo-Ulugbek District Court in Tashkent, according to local and international press reports.

Judge Ganisher Makhmudov ruled that the trial would be closed to the public to protect the privacy of minors who were allegedly victims in the case. Human rights advocates, however, believe that the trial was closed to prevent public scrutiny of the case.

Sharipov's lawyers argued that their client could not receive a fair trial because he had criticized the Mirzo-Ulugbek District Court and police in previous articles. Judge Makhmudov rejected the lawyers' request to have the trial moved to a different court in Tashkent.

On August 8, 2003, the trial took a bizarre turn when Sharipov reportedly pleaded guilty to sodomy, waived his right to legal counsel, and expressed his readiness to apologize for criticizing President Islam Karimov and other Uzbek authorities in his articles, according to a member of Sharipov's defense team. On August 13, the Mirzo-Ulugbek District Court convicted Sharipov on all three charges and sentenced him to five-and-a-half years in prison.

On September 5, 2003, Sharipov issued a statement from prison saying that he pleaded guilty to sodomy in his August trial because officials had tortured him into confessing. His statement, which was addressed to U.N. Secretary-General Kofi Annan, was posted on the Web site of the Moscow-based Center for Journalism in Extreme Situations (*www.cjes.ru*) on September 9. A member of Sharipov's family confirmed to CPJ that the statement is authentic.

In the statement, Sharipov wrote, "I was tortured and pressured in ways I cannot describe with the aim of forcing me to confess and plead guilty at the trial for a crime I hadn't committed." He continued, "They put a gas mask on my head and sprayed an unknown substance into my throat. ... After that I could hardly breath, they injected an unknown substance into my veins and said they will inject me with the AIDs virus if I did not follow their instructions." Sharipov also wrote that before he pled guilty at his trial, he was forced to write a "death note" declaring he had "committed suicide of my own volition."

At a closed hearing on September 25, the City Court in Tashkent rejected an appeal by Sharipov to have his conviction and prison sentence overturned, according to local and international press reports. Instead, the court dropped one of the three charges against the journalist and reduced his prison sentence to four years.

A member of Sharipov's family told CPJ that Sharipov arrived at the court hearing with serious injuries to his eye and broken glasses, and that the police claimed that the injuries were from a car accident.

Surat Ikramov, a human rights activist on Sharipov's defense team, said that Sharipov was planning to appeal the case to a higher court, the AP reported. Sharipov is currently serving his sentence in Tavaksay Prison, about 40 miles (70 kilometers) northeast of Tashkent.

In his first interview since his conviction, Sharipov repeated to the AP that he had been coerced into confessing during his trial because of police torture. On December 22, Mikhail Gurevich, chief of staff of the country's prison system, announced that Sharipov would not be eligible for a wide-ranging presidential pardon scheduled to be carried out that month, the AP reported.

VIETNAM: 9

Ha Sy Phu, freelance
Imprisoned: May 12, 2000

Nguyen Xuan Tu, a scientist and political essayist better known by his pen name, Ha Sy Phu, was placed under house arrest and charged with treason. The arrest came after an April 28, 2000, raid on Ha Sy Phu's home in Dalat, Lam Dong Province, during which police confiscated a computer, a printer, and several diskettes. They returned on May 12 with orders for his arrest signed by Col. Nguyen Van Do, police chief of Lam Dong Province.

Officials suspected that Ha Sy Phu had helped draft a pro-democracy declaration, according to CPJ sources, and his arrest followed the government's long-standing harassment of the writer. Ha Sy Phu was held under Administrative Detention Directive 31/CP, which allows the government to put individuals under house arrest for two years without due process, and was required to report daily to the Dalat police for interrogation.

In January 2002, police searched Ha Sy Phu's home and again confiscated his computer. The raid came during a period of escalating harassment of dissidents in Vietnam. Though the treason charge against Ha Sy Phu was withdrawn in January 2001, authorities renewed his administrative detention order for two years. Although the detention order expired in early 2003, officials refused to officially clarify if he was free from house arrest, so he remained under effective detention at the end of 2003, according to CPJ sources.

Tran Khue, freelance
Imprisoned: October 9, 2001

On October 22, 2002, the Foreign Ministry announced that writer Tran Khue, also known as Tran Van Khue, had been placed under administrative detention, or house arrest, for two years, and that his term had begun on October 9, 2001. Administrative Detention Directive 31/CP allows the government to put individuals under house arrest for two years without due process.

In September 2001, Khue had been active in failed efforts to legally register the independent National Association to Fight Corruption. He had also established online publications, called *Dialogue 2000* and *Dialogue 2001*, which included articles by himself and others advocating political reform. In January 2002, the Vietnamese government ordered local officials to confiscate and destroy all printed copies of the publications.

On March 8, 2002, seven police officers entered and searched Khue's home in Ho Chi Minh City and confiscated his computer equipment and several documents, according to CPJ sources. On March 10, Khue sent a message via cell phone to a friend indicating that he was in danger. Immediately after the message was sent, all means of communication with Khue were cut.

According to CPJ sources, police had searched Khue's house for materials relating to an open letter he sent to Chinese President Jiang Zemin during Jiang's visit to Vietnam in late February 2002. The letter, which was distributed over the Internet, protested recent border accords between the two countries.

On December 29, 2002, about 20 security officials came to Khue's house and detained him after he met with Hanoi-based democracy activist Pham Que Duong and his wife. The officers also confiscated his computer and computer disks. The day before, Duong was arrested at the Ho Chi Minh City train station while he was returning to Hanoi. A government official stated that the two men had been "caught red-handed while carrying out activities that seriously violate Vietnamese laws." She said that Khue and Duong will be tried but did not clarify on what charges or when the trial will take place.

Although Khue's administrative detention order expired in 2003, he remained in detention at year's end.

Nguyen Khac Toan, freelance
Imprisoned January 8, 2002

Toan was arrested at an Internet café in the capital, Hanoi. He had reported on protests by disgruntled farmers, and then he transmitted his reports via the Internet to overseas pro-democracy groups. Authorities later charged him with espionage. On December 20, 2002, Toan was sentenced to 12 years in prison, one of the harshest sentences given to a Vietnamese democracy activist in recent years.

Toan, 47, served in the North Vietnamese army in the 1970s. After becoming active in Vietnam's pro-democracy movement, he began to write articles using the pen name Veteran Tran Minh Tam.

During the National Assembly's December 2001 and January 2002 meeting, large numbers of peasants gathered in front of the meeting hall to demand compensation for land that the government had wrongfully confiscated from them during recent redevelopment efforts. Toan helped the protesters write their grievances to present to government officials. He also wrote several news reports about the demonstrations and sent the articles to overseas pro-democracy publications.

Toan's trial took less than one day, and his lawyer was not allowed to meet with him alone until the day before proceedings began. The day after Toan was sentenced, the official Vietnamese press carried reports stating that he had "slandered and denigrated executives of the party and the state by sending electronic letters and by providing information to certain exiled Vietnamese reactionaries in France." He is currently being held in B14 Prison, in Thanh Tri District, outside Hanoi.

Bui Minh Quoc, freelance
Imprisoned January 14, 2002

Freelancer Bui Minh Quoc was charged with "possessing anti-government literature," including his own writings, and put under administrative detention, or house arrest, for two years in Dalat District. Administrative Detention Directive 31/CP allows the Vietnamese government to put individuals under house arrest for two years without due process. Prior to Quoc's arrest, he had conducted extensive research on Vietnam's territorial concessions to China, according to international news reports.

A Foreign Ministry spokesperson told journalists that, "The competent authorities told me that Quoc had violated Vietnamese law and they will provide more specifics on his violations in the coming time." Quoc, a poet and journalist who was a North Vietnamese Radio correspondent during the Vietnam War, was also under house arrest between 1997 and 1999.

Le Chi Quang, freelance
Imprisoned February 21, 2002

Le Chi Quang, 32, was detained at an Internet café in the capital, Hanoi. He had written and posted several articles online criticizing government policy. According to Vietnamese authorities, officials at a popular domestic Internet service provider notified the Public Security Bureau that Quang had used computers at a specific Internet café in Hanoi to communicate with "reactionaries" living abroad. Security officials then tracked him down at the café.

On September 24, 2002, the state prosecutor's office, known as the Supreme People's Organ of Control, issued a document outlining specific charges against Quang. The document cites several articles by Quang as evidence of his "anti-government" activities, including an essay titled "Beware of Imperialist China," which criticized land and sea border agreements between China and Vietnam; essays praising well-known dissidents Nguyen Thanh Giang and Vu Cao Quan; and an article about the U.S.-Vietnam bilateral trade agreement.

On November 8, after a three-hour trial on national security charges, the Hanoi People's Court sentenced Le Chi Quang to four years in prison followed by three years of house arrest. Quang was charged under articles 88 and 92 of the Criminal Code, which ban the distribution of information that opposes the government. Quang's parents were the only observers allowed into the courtroom, and his lawyer was not allowed to present a defense before the court, according to CPJ sources. While the chief judge in the case told foreign reporters that Quang had pleaded guilty, CPJ sources said he admitted in court to having written the articles mentioned by the prosecution but denied committing any crime.

During Quang's trial, about 100 family members and supporters gathered outside the courthouse. In December 2002, he was transferred to Sao Do Prison in Phu Ly, south of Hanoi.

Pham Hong Son, freelance
Imprisoned March 27, 2002

Son, a medical doctor, was arrested after he posted an essay online about democracy. Authorities also searched his home and confiscated his computer and several documents, according to the Democracy Club for Vietnam, an organization based in both California and Hanoi, Vietnam's capital.

Prior to his arrest, Son translated into Vietnamese and posted an essay titled "What Is Democracy?" (The article first appeared on the U.S. State Department's Web site.) Son had previously written several essays promoting democracy and human rights, all of which appeared on Vietnamese-language online forums.

After Son's arrest, the government issued a statement claiming that his work was "anti-state and anti-Vietnam Communist Party," according to international press reports.

On June 18, 2003, the Hanoi People's Court sentenced Son to 13 years in prison, plus an additional three years of administrative detention, or house arrest. The trial was closed to foreign diplomats and correspondents. Son's wife, Vu Thuy Ha, was also barred from the courtroom, except when she was called to testify.

In an appeal trial on August 26, 2003, the Hanoi Supreme Court reduced Son's sentence to five years. Son is still required to serve three years of house arrest upon release.

Nguyen Vu Binh, freelance
Imprisoned September 25, 2002

Security officials searched Binh's home in Vietnam's capital, Hanoi, before arresting him, said CPJ sources. Police did not disclose the reasons for the writer's arrest, although CPJ sources believe that his detention may be linked to an essay he wrote criticizing border agreements between China and Vietnam.

In a trial on December 31, 2003, the Hanoi People's Court sentenced Binh on espionage charges to seven years in prison, followed by three years of house arrest upon release. Binh's wife was the only family member allowed in the courtroom. Foreign diplomats and journalists were barred from the trial.

Following the proceedings, the official Vietnam News Agency reported that Binh was sentenced because he had "written and exchanged, with various opportunist elements in the country, information and materials that distorted the party and state policies." He was also accused of communicating with "reactionary" organizations abroad.

Binh is a former journalist who worked for almost 10 years at *Tap Chi Cong San* (Journal of Communism), an official publication of Vietnam's Communist Party. In January 2001, he left his position there after applying to form an independent opposition group called the Liberal Democratic Party.

Since then, Binh has written several articles calling for political reform and criticizing current government policy. In August 2002, he wrote an article titled, "Some Thoughts on the China-Vietnam Border Agreement," which was distributed online.

In late July 2002, Binh was briefly detained after submitting written testimony to a U.S. Congressional Human Rights Caucus briefing on freedom of expression in Vietnam. Authorities then required him to report to the local police station daily. He was also subjected to frequent, daylong interrogation sessions.

In 2002, Vietnamese authorities cracked down on critics of land and sea border agreements signed by China and Vietnam as part of a rapprochement following a 1979 war between the two countries. Several writers have criticized the government for agreeing to border concessions without consulting the Vietnamese people.

Pham Que Duong, freelance
Imprisoned: December 28, 2002

Military historian Duong was arrested at a train station in Ho Chi Minh City while en route to his home in the capital, Hanoi, after meeting with writer Tran Khue. Khue, who has been under house arrest since October 2001, was detained on December 29, 2002, at his home in Ho Chi Minh City. A government official stated that the two men had been "caught red-handed while carrying out activities that seriously violate Vietnamese laws."

She said that Khue and Duong will be tried but did not clarify on what charges or when the trial will take place.

Duong and Khue had both signed a petition sent to the Vietnamese Parliament in August 2002 calling for democratic reforms. Prior to his arrest, Duong had written a number of articles calling for political reforms and support for human rights, according to CPJ sources.

Duong, a former colonel in the Vietnamese military, served as editor of *Tap Chi Lich Su Quan Su* (Military History Review) from 1982 to 1986. In 1990, he resigned from the Vietnamese Communist Party and began writing articles that criticized the current political system.

Duong was also involved in the failed attempt to launch an independent anti-corruption organization in 2001.

According to CPJ sources, Duong has been under tight surveillance in recent years because he became well known for his expressions of political dissent.

By year's end, Duong had not been tried and the government had not announced any formal charges against him.

Nguyen Dan Que, freelance
Imprisoned March 17, 2003

On March 17, Que was arrested outside his home in Ho Chi Minh City. Police also confiscated several documents and a computer from his house. Que is being held at the Nguyen Van Cu detention center, according to CPJ sources.

On March 20, a Foreign Ministry spokesperson announced that, "Nguyen Dan Que was arrested red-handed while carrying out activities that violate Vietnamese law," according to international news reports. She added that Que will be tried but did not clarify when or on what charges.

On March 13, Que issued a statement, titled, "Communiqué on Freedom of Information in Vietnam," in which he criticized the Vietnamese government's refusal to implement political reforms and lift controls on the media. Que wrote that, "The state hopes to cling to power by brainwashing the Vietnamese people through stringent censorship and through its absolutist control over what information the public can receive."

Que's statement also declared support for a bill submitted to the U.S. House of Representatives on February 27, 2003, the Freedom of Information in Vietnam Act of 2003. The bill would support enhanced broadcasts from the U.S. government–funded Radio Free Asia into Vietnam and would allow the United States to counter Vietnamese government blocks on Internet access.

Que, an endocrinologist, is a prominent writer who has spent a total of 18 years in prison for his political activism since his first arrest in 1978. After he was arrested in 1998, authorities began keeping him under strict surveillance and tightly restricting his movements. However, Que has remained active in recent years by writing a number of essays and letters calling for political reforms.

Que had not been formally charged or tried by year's end. In May, during a meeting with the U.S. ambassador to Vietnam, Raymond Burghardt, Deputy Prime Minister Nguyen Tan Dung said that Que will be released only if he agrees to leave Vietnam permanently and live in exile, according to a Radio Free Asia report.

Que's brother Nguyen Quoc Quan told CPJ that Que refused a similar offer of exile when he was amnestied from prison in 1998, telling him at that time that "exile is not freedom." ■

CPJ INTERNATIONAL PRESS FREEDOM AWARDS

SINCE 1991, CPJ HAS HONORED SEVERAL JOURNALISTS EACH YEAR from around the world with its International Press Freedom Awards. Recipients have shown extraordinary courage in the face of enormous risks, bravely standing up to tyrants who refuse to allow free discussion in order to hide corruption or keep the world from witnessing their deeds. These journalists have endured terrible difficulties, including jail or physical violence, simply for working to uncover and report the truth, or because they have expressed opinions that the leaders of their countries deem to be dangerous.

INTERNATIONAL PRESS FREEDOM AWARD RECIPIENTS 1991-2003

1991

Byron Barrera, *La Época*, Guatemala
Bill Foley and Cary Vaughan, United States
Tatyana Mitkova, TSN, former Soviet Union
Pius Njawe, *Le Messager*, Cameroon
Imprisoned: Wang Juntao and Chen Ziming, *Economics Weekly*, China

1992

Muhammad al-Saqr, *Al-Qabas*, Kuwait
Sony Esteus, Radio Tropic FM, Haiti
David Kaplan, ABC News, United States
Gwendolyn Lister, *The Namibian*, Namibia
Thepchai Yong, *The Nation*, Thailand

1993

Omar Belhouchet, *El Watan*, Algeria
Nosa Igiebor, *Tell*, Nigeria
Veran Matic, Radio B92, Yugoslavia
Ricardo Uceda, *Si*, Peru
Imprisoned: Doan Viet Hoat, *Freedom Forum*, Vietnam

1994

Iqbal Athas, *The Sunday Leader*, Sri Lanka
Daisy Li Yuet-wah, Hong Kong Journalists Association, Hong Kong
Aziz Nesin, *Aydinlik*, Turkey
In memory of staff journalists, *Navidi Vakhsh*, Tajikistan
Imprisoned: Yndamiro Restano, freelance, Cuba

1995

Veronica Guerin, *Sunday Independent*, Ireland
Yevgeny Kiselyov, NTV, Russia
Fred M'membe, *The Post*, Zambia
José Rubén Zamora Marroquín, *Siglo Veintiuno*, Guatemala
Imprisoned: Ahmad Taufik, Alliance of Independent Journalists, Indonesia

1996
J. Jesús Blancornelas, *Zeta*, Mexico
Yusuf Jameel, *Asian Age*, India
Daoud Kuttab, Internews Middle East, Palestinian Authority Territories
Imprisoned: Ocak Isik Yurtcu, *Ozgur Gundem*, Turkey

1997
Ying Chan, *Yazhou Zhoukan*, United States
Shieh Chung-liang, *Yazhou Zhoukan*, Taiwan
Victor Ivancic, *Feral Tribune*, Croatia
Yelena Masyuk, NTV, Russia
Freedom Neruda, *La Voie*, Ivory Coast
Imprisoned: Christine Anyanwu, *The Sunday Magazine*, Nigeria

1998
Grémah Boucar, Radio Anfani, Niger
Gustavo Gorriti, *La Prensa*, Panama
Goenawan Mohamad, *Tempo*, Indonesia
Pavel Sheremet, ORT, *Belorusskaya Delovaya Gazeta*, Belarus
Imprisoned: Ruth Simon, Agence France-Presse, Eritrea

1999
María Cristina Caballero, *Semana*, Colombia
Baton Haxhiu, *Koha Ditore*, Kosovo
Jugnu Mohsin and Najam Sethi, *The Friday Times*, Pakistan
Imprisoned: Jesús Joel Díaz Hernández, Cooperativa Avileña de Periodistas Independientes, Cuba

2000
Steven Gan, *Malaysiakini*, Malaysia
Zeljko Kopanja, *Nezavine Novine*, Bosnia-Herzegovina
Modeste Mutinga, *Le Potentiel*, Democratic Republic of Congo
Imprisoned: Mashallah Shamsolvaezin, *Asr-e-Azadegan, Neshat*, Iran

2001
Mazen Dana, Reuters, West Bank
Geoff Nyarota, *The Daily News*, Zimbabwe
Horacio Verbitsky, freelance, Argentina
Imprisoned: Jiang Weiping, *Qianshao*, China

2002
Ignacio Gómez, "Noticias Uno," Colombia
Irina Petrushova, *Respublika*, Kazakhstan
Tipu Sultan, freelance, Bangladesh
Imprisoned: Fesshaye Yohannes, *Setit*, Eritrea

2003
Abdul Samay Hamed, Afghanistan
Aboubakr Jamai, *Le Journal Hebdomadaire* and *Assahifa al-Ousbouiya*, Morocco
Musa Muradov, *Groznensky Rabochy*, Russia
Imprisoned: Manuel Vázquez Portal, Grupo de Trabajo Decoro, Cuba

BURTON BENJAMIN AWARD

SINCE 1991, CPJ HAS GIVEN THE BURTON BENJAMIN MEMORIAL AWARD to an individual in recognition of a lifetime of distinguished achievement for the cause of press freedom. The award honors Burton Benjamin, the late CBS News senior producer and former CPJ chairman, who died in 1988.

BURTON BENJAMIN MEMORIAL AWARD RECIPIENTS 1991–2003

1991
Walter Cronkite
CBS News

1992
Katherine Graham
The Washington Post Company

1993
R.E. (Ted) Turner
CNN

1994
George Soros
Open Society Institute

1995
Benjamin C. Bradlee
The Washington Post

1996
Arthur Ochs Sulzberger
The New York Times

1997
Ted Koppel
ABC News

1998
Brian Lamb
C-SPAN

1999
Don Hewitt
CBS News

2000
Otis Chandler
Los Angeles Times
Times Mirror Company

2001
Joseph Lelyveld
The New York Times

2002
Daniel Pearl
The Wall Street Journal

2003
John F. Burns
The New York Times

CONTRIBUTORS

THE COMMITTEE TO PROTECT JOURNALISTS IS EXTREMELY GRATEFUL to the foundations, corporations, and individuals whose generosity made our press freedom work possible in 2003:

Foundations & Corporations:

ABC News
Advance Publications
American Federation of Television and Radio Artists
The Annenberg Foundation
Argus Media Inc.
Around Foundation
The Associated Press
The Atlantic Monthly
The Baltimore Sun
Bankrate.com
The Belo Foundation
Bloomberg
Bridgewater Fieldwater Foundation
British Airways, PLC
Brokaw Family Foundation
Burson-Marsteller
BusinessWeek
CameraPlanet Pictures
CBS News
Cisco Systems Inc.
Citigroup Inc.
Clifford Chance U.S. LLP
CNBC
CNN
Columbia University Graduate School of Journalism
Communication Workers of America
Community Counselling Service Co.
Continental Airlines
Copley Newspapers
Court TV
Cox Newspapers
Crowell & Moring LLP
Daily News L.P.
Debevoise & Plimpton
Deloitte
Delphos Herald Incorporated
Dow Jones & Company
Dow Jones Foundation
Stanley Eisenberg Charitable Gift Fund
Ethics and Excellence in Journalism Foundation
Forbes Inc.
Fortune
Fox News Channel
The Freedom Forum
Freshfields Bruckhaus Deringer
Fried, Frank, Harris, Shriver & Jacobson
Philip L. Graham Fund
Hearst Newspapers
Drue Heinz Trust
Vira I. Heinz Endowment
Internews Network
Johnson & Johnson
Kekst and Company, Incorporated
John S. and James L. Knight Foundation
Knight Ridder
Lexis-Nexis
Los Angeles Times
The McClatchy Company
Robert R. McCormick Tribune Foundation
Andrews McMeel Publishing
MediaNews Group Inc.
Merrill Lynch & Co., Inc
The Miami Herald
Morgan Stanley
MSNBC.com
The Nation
NBC News
The New York Times Company Foundation
The New York Times Company
The New Yorker
Samuel I. Newhouse Foundation Inc.
Newhouse Newspapers
Newsday
Newsweek
The Nieman Foundation for Journalism
The North Jersey Media Group Foundation Inc.
Oak Foundation USA
Open Media Fund for Afghanistan
Open Society Institute

The Overbrook Foundation
The David and Lucile Packard Foundation
Pew Charitable Trusts
Philip Morris/Altria Group Inc.
The Playboy Foundation
Poynter Institute
Public Concern Foundation
PublicAffairs
Pulitzer Foundation
RealNetworks Foundation
Reebok Human Rights Foundation
The Rendon Group
Reuters Group PLC
Rubin & Associates P.C.
The Rudin Foundation, Inc.
Scholastic
Slate
Sony Corporation of America
St. Petersburg Times
J. Walter Thompson U.S.A., Inc.
Time Inc.
Time
Time Warner Inc.
The Torrenzano Group
Tribune Company
TRIO
UBS AG
Verizon Foundation
Viacom
The Washington Post Company

Individuals:
Marcia and Franz Allina
Deborah Amos and Rick Davis
Terry Anderson
Carol Ash and Josh Friedman
Ken Auletta
Eva and Tobias Bermant
Carl Bernstein
Mary Billard/Barry Cooper
Molly Bingham
Mr. and Mrs. Barry Bingham Jr.
Mark Bowden
Meredith and Tom Brokaw
Jerry and Linda Bruckheimer
Stephen Capus
Virginia Carter
Terry Chabrowe
Ken Chenault
Lisa Church
Joe Conason and Elizabeth Wagley
Arthur Cooper
David F. Cooper
Rabbi Scott Corngold
Katie Couric
Paul C. Critchlow
Frank del Olmo
Phil Donahue and Marlo Thomas
Stuart and Randi Epstein
David Evans
Pamela Falk and Ed Wallace
Robert R. Fenichel, M.D.
Jennifer Fiore and John Merz
Ruth Friendly
Anne Garrels and Vint Lawrence
Robert Giles
James C. and Toni K. Goodale
Cheryl Gould
Henry Grunwald
Harry B. Gutman
Ruth Ann and William F. Harnisch
Michael J. Hirschhorn and Jimena P. Martinez
Brant Houston
Pamela Howard
Benjamin W. Hulse
Kathleen E. Hunt
Charlayne Hunter-Gault
Alberto Ibargüen
Steven L. Isenberg
Samuel Jameson
Peter Jennings
Alex S. Jones
Eduardo Kaplan
David A. Katz, Esq.
Bob and Maureen Keller
Mr. and Mrs. George M. Keller
Faun Kiddle
Donald Kimelman
Michael Kinsley
Kevin Klose
Matt Lauer
David Laventhol

Carolyn Lee
Richard A. Leibner and Carole Cooper
Anthony Lewis
Robert Lenzner
Steve and Amy Lipin
Joseph Lovett
Robert and Donna MacNeil
Joaquin A. Martinez
Kati Marton
Christopher Matthews
Michael McCurry
Geraldine Fabrikant Metz and Robert T. Metz
Anne and Victor Navasky
Hermine F. Nessen
Bill O'Reilly
James Ottaway
Clarence Page
Jane Pauley and Garry Trudeau
Jane Perlez
Stone Phillips
Karl Putnam
Jonathan Randal
Jean and Dan Rather
Warren Reintzel
Susan and Gene Roberts
Arthur Rosenzweig
Charles Rowe
Tim Russert
Robert J. Samuelson
Diane Sawyer
Dame Marjorie Scardino
Neal Shapiro
Allan M. Siegal and Gretchen M-P. Leefmans
Joseph Simone
Anita Snow
Jerry and Linda Speyer
Jean Stein
Matthew V. Storin
Paul C. Tash
Seymour Topping
Robert C. Waggoner

We also extend our gratitude to the many individuals and organizations who supported the Committee to Protect Journalists with gifts under $500, not listed here due to space limitations.

The Committee to Protect Journalists is grateful to the friends and family of the following people, in whose names generous contributions were made.

MEMORIAL GIFTS (gifts of all amounts listed):

Vicky Burrows
The staff of *LIFE* magazine
Mark Chavunduka
Jim Morrill
Art Cooper
Giorgio Armani Corp.
Elizabeth Barrere and Dennis M. Cass
Peter Bloch and Nanette Varian
John and Patricia Brunelle
Burberry Limited
Joseph Calluori
Giulio Capua
Betsy L. Castenir
Kenneth Cole Productions Foundation
Peggy Daitch
Lucy Schulte Danziger
Wendi and Arem Duplessis
Jennifer C. Egan
Alan M. and Ann A. Fleishman
Gourmet Magazine
Pamela Hanson
Arnold M. Huberman
Michael and Tina Ienna
Imperia Trading Inc.
Mervyn D. and Nancy S. Kaufman
Jim Kelly and Lisa Henricksson
Kaija Korpijaakko
Robert L. and Sandra G. Krakoff
Kate Larkworthy
Guy C. Lawson
Michael Luz
Amy McIntosh and Jeffrey Toobin
David Orlin
Rodale Publishing

Valerie Salembier
Mark Seliger Photography
Mary F. Shanahan
Paul Scherer
Yvonne Silverman
Cyndi Stivers
Charles H. Townsend

Mazen Dana
Mona Eltahawy
Jennifer Friedlin
Evelyn Hockstein
Rodney Palmer
Aimee Rhodes

Mark Fineman
Associated Counseling Professionals
Susan Blaustein
Lawrence H. Brown
Chris Buzard
California Community Foundation
John S. Carroll
Mark Chamberlin
Chicago Tribune Press Service, Inc.
Lynn Fryer
Gambs Family Foundation
Joan (Jody) Gambs
James Gerstenzang
Samuel Jameson
Katherine M. Johnston
Vicki Kemper
Kamala Shirin Lakhdhin
Dexter Leong
Lexington Habitat for Humanity
Thomas and Marcia Little
Los Angeles Times
Foreign Correspondents and Editors at the *Los Angeles Times*
Doyle McManus
Alan Miller
Marjorie Miller
Jack and Barbara Nelson
Florence Nemkov
Lucy Overall
Julia Preston
Robert Rosenblatt
Kevin Sack
Jen and Ajay Shah
Joel R. Simons
Anita Snow
Robert Tischenkel
Mary Jo Vortuba
Valerie Werlich
Nick Williams

Larry LeSueur
Elizabeth Likert David
Elizabeth Fisher
Marie A. Haralson
Alan and Dorothy Heil
Wilbur Levin
Hilda and Mary Rosenbaum
C. Fairley Spillman
Paul Sullivan

(Tia) Pola Marchant
Robert Marchant

Paul Moran
The Rendon Group

Lars-Erik Nelson
Mary Santarcangelo

Daniel Pearl
Thomas & Carolyn Langfitt Family Foundation

Jonah Richman
The Medill Club of Greater New York

Howard K. Smith
Charles B. Holstein

HOW TO REPORT AN ATTACK ON THE PRESS

CPJ needs accurate, detailed information in order to document press freedom abuses and help journalists in trouble. CPJ corroborates the information and takes appropriate action on behalf of the journalists and news organizations involved.

What to report:

Journalists who are:

- Arrested
- Assaulted
- Censored
- Denied credentials
- Harassed
- Kidnapped
- Killed
- Missing
- Threatened
- Wounded
- Wrongfully expelled
- Wrongfully sued for libel or defamation

News organizations that are:

- Attacked or illegally searched
- Censored
- Closed by force
- Editions confiscated or transmissions jammed
- Materials confiscated or damaged
- Wrongfully sued for libel or defamation

Information needed:

CPJ needs accurate, detailed information about:

- Journalists and news organizations involved
- Date and circumstances of incident
- Background information

Anyone with information about an attack on the press should call CPJ.

Call collect if necessary: (212) 465-1004, or send us a fax at (212) 465-9568.

Contact information for regional programs:

Africa: (212) 465-9344, ext. 112
E-mail: africa@cpj.org
Americas: (212) 465-9344, ext. 120
E-mail: americas@cpj.org
Asia: (212) 465-9344, ext. 140
E-mail: asiaprogram@cpj.org
Europe and Central Asia: (212) 465-9344, ext. 101
E-mail: europe@cpj.org
Middle East and North Africa: (212) 465-9344, ext. 104
E-mail: mideast@cpj.org

What happens next:

Depending on the case, CPJ will:

- Investigate and confirm the report
- Pressure authorities to respond
- Notify human rights groups and press organizations around the world
- Increase public awareness through the press
- Publish advisories to warn other journalists about potential dangers
- Send a fact-finding mission to investigate

CPJ STAFF

Executive Director Ann Cooper
Deputy Director Joel Simon
Editorial Director Susan Ellingwood
Director of Development and Outreach Julia Pimsleur
Director of Finance and Administration Lade Kadejo
Journalist Assistance Coordinator Elisabeth Witchel
Communications Coordinator Wacuka Mungai
Washington, D.C., Representative Frank Smyth
Deputy Editor Amanda Watson-Boles
Webmaster and Systems Administrator Mick Stern
Development Associate Dan Bolger
Development Assistant Elena Snyder
Research and Special Projects Associate Alexis Arieff
Receptionist and Office Manager Janet Mason

REGIONAL PROGRAMS

AFRICA
Program Coordinator Julia Crawford
Research Associate Adam Posluns

THE AMERICAS
Program Coordinator Carlos Lauría
Research Associate Sauro González Rodríguez

ASIA
Program Coordinator Abi Wright
Senior Research Associate Sophie Beach
Program Consultant A. Lin Neumann

EUROPE AND CENTRAL ASIA
Program Coordinator Alex Lupis
Research Associate Nina Ognianova

MIDDLE EAST AND NORTH AFRICA
Senior Program Coordinator Joel Campagna
Research Associate Hani Sabra

| INDEX OF COUNTRIES |

NOTES

NOTES